THE
MATRIARCH

THE MATRIARCH

—✦—

BARBARA BUSH AND THE
MAKING OF AN AMERICAN DYNASTY

SUSAN PAGE

TWELVE

NEW YORK   BOSTON

Twelve
Hachette Book Group
1290 Avenue of the Americas, New York, NY 10104
twelvebooks.com
twitter.com/twelvebooks

First Edition: April 2019

Twelve is an imprint of Grand Central Publishing. The Twelve name and logo are trademarks of Hachette Book Group, Inc.

The publisher is not responsible for websites (or their content) that are not owned by the publisher.

The Hachette Speakers Bureau provides a wide range of authors for speaking events. To find out more, go to www.hachettespeakersbureau.com or call (866) 376-6591.

Library of Congress Control Number: 2018959120

ISBNs: 978-1-5387-1364-8 (hardcover), 978-1-5387-1552-9 (large print hardcover), 978-1-5387-1365-5 (ebook)

Printed in the United States of America

LSC-C

10 9 8 7 6 5 4 3 2 1

To Carl, Ben, and Will

Contents

THE
MATRIARCH

Introduction

—✦—

The congregation that filled St. Martin's Episcopal Church in Houston for Barbara Bush's memorial service on April 21, 2018, was invitation-only. Seated in the pews were family, friends, and dignitaries, four former presidents, and the current First Lady. Television networks broadcast the service live; cable news channels featured retrospectives; world leaders issued tributes.

But most remarkable was what happened outside the spotlight. A day before the memorial service, thousands of mourners had stood in line to file past her silver casket and pay their respects. For a time, her widowed husband, former president George H. W. Bush, insisted on being there in his wheelchair to thank them. After the service, when the hearse pulled away for the one-hundred-mile drive to her burial site at the George H. W. Bush Presidential Library in College Station, the roads along the route were lined with regular folks saying farewell. Some held aloft signs they had written. "Welcome Home Barbara," one read. "Pearls & Grace: Her Legacy Lives On!" said another. Many of the women wore pearls, real and fake, as an affectionate salute.

Two months later, her oldest son, George W. Bush, marveled at the memory. "It was unbelievable, an unbelievable outpouring of affection," the nation's forty-third president told me in an interview in his Dallas office. His mother had been largely out of the public eye for a quarter century, he noted. "What caused her, the wife of a one-term president, to be not only heralded as a great First Lady but loved? I don't think there have been many of them like that."

What made Barbara Pierce Bush resonate so with Americans?

She wasn't a charismatic speaker or a classic beauty. Indeed, her self-deprecating humor about her cloud of white hair and her endless efforts to lose a few pounds were part of her signature. She never held public office.

But she was formidable, and she was fearless.

In the spring of 2000, billionaire financier and philanthropist David Rubenstein accompanied a group that included the former First Lady and two of her granddaughters, Lauren and Ashley, on safari in Africa. At one point during their stay at the Maasai Mara National Reserve in Kenya, a hippopotamus emerged from a watering hole in a way that looked threatening. "The Secret Service is saying, 'It's heading to Mrs. Bush. What do we do? Do we shoot it?'" Rubenstein told me.

Amid the fuss, Barbara Bush stood her ground.

"She didn't seem to worry about a hippopotamus that might be charging at her," Rubenstein recalled. "I think she felt she could out-intimidate the hippopotamus."

Indeed, the hippo retreated.

Throughout her life, Barbara Bush spoke with strength, passion, and authority about both uncontroversial topics such as literacy and controversial ones including HIV/AIDS. She was quick with a quip—"Never ask anyone over seventy how they are feeling," she cautioned, adding, "They'll tell you"—and had a tongue that sometimes got ahead of her. With all that, she emerged as one of the most authentic voices of her era. She also became one of the more influential women in American history, though her role often went unrecognized.

Her death came at a time when many Americans were worried about the nation's embattled politics, which were becoming so fiercely partisan that few people in the public arena were by consensus deemed to be decent, honorable, and worthy of respect. Barbara Pierce Bush was clearly one of those few. One sign of the country's poisonous climate was the quiet relief among many who loved her when President Donald Trump announced he wouldn't attend the memorial service, citing a desire to avoid the disruptions of the added security, though First Lady Melania Trump was there.

Also seated in a front pew was Bill Clinton, a political foe who had become a family friend.

The Democratic opponent who ousted George H. W. Bush from the White House became an annual visitor to their summer home in Maine, although he acknowledged that Barbara Bush took more time to win over than her husband. She was "a person with a strong sense of right and wrong, not so much about political issues but about how to live a life, how to organize a family, how to persevere in the face of adversity, how to deal with the things that come to everyone," Clinton told me. "She had a sense of how it ought to be done."

Barbara Pierce was born to privilege in a tony New York City suburb, an indifferent student despite a high IQ, happily dropping out of college to marry the first boy she ever kissed. She followed George Bush to West Texas, where she was the parent who stayed home to raise their sizable family while her husband set off to make a name for himself. She was his essential partner as he built an oil business, won a seat in Congress, served as the top US diplomat at the United Nations and in China, was named director of the CIA, was elected vice president, and then ran for and won the White House. She would become only the second woman in history to be both the wife and the mother of presidents, and the only woman to live to see both her husband and a son in that high office.

Her life spanned a revolution in the roles of and opportunities for women. Her marriage, like many of its time, wasn't a partnership of equals. She ran the household; he called the shots everywhere else. But over time she emerged from being a helpmate, willing to follow her husband's decisions on where they would live and what he should do, to becoming a crucial adviser—perhaps his most crucial. "She's about the only voice that he 100 percent trusted," one of his closest White House aides said.

Most of those who knew them best say George Bush would have

been unlikely to accomplish all he did, including becoming president, if he hadn't married Barbara Pierce. "There is no George H. W. Bush without Barbara Bush," grandson Pierce Bush told me. "Really, I don't see my grandfather being able to attain what he did in life without my grandmother being there."

Beyond the achievements, few knew about the grief Barbara Bush also suffered. The social bloodlines and the affluence and the political position were no protection from pain.

Her difficult mother left her with lifelong insecurities about her looks and her weight. The death from leukemia of daughter Robin, at age three, devastated her; for the rest of her life it would help shape everything from her impatience with prattle to her beliefs on abortion. Persistent rumors of infidelity involving the husband she adored were a source of anguish. She would suffer from serious depression for a time. Two of her children would go through messy divorces. One son would become ensnared in a savings and loan scandal. Another would battle a chronic, life-threatening disease. A beloved granddaughter would struggle with mental illness and drug abuse.

Through it all, she persevered. She was the glue that held her boisterous family together, in good times and bad. Like so many women of her day, her influence and her contribution to her husband's successes were consistently undervalued—even by her fans. And by him. And by her.

After covering national politics over four decades, including six presidencies, I concluded that Barbara Bush was the public figure Americans felt they knew most but really understood least. Many embraced her as a down-to-earth grandmother who sported a triple strand of faux pearls and joked about her wrinkles. That soft-focus impression wasn't inaccurate, but it was decidedly incomplete. In my view, she stands as the most underestimated First Lady of modern times.

And perhaps the most interesting.

In the summer of 2017, I wrote Barbara Bush, then ninety-two years old, to let her know that I was going to write this biography. She initially agreed to give me one interview, then a second, and then a third—five in all, once a month, in the living room or the den of her home in Houston. Her two tiny dogs, Bibi and Mini Me, notoriously ill-tempered to everyone but their mistress, were always in her lap or at her feet. (They were half Maltese, half poodle; the senior George Bush gave Mini Me her name because he said the dog that was a puff of white fur looked like his wife.)

At the end of our fifth interview, which turned out to be the last time I saw her, Barbara Bush unexpectedly granted me access to her diaries. She had begun collecting this account of her life in 1948. She had declared at the start that I wouldn't be allowed to read the daily and weekly entries, and the personal papers and letters tucked in with them, that were archived at the George H. W. Bush Presidential Library and Museum. Those boxes and binders won't be open to public view until 2053, thirty-five years after her death.

That meant I was able to read her diary entries about everything—even about this book. After our third interview, she wrote, "I talked to Susan Page who is writing a book about me. Boring." (I hope "boring" was a bit of self-deprecation about herself and not a description of me, but I never had a chance to ask her.) After our final interview, she wrote, "I like her and hope she is kind to me."

She encouraged family members and friends and former aides to talk with me. When her brother Scott Pierce asked her what he should say, she replied, "Just tell the truth." I sat down with both presidents named Bush, and with President Clinton, and with her children and grandchildren—in all, with more than one hundred people whose lives intersected with hers.

I discovered that there was more about Barbara Bush, and her role in some of the most important events of our age, than I would have even guessed. This book is about what I found.

———

America's saga was in her DNA.

Her direct ancestor Henry Samson, then sixteen years old, was one of the Pilgrims who arrived in the New World aboard the first voyage of the *Mayflower*, in 1620. During the Industrial Revolution, her paternal great-great-grandfather, General James Pierce, made a fortune in pig iron—that is, the first crude iron from a smelting furnace, shaped into bricks—though his sons would squander their inheritance. Her distant cousin Franklin Pierce was elected president during the years leading up to the Civil War, an unsettled time and one that historians would conclude he handled with catastrophic ineptitude.

She was born during the Roaring Twenties—just five years after women won the right to vote—and grew up during the Great Depression. Her father served in World War I, her boyfriend and her brother in World War II, and two of her grandsons in Afghanistan. As a teenager during World War II, she became one of the millions of women who joined the war effort at home, working one summer at a nuts-and-bolts factory; she fetched coffee for some of the same workers who on evenings and weekends would wait on her family at their private club. As a bride, she and her husband were among the flood of migrants who moved west for opportunity in the Sunbelt. Later, she would play a personal role in seven presidential campaigns.

No accounting of the era that stretches from the Reagan Revolution to the election of Donald Trump would be complete without an understanding of Barbara Pierce Bush.

For one thing, no other woman in American history has played such an intimate part in two White House administrations. Abigail Adams, like Barbara Bush, was the wife of one president and the mother of another. But of the two women, only Barbara could claim a role in both presidencies; Abigail died of typhoid six years before her son John Quincy Adams moved into the White House in 1825.

During the twelve years that a President Bush lived in the White House, the world would be transformed, then transformed again. George H. W. Bush managed with diplomatic finesse the collapse of the Soviet Union and the end of the Cold War. George W. Bush led the nation's response to the most devastating terror attack in its history and launched a war that would be vehemently disputed. Barbara Bush stood near the center of both administrations, forty-one and forty-three. She was never an ornament or a bystander, never just a leaf on the family tree. She had the ear of a pair of presidents in a way no other American has had, even if they weren't always enthusiastic about hearing from her. She used her unique position to act at times as their protector, at times as their conscience.

She pressed her husband to pay more attention to homelessness and HIV/AIDS. She set out to forge a friendship with the didactic Raisa Gorbachev, an act of will that the German chancellor and Canadian prime minister credited with helping ease the superpower negotiations that closed the Cold War. She raised alarms with her son about the advice he was heeding on Iraq, a war that would undermine public support for his presidency. She cautioned both presidents about phonies and users. She could unnerve their senior aides with a pointed question or a dyspeptic look. She kept scores. Her words could sting and leave scars, even with those she loved.

"She is a strong woman, not ego-driven but protective of kith and kin," White House speechwriter Peggy Noonan observed in *What I Saw at the Revolution*, her account of the Reagan era. "Those merry eyes, the warmth, the ability to get the help cracking in a jolly way, and then not so jolly. A lack of pretension, a breeziness, but underneath she is Greenwich granite, one of the women who settled the hard gray shores of the East and summoned roses from the rocks."

Barbara Bush was both warm and tough, simultaneously grandmother and enforcer. She was organized and disciplined, focused and flexible. She built sprawling networks of friends and easily socialized with strangers, from foreign ambassadors at state dinners to factory workers on the campaign trail. She wasn't flummoxed by abrupt changes in circumstance and locale, from Rye (New York) to Odessa (Texas) to Beijing (China) to the White House. She was comfortable with risk. Those are the qualities of successful CEOs and military commanders and political strategists and, indeed, presidents.

Had she been born a generation or two later, when opportunities were exploding for women in America, she might well have been any of those. "In a different time and a different era, my mother might have been president," Jeb Bush told me in an interview in 1990, when it was his father who was president. She might have seen more room for personal ambition. She might have been less Barbara Pierce Bush and more, say, Hillary Rodham Clinton.

Hillary Rodham was born a generation later. Just twenty-two years apart in age, she and Barbara Pierce stood on opposite sides of a social revolution. "She lived a full and exemplary life in every way, but she was of my mother's generation," Hillary Clinton told me. "It was just a divide that had really significant repercussions for young women my age, coming up at the time we did." Clinton would succeed Barbara Bush as First Lady but then become a US senator, a secretary of state, and the first woman nominated for the presidency by a major political party. In a peculiar turn, one of the Republicans vying to oppose her in 2016 would be Barbara Bush's second son, Jeb.

Barbara Bush's profile was more traditional, her influence less direct, her power wielded more often in private, even clandestinely. Still, she stands as a historic figure. A list of the presidential spouses who have had the greatest impact on America would include her alongside such women as Abigail Adams, Edith Wilson, Eleanor Roosevelt, Nancy Reagan, and Hillary Clinton.

Her appeal transcended party lines in a way the candidates in her family could only yearn to emulate. Jeb Bush, the two-term governor of Florida and a GOP presidential hopeful in 2016, described a common phenomenon he encountered while waiting at airports. "I love your mother," strangers would come up to tell him. "Occasionally I would say, 'Well, what about my dad?' 'No, I love your mother.' 'What about my brother?' 'I really love your mother.' 'What about me?' 'Your mom is great.'"

That said, during the time she was most in the public eye, Barbara Bush did catch flak from critics—from *Saturday Night Live* comics who mocked her, and from young women in Wellesley's class of 1990 who protested her as a commencement speaker. Some saw her as a throwback, "just a housewife," defined by her marriage to a powerful man.

That's one reason she had a complicated and not entirely friendly view of feminism and the women's movement. She was wounded by the protests at Wellesley. She responded by delivering an enduring message that has been quoted in commencement addresses ever since: "At the end of your life, you will never regret not having passed one more test, winning one more verdict, or not closing one more deal," she said then. "You will regret time not spent with a husband, a child, a friend, or a parent."

At the end of her life, Barbara Bush had few regrets.

The ranks of America's political matriarchs include remarkable women, among them Sara Delano Roosevelt and Rose Kennedy. But "matriarch" was a title Barbara Bush rejected for herself, along with any suggestion that she led a dynasty. "Mother was pretty good about dealing with big shot–itis," George W. Bush told me, "and there's nothing more big-shotty than saying, 'This is a dynasty.'"

Whether she liked the word or not, though, it is undeniable that Barbara Bush was the matriarch of an American dynasty—a dynasty defined not only by political office but also by public service of all sorts by her children and her grandchildren and others she influenced. Besides the White House, her sons were elected and reelected as governors of two of the nation's largest states. One grandson was elected to statewide office in Texas. Another enlisted in the US Marines and was deployed to Afghanistan, dangerous duty that was never publicly disclosed. A third left a business career to become a leader in the Big Brothers Big Sisters program. She bragged about the global health program one granddaughter cofounded, and the campaign to feed hungry children around the world that another granddaughter helped launch.

Her mind was sharp to the end, but her physical health was failing, her breathing more labored and her pain more apparent with each visit. She would pass away, peacefully, on April 17, 2018; her husband would die seven months later, on November 30. At the end of our first interview, in the autumn of 2017, I asked her, "What do you think the title of this book should be?"

She answered without missing a beat. "*The Fat Lady Sings Again*," she said. And she smiled, pleased with herself.

Chapter One

—⭐—

Six Brutal Months

I don't know what to do this morning," three-year-old Robin told her mother on that March day in Midland. "I may go out and lie on the grass and watch the cars go by, or I might just stay in bed."

Barbara Bush was preoccupied with Jebby, the baby brother who had been born just a few weeks earlier on February 11, 1953, and wasn't yet sleeping through the night. Georgie was attending first grade at Sam Houston Elementary School, but Robin was still home with her mother all day, at the new house on West Ohio Street. Her giggly daughter had blond curls and chipmunk cheeks and, usually, a quick smile. The notion that she was listless and exhausted, with more than just a dreamy spring fever, didn't sound right. Barbara made an appointment with the children's doctor, who examined Robin and drew some blood. Dr. Dorothy Wyvell, the pediatrician just about every family in Midland trusted, immediately spotted signs of something serious, but she didn't put a name to it, not until she was sure. When the test results came back, she would call her, she told Barbara. She suggested that the parents return together that afternoon to talk, without Robin. That sounded ominous, Barbara thought, but she couldn't imagine that something was seriously amiss.

George Bush, then twenty-eight years old, was checking land records at the Ector County courthouse, twenty miles from Midland, when

Barbara called him. Dr. Wyvell wanted to see them right away. In late afternoon, as daylight ebbed, they sat down in her small office. George Bush could tell something was wrong. The pediatrician, a family friend, had been a composed and reassuring figure in dealing with the standard childhood scrapes and ailments. This time, she was struggling to find words, and her eyes were misting with tears.

The doctor finally spoke. The test results were back. Robin had leukemia.

Neither parent had ever heard of it. What was it? How do we cure her? What can we do? Nothing, Dr. Wyvell told them. Robin's white blood cell count was the highest she had ever seen, a sign that the disease was rampant. Robin might have a few weeks to live, or even just a few days. They could choose to treat her, though the research into leukemia was very preliminary. There was no cure. The doctor's advice was to let nature take its course. Tell no one about their daughter's terrifying diagnosis. Take her home. Make her comfortable. Let her slip away.

They were stunned, but they were hardly ready to accept that advice. They already had demonstrated they were more comfortable taking action than sitting still. He had enlisted at age eighteen to fight in World War II; at age twenty-two, she had left the comforts of upper-crust society in Connecticut to set up a string of households in the Oil Patch. They weren't ready to give up on their daughter without a fight. They had moved to Texas in a sort of declaration of independence, but now they were grateful for their family connections back east. Bush called his uncle, Dr. John Walker, a renowned surgeon at Memorial Hospital in New York.

Walker urged them to bring Robin to New York, where doctors had just begun some of the early research into leukemia. Perhaps nothing could be done, he said, but they would never forgive themselves if they didn't try. "You don't have a choice," he told them. Even if the odds were a hundred million to one, "you've got to give life a chance."

They left Dr. Wyvell's office with the news still sinking in. They had driven there in separate cars. Barbara headed home; Bush told her he needed to stop by his office for a moment. In fact, he dropped by the house of some friends, the Fowlers, and asked Liz Fowler to come over to be with Barbara. More friends gathered at the house as the news spread through the neighborhood.

Decades later, Barbara Bush would remember every bit of it, with the crystalline recall that comes with the unfolding of catastrophic events. When their teetotaling minister and his wife arrived, George Bush offered them a drink—though they "would no more take a drink than fly," Barbara said. The Reverend Dr. Matthew Lynn demurred. "Not *now*, George," he said. The "now" deflected any sense of discomfort, as though perhaps another time the pastor might well accept. "Such a silly, small thing to remember," Barbara would say later, and yet she did remember.

Hurriedly, frantically, plans were made. Little George would stay with one friend; baby Jeb would stay with another. The next morning, George and Barbara Bush were on a plane to New York with their daughter. Not even twenty-four hours had passed since they had received the most devastating news of their lives.

Robin's illness and her death six brutal months later would forever change Barbara Bush. The experience would steel her resolve and broaden her understanding of the ways the innocent can be caught and crushed by the unfairness of life. It would leave an indelible stamp on her about what matters, and what doesn't. It would cement a bond between her and her firstborn son that would last until Barbara's passing. And it would test her marriage. George's and Barbara's responses to Robin's illness and eventual death would forge a template that they would follow through the ebbs and flows of their long union.

Barbara was the strong one during Robin's painful treatment as George dissolved in tears. With Robin's death, Barbara was the one who collapsed into sorrow, and George became her rock. The pattern of one stepping up when the other was struggling—and of being able to switch those roles between them—would sustain the couple during times of political defeat and personal pain. It would prove to be crucial decades later when Barbara Bush struggled with depression and again when the elder George Bush was embittered by his defeat for reelection to the White House.

But nothing would ever match the heartbreaking struggle that robbed them of any sense of the seasons in 1953.

The morning after Robin died, on October 11, 1953, Barbara was shocked when she suddenly noticed that the leaves on the trees in her hometown of Rye, in suburban New York, were at the peak of their fall colors. The last time she had paid any attention to such things was six months earlier, in Midland, on that March day. "I remember realizing life went on," she said, "whether we were looking or not."

When Robin was diagnosed with leukemia, no medical journal had recorded even a single case of a patient being cured of the disease, nor of anyone surviving for more than a few months after being diagnosed. But the first breakthroughs were being made.

For more than a century, childhood leukemia had perplexed and frustrated doctors. The disease was like "a wax-museum doll," Siddhartha Mukherjee wrote in the opening chapter of his epic 2010 tome, *The Emperor of All Maladies: A Biography of Cancer*. The disease had been studied in detail but without achieving any therapeutic advances. Patients were "diagnosed, transfused—and sent home to die," a medical magazine noted. Indeed, that was close to the advice Dr. Wyvell had given the Bushes.

In 1948, researcher Sidney Farber at Children's Hospital in Boston managed to push leukemia into remission by using an early form of chemotherapy—a dramatic breakthrough and a welcome one, but only a temporary respite. Within a few months, the patients invariably would suffer a relapse and die. In the early 1950s, two scientists at Sloan Kettering began clinical trials on a similar approach, using a different drug. They succeeded in bringing about a remission after only a few days of treatment, but the remission was limited to weeks.

Even so, that was enough to give Barbara and George Bush a spark of light during a dark time. "Robin does unfortunately have Leukemia, and although there is little hope for her we have taken her to Memorial Hospital for treatments," her father wrote in a letter that summer. "Our big hope is that some new cure will be discovered for this horrible disease." That somehow Robin could be kept alive long enough for a cure to be found.

Five years after George and Barbara Bush had left the East Coast to make their own way, they were back. John Walker, the brother of Bush's mother, Dorothy, was a prominent doctor who would later serve as the president of the prestigious Memorial Sloan Kettering Hospital. (He had personal experience in the trials and tribulations of serious disease; three years earlier he had begun his own battle with polio.) Dorothy Walker Bush dispatched Marion Fraser, the nurse who had helped when her own children were growing up, to Texas to care for Georgie and Jebby. Barbara Bush moved into the grand apartment at One Sutton Place that was owned by her husband's eccentric grandparents, Bert and Loulie Walker, just nine blocks from the hospital. She would spend just about every waking moment by Robin's side while her husband shuttled between New York and Texas, where he was scrambling to launch his new oil venture.

Robin was very sick from the start. When she was checked into Sloan Kettering, the doctors there were sure the pediatrician in little Midland had gotten the blood test wrong; Robin's white blood cell count was just too high to be accurate. But when they retested her blood, they registered the same results. It was the highest white blood cell count the experts had ever seen.

The treatments were torturous, the odds they would succeed remote. "How we hated bone marrow tests," Barbara Bush recalled, an agonizing procedure even for adults. Robin would be awake as doctors used a biopsy needle to collect a sample of marrow from a bone. Sometimes Robin would be "panicked, crying," George Bush said. There were endless, painful blood transfusions, and as the hospital had requested, a parade of family members and friends journeyed to Sloan Kettering to replace the pints of blood that Robin used. More than once Barbara would be called to help when her sister or a friend passed out while donating blood.

She set one rule: No crying in front of Robin.

Barbara Bush didn't want the little girl unsettled by seeing the adults in her life in tears. But George Bush, a man of open emotion, found it almost impossible to comply. Again and again, he would tell Robin he had to go to the bathroom and then step into the hallway to regain his composure. "We used to laugh and wonder if Robin thought he had the weakest bladder in the world," Barbara Bush said. "Not true. He just had the most tender heart."

He knew how hard it was on Barbara to be the stoic, to be the one in control. Years later, George Bush wrote a revealing aside in a letter to a constituent in his congressional district who had been diagnosed with cancer. "Someone had to look into Robin's eyes and give her comfort and love," he said, "and somehow, Paul, I didn't have the guts."

Every morning when he was in Midland, George Bush would drop by First Presbyterian Church at 6:30 a.m. to pray for Robin. In the beginning, only the custodian was around to notice. Then the minister began showing up to join him. The two men never talked. They would sit quietly until Bush felt ready to face the day.

At the time, Bush was teaching a Sunday school class for teenagers at the church. He often would arrive disheveled and unshaven, with no lesson prepared. Instead, he would sit with the small group of students and talk about life, death, war, faith, hope, and despair. There was no stricture against crying there.

⁓ ⁓

In New York, one of Bush's college pals began dropping by the hospital after work each night to check on Robin and to see if Barbara needed anything.

Lud Ashley had been Bush's classmate at Yale as well as a fellow member of the secret Skull and Bones society. Like Bush, he had served in World War II, a US Army corporal in the Pacific theater. Each had a distinguished political lineage. Bush's father, Prescott Bush, had been elected to the US Senate from Connecticut the previous November. Ashley's great-grandfather James Mitchell Ashley was a noted abolitionist and Ohio congressman during the Civil War. Lud Ashley recently had graduated from Ohio State University Law School and soon would move back to Ohio to launch his own long congressional career.

At the moment, though, he had taken a job in New York at Radio Free Europe, a few blocks from Sloan Kettering. He stopped by the hospital so regularly that one of the night nurses assumed he was Robin's father. "What does your husband do, Mrs. Bush?" the nurse asked her one day. "I meet him every morning around 2 a.m. when he comes in to check on Robin before going to bed." If Robin's door was closed, presumably for some treatment, Ashley would wander over to the waiting room, which overlooked the East River, and watch the lights on the water for a half hour or so before going back to check on her again.

When she was awake, Robin recognized Ashley, but it was clear she was failing. "Her eyes didn't sparkle or anything of that kind," he recalled, "and she had things sticking out of her and really, she wasn't in good shape at all. It was really tough going for her."

It was tough going for all of them. Once, when the end was near, Barbara Bush slipped out to the cold rooftop terrace off the parents' waiting room to be alone, to smoke a cigarette, to cry. She found Ashley, huddled outside in the freezing cold. He didn't want to intrude, but he did want to be nearby, just in case. In the decades that followed, the Bushes would never forget. He would remain one of their most treasured friends for life.

Barbara Bush became part of the hospital's community of parents, an involuntary club bound by pain and hope. "We understood each other," she said. The journey to Texas had broadened Barbara's horizons from her days of growing up in affluent Rye and attending boarding school at Ashley Hall, in South Carolina. The long days in the hospital ward were eye-opening in a whole new dimension.

She realized how lucky she was in some ways. She had a stable home and a supportive spouse. They had health insurance and family assets. Some of the other mothers were dealing with family fissures and financial strains, which made their ordeal even harder. Sloan Kettering didn't charge those who couldn't pay, but there were other expenses and dislocations that debilitated some.

"I remember one precious little boy named Joey, whose mother had a big family in upstate New York," she said. "Her husband was a laborer and was trying to cope with schools, bills, and meals. She worried all the time." Joey's mom rented a cheap room in the Bronx and would commute to the hospital by bus and subway each day, wearing her bedroom slippers for comfort.

"As Joey's time drew near, I met her one day in the parents' room and asked about her son. 'Joey's bad, Barbara,' she said, then unintentionally mangled a Bible verse; Barbara realized she found her version of it comforting. 'Do you remember in the Bible where it says, "Let the little children suffer and they will come unto me"? Joey is really suffering.'" (Years later, Barbara Bush would remember Joey when Ronald McDonald House Charities, which provides housing and support for the families of hospitalized children, asked her to help headline their annual fundraising dinner. She accepted. What a difference the organization could have made for Joey's mom if it had existed then, she thought.)

Cancer proved to be a terrible equalizer. Neither money nor power nor position had given Robin any more refuge from leukemia than Joey had.

Like every other parent at the hospital, the Bushes were desperate, ready to grasp at straws. One day, several friends phoned George Bush after hearing Paul Harvey on his radio program describe a doctor in Kansas who had discovered a cure for leukemia. After five frantic hours, Bush managed to get through to the doctor on the phone. He had been swamped by calls from parents who would do anything to save their children, but all he had to offer was one more unproven medicine then being tested. Barbara Bush later chastised Paul Harvey for causing such heartbreak. "He raised our hopes only to have them dashed," she said.

True to form, Robin's disease did go into remission for a time. Once in a while, she could visit the Walkers' apartment with her mother. George Bush's maternal grandfather, known as Gampy Walker, was a flamboyant and forbidding figure with a mercurial temper that had estranged him from his own children. But he was putty in Robin's hands. He taught the three-year-old to play a simplified version of gin rummy. She thought he had called it "gin mummy," a name she gleefully changed to gin poppy, after her father.

She could also take the rare trip to her grandparents' home in Greenwich, Connecticut. One day she went for a walk with her father, headed to the bank, holding hands and laughing. They ran into an acquaintance of his, and the two men chatted. "George, how is your other little kid doing—the one sick, with leukemia?" the other man asked. It didn't occur to him that the patient could be this sunny little girl. Once that summer, they traveled to the family home in Kennebunkport, Maine, and Robin got to see her brothers. Then she made a brief trip to Texas, the farthest the hospital had let a leukemia patient go. It was a chance for her to see her home in Midland, and for her family and friends to see her, one more time.

Many in Midland shied away, worried that leukemia might be contagious. Barbara Bush never forgot the pain that caused her. Later, as First Lady, she would make a point of embracing HIV/AIDS patients at a time when many were skittish. Then, her friend Betty Liedtke "saved my life," Barbara Bush recalled, spending hours at the Bush house to make Robin laugh or encourage her to eat.

Robin had to return to the hospital in New York, her health failing, the treatments no longer working. She caught pneumonia and spent time in an oxygen tent. Her legs were covered with bruises. There were dozens of painful open sores on her torso. She was bleeding internally. Barbara and the doctors called George Bush in Texas to discuss one more operation. "I said, 'No, we've done enough to her,'" Bush told them. There was nothing more that could be done. "We thought it was time to let her go."

He flew back to New York. By the time he arrived, Robin had slipped into a coma.

"One minute she was there, and the next she was gone," Barbara Bush said. "I truly felt her soul go out of that beautiful little body." Her mother combed Robin's curly blond hair for one last time. Barbara was twenty-eight years old when her daughter died in her arms.

"Like an oak in the wind, she was tossed, but she would not be moved," author Richard Ben Cramer would write of Barbara's forbearance. She had accomplished her mission. She had never cried in front of her frail little girl, not once. Now the tears could flow, and they did.

The next day, her father, Marvin Pierce, suggested Barbara and George come to Rye to play golf, a chance to be outdoors, a brief respite from the hospital and the flood of demands and decisions that were about to follow. In the ladies' locker room at the club, she ran into a friend, Marilyn Peterson. They chatted, but Barbara didn't mention Robin. She wondered later, *Would Marilyn think that was strange?*

The Bushes already had decided to donate Robin's body to research in hopes that it would speed understanding of the disease, that it might help save some other child. While she had been sick, they had overheard grieving family members in the next room berate a doctor who had asked if they would give their child's body to science. They took a lesson from that, and applied it when their time came to answer that hard question.

They also had made preparations for her burial site.

George Bush's father, Prescott Bush, had broached the difficult topic in a delicate way. One day, he asked Barbara to go with him to a cemetery in Greenwich to show her where he would be buried. When they arrived, he poked fun at the gravesites with huge headstones and mausoleum-style structures. "I knew old so-and-so," he told her. "He certainly thought highly of himself, didn't he, Bar?"

A modest headstone that read "BUSH" already marked the plot he had bought on a hillside. On one side of the headstone was a freshly planted lilac bush; on the other, a dogwood tree. She understood that he had prepared the gravesite not only for him and his wife but also for Robin, to give her a tranquil place to rest in peace.

Robin's burial would be delayed to allow time for the researchers to examine her. George and Barbara scheduled a memorial service for family and a handful of friends at Christ Church in Greenwich before they returned to Midland. They were at the home of George's parents, getting ready in an upstairs bedroom. They could hear the others gathering on the first floor. Suddenly, Barbara's stoicism evaporated. She couldn't face anyone, she told her husband. She couldn't do it. She was done.

George looked out the window and saw Barbara's sister and brother-in-law, Martha and Walt Rafferty, walking up the driveway. "Sure, and with the O'Raffertys, it is going to be a grand wake!" he told her. It was the sort of deliberately goofy comment that could make her laugh, that would help her to hold it together one more time.

As soon as the service was over, Barbara and George flew home to Texas to explain to Georgie what had happened to his little sister. In the Greenwich cemetery a few days later, George Bush's mother and the faithful Lud Ashley stood by as Robin's remains were laid to rest.

~ ~

It would be the first vivid memory of his life.

George W. Bush, now in the second grade, had been dispatched by his teacher to help carry a Victrola phonograph back to the principal's office. He and classmate Bill Sallee were lugging it down a covered walkway when George spotted his parents' car pulling into the parking lot. They had been away on one of their frequent trips to New York. "I remember the pea-green car," George W. Bush told me in an interview sixty-five years later. "I saw him pull up. I thought I saw Robin in the back." He asked his teacher if he could go say hello to his parents and his sister.

He knew Robin had been sick, but he had no idea that she might die. She wasn't with them, his parents told him in the car. She was never coming home.

Decades later, in an interview in the living room of her Houston home, Barbara Bush was still torn over whether they had made the right decision, trying to protect their young son by not being candid about what was going on. "We should have told him that she was very, very sick," she told me, tears welling in her eyes. I apologized for making her cry. "That's normal," she replied. "Don't worry about that." A pastel portrait of Robin was hanging on the wall, within her line of sight. "He's never really forgiven me for that, or us. I can understand that. We just didn't know what to do. He was a little boy."

George W. Bush told me he understood why they didn't tell him in advance. "Why would you burden a six-year-old kid?" he said. In the end, he added, "I turned out okay."

At the moment, they were all reeling. No one was sleeping through the night.

In those first weeks, Georgie struggled. Not long after Robin's death, he went over to the house of a friend, Randall Roden, for a sleepover, but he had such terrifying nightmares that his mother had to come over to the house to comfort him.

Barbara Bush herself would wake up with a wave of grief so fierce that the pain felt physical. During the day, she hated it when friends avoided saying Robin's name, as though the little girl could or should be forgotten. She was exhausted by condolence calls from people she hardly knew, and by the awkward comments some would make in an effort to comfort her. Once, walking into the living room, she got a glimpse of a friend practicing sad expressions in a mirror; Barbara backed out of the room and came in again, more noisily. "At least it wasn't your firstborn and a boy at that," a visitor said. Barbara was speechless and enraged. "I just needed somebody to blame," she said.

In an instant, Barbara and George had switched roles. She had been the strong one when Robin was sick, with the fierce discipline to maintain her composure in the hospital room while he had to retreat into the hallway to weep. "I wouldn't let them cry in front of her, and I was very strong then," she said. "But then it was all over, and he took over."

She fell apart. "Time after time during the next six months," she said, "George would put me together again."

The death of a child can pressure any marriage, even a strong one. A study in the 1970s estimated that as many as 90 percent of bereaved couples found themselves in serious marital difficulty within months after the death of a child. A decade later, another study concluded that "all indicators of marital happiness deteriorated over time" among bereaved parents. The most serious problems developed when the mother and the father coped differently with their grief. Often fathers would take refuge in their work and try not to dwell on the loss, the researchers found, while mothers wanted to talk about their child, to express their pain. That disconnect would fray their bonds, sometimes irreparably.

But George Bush defied that stereotype of his gender and his times. It was Barbara who wanted to rush through a grieving process that could not be hurried; he refused to let her do that. "I wanted to get back to real life, but there is a dance that you have to go through to get there," she said. "When I wanted to cut out, George made me talk to him, and he shared with me." He reminded her that others were feeling the same pain she felt. He felt it, as did their son, and their relatives back east, and their friends in Texas. Night after night, he would hold her as she cried herself to sleep.

Robin's illness strained her parents' marriage, then strengthened it. It deepened her young mother's faith, and it made her both harder and softer. On the inside, Barbara Bush emerged more aware of the fragility of life and the universality of grief. She felt a newfound sympathy and understanding for her mother, who had to deal with the repeated hospitalizations of Barbara's brother. On the outside, she developed a survivor's armor, and with it even less patience for the general boneheadedness of people. She had never been one to suffer fools gladly. Now her impatience was sharpened, even if those fools were well-meaning. She no longer had the time or stomach for them.

She had never paid much attention to what she wore or how her hair looked. Now she cared even less. All that seemed so unimportant. "There is a sad part of my mom and dad that those of us who have never lost a young child could never understand," said Dorothy Bush Koch, the daughter known as Doro who was born six years later.

For the rest of her life, Robin's death would heighten Barbara Bush's empathy for those who were struggling with life's injustices.

"That, I think, was maybe one of the things that made Barbara so tender to others after she got through it," Susan Baker, one of her closest friends, told me. Barbara Bush chose Susan, the wife of former secretary of state James A. Baker III, to deliver one of three eulogies at her funeral. "It scarred her in a way that's benefited many, many people. I shouldn't say scarred—it's tenderized her in a way that has benefited so many people." When tragedy strikes, "there are many people that run the opposite direction," Susan Baker said. "But not Barbara Bush."

The innocent queries of seven-year-old Georgie helped the adults around him chart a path forward.

When George Bush took his son to a football game that fall, the youngster declared that he wished he were Robin. The adults who heard him stiffened uncomfortably. His father asked him why. "I bet she can see the game better from up there than we can here," Georgie explained. That brought a smile to everyone.

Another time, he asked his father a question that again momentarily shocked the adults: Had they buried Robin lying down or standing up? George Bush said he wasn't sure. Why did he want to know? In school, Georgie had just learned that the earth rotated. Did that mean his sister was spending some of her time standing on her head? And wouldn't that be neat?

"He taught me something," Barbara Bush told me, decades later.

George W. mentioned Robin easily, naturally, while others were afraid to say her name. "It taught me that when someone dies you ought to talk about them. That's hard to do."

It is hard, I agreed.

"But you should talk about them. Otherwise I thought that she was a nobody, when nobody talked about her. I thought, *Why don't people act like she was there?*"

Barbara Bush and her firstborn son already were exceptionally close, a result of those early years when it was often just the two of them while the senior George Bush was on the road, building his business. Now Robin's loss made their ties even stronger. He was the only one of the children who could share with their parents his own memories of Robin. "I feel very close to George, very," Barbara Bush told me. "He went all through the Robin thing. He really took care of me." He agreed. "We had a very, very close relationship," George W. Bush said. "My brothers and sister did, too, but it was just different."

In the days before her own death in April 2018, Barbara Bush worried that George W. would take her passing the hardest "because of Robin."

During the fall of 1953, after being away for most of the past six months in New York, she focused on Georgie and little Jeb. "Mother's reaction was to envelop herself totally around me," George W. Bush recalled. "She kind of smothered me and then recognized that it was the wrong thing to do." One breezy day, Barbara was in her bedroom when she overheard Mike Proctor, the boy who lived across the street, ask Georgie if he wanted to come over and play. He did, he replied, but he couldn't leave his mother. She needed him. "That started my cure," Barbara Bush said. "I realized I was too much of a burden for a little seven-year-old boy to carry."

Robin's death extended the age gap between George W. and his closest sibling. Jeb was seven years his junior. Jeb and the three who followed—Neil, Marvin, and Doro—were clustered, all born in the space of six and a half years. George W. stood apart. "For a while after Robin's death I felt like an only child," he said. Relatives back east worried that he might see it as his job to cheer up his grieving parents, to be the family clown. "I think kids who lose a sibling often try and find ways to, you know, make things easier in the family," said a cousin, Elsie Walker, who herself had lost a sister.

"He felt he had to be the caretaker," Betsy Heminway, one of Barbara Bush's closest friends from Greenwich and Kennebunkport, told me. She thought the role Georgie filled then to cheer up those around him helped shape his personality. "He was the cheerleader—which he was at Yale, so he started early. I think that's part of it." Some of his relatives would wonder if Robin's death, and perhaps his own sense of survivor's guilt, contributed to the years when George W. as a young man would be known more for his partying than his sense of purpose.

George W. Bush would always be the one who could tease his mother and get a rise from her. The sarcastic patter between them would persist for the rest of their lives. Barbara Pierce Bush, the daughter of George W. and the namesake of her grandmother, had often heard the story about her father as a little boy, telling his friend he had to stay home to cheer up his mom. "I always thought that was so sweet and I feel like, oddly, that's how their relationship remains," she told me. "It was very playful; it was very funny. My dad's role really was to make my grandmother laugh— like he got so much joy out of making her laugh."

Robin's death had an impact even on her brothers and sister not yet born.

"She was a constant memory," Neil Bush, the first child born after Robin died, told me.

"It's a strange thing to mourn someone you never met, but my heart still feels heavy when I think of what might have been," Doro Bush Koch said about the big sister who wasn't there. She once told her mother that she felt bad because she had straight, brunette hair instead of the blond curls Robin had.

～～

A year before Doro was born, the elder George Bush told his mother about the hole in his heart.

"There is about our house a need," he wrote Dorothy Walker Bush in a letter in the summer of 1958 that he described as "kind of like a confessional." It was found among his mother's possessions when she died in 1992. "We need some starched crisp frocks to go with all our torn-kneed blue jeans and helmets. We need some soft blond hair to offset those crew cuts. We need a doll house to stand firm against our forts and rackets and thousand baseball cards...

"We need a girl."

Bessie Liedtke, the wife of George Bush's business partner and one of Barbara Bush's friends in Midland, believes that Robin's death expanded her father's drive and his aspirations. "He just said, 'I've got to do something that's bigger than just the oil business,'" she told me. "I think that was a big factor in his running for office and trying to do good for people." Barbara thought being shot down in the Pacific during World War II had sparked his determination to do big things, but Robin's death could have contributed as well. "Maybe all those things add up," she told me.

Bush biographer Jon Meacham once asked the former president what lessons his daughter Robin's death had taught him.

"It taught me that no matter how innocent or perfect the child, she can still be taken away from you by horrible illness," Bush said. "That gets into 'the Lord works in strange ways,' if you believe in that. I've never gotten a real answer to that one. But I learned a lot from it. Keep going, charging ahead."

When George W. Bush spoke at his father's memorial service at Washington's National Cathedral in December 2018, he closed his eulogy with words that made him choke back tears. "In our grief," he said, "let us smile knowing that Dad is hugging Robin and holding Mom's hand again."

A year earlier, amid preparations for what would turn out to be the final Christmas of her life, Barbara Bush, then ninety-two, had her lost daughter on her mind. On December 20, 2017, she wrote in her diary: "I believe this is our precious Robin's birthday."

Chapter Two

—★—

"The Fighting Pierces"

Barbara Pierce Bush's strength and perseverance may have been imprinted in her genes, in a family whose story tracked America's history from the start.

Robert Coe was one ancestor of note. A restless and ambitious man, he was thirty-eight years old in 1634 when he boarded the *Francis* in Ipswich, northeast of London, with wife Anne and three young children, heading to America. The ship's departure was delayed for two weeks by customs bailiffs, but the journey finally began in April, lasted ten long weeks on the Atlantic Ocean, and was "marked by seasickness, monotony, boredom, bad weather and a steadily deteriorating diet." Tickets cost £5 per adult (just over $1,000 in 2018 dollars), with children charged at half price. In late July, the square-rigged ship, 100 feet long, sailed into Massachusetts Bay. Notably for the time, all ninety-four passengers survived the voyage.

The *Mayflower* had made its historic journey just fourteen years earlier. Coe was part of a second great surge of religious dissidents from England settling a new land. He would live a remarkably long life, especially for the era, surviving into his nineties after playing a key role in establishing churches and communities in Massachusetts, Connecticut, and New York.

He would spawn a distinguished family. His direct descendants included Charles Dawes, President Calvin Coolidge's vice president and

the corecipient of the Nobel Peace Prize in 1925 for his work on repa-
rations after World War I. British prime minister Winston Churchill,
whose leadership during World War II made him a hero on both sides of
the Atlantic, was another, through Churchill's American-born mother,
Jennie Jerome.

Barbara Pierce Bush was also a descendant, through her mother.

By the time Coe came ashore in the new world, a direct ancestor of
Barbara Bush through her father was already there. Henry Samson, sixteen years old, had arrived on the *Mayflower,* perhaps as an apprentice to
his uncle. By the end of their first ferocious winter in America, almost
half of the 102 passengers had died, among them Henry's uncle and aunt,
Edward and Ann Tilley. Samson, though, would live into his eighties,
fathering nine children. (One curious note: Samson's direct descendants
include not only Barbara Pierce Bush but also the poet Henry Wadsworth Longfellow and Sarah Palin, the 2008 Republican nominee for
the vice presidency, the job George Bush once held. Barbara Bush and
Sarah Palin were sixth cousins once removed.)

Barbara Bush's lineage underscores the depth and breadth of her links
to the history of the United States, and the energy and independence
that was part of her heritage. Her ancestors helped settle New England.
They fought for independence in the Revolutionary War and for the
Union in the Civil War. They amassed a fortune during the Industrial
Revolution. They served in World War I and World War II.

There were imposing women in one generation of the family after
another.

A great-great-grandmother on her father's side endowed a chair at
Buchtel College in Akron, Ohio, for a female professor at a time when
few women could aspire to higher education. Her grandmother on her
mother's side ignored the conventions of the day after the death of her
husband, a state Supreme Court justice in Ohio. With three fellow widows, she packed up a trailer and set off on an adventurous journey across
the United States, Canada, and Mexico. Her tales would delight her
granddaughter, a little girl growing up in Rye, New York.

As for Robert Coe, his ancestry traces back to John Coe, a resident of Gestingthorpe, in England's Essex County. In the fourteenth century, John Coe served under Sir John Hawkwood, a veteran of the Hundred Years' War, when he led an infamous mercenary unit that battled for various city-states in Italy.

Robert Coe was born in 1596, after his father had moved the family to Suffolk County. Coe worked as a weaver and a questman, a local person empowered to look into abuses and disputes. But the textile industry was in precipitous decline. Many Puritans saw God's hand, arguing that the economic dislocations were divine punishment because England had not created a reformed Protestant Church, and that more hard times were likely to follow. Puritans like Coe from Suffolk, Essex, and Norfolk Counties became the heart of the American migration.

After arriving in America, he became a peripatetic figure, sometimes propelled to move on after disputes over church governance, emerging as a leader in religious and civic affairs wherever he went. He traveled first to Watertown, now part of the Boston area, where others from his hometown already had settled. A year later, he helped found a new plantation at Wethersfield, one of Connecticut's three founding towns and the site of a bloody battle with the Pequot tribe while he was there. Five years later, in the wake of a disagreement over what rules should govern the local church, he moved to Stamford, Connecticut. There, he was appointed town magistrate and a deputy to the General Court in New Haven.

Robert Coe was "a fine example of the Puritan of his day; a man of vigorous physique, restless energy, strict integrity, strong convictions, and great force of character," the American genealogist Joseph Gardner Bartlett recorded. By all accounts, Coe was outspoken and adventurous, words that could be used seven generations later to describe Barbara Bush.

After yet another battle over church governance, Coe and the Reverend Richard Denton, famed for the passion of his preaching, decided to move across Long Island Sound to the new settlement of Hempstead, on Long Island.

Coe would stay in Hempstead for eight years, his longest stretch in one place since leaving England. He acquired large tracts of land and served as magistrate of the town under the Dutch. At age fifty-six, Coe founded yet another new settlement a few miles west, then called Mespat and now called Newtown, part of Queens. He served as magistrate of Newtown for four years, and as an elder in the new church there.

At the time, Long Island was divided, the eastern end under English authority, the western under Dutch. There were rumors that Peter Stuyvesant, the Dutch director general of the colony of New Netherland, had offered to pay local Native Americans to slaughter the English settlers. As the town deputy, Coe traveled first to Boston to urge the Massachusetts Bay Colony to protect their fellow English settlers on Long Island, then to New Amsterdam to meet with Dutch officials. Governor Stuyvesant confirmed the unsettling rumors; Coe negotiated an agreement to safeguard the settlers. His efforts and the end of the First Anglo-Dutch War brought peace for a time.

Not all of the family's actions were heroic. There are indications that one of Robert Coe's sons, John, owned slaves. The religious liberty that Robert Coe espoused applied to Puritans; other religious minorities like Quakers, Baptists, and Catholics were often not welcome. His son Benjamin was among those who signed a letter pledging to help the Dutch crack down on Quakers. (It was Benjamin, the son of Robert Coe and his first wife, Mary, who continued the direct line of ancestry to Barbara Bush.)

By then, Benjamin had moved with his father to help found the town of Jamaica, now part of Queens. In 1662, Robert's son John joined in leading a successful revolt against the Dutch government of Long Island. Robert Coe had served as magistrate in Jamaica under the Dutch, and he was reappointed magistrate under the British. He was named to other grand-sounding posts of authority: Judge of the Courts of Oyer and Terminer, and High Sheriff of Yorkshire.

By then, he was the oldest resident in town. At age seventy-five, in 1671, he finally retired from public life. Seventeen years later, at ninety-two, he passed away, his influence and his progeny established in this new land.

—— ——

In the seventeenth century, Robert Coe, Barbara Pierce's ancestor through her mother, was a leader in the first movement of Europeans to America.

In the nineteenth century, James Pierce, Barbara's ancestor through her father, was a pioneer in traversing the upheaval and opportunities of the Industrial Revolution. It was through this family line that she would be born the distant cousin of the nation's disastrous fourteenth president, Franklin Pierce, who served in the White House during the lead-up to the Civil War. With the Pierce family saga—wealth gained, then lost—her forebears once again were caught up in the narrative of the nation.

In his day, everyone referred to her great-great-grandfather as General Pierce. The title was an honorific, but after he built a town and a fortune, it seemed to fit.

When James Pierce was born in 1810 in Swanzey, New Hampshire, he inherited no particular assets beyond quick wits and an entrepreneurial spirit. He worked on the family farm, attended local country schools, and at age seventeen got a job in the lumber business. He and his cousin formed a merchant business, trading cotton, horses, clocks, and stoves between New Hampshire and Erie, Pennsylvania. He began expanding into mining and eventually moved to Sharpsville, in western Pennsylvania, near the Ohio border.

At the time, Sharpsville was no more than a few houses around a gristmill and a sawmill. The town was established in 1820 by James Sharp, who fled west in 1847 when the sheriff seized the gristmill for debts. Pierce, who arrived in 1856, would build the small community into an industrial center. He was "a wiry, well-spoken man with a driving personality and immense 'know-how,'" reputed to have a voice that carried well, the Sharon *Herald* approvingly noted. In his obituary, the Greenville *Record-Argus* described him as "a fine specimen of true New

England manhood," a man with "indomitable energy and fixed purpose in life."

That purpose was doing the heavy work of the Industrial Revolution, and profiting handsomely from it.

General Pierce made money from coal mining, from iron foundries, and from railroads. He built a railroad to carry raw materials to his foundries from Lake Superior, in Michigan. He opened a coal mine near Hickory Township, where his homestead was located. He built furnaces in Mount Hickory with William Lawrence Scott, a multimillionaire railroad tycoon and the mayor of Erie. Pierce was the leader of a group that built the Sharpsville and Oakland Railroad, the first railroad in the Shenango Valley. He founded the Iron Banking Company, which would become the First National Bank of Sharpsville.

Pierce became a millionaire when that status signaled something big. By the time he died, he was worth $1.5 million, the equivalent of more than $33 million in 2018 dollars.

He lived like a millionaire too. During his final years, he focused his attention on constructing a mansion the likes of which Sharpsville had never seen. A local newspaper reported the jaw-dropping cost: He spent $110,000 on the house, which translates to about $2.4 million in 2018 dollars.

The *Record-Argus* praised its "great taste and durability, being a combination of the Gothic and Corinthian orders of architecture." The three-story mansion boasted thirty rooms, oak woodwork, and custom wrought iron. The ceilings were painted with frescoes.

General Pierce became the local Rockefeller of Sharpsville, the business magnate whose financial support was sought for civic projects. He contributed land for the First Baptist Church of Sharpsville. He convinced the Universalist Church to locate in Sharpsville. His wife, Chloe Holbrook Pierce, contributed money to erect the Universalist building that stands today; a plaque on the organ memorializes her sister. When Pierce built the headquarters for the Iron Banking Company, he included a space upstairs to host opera performances. (The refurbished

Pierce Opera House offered community productions of operas and plays into the twenty-first century.)

Education was of particular interest to Pierce and his wife. He served as a director for the local public schools, donated land for a new school building, and contributed $1,000 for its construction. His wife was a major supporter of Buchtel College, in Akron. In 1873, at a time when few women even sought higher education, she contributed $10,000 to establish an endowed chair for a female professor at the school. The Pierce Professorship of English Literature would continue for four decades, until Buchtel became the Municipal University of Akron.

But General Pierce's late-in-life passion, his mansion, would be his undoing. Soon after construction had been completed, while his wife was on a shopping trip to Baltimore to buy furniture to fill its grand rooms, he tripped and fell down the cellar steps. The injury to his head was severe. A week later, at age sixty-five, he died.

His funeral was held in his new home, the casket placed in the library, the religious services conducted in the broad hall. The Universalist Church choir sang "He's Gone, He's Gone, Gone to the Silent Land." More than two thousand people gathered, a huge crowd for the small town. Even the children who attended would file somberly by his open casket.

That misstep down the cellar steps would cost General Pierce his life, and it would open the door to the loss of his fortune. The financial strains that followed would reverberate into Barbara Pierce's childhood.

Jonas Pierce—Barbara Bush's great-grandfather—was the firstborn of General James and Chloe Pierce. Their five children would all be boys: Jonas, twins Walter and Wallace, Frank, and James. All of them would be locally prominent. All except Walter would at one time or another be accused of extortion, fraud, or other wrongdoings. Weirdly, all except Frank had six fingers on each hand, a congenital anomaly known as poly-dactyly. (That would be the source of fascination and dispute between

Barbara and her brother Scott concerning the distinguishing defect of the great-great-uncle who sometimes visited their grandfather.)

Jonas was working at his father's coal and iron furnace when the Battle of Fort Sumter opened the Civil War. He was twenty-one, a prime age to join the Union cause. But Jonas, who never seemed to emerge as a heroic or even particularly honorable figure, wasn't among those who rushed to enlist. He "withstood the war fever which was raging around him," the *History of Mercer County* noted without comment. Three months after the First Battle of Bull Run in July, taken by both sides as a sign that a long and bloody war was ahead, Pierce joined the 63rd Pennsylvania Volunteer Infantry. He was transferred to the 111th Pennsylvania Volunteer Infantry and was promoted from corporal to lieutenant to captain.

His unit struggled. They trained at Camp Reed in Pennsylvania, which one soldier described as "the roughest and wickedest place I ever saw." The first engagement with the enemy was "not a roaring success," a historian observed drily. A reconnaissance mission to Charles Town, West Virginia, was attacked by Confederate forces; the Union soldiers retreated in disarray. Pierce's unit then fought under General John Pope as part of the Army of Virginia. The hardtack biscuits, the mainstay of their diet, were "so hard that we have almost to break it with stones so that we can eat it," one soldier complained in a letter home. Half of the regiment had dysentery by July 1862. An outbreak of typhoid decimated its ranks.

After little more than nine months in the military, in July 1862, Jonas Pierce was discharged. The corps commander approved his resignation for reasons not explained in the official documents. It wasn't an easy time to leave the ranks; the Union war effort was at a low ebb. Just two weeks earlier, in the Seven Days Battles, Confederate general Robert E. Lee had pushed the Union Army of the Potomac into retreat in Virginia.

Whatever the reason, Jonas Pierce could count himself as lucky to get out. The 111th Pennsylvania Volunteer Infantry became one of the three hundred regiments that sustained the heaviest losses of any on the Union side. Of the 1,549 men who served in its ranks, 304 died in battle, 304 died of disease or accidents, and 245 were wounded.

He returned home to manage his father's Sharpsville foundry. They established James Pierce and Sons, an iron furnace company. Father James Pierce was a leader of the local Democratic Party, and ran once, unsuccessfully, for the state legislature. Son Jonas Pierce had been a Democrat but switched to the Republican Party in 1884 to protest the failure of the Democratic platform to support higher tariffs on the import of pig iron. He joined the executive committee of the state GOP in 1888. Jonas also served as a town burgess and as president of the school board.

After his father's death in 1874, though, family feuds and larger economic forces would undermine the Pierces' harmony and their finances.

General Pierce hadn't left a clear will or succession plan. After he died, his widow and sons agreed that Jonas and Wallace would be appointed administrators, but that the estate should not be divided. Each son was to take charge of some portion and manage it for their common benefit. As it turned out, his sons lacked the competence to handle the family business, especially during challenging times.

The economics of railroads and pig iron were changing. Efforts to dominate major railroad routes sparked an epic conflict among the nation's robber barons, men like John D. Rockefeller and Andrew Carnegie and William Vanderbilt. The battles within the Pierce family became a small front in their larger war over control of the railroads.

In 1877, the Pierces were united in a lawsuit between the Sharpsville Railroad, which they owned, and the Erie & Pennsylvania Railroad, leased to the dominant Pennsylvania Railroad. But six years later, a pair of additional lawsuits sparked a civil war within the Pierce family. Jonas Pierce supported sending traffic to the Pennsylvania Railroad Company. His four brothers and his mother backed the rival railroads owned by the Vanderbilts.

"Sharpsville will go down in history as a town that had a war wholly her own," a 1924 history of the town would report, "namely a railroad war, where they shed blood, took prisoners and paroled them, but took no lives."

A lawsuit filed by Jonas Pierce and railroad magnate William Lawrence Scott over the election of six directors to the Sharpsville Railroad board went all the way to the Pennsylvania Supreme Court, where they lost. A second lawsuit, over 414 critical shares of capital stock, became a saga of duplicity, blackmail, and fraud.

The stock was owned by the First National Bank of West Greenville. On November 24, 1882, Jonas went to the bank and offered to buy the stock at 60 cents a share, saying they had "but little value" for a railroad that was "largely in debt." He didn't mention that he was being backed by William Scott. Bank officials tentatively accepted but, unhappy about the price, didn't agree to a firm contract. Soon afterward, they sent a letter to Jonas saying they reserved the right to sell to the highest bidder.

Jonas destroyed the bank's letter and testified in later depositions that he had never received it—a claim undercut by a menacing letter he had sent to the bank president dated November 29, 1882. "Would advise you to keep that Rail Road stock matter quiet should you ask for offers it might be unprofitable," the letter said, not specifying exactly what "unprofitable" consequences might follow. "Yours Truly, J.J. Pierce."

The next week, Jonas signed a contract to deliver the stock to William Scott, who wanted a monopoly on the coal trade in the Shenango Valley. Then Jonas and the bank president had an ominous conversation in a back room, their private and apparently threatening exchange later the subject of dispute. A few days later, Frank Pierce walked into the bank and offered a better price, 70 cents a share. The bank officers accepted. When Jonas's business partner, George D. Kelley, showed up two days later to buy the shares, he was told they already had been sold.

Jonas filed a lawsuit; the Mercer County Court of Common Pleas ruled against him. But he wasn't ready to give up without, literally, a fight.

The violent brother-versus-brother brawl that followed in Sharpsville became infamous, drawing coverage by not only the local newspapers but those as far as away as New York City. The *Pittsburgh Post-Gazette* headlined its story "The Fighting Pierces." It started when Jonas Pierce and workers from the Pennsylvania Railroad began to build tracks from his iron furnaces to the Pennsylvania line, a route that required crossing the Sharpsville Railroad tracks.

Jonas's brother Wallace and Sharpsville Railroad workers responded with a show of force. "Wallace Pierce attacked his brother Jonas, striking him a brutal blow in the face," the newspaper reported. "James Pierce, son of Jonas Pierce, came to his father's rescue and vanquished his pugnacious uncle by knocking him down with a stone. A general riot was imminent, but cool heads and police interference brought about a parley which prevented further bloodshed."

The story ended ominously: "More trouble is anticipated."

Local law enforcement was less effective in handling the near riot than the newspaper article suggested. In a scene that sounds comical, local sheriff's deputies sympathetic to the Sharpsville Railroad were sworn in and began to arrest the Pennsylvania Railroad workers. They converted a railroad caboose into a makeshift magistrate's office. Each time the deputies brought a new set of prisoners through the front, however, the men who already had been arrested would slip out the back and return to work on the tracks. A local history reported one man was arrested fourteen times.

More lawsuits followed. Jonas's brothers twice took him to court to allege fraud and financial malfeasance in connection with his management of a mine in Marquette, Michigan. Both cases went to the Michigan Supreme Court. Both times, Jonas Pierce lost and was ordered to make payments to his brothers.

Unpaid debts mounted against his company. One day in February 1892, Jonas's business partner, George Kelley, "left the company's works at Sharpsville in good spirits and walked to an empty car on a siding nearby," the *Altoona Tribune* reported, before "shooting himself through the head with a bullet from a revolver." Forty-eight years old, he left behind a wife, children, and a legal and financial mess. A story in the *Pittsburgh Dispatch* a few days later, headlined "Trouble Following a Suicide," noted financial judgments against the company from the First National Bank of Youngstown and the Iron Banking Company.

At a meeting in March, the creditors agreed to give Pierce, Kelley, and Co. two years to repay liabilities that totaled between $100,000 and $150,000. Frank Pierce was given control. The factory was shut down to wait for improvements in the price of iron—which never came.

The family's fissures distracted the Pierces from responding to economic trends that ultimately would crush their iron companies. Southern competition and overproduction were undercutting pig-iron prices. Steel production was on the rise, but the Pierces didn't adjust to meet the new demand. Then the Panic of 1893 contributed to the collapse of railroads and banks, and a wave of mergers hastened the demise of independent iron manufacturers. That was the final straw for the industrial empire that General James Pierce had built.

The Pierce businesses were beset by creditors and lawsuits. Their unpaid debts were a factor in the collapse of the Commercial National Bank in Milwaukee. The city of Sharpsville filed a lien against property Jonas owned on Main Street. The glorious mansion his father had built eventually was abandoned and finally demolished.

Jonas's five children—Scott, James, Chloe, Jonas Jr., and Frederick—would not have the privileged life of their father. For Scott, the grandfather of Barbara Pierce, acquiring money would be a constant struggle until he could rely on his son, Marvin, to support him.

In 1905, a bankrupt Jonas, who had been so reluctant to enlist, applied for a Civil War soldier's pension as a "partial invalid." The onetime scion of an industrial fortune was relieved to get it: $8 a month.

Chapter Three

The Football Star and the Campus Beauty

Marvin Pierce, who would become Barbara's father, was born as his family's fortune was unraveling.

A year earlier, in 1892, his grandfather's business partner, George Kelley, had committed suicide, leading to revelations about the crushing debts their company had accumulated. Marvin was born on June 17, 1893, six months after the Panic of 1893 had sent the economy into a depression that would last for the next four years. Gone was the comfortable life that Marvin's father, Scott, had enjoyed during his childhood in Sharpsville, Pennsylvania, courtesy of the industrial empire built by General James Pierce.

Scott met his wife, Mabel Marvin, who would become Barbara Pierce's grandmother, when they were students at Buchtel College in Akron, Ohio, sixty-five miles or so west of Sharpsville. He dropped out of college after two years, worked for his father's company in Sharpsville for five years, and then spent a year at a job in Chicago for a pig-iron dealership that was doing business with the family's firm. At that point, his career took a tumble from which it never recovered, and his family was no longer in any position to bail him out.

Scott didn't inherit the fervor or skill for business that marked the lives of his grandfather and his son. When he moved back to Akron to sell insurance, the local newspapers published items not about Scott's financial prowess but about his performances in local music productions. The *Akron Beacon Journal* ran a correction, presumably after he complained, that apologized for failing to mention him in a story about a recital. "Mr. Pierce sang a beautiful baritone solo," the correction read. Another story chronicled a whist club he formed for fellow enthusiasts of the English card game.

In 1898, Scott and Mabel and their two children, Marvin and Charlotte, settled near Dayton, Ohio, in Harrison Township. Scott moved to New York City for a year or two—just what he was doing there isn't clear—and the rest of his family moved in with his in-laws. (Mabel's father, Dr. Jerome Marvin, manufactured baking powder and sold it for five cents a bag at his pharmacy.) Finally, Scott returned to Dayton, and stayed. For a half dozen years, he taught a salesmanship class at the Dayton YMCA.

He never seemed to hit his stride. "Daddy's father, Scott Pierce, was not a success in life," Barbara Bush acknowledged, making the success of his son Marvin all the more impressive. As a little girl growing up in Rye, New York, she would sometimes take the overnight train with her father to Dayton, where he was overseeing construction at the McCall's publishing plant, to visit her grandparents. She remembered her grandfather as an eccentric figure who would take her downtown on the bus wearing his bedroom slippers.

"They had a tiny little house, and it was very, very hot in Dayton, and he would sleep in the basement," she said. She would sleep in a Murphy bed that pulled out of the wall in a downstairs bedroom. "My auntie, the hunchback, stayed upstairs. My grandmother Mabel did, too, and my great-grandmother." Her great-grandmother would lock her bedroom door at night so she could take off her wig. "The lady with the white hair," Barbara called her.

The family had settled in Riverdale, Ohio, a Dayton suburb that happened to be home to industrial giants including Thomas J. Watson, who built IBM, and Edward Andrew Deeds, an engineer and inventor involved in the development of early cars and planes. Marvin was drawn to engineering and eventually earned a master's degree in engineering from a joint program at MIT and Harvard.

But it was football that first propelled his future.

Handsome, graceful, and six feet tall, "Monk" Pierce was "the best all around athlete that the Gem City ever developed," the *Xenia Daily Gazette* raved in 1914, calling Dayton by its nickname. "Pierce is a handsome young fellow with ability in every line of sport. Newspapers claim him to be the best all-around athlete in Ohio."

The renowned West Point football coach Earl "Red" Blaik grew up six houses down the street and became a lifelong friend. He counted Marvin, who was four years older, as a role model and a hero. None of the industrial titans in Dayton "loomed as large in my boyhood eyes as Steele High's star back and pitcher, Marvin 'Monk' Pierce," Blaik wrote in his autobiography. "By example at Steele and more directly later at Miami [University], Monk exerted considerable influence on my career as an athlete."

As a high school athletic star, Marvin Pierce was recruited for college ball in violation of National Collegiate Athletic Association regulations at the time, albeit rules that were widely flouted. Athletic scholarships didn't exist; schools were required to draw athletes from the general student body. In response, colleges with competitive sports programs often arranged undemanding jobs for the best prospects or offered them under-the-table payments.

That's what Miami University in Oxford, Ohio, apparently negotiated with Scott Pierce. A handwritten letter from George R. Eastman, who worked for the Ohio High School Athletic Association, reported to a professor at the school that he had met with Scott. (The letter was found in the college's files on Marvin.) Scott told Eastman that his son would be inclined to enroll at Miami "*if there should be $300.00 a year in it*" (emphasis added). He would keep Marvin "completely in the dark" until the school was ready to make an offer, Scott told him.

The effort by a father to cash in on his son's athletic prowess wasn't unusual in that day nor, for that matter, in more modern times. Marvin would support his parents financially for the rest of their lives, even when he was newly married and living on an Army salary. His new wife made it clear she was annoyed when Scott wrote them about taking up golf while his son was deployed in Europe during World War I, but Marvin never seemed to mind.

He never complained about his father's dependency or the instability of his early years. He had an expansive embrace and unconditional love for him, as he would have later for his daughter. On his father's sixtieth birthday, Marvin wrote a tribute to him, a poem titled "Lines on My Best Friend Turning Sixty."

His father warned Eastman that other schools were interested in Marvin. The University of Pennsylvania had offered to pay all his expenses if he would go to a fake job at a downtown office for thirty minutes a day. The University of Chicago made a similar pitch. "His own and his parents' sense of honor were too high to accept," Eastman reported, saying the Miami University offer would have to be "above board."

Professor A. E. Young forwarded the letter to the president of the school, Raymond Hughes, with an encouraging note that described Marvin as "one of the best all-round men that will enter college anywhere this fall." In his reply, Hughes didn't explicitly approve the payment. "I appreciate, however, the value of getting this man here," he wrote, "and I shall give this careful thought."

Whatever happened next, Miami University was where Marvin Pierce enrolled that fall, and he became the school's marquee player. Blaik described him as "Miami's star pitcher as well as backfield ace, a Big Man on Campus." By his senior year, he was captain of the football team and an All-Ohio running back. He played not only football but also baseball, basketball, and tennis—a nine-letter man, his daughter would later brag.

Money would become an issue again, threatening his college career. During the summer between his sophomore and junior years, Marvin began playing for a minor-league team, the Dayton Shilohs. "Pierce

Pitching Fine Ball," a *Lima News* headline read. The story of a 5–0 victory over a local team described him as "one 'Monk' Pierce, Dayton citizen, whose pastime is heaving the horsehide for the Shiloh base ball crowd."

Then he was notified that playing for the semipro team broke collegiate rules. "He will be declared ineligible to participate in further intercollegiate athletics and will be relieved of all his athletic laurels," he was warned. The alarming headline in the *Daily Gazette* declared: "Pierce May Be Black Listed." Two other students who were playing for the Dayton Shilohs received similar warnings. But Marvin was allowed to continue to play after the team assured the university that the students were receiving no compensation beyond expenses. Given Marvin's financial strains, that denial may stretch credulity, and it's possible he received special treatment because of his standing. The other two players didn't return to school in the fall.

Marvin was an outstanding student and a popular figure on campus as well as a star athlete. A local newspaper described him as "a fine specimen of all around well balanced young man." In 1916, he graduated magna cum laude and Phi Beta Kappa. He was elected class president as a freshman, vice president of the Student Forum as a junior, and a three-year representative on the student senate. As a freshman, he formed the Wildmen Club, which seemed to be devoted mostly to chewing tobacco. He was a leader of the Beta Theta Pi fraternity; that would prove to be crucial when he was trying to land a job after graduate school.

He was ambitious and driven in a way that was more reminiscent of his great-grandfather General James Pierce than of his hapless father— qualities Marvin would need for his rise in business and society. In photographs taken during his years in college, his eyes are intensely focused, even penetrating.

The praise from professors and classmates for his achievements, his athleticism, and his character was similar to the praise that a generation later would greet another golden boy, George Herbert Walker Bush, at Andover and Yale. When Pierce was a senior, the university president volunteered some advice, never taken, on what line of work he should try "in the new big world" he was about to face.

"President Hughes thought I should go into politics," Marvin Pierce recalled.

~ ~ ~

Pauline Robinson, who would become Barbara's mother, seemed to define the proper young lady.

She was a campus beauty, a natural fit with the school's star athlete. In the college yearbook, the *Recensio*, she attracted more attention for her looks than her studies. "March 8th—Pauline Robinson wears her hair back and looks like a Madonna," an entry in the 1915 yearbook sighed. Another entry seemed to make a juvenile joke about ogling her breasts: "Pauline Robinson does her regular weekly darning in history of Education. Chapel Speaker says 'I'm glad Miss to look into your bright -------.' Loud applause."

As a freshman, Pauline accompanied Red Blaik to a dance at Beta Theta Pi; the dance card listed Miss Robinson and Mr. Blaik as doing the waltz and the two-step. That was also Monk's fraternity; it's possible she encountered the handsome upperclassman then. She played first violin in the school orchestra and sang in the choir, graduating with a two-year teacher's diploma in 1916. Then she moved back to her hometown of Marysville, Ohio, where she taught sixth grade and led the Christian Endeavor Society at the First Presbyterian Church.

When Marvin Pierce came courting, his visits were considered notable enough to warrant gossipy mentions in the *Union County Journal* and the *Marysville Journal-Tribune*. World War I complicated their romance, as World War II would for their daughter's. A month after Congress declared war on Germany, in April 1917, Marvin registered for the draft. He was then studying for a master's degree in engineering, and he asked for an exemption to finish his courses. The Army agreed. A year later, he reported for duty in the Army Corps of Engineers Reserves.

Late that summer, in August 1918, Second Lieutenant Marvin Pierce and Pauline Robinson would have a small, wartime wedding—one that their daughter Barbara would echo a generation and a war later. They were married at the bride's hometown Presbyterian church, in Marysville. Only weeks later, he would be deployed to Europe.

World War I was entering its final months after four long and bloody years of battle. Allied forces had just launched the Hundred Days Offensive, which would force the Germans to seek an end to the war. Marvin and his unit boarded the transport ship HMS *Plassy*, headed to the English port of Liverpool, to fill the gaps "left by the heroic youths who had fallen beneath the mailed fist of Prussian autocracy." He was in Company One, 284 men who were part of the Washington Barracks SARD (September Automatic Replacement Draft) Engineers. After landing, his company was detached to construct the American Rest Camp, being built to accommodate a larger army.

They were still at work when news of the Armistice arrived on November 11, 1918. The Great War was finally over. Marvin was made head of the unit, which served as the honor guard for President Woodrow Wilson when he visited Manchester, England, in January 1919, during a European tour before the Versailles negotiations that officially ended the war. Once again, Marvin's athletic prowess boosted his profile. He created and coached a US-style football team, which won the American Championship of England, then competed against American teams in France.

A few months after the Armistice, he was shipped stateside, arriving in Hoboken, New Jersey, in April 1919 and then honorably discharged in May. Within a year, daughter Martha would arrive, his new family with Pauline Robinson Pierce begun. On June 8, 1925, Barbara was born at Booth Memorial Hospital, then on Manhattan's Lower East Side.

Pauline's father, James E. Robinson, was a notable man, and ahead of his time.

The man who would become Barbara Bush's maternal grandfather was a lawyer, prosecutor, and judge known as having a sunny disposition and as being unpretentious, fearless, and fair. For decades, he took the side of women who accused their husbands of abuse, even when those men were prominent in the community—not a stance followed by everyone in law enforcement at the time, or since. The blowback from one case may have nearly cost him an election. When his daughter married Marvin Pierce, he was in the middle of what would be a successful campaign for a seat on the Ohio Supreme Court.

Robinson was born on his family's farm near Marysville in 1868, little more than three years after the Civil War had ended. Robinson's mother was Sarah Coe, a descendant of the colonial leader Robert Coe. He graduated from Marysville High School but struggled to scrape together the funds to go to college, attending Ohio Wesleyan for a time but then dropping out when he ran out of money. He traveled as a salesman in Kansas for a firm that faltered, then returned to the farm. In time, he began working at the law firm of Robinson and Woodburn in Marysville. His uncle James W. Robinson, a former state legislator and one-term member of Congress, was a partner.

In the fall of 1890, James E. Robinson began studying law at Ohio State University in Columbus, a member of the law school's first graduating class. He passed the bar in 1892, returned to the Marysville area, and began running ads in local newspapers, promising "prompt attention given all business entrusted to his care."

He managed all sorts of legal work, from writing wills to defending bootleggers and murderers. ("Always eloquent, Attorney James E. Robinson out-did himself," the *Marysville Journal-Tribune* gushed in a story about his three-hour speech to the jury, although the defendant may not have agreed; he was convicted.) Robinson also began to handle divorces, sometimes representing husbands who accused their wives of cheating on them but more often working on behalf of wives who accused their husbands of beating them.

Her husband threatened to shoot her and "to pound her into mince meat," one woman he was representing told the court. Another said her husband, a schoolteacher, was writing "many spicy love letters" to a student and had "choked her until she became black in the face." There was a woman who sued for divorce after twenty-three years of marriage and bearing eight children. She said her husband had choked her and beaten her, then threatened to burn down the house and the barn. When he attended a revivalist tent meeting and the minister preached a sermon against husbands abusing their wives, he attacked the minister and tore down his tent.

In 1899, Robinson was elected prosecuting attorney of Union County, a post responsible for prosecuting defendants on all sorts of charges, from fraud to murder. "Mr. Robinson's hustling qualities are well known," a local newspaper noted approvingly during the campaign. "Robinson has youthful energy and vim to devote to public service, his honesty and probity are unquestioned." In his new post, he continued to act to protect women who felt they were in peril. In one case, an accused wife-beater came to his office to tearfully plead his case, then took out a revolver and tried to shoot himself in the head. (Fortunately, the rusty gun didn't fire.)

When he was county prosecutor, Robinson took the case of Mary Rodgers, who was seeking a divorce from Joseph Rodgers, a wealthy and prominent farmer. The details of his alleged mistreatment apparently were too shocking to repeat. The *Richwood Gazette* called her description of them "sensational, so much so we think it best for those interested not to give it in full."

Taking on Joseph Rodgers may have nearly cost Robinson his job as county attorney. A few months later, he won a second term by just 314 votes after several influential Republicans in the area openly campaigned against him, even though he was the party's nominee and the incumbent. After the election, Robinson brought charges of voter fraud against another leading Republican farmer who somehow had managed to cast a ballot in every precinct in town; the official records don't make it clear whose side he was on.

In that election, Robinson also was opposed by African Americans in the county, a small voter bloc but one considered solidly Republican. They objected to "some of his remarks, concerning their race, to the court in a recent trial." What he had said to spark accusations of racism isn't detailed.

Two years later, he didn't run for a third term, instead returning to private practice. He briefly sought the Republican nomination for Congress in 1909. In 1915, the Ohio governor appointed him to a seat on the state court of appeals in a Democratic-dominated district; he lost his reelection bid in 1916. In 1918, he won a seat on the Ohio Supreme Court, where accounts of the day praised him as being a thoughtful and respected jurist. His judicial philosophy was reliably conservative, pro-business, and antiregulation. In at least two cases, his dissenting opinions ended up being upheld by the US Supreme Court.

During his third term, in 1932, he fell ill and died of a heart ailment ten days later. He was sixty-three years old.

⌒ ⌒

Barbara Pierce, six years old when her grandfather died, had little memory of him. But Robinson's widow, Lulu Dell Flickinger Robinson, would become Barbara's favorite grandparent and a model for how women could defy society's expectations. After her husband died, Lulu and three friends, all widows in their sixties, bought a small trailer and drove it across the United States, toured Canada and Mexico, and tried, unsuccessfully, to make it to Argentina. They packed a knife for protection, Barbara's brother Scott recalled.

The whole notion seemed so outlandish that wire services filed incredulous stories about them. The headline in the *Indianapolis Star* sounded slightly ominous: "Mexico Lures Four Widowed Grandmothers." The United Press story quoted Mrs. James E. Robinson (in the style of the day, not bothering to mention her given name) as saying cheerfully, "We think life begins at 60."

In Rye, those adventures alarmed her daughter and thrilled her granddaughter. "She was very adventurous," Barbara Bush recalled, her grandmother's appeal enhanced because her mother didn't quite approve. "Pretty frisky."

Chapter Four

——⋆——

Stuck in the Middle

She was easy to overlook.

Barbara Pierce was stuck in the middle, the third child of four, and overshadowed by siblings who seemed to have more problems or more prospects than she did. Her older sister, Martha, was the family beauty, so striking that she appeared on the cover of *Vogue* for its 1940 college fashion issue. Her older brother, Jimmy, was the troublemaker who once accidentally shot his little sister in the leg with his BB gun and threatened to "kill" her if she told their mother. ("For a week, I wore long, high woolen socks and feared death," she said later.) Her younger brother, sweet-tempered Scott, spent much of his childhood in hospitals for an ailment that left one arm deformed and his family deeply in debt.

Barbara described her childhood as idyllic, although like just about every childhood it was also complicated. It made her independent-minded and competitive, at athletics and everything else, and a sharp judge of people. She was popular, the leader of a close-knit clique of girls in elementary school who would remain her friends for life. She learned to wield humor as both a shield and a weapon. And there were hard lessons for the future on the costs, financial and emotional, of caring for a child undergoing painful stints in the hospital.

The redoubtable woman Barbara Pierce would become was shaped in Rye, a fast-growing Westchester County suburb during the years between World War I and World War II. It was filled with up-and-coming company men who commuted to New York City and their stay-at-home wives, the revolution in women's roles decades away. She sparred with her siblings, clashed with her mother, Pauline, and adored her father, Marvin. "He was the fairest man I knew until I met George Bush," she said.

Luckily, her father adored her too.

With her mother, though, there was constant conflict.

Pauline Robinson's good looks had been her calling card; she had caught Marvin Pierce's eye when she was the prettiest girl on campus at Miami University. That may help explain why she put such store by her daughters' appearances, even at the cost of Barbara's self-confidence. She had what her children called "enthusiasms." Flowers were her passion and the pollination of lilies her special expertise. She was president of the Rye Garden Club and conservation chairman of the Garden Club of America. (Her husband was not a fan of the group. In a letter to a friend, Marvin described the Garden Club as "an association of the snottiest outfits engaged in that sort of work.") Local newspaper gossip columns faithfully recorded the teas, luncheons, dinners, and debutante parties she hosted or attended at their club, the Apawamis—a nice club, to be sure, but not the most elite. She fretted about her family's social standing and spent more money than they had to spare. Even those who loved her acknowledged she had little apparent sense of humor.

"Mrs. Pierce, she was tough to get along with," recalled William "Bucky" Bush, George Bush's youngest brother. "She was kind of a gloomy person, and she thought Martha, Barbara's older sister, had hung the moon—tall and beautiful and long, curly hair. Barbara got kind of second shrift with her mother, which I don't think she ever got over," he told me. But he described Barbara's father as "a really all-time wonderful man—bright, funny, literate, well-read, beautiful athlete and just fun to be around."

Pauline Pierce could hardly have been more different from her younger daughter, who was funny and irreverent, athletic and pugnacious, not particularly concerned about fashion, and prone to pudginess. "I loved her very much, but was hurt by her," Barbara Bush would write in her memoir. "(I am sure that I hurt her a lot, too.)" She told me she felt her father favored her over her sister, but she was "probably the child least close to my mother."

Even Miss Covington's Dancing School, held at the Episcopal Church in Rye on Friday afternoons and evenings, was a source of conflict between them. Barbara would put on a party dress; Pauline would sit in the balcony with the other mothers to watch. The problem was that girls always outnumbered boys in the class. When the boys were told to pick their partners—a merciless early lesson in gender roles and power—Pauline would watch in horror as her daughter raised her hand to play the part of a boy. Barbara was taller than most of the boys; she was trying to preempt the humiliation of being the last girl left on the sidelines. Her mother found the idea of playing a boy more humiliating. She finally forbade her daughter to volunteer again, no matter what.

They were always at odds. Barbara and her father struggled with their weight, a bond between them; Martha and Scott were naturally slender. "I remember my mother saying, all in one breath, 'Eat up, Martha! Not you, Barbara!'" she recalled. Her mother joked that Barbara had weighed a hundred pounds at birth—a needle more pointed than funny. When she went to summer camp at age twelve, Barbara recalled with chagrin, she weighed 148 pounds.

In her memoir, Barbara's fondest childhood memories seemed to revolve around eating. "The best food in the world came out of our kitchen," she wrote, prepared not by her mother but by the household staff of two. On Sundays, when the cook had the afternoon off, the Pierce family would eat a big lunch—"baked chicken with the world's best stuffing and mashed potatoes"—and make do in the evening with graham crackers and cream. "A glorious dish," she exulted.

In a youthful episode that became family lore, Barbara at age ten bought a can of Marshmallow Fluff—the name is an apt clue of its sticky sweetness—and happily dug into the tin with her fingers to eat as she walked home. By the time she arrived there, her mother had gotten three phone calls from neighbors reporting the cute scene.

"Mother did not think it was quite so cute," she recalled. Pauline felt humiliated. Barbara became violently sick. She could never bring herself to eat Marshmallow Fluff again.

The friction between them was hard to miss, especially given how Pauline doted on her older daughter. June Biedler, a childhood pal, described Barbara's exacting mother as "a little mean to her," perhaps one reason Barbara could be a little mean to others. At the local public elementary school, the Milton School, Barbara emerged as the ringleader of a posse of girls—Joan Herman, Posy Morgan, Lucille Schoolfield, Kate Siedle, and June. While she remembered Barbara fondly, June as an adult recalled in a 1992 *Vanity Fair* profile that her friend could be cutting, "kind of a gang leader." She teased June about her childhood stammer. She would summarily declare one of the girls persona non grata for the day, and the others would follow her dictate.

The *Vanity Fair* article angered Barbara Bush and hurt her. The headline included a comparison she found particularly galling: "Barbara's Backlash: Suddenly the First Lady Is Reported to Be a Woman So Fiercely Calculating She Puts Nancy Reagan to Shame." Her aide, Peggy Swift, had brought her a copy when it hit the newsstands. "The meanest article I have ever read about me," she wrote in her diary, wounded and sarcastic in response. "There are quotes from 'people who want to remain anonymous because they are afraid that I will kill them.' I hate that."

In an interview a quarter century later, she mentioned the article to me, saying a childhood friend (it was June, but she remembered it as being Posy) had portrayed her as "sort of a pain." I replied, "It just made it sound like you were the alpha." That sounded better, she said, adding, "I probably needed to do that"—that is, to be the one in charge.

The life lessons Barbara took from her mother were more often about what not to do, how not to behave.

The mother overspent; the daughter would be frugal. "She begged and borrowed, and she never paid her bills, and she'd say, 'Don't shop at Macy's, go to Lord and Taylor's,'" because of overdue accounts at one store or the other, Barbara Bush told me. Her mother kept a stack of unpaid bills in a drawer next to her bed; when she died in a freak auto accident, her husband discovered that she had left deposits on items at antique shops all over the county. Barbara and her brother Scott "pay our bills the day they come, because we don't want to be like Mother," she said.

The mother was perpetually dissatisfied with her lot in life; the daughter would declare herself delighted with the turn of events, whether that meant moving to the wilds of Texas or soldiering through another campaign. Pauline often talked about what she would do "when her ship came in." Even as a child, Barbara thought that was misguided. Her mother had a wonderful husband and four children and good friends. What more could she want? Hadn't her ship already come in?

"Probably her most important lesson was an inadvertent one," Barbara Bush said later, stating what came close to being her mantra. "You have two choices in life: You can like what you do, or you can dislike it. I have chosen to like it."

They lived at 31 Onondaga Street, a street named for one of the Iroquois nations in a neighborhood known as Indian Village. The three-story, five-bedroom house was a Georgian Revival, a stately brick house in an affluent suburb. It was a step up for the Pierces, who moved there from an apartment in the Bronx shortly before Barbara was born. Even so, the houses were nothing like the grand old-money mansions in nearby Greenwich, Connecticut, where George Bush and his family lived.

As in many upscale suburbs of the day and later, there were no African Americans living in the neighborhood, except as servants. There were Jewish families, but anti-Semitism was rife. As a girl, Barbara was shocked when she learned that her friend Joan Herman wasn't allowed to go to the private clubs favored by the other girls' families because she was Jewish. "Mother said, 'Well, she has her own club,'" Barbara Bush recalled. "That didn't cut it with me." In modern-day Houston, she noted, "the biggest philanthropists, the most giving people, are Jewish."

Her father was a success, albeit in an unexpected career. Marvin Pierce had been trained as an engineer but had trouble finding a job when he finished graduate school. He landed one at the McCall Corporation, apparently through a fraternity brother from Miami University, John Simpson. Simpson was the comptroller at Filene's Department Store and would soon join the board of directors of McCall, the publisher of leading women's magazines. Pierce was hired as a clerk at McCall in 1921 and rose fast. Within a year he was appointed assistant to the president. By 1926, he was a vice president.

Pierce didn't know much about recipes or fashion, but his engineering background was invaluable in overseeing the expansion of the company's printing plant in Dayton, and he was a tough negotiator with paper suppliers and others. He played a major role in the early history of *Newsweek*, serving as the provisional publisher during a dispute between the magazine's founder and its owners in 1937. In December 1945, he became president of the McCall Corporation, and later publisher of *McCall's* magazine. He eventually joined the company's board of directors.

Marvin Pierce would make the fifteen- to twenty-minute walk from home to the station each morning to catch the train into the city; Barbara would delight in walking with him, then board the bus for school. On the morning ride into the city, Marvin Pierce would read the newspapers; in the evening, he'd take a seat in the club car to have a drink and play bridge. (George Bush's father, Prescott, was commuting on the same train, getting off two stops down the line, in Greenwich, although the two men didn't know each other then.) The Great Depression forced the Pierce family to pinch pennies, but they never faced the devastating financial hardship that beset many Americans. Pierce was making the impressive salary of a rising New York City executive—$22,500 in 1935, about $417,000 in 2018 dollars.

Even so, money was a constant source of tension at home. The week before Barbara Bush was married, Marvin Pierce took her to New York for a father-daughter luncheon, just the two of them, and gave her some advice. "The thing that will break up most marriages is money," he cautioned her. The two had a close and candid relationship; unlike her mother, he wasn't taken aback by her bluntness. She replied, "You're a fine one to be talking. Mother has a whole drawer of unpaid bills."

Then he told her how he had managed to keep the family finances under at least a modicum of control. "I know what I'm going to give her every year," he said. "I cut it in half and I give her the half," pretending that's the total for the year. At Christmas and at their anniversary in August, he would dispense the other half to bail her out of her debts, "and she thinks I'm a great hero."

⁓ ⸺

Scott Pierce was two years old when he fell off the back of his brother's bike and broke his collarbone. On an X-ray, doctors spotted a growth on the bone of his right arm, a cyst. They told his parents it was a perilous condition.

He was almost three when the first operation took place; he was nine by the time the last one was over. There were five operations in all. They dug out the cyst, then transplanted bone chips from his shins and a hip to reinforce the weakened spot. The operations required him to spend months at a time in the hospital, then months at home in bed wearing a cast, and sometimes two casts. When he was home, his parents were vigilant about protecting him from childhood illnesses. If Barbara was sick, she had to move in with her friend Lucille Schoolfield until the risk that she could infect her brother was over. He missed second grade entirely; his mother taught him his lessons. She was always by his side, which left her even less time for Barbara and the other children, a skewed family dynamic that created some childhood resentments.

"Part of my job after the operations would be [to be] wheeled around and cheer up everybody else" in the hospital ward, Scott Pierce recalled years later in an interview at his winter home in Fernandina Beach, Florida. By then, Pierce, a retiree who had been president of the stockbrokerage firm EF Hutton, was eighty-seven years old. A few months earlier, his left leg had been amputated after knee replacement surgery went awry, and he was still getting used to being in a wheelchair. Despite all that, he still displayed the sunny disposition that had made him everyone's favorite as a child, even as a patient.

Once, driving Scott to the hospital to have yet another set of X-rays taken, Marvin Pierce was pulled over for speeding. Scott, then nine years old, watched his father break down into tears as he told the police officer that they were on their way to see if his son was going to lose his arm. The officer was so touched that he didn't write a speeding ticket; instead, he provided a police escort for the rest of the way. Thankfully, the X-ray showed that the surgeons had successfully removed the suspicious cells, leaving a thin upper shoulder bone and preserving Scott's arm.

Years later, when she was a young mother caring for her own desperately sick child, Barbara Bush felt a new sympathy for the burden her mother had carried, whatever their other conflicts. "In retrospect, I realize that she had a terrible problem, my brother being so sick," she told me. "She drove into New York every single day to see the boy for three months in the hospital, [then] brought him home. They were scared to death, always, about his health."

The operations left Scott with a malformed upper right arm, three and a half inches shorter than his left, and his parents deeply in debt. They didn't have health insurance, and there was no government program they could tap. Marvin Pierce took out a $100,000 loan from McCall to pay for the medical bills—an enormous sum, equal to more than $1.8 million in 2018 dollars, and one that had to be reported to stockholders. He would spend years repaying it.

The treatment Scott received was considered appropriate at the time. "The treatment of solitary bone cyst is surgical," a study in the *Annals of Surgery* declared flatly in 1934, citing "striking agreement upon this point among the many who have made important contributions to our knowledge of this disease." But under today's protocols, doctors probably would have taken a much less aggressive approach. They would have waited to see if the lesion resolved itself, then tried steroids, a treatment not available at the time. Only as a last resort would they do surgery, especially when the bone affected was tied to growth plates. That could stunt the growth of the limb, as it did with Scott.

There would be striking parallels with Robin's diagnosis of leukemia two decades later. Medical advances made within a generation could have made a world of difference. Today, there might well have been no need for Scott to undergo a series of painful operations. No need for his parents to face years of anguish and worry. No need to endure the repercussions, emotional and physical and financial, that affected them all.

Jimmy Pierce had his own problems, mostly of his own doing. Barbara's older brother didn't like following the rules, and he didn't work particularly well with others, as a child or an adult. He received the most spankings of any of the Pierce children, delivered by his mother with the back of a hairbrush or a wooden clothes hanger. He came in for more disciplinary punishment when he was sent to the Taft School in Watertown, Connecticut, a bucolic prep school for boys.

"He was charming," Barbara Bush told me. "Everybody adored him, but he was at the Taft School and he would write home to Mother: 'Dearest Mother, I have small problems. Caught smoking behind the so-and-so, and I've been put on probation. My marks aren't very good.' And he would end with, 'And I love you, Mother, more than anything.' And she would say, 'Isn't that the sweetest letter?'"

He failed to graduate from Taft on time; his father made him return to campus after his classmates had departed to finish his high school degree. A year after the attack on Pearl Harbor, at age twenty-one, he enlisted in the US Army Air Corps, then was honorably discharged eighteen months later with a diagnosis of bronchiectasis, or damaged lungs. He worked for a time as a trainee at a nuts-and-bolts factory in Port Chester—presumably the same one his sister worked at one summer during the war—then enlisted in the Navy Reserves, serving for almost two years and based for a time in the Philippines.

Martha had been sent to Ashley Hall, in Charleston, South Carolina, and Barbara followed her older sister there. The girls' school had been founded on the grounds of an old plantation, an estate once owned by George Trenholm, a secretary of the Treasury of the Confederacy and a dashing figure who was rumored to be novelist Margaret Mitchell's inspiration for Rhett Butler in *Gone with the Wind*. The rules were strict and the standards traditional: Girls were not allowed to wear pants; they were required to wear stockings; bare ankles were forbidden.

A sanctioned history of Ashley Hall reported that some boarding students still managed to engage in "unladylike-fun"—pranks like sneaking downstairs with flashlights to raid the pantry, or throwing water balloons on people walking down the street. Letters home written by Kathryn Noble, a student there in 1940, said that three girls were caught and punished for leaning out of a window and talking to some boys until 11:05 p.m. "The girls didn't seem to care," she noted.

In those days before the surgeon general had warned of its risks, smoking was permitted. Barbara started smoking when she was a senior at Ashley Hall and spent Thanksgiving with a friend in Beaufort, South Carolina. Wartime made it difficult for her to go home to Rye; her friend's aunt had an inn near the Parris Island Marine Corps base. The girls were forbidden from going outside because the streets were teeming with Marines—who knew what might happen?—so they stayed inside and smoked.

She wouldn't stop smoking for a quarter century. Decades later, she would blame it for the congestive heart failure and chronic lung disease that ultimately took her life at the age of ninety-two.

Once again, she lived in the segregated society of the day; South Carolina still had Jim Crow laws on the books. There were no African American students at Ashley Hall when Barbara Pierce attended; the first black student wouldn't graduate for more than three decades, in 1974. Jewish girls were allowed to attend, but only as day students, not as boarders. "There was always that undercurrent of anti-Semitism there," said Shera Lee Ellison Berlin, who was one of two Jewish students in the lower school in the late 1930s; there was one Jewish girl in the upper school at the time. "I always felt that I was not wanted there."

Martha was a campus star nicknamed "Chicky"—active in the student council, the drama club, the French club. She played on the varsity teams for basketball, tennis, and swimming. She won the school's poetry prize. She was assistant editor of the *Cerberus*, the combination literary magazine and yearbook; the editor that year was Madeleine L'Engle, who would gain fame as the author of *A Wrinkle in Time*.

Still, Martha was always "somewhat of a loner," her sister said. Her writings for the *Cerberus* were full of teen angst. In a short story titled "Flashy," her protagonist softly cries herself to sleep each night; her mother is described as "pretty, frivolous, foolish." As a senior, she wrote a dark poem, titled "Black and White," that seems to be about an engagement ring, a "white stone torn from black dust." It concluded: "Men do her heart desire/Souls burnt by simple fire/Slaves cringing at her ire/They give their all./First came a ribbon red/Years ago—now a shred./Long has her soul been dead—Love, and let fall./She smiles at her conquest; the hard/hard cold band,/Symbol of foul greed, shines pure in/her hand."

When they were adults, the tables would be turned for the two sisters, something that didn't always sit well with Martha. Martha tried a brief foray into politics, heading the Federation of Alsop Citizens Efforts in 1962. The group coordinated campaign volunteers for John Alsop, the Republican nominee for governor of Connecticut; he lost. That was just about the time George Bush was beginning his political climb in Houston. Eventually, Barbara, not Martha, would be the famous one whose picture was on the cover of magazines. Family members would worry that Martha and her husband, Walt, both drank too much.

At Ashley Hall, though, Barbara didn't leave an imprint as big as her older sister. "Everybody liked her," recalled Jane Lucas Thornhill, also a member of the class of 1943, though she couldn't recall anything memorable that the girl they called Barbi did, exactly. Her school awards were mostly small bore. She won the "Promptness Pin" and the Rosalie McCabe Cup for general sportsmanship. She was a champion knitter and the school's underwater swimming champion. She served on the student council and, like all the students, participated in the school's productions of Shakespearean plays. A school test measured her IQ at an impressive 120, edging into the "superior" range. But her grades were mediocre, a mix of Bs and Cs. She once again was stuck in the middle, graduating thirteenth in a class of thirty.

(She had no illusions about her grades. When I asked for permission to see her high school transcript, she wrote a letter on her personal stationery to the College of Charleston, which held the Ashley Hall archives. "Although I fear she will be unimpressed," she wrote in classic Barbara Bush fashion, "I am giving my permission for Susan Page to have access to my academic records at Ashley Hall.")

In four years of high school—the first two at the private Rye Country Day School, when she lived at home, and the last two at Ashley Hall, where she boarded—Barbara received only one A grade. It was an A+ in physical education, as a senior. That year, she had Bs or B-minuses in her other classes—chemistry, English, history, and Latin. She had never been particularly studious, and by then she was even less focused on her schoolwork than before. She had met George Bush at a Christmas dance back home, and she was intoxicated. Her future was with him, she dreamed, not in some classroom or career.

"B. Pierce likes flowers," the 1942 yearbook teased, then used George Bush's nickname. "Her favorite is the poppy!"

— —

When Barbara Bush was ninety-two years old, I asked her to characterize her siblings, to cast them into the roles they had played when they were growing up. She called Martha the pretty one; Jimmy the "Peck's bad boy" (from the children's serial about a lad who was constantly in scrapes); and Scott "the best." And herself? "The little fat one," she said.

That was the image of herself that she kept in her mind's eye throughout her life, but to judge by family and school photos, her sensitivity was at the least an exaggeration. They show Barbara as no more than pleasingly plump when she was a little girl; by the time she was at Ashley Hall she was slender, dark-eyed, and pretty. She was a lissome figure in her wedding photos. In middle age and after bearing six children, she was athletic and sturdy, not morbidly obese. It's just that she was closer to the size of an average American woman than to a fashion model—than, say, her photogenic sister.

Her mother's barbs help explain why Barbara never saw it that way. She was critical of herself and of family, friends, and staffers for their size; her bluntness when she thought they needed to lose weight sometimes hurt feelings, even brought tears. In her diaries, the first thing Barbara Bush often admired about a woman, whether a pal or a prime minister, was that she was slender. She would use self-deprecating humor to make fun of her weight and her wrinkles before anyone else could. And she could almost never accept a compliment about her appearance at face value, even when it came from her enchanted fiancé.

"Goodnite, my beautiful," George Bush said in the only one of his wartime letters to her that survived. He wrote it on the day their engagement announcement was published in the *New York Times*, and he signed it, "Poppy/public fiance as of 12/12/43." She tucked it into the scrapbook she kept chronicling their engagement. "Everytime I say beautiful you about kill me but you'll have to accept it—"

That may help explain this: Then and for the rest of her life, Barbara Pierce would feel grateful and perhaps a little surprised that Poppy Bush, the charismatic young man from the prominent Greenwich family who could have the pick of just about any young woman around, had chosen her.

Chapter Five

———★———

Love and War

Their romance was bracketed by war.

Weeks after the Japanese bombed Pearl Harbor, Barbara Pierce and George Bush met for the first time, their attraction across a crowded room practically cinematic. Months before World War II finally ended, they would be married in her hometown church. He wore his Navy dress blues.

World War II affected everything for their generation. It disrupted their plans, broadened their horizons, and accelerated their timetables. George Bush was so young when they married (he was twenty; she was nineteen) that his parents had to sign papers to authorize the wedding; the age of consent in New York for men then was twenty-one, though for women it was eighteen. "In wartime, the rules change. You don't wait until tomorrow to do anything," Barbara Bush would explain to their children years later. George Bush said they were living with "heightened awareness, on the edge."

Their instant connection sparked a marriage that would endure for more than seven decades. When Barbara Bush died in 2018, they could boast the longest union of any presidential couple in American history. The characteristics that marked the start were apparent for the rest of their lives. They took risks. They trusted their instincts. They rolled with the punches. When her fiancé's return from a war zone was delayed,

Barbara scratched out the date on their engraved wedding invitations to write in a new one by hand.

To be sure, their marriage wouldn't always be a storybook one. There would be heartbreak and strain, including rumors of his infidelity, which he would deny. It would evolve over time from the most traditional of marriages—husband and homemaker, and no question who was in charge—to a partnership in which they would take turns being the strong one at moments of uncertainty, grief, and defeat. At crossroads during his presidential campaigns, hers was the final voice he sought to hear. Their devotion would be particularly fierce at the beginning and near the end.

It all started at the annual Christmas dance at the Greenwich Country Club.

Two weeks earlier, on December 7, 1941, the Japanese had attacked Pearl Harbor on what President Franklin D. Roosevelt proclaimed as "a date which will live in infamy." George heard the news as he was walking across campus at Phillips Academy Andover, in Massachusetts, where he was a senior. His reaction "was the same as every other American— 'We gotta do something about this one.'" Barbara was at Ashley Hall, in Charleston, South Carolina, where she was a junior. "Although fighting had been going on in Europe for several years, war seemed very far away," she said. That was no longer going to be true.

Both had gone home for the holidays. At the dance, the boys wore tuxedos and the girls donned bright party attire. Decades later, George Bush could recall that the pretty girl across the room was wearing a green-and-red holiday dress. He went up to Jack Wozencraft, a friend from Rye who was home from Deerfield Academy. Did he know her? Yes, Jack said; that was Barbara Pierce, who lived in Rye and went to school in South Carolina. Would you like an introduction? "I told him that was the general idea," Bush said, "and he introduced us."

When he was ninety-three years old, his health frail, I asked Bush if he remembered that night, and what had drawn his eye.

Yes, he nodded: "She was so beautiful."

Just as Jack introduced them, the band, which had been playing Glenn Miller tunes, changed tempos from the fox-trot. "He asked if I'd mind sitting out the next dance, as it was a waltz and he didn't know how," Barbara Bush recalled. They talked, and danced, and he asked what she was doing the next night. She told him she was going to another dance, this time at the Apawamis Club in Rye.

When he got home to Greenwich that night, George told his sister, Nancy, that he had met "a wonderful girl...beautiful and funny." When she got home to Rye, Barbara sat on the edge of her mother's bed for a debriefing—a routine Pauline Pierce insisted on after a night out—and told her she had met "the nicest, cutest boy, named Poppy Bush."

He came from an old-money family that bestowed preppy nicknames on just about everyone. His legal name was a mouthful, George Herbert Walker Bush, but everyone called him Poppy. He had been named after his maternal grandfather, George Herbert Walker, a St. Louis investment banker and businessman whose four sons called their father "Pops." That made their nephew "Little Pops," which soon became "Poppy."

George Bush had bloodlines to match those of Barbara Pierce. He had ancestors who had arrived aboard the *Mayflower* too. His fraternal grandfather, Samuel Prescott Bush, made a fortune in iron and steel in Ohio. His father, Prescott Bush, was an investment banker who would be elected to the US Senate from Connecticut. His mother, Dorothy Walker Bush, was the competitive and athletic daughter of Bert Walker, a flamboyant financier who established golf's Walker Cup. Prescott and Dorothy had been married at St. Ann's Episcopal Church in Kennebunkport, Maine, where her family spent summers on a jut of land called Walker's Point.

The night after George met Barbara at the Greenwich Country Club, he showed up at the Rye dance, looking for her. He brought along Nancy, the sister two years his junior, who was curious about the new girl who had caught her big brother's attention. By the time Barbara had gotten up that morning, her mother had been on the case. She "should have been an FBI agent with her superior intelligence network," her exasperated daughter complained. Pauline Pierce had determined that he was "a wonderful boy" from "a very nice family."

It was another member of her family who complicated matters that second night. George asked Barbara to dance. But Barbara's big brother, Jimmy, always the troublemaker, almost immediately cut in. "Aren't you Poppy Bush?" Jimmy demanded. "Please go over and wait on the side. When I get rid of her, I want to talk to you." As it turned out, Jimmy was recruiting George to play in a basketball game between prep school boys and the Rye High School championship team. George agreed, and he asked Barbara if she would go out with him after the game.

The entire Pierce family showed up to watch the basketball game that next Thursday.

George had borrowed his mother's Oldsmobile for their first date after the game, begging his mother to let him use it because it had a radio and the family's other car didn't. "He was so afraid we would sit in stony silence and have nothing to say to each other," Barbara said. "For years he has teased me that there was no silence that night and I haven't stopped talking since."

After the holiday break, Barbara and George exchanged letters through the winter. At spring break in 1942, their time at home over-lapped for only a single day. They double-dated to see *Citizen Kane*, the movie classic that had been released the previous fall. Then George invited Barbara to be his date at Andover's spring prom.

"I think it was perfectly swell of you to invite me to the dance and I would love to come or go or whatever you say," Barbara wrote him on Ashley Hall stationery from South Carolina. "I really am excited but scared to death, too. If you hear a big noise up there, don't worry, it's just my knees knocking."

"I would love to come or go or whatever you say."

She would become more confident in her own views over time, and more direct about expressing them. But the declaration in a sixteen-year-old's hand was one she would follow for decades during his peripa-tetic career, from Texas to New York to China to Washington.

After the prom, George walked Barbara back to her dorm, where she was staying with a housemaster and his wife who were friends of her sister. George kissed her on the cheek "in front of the whole world," she exulted. "I floated into my room and kept the poor girl I was rooming with awake all night while I made her listen to how Poppy Bush was the greatest living human on the face of the earth."

She was besotted. So was he.

During baseball practice that spring at Andover, George was standing just off first base, chatting with a teammate, Junie O'Brien. George reached into his right pocket and pulled out a photo of Barbara Pierce. "I told him she was a winner," O'Brien recalled, "and he said, 'You're telling me. I'm going to marry her.'"

"I couldn't breathe when I was in the room with him; that's how I knew I was in love," Barbara Bush told me decades later. At the time, her health was failing; she was dependent on oxygen as she struggled with congestive heart failure and chronic lung disease. "Here I am, back to not breathing again," she said.

～ ⌣

Ashley Hall was bracing for war. The dining room, fortified with sandbags, became a bomb shelter. Fire drills were replaced by air-raid drills. There were fears along the Atlantic Coast of an enemy attack. In the spring of 1942, German U-boats sank so many freighters off the Outer Banks of North Carolina that it became known as "Torpedo Junction." (That was a twist on "Tuxedo Junction," a Glenn Miller hit song of the day.) A rumor swept the Ashley Hall campus that a German submarine had been sighted offshore. A year would pass before the Navy would confirm that the Coast Guard had sunk a sub, *U-352*, off Cape Lookout on May 9, 1942.

At Andover, too, all the talk was of war.

Secretary of War Henry Stimson delivered the commencement address that spring. He told the graduating class, including George Bush, that the war would be a long one, and that they could serve their country by getting more education before they got into uniform. Bush was not deterred. On June 12, 1942, the day he turned eighteen years old, he took the train to New York with his father to enlist in the US Navy. By August, he was on another train, heading south for preflight training in Chapel Hill, North Carolina. He was a seaman second class, assigned to the 6th Battalion, Company K, Second Platoon.

Back home, Barbara Pierce would do her part for the war effort too. One summer, she worked as a gofer at a nuts-and-bolts factory in Port Chester, riding her bike there with a friend each day. "We went in and delivered coffee and were ordered around by the same people who waited on me in the summers at the Apawamis Club," she told me.

As a farewell present, George bought her a small watch, which she pinned to her dress. They kissed—a real kiss, and a first for both. "I kissed Barbara and I am glad of it," Bush wrote his mother, who had expressed dismay when she caught daughter Nancy kissing a boy. George invited Barbara to stop in Chapel Hill for an afternoon when she was on her way back to Ashley Hall for the fall semester. His mother assured Barbara's mother that a visit was a "grand idea."

Barbara took the train from New York to Raleigh, then a cab to the Carolina Inn in Chapel Hill. They met at noon and strolled across the University of North Carolina campus.

"She looked too cute for words—really beautiful," Bush wrote his mother that night with almost novelistic detail. "We had a sandwich in town and then walked. I showed her the plant and then we walked over to Keenan [Kenan] Stadium. When we started it was clear, but once there it poured—just buckets. We got some protections from the canvas covered press box, but couldn't leave there."

He was younger than the others in his squadron, and sensitive about it. "He looked like a baby," Barbara Bush remembered, and she was a year younger than he was. When she visited that day, he asked her to add a few months to her age if anyone asked. "He said, 'Please tell them you're eighteen,'" she told me, laughing. "Do you know how many people asked how old I was? Not one person."

George had to report to the base for formation at 6 p.m. He escorted Barbara back to the inn, where she caught a bus to Raleigh to stay overnight with a friend from school. She was on her way to Ashley Hall to start her senior year; he had begun a year of flight training before he would be deployed to a war zone.

It was a September afternoon filled with the most ordinary of activities: sharing a sandwich, walking around the campus, dodging the rain, talking. It was enough. "Not thrilling but such fun just seeing her," Bush wrote. "We laughed at everything."

~ ~

He worried about getting a "Dear John" letter.

"If she 'fluffed me off' without warning I would be absolutely sick no kidding," George Bush wrote his mother the following spring, in June 1943, sounding almost frantic in a letter from the US Naval Air Station in Corpus Christi, Texas. He had seen it happen with fellow servicemen as they tried to hold on to girlfriends back home. "Every day practically guys are getting 'fluffed off' from girls they've left," he stewed. "All the time it happens."

He was certain of his feelings for her; he was less certain about her feelings for him. "I do still *love* (I honestly feel very sure of it) Barbara, Mum, yet I know that there is such a chance of her meeting some other guys. She is so very young and so darn attractive and I could hardly expect her to keep caring about me for years."

Then and for the rest of his life, Bush would be a constant correspondent, penning short notes and long ruminations to family and friends. He could write more eloquently than he could speak. In the stress of training for war, he poured out his heart to his mother and wrote his girlfriend nearly every day. But Barbara sometimes would let days or weeks go by without writing him back.

"Mum, I'm really worried," Bush wrote that summer. "I hope it's one of her lapses which she falls in occasionally either because she's busy or just to keep me anxious and interested; but I haven't gotten but 1 letter in

3 ½ weeks. Before there were a couple of 2 week famines but never this. I don't know, hope it's not the 'fluff.' "

He realized that Barbara Pierce shouldn't be underestimated. "As I've said before," he fretted, "Barb is really a smart girl in that she can be sweet and all that without committing herself to any great degree."

By then, he had completed his preflight training in Chapel Hill, North Carolina, then been transferred to Minnesota to learn how to fly. He finished basic training in Corpus Christi, Texas, and advanced training in Fort Lauderdale, Florida. He bounced around for additional training, in Norfolk and Chincoteague, Virginia; Hyannis, Massachusetts; and Charlestown, Rhode Island.

On July 9, 1943, Ensign George Bush became one of the youngest pilots in the Navy. (Bush biographies often say he was the youngest, but Chuck Downey of Poplar Grove, Illinois, was younger by twelve days when he earned his wings.) Bush was assigned to VT-51, a torpedo squadron getting ready for active duty in the Pacific.

That summer, he came home on a seventeen-day leave—an opportunity to see his family and, he hoped, to make his intentions clear to his girl. His mother had invited her to join the Walker clan at their retreat in Kennebunkport, Maine. Now it was Barbara's turn to be nervous. The extended family would be there: George's grandmother and grandfather, all six of their children and their spouses, plus a collection of cousins so numerous they were hard to keep straight.

"I knew, of course, they would hate me," she said.

They didn't, of course. Athletic, resilient, and funny, she was a good fit with his family. "He could kid her, and she could take it and give it right back," Bush's brother Jonathan recalled. His sister, Nancy, never got over thinking how prescient her brother had been to recognize in Barbara the qualities he admired and would later depend on so much. "I think he saw a person sure enough of herself to reach out to others and not be worried about herself all the time," Nancy Bush Ellis said. "And they're much the same qualities that my mother had."

Her unofficial admission to the family included getting a nickname.

George had called her "Bobsie" in some letters, but it didn't stick. "Bar" did. For the rest of her life, newcomers and outsiders would simply assume it was short for Barbara. But in the family tradition, the nickname was more complicated than that, and less flattering. Because gasoline and tires were rationed during the war, the Walkers had hired a horse-drawn wagon to take them in and out of town. The horse's name was Barsil, and George's big brother Prescott teasingly called Barbara "Barsil." The name, just short of mean, would be shortened forevermore to Bar.

Barbara and George spent the days riding bikes, playing tennis, walking on the beach, boating, and fishing. It was during this visit, walking up the driveway at Walker's Point, that they got engaged. Seventy-five years later, in 2018, George Bush could remember the moment as he reminisced on the porch of the Kennebunkport house, that same driveway in sight. It was the summer after Barbara had died. "I didn't get down on one knee kind of thing," he said. He hadn't asked her father for permission, and he didn't have a ring. They both just knew.

"We were secretly engaged," he would explain. "Secret, to the extent that the German and Japanese high commands weren't aware of it." Their feelings were apparent to just about everyone around them. It was scarcely a year and a half since the first time they had seen each other across the dance floor. Both were still teenagers.

When Barbara's older sister, Martha, announced she was getting engaged, their parents had heated deliberations about whether she was too young to get married. She was then a senior at Smith, and her fiancé, Walter Rafferty, was a junior at Yale. Like George Bush, he was from a prominent Greenwich family and an alumnus of Phillips Academy Andover. "When she came home, they carried on like nothing you've ever known: 'Oh, no, it's way too early,'" Barbara Bush told me, rolling her eyes. "They said, 'Sorry, it just couldn't be.'"

But Barbara got a different reaction, perhaps one more effect of being the third child, and not her mother's favored daughter. "So when I came home and told them I wanted to marry an eighteen-year-old, or a nineteen-year old, they said, 'Great.'" Although she was getting what she wanted, it was "a little disappointing," she said, a sign her big news was somehow less momentous than it had been for her sister.

Her father, Marvin, was impressed by his future son-in-law from the start. "My dad knew he was going to be" president, Barbara Bush declared later. But her mother, Pauline, was not. Perhaps that reflected the limits of her expectations for her younger daughter generally. "I don't think my mother expected I was going to amount to anything," she said, "and I know she didn't think that George was."

——— ——

"Do you know the story about why we announced our engagement?" Barbara Bush asked me as she and her husband were about to celebrate their seventy-third wedding anniversary. "It's so terrible."

She had arrived at Smith to start her freshman year of college, smitten with George Bush and secretly committed to him. They assumed their marriage would be years away, after the war had ended. A sophomore at her dorm, Tyler House, "a very cute-looking young thing with blond hair and curves," presented an invitation that apparently couldn't be refused. She told Barbara Pierce, "I've looked all around, and you're the freshman I'd like to take with me...over to Amherst; there's a blind date over there." Barbara demurred, without an explanation. "No, I'm sorry; I can't do that," she said. The sophomore asked her another time, and Barbara again said no.

The sophomore then told Barbara's roommate, Margie Boyce, that their secret was out: Barbara was a lesbian, and she and Margie were lovers. Margie panicked. She ran to Barbara with the rumor and began denying it to others by spilling the beans. Her roommate was no lesbian; she was engaged. While traditional gender boundaries could be blurred at all-women colleges like Smith, homophobia was still common then.

"I told George, and we decided maybe we should announce our engagement," Barbara Bush said, adding, "What a mean little girl." That evening in Kennebunkport, they already had come to an understanding that they would marry, but they had planned to keep it secret until closer to their wedding date, whenever that would be. Now the announcement of their engagement ran in the *New York Times* on December 12, 1943. "Barbara Pierce Engaged to Wed," the headline read. "Student at Smith College Will Be Bride of Ensign George Bush of Naval Air Arm." The caption above her photo said, "Fiancee of Ensign."

Bush wrote Barbara an emotional letter that day. "How lucky our children will be to have a mother like you," he wrote. "Bar, you have made my life full of everything I could ever dream of—my complete happiness should be a token of my love for you."

He worried about whether they could afford to get married, and when. He came from an affluent and well-connected family that gave him a safety net, to be sure, but he and his brothers were expected to earn their own living. George Bush wasn't sure what he wanted to do, but he knew he didn't want to glide along the easy path his family had cleared. After graduating from Yale, he would decline job offers at his father's private bank, Brown Brothers Harriman, and at his grandfather's investment firm, G. H. Walker & Company.

"What do you both think I should have to offer Bar before we can get married?" he asked his mother in a letter. "She does not expect us to have a thing, but I wonder if it would be fair to her to get married with what I have saved, say in a year after I get back I will have well over $2,000 by then," accumulated from his Navy pay. "Perhaps I should have a talk with Mr. P after shakedown"—that is, talk to Barbara's father after the first shakedown cruise of the USS *San Jacinto*. His squadron had been assigned to the new carrier.

George had been trying to find a proper engagement ring. "Incidentally if you see any shiny rocks on our driveway collect them," he joked. "Seriously, though, Mum just for interests sake what does a fairly decent looking ring cost?" His mother offered him a star sapphire ring that belonged to her sister, Nancy Walker.

In December 1943, Dorothy Walker Bush surreptitiously brought the ring with her when she and Barbara took the train together to Philadelphia for the commissioning ceremony of the *San Jacinto*. During the trip,

Dorothy delicately tried to make sure Barbara didn't have her heart set on a diamond engagement ring. What kind of ring did she want? Barbara, who was no fool about what was afoot, assured her that any ring would be wonderful.

In the shipyard, George gave Barbara the sapphire ring. She would wear it until the day she died, when he took it off her finger to keep and treasure.

⌐ ⌐

Aboard the *San Jacinto*, part of the fast carrier strike force of the Navy's Fifth Fleet, Bush was in the thick of the war. During the June 1944 campaign in the Marianas, he helped provide air cover for Marines who were landing on the island of Saipan, having been airborne for more than thirty-two hours as they bombed Japanese fortifications. After one takeoff during the battle, Bush had to ditch his plane in the ocean. In the campaign that followed, he flew airstrikes on islands whose names were becoming familiar to Americans back home who were trying to follow the war's course, places like Iwo Jima.

"We were all worried," Barbara Bush recalled, for her fiancé and others. Her older brother, Jimmy Pierce, had enlisted in the Army Air Corps and later served in the Navy Reserves. Her sister's husband, Walter Rafferty, joined the Marines and shipped out to the Pacific, landing on Guadalcanal in the first major offensive by Allied forces against Japan. Walt's brother, Kevin Rafferty, a pilot, was lost in Europe, his body never found. With more than sixteen million Americans in military service, the whole nation was on edge. "We listened for every piece of news from the Pacific," Barbara said, "and rumors ran wild."

For Bush, the most perilous episode of the war came on September 2, 1944, when he and his two-man crew were sent to bomb an enemy radio site at Chichi Jima, in the Bonin Islands.

As he began the dive toward his target, the radio tower, the Avenger was hit by Japanese fire. "The minute we pushed over to dive, you could just feel the danger," Bush would recall. "Some way about halfway down the run I was hit." What happened next was a crush of chaos and adrenaline. "The cockpit filled with smoke and I told the boys in the back to get their parachutes on," he wrote his parents the following day. He told crewmates John Delaney and Ted White to jump; he thought they had gotten out, then he bailed out himself. But they hadn't. Both were killed when the plane crashed into the ocean, a loss he would forever remember and always regret.

Back home, there had been no letters from George that September, but that wasn't unusual. Mail from war zones was understandably slow. Barbara was getting ready for their wedding, though a date hadn't been set.

Then she received a heart-stopping letter from Doug West, a pilot in George's squadron. He told her that George's plane had been shot down off Chichi Jima. Bush had forgotten to tie his parachute to his life raft before he bailed out. West had buzzed him overhead to signal where the raft had landed; he had seen Bush swimming toward it. Then West's plane and another moved off to strafe an enemy boat that had set out from the Japanese-held island toward the area of the ocean where Bush's plane had gone down.

She called Bush's parents, who had been notified several days earlier that George's plane had been shot down. Without word of his condition, and not wanting to worry her until they knew more, they had delayed telling her.

"We were frantic, but Doug's letter held out hope that a submarine had been alerted and might have rescued George," Barbara said. "I really don't remember the next three days—they are just a blur—but the Navy got a message to the Bushes that George had in fact been picked up and was in Hawaii for some R & R before being returned to the *San Jac*."

A submarine in the area, the USS *Finback*, had picked him up about three hours after his plane crashed into the ocean, a rescue immortalized in a video recording that one day would be used in his TV ads campaigning for the presidency. If he hadn't been found, tides likely would have carried him to Chichi Jima, held by the Japanese. In the prisons there, American captives were subjected to horrific war crimes, including cannibalism.

Bush could have gotten an immediate home leave, but he decided instead to go back to his ship. He was needed. Of the fourteen original pilots in his squadron, four were dead. Two months later, in November 1944, Bush was allowed to return stateside before getting orders for his new deployment. He began the journey home on a troop ship headed to San Diego from Hawaii.

"This is the letter I have wanted to write to you for a long long time," George wrote to his parents on December 1, 1944. "At least I can tell you that we're coming home." Soon he would be able to tell Barbara "when I'll definitely be in Greenwich, and she can set the wedding date."

Barbara Pierce had enrolled in classes at Smith during the summer of 1944, hoping to graduate early, but by the fall she had dropped out and never returned. ("Don't do what I did," she would caution students at Columbia College in South Carolina a half century later. "Stay in school.") She was one of six students to withdraw from Smith in the wartime summer of 1944. In all, about 25 percent of her class didn't graduate, a higher dropout rate than the school would record before or after the war.

She hadn't declared a major yet. Her freshman year, she took classes in English, Spanish, psychology, history, physical education, and "hygiene," described as "the hygiene of body mechanics." She was smart, but she had never been a diligent student, and now her mind was elsewhere. As she ruefully told an interviewer decades later: "Barbara Bush majored in George Bush at Smith College."

Her father would call Virginia Corwin, the freshman dean, and plead for understanding about his daughter's distraction. Barbara's fiancé is overseas, he would tell her, and she's so worried. She had begun addressing wedding invitations and buying a trousseau. Her mother "begged and borrowed" shoe coupons from friends, since shoes were among the items rationed during the war.

The wedding date was set—December 19, 1944—and the invitations printed. But the groom hadn't managed to arrive home by then. Finally, on Christmas Eve, George called. He had gotten a cross-country flight to New York from California, and he was at Grand Central Station, boarding a train for Rye. He would be at the Westchester County station in an hour. Barbara raced to get dressed and meet the train. "There were tears, laughs, hugs, joy," George Bush said.

They had set a new wedding date, for January 8, but that had to be changed as well. Amid the press of wartime weddings across the country, George's older brother, Prescott, was getting married in Miami on New Year's Eve. George's wedding was moved closer in time to that, to accommodate travel plans for family members from out of town who wanted to attend both ceremonies. The sensible Dorothy Walker Bush wore the same dress and hat to both sons' weddings.

On January 6, 1945, at Rye Presbyterian Church, the wedding finally was ready to start. The organist began to play the wedding march. Eight bridal attendants, dressed in emerald-green satin gowns with matching green ostrich feathers in their hair, were poised to begin walking down the aisle, carrying bouquets of red and white carnations.

Suddenly, a young man in a Navy midshipman's uniform rushed into the vestibule. It was FitzGerald Bemiss, a pal of Prescott Bush from Kennebunkport. He had battled bad weather to get there from Cornell University. He was supposed to be in the wedding party, he told them. Marvin Pierce, suspecting he was drunk, told him he was too late. But Barbara helped him strip off his coat and sent him hurrying down the aisle, just ahead of the attendants. Prescott, best man for his brother, could be heard exclaiming, "Bemiss!"

Barbara wore what the *New York Times* described in the wedding announcement as "a gown of ivory satin, made with a fitted bodice embroidered with seed pearls and a full skirt." Her veil of heirloom princess and rosepoint lace had been worn by Dorothy Walker at her wedding to Prescott Bush in Kennebunkport in 1921. The long train of Barbara's gown is draped over her left arm in the photo of her first dance with George as his wife. They are gazing into each other's eyes as though there was no one else in the room, or the world.

George Bush, twenty years old, was by then a veteran of fifty-eight combat missions and a survivor of a deadly crash in a war that wasn't over yet. Barbara Pierce, nineteen years old, was thrilled to be marrying Poppy Bush with no particular plans beyond sharing his life and rearing their children.

"When I fell in love with George Bush, I didn't know a damn thing, and he trained me, truthfully," Barbara Bush told me. "I was so stupid. I didn't know anything, and he took care of me. He grew me up."

She would help grow him up too.

—★—

Chapter Six

"The Street Cop"

When George Bush decided to leave the comfort of New England for the wilds of Texas, it didn't occur to him to ask Barbara what she thought about it.

"Well, I never, never wondered about whether she'd want to go," the former president, by then ninety-three years old, told me in an interview during November 2017 in his Houston office. (For the record, he never exactly asked Barbara Pierce to marry him, either, and years later he didn't ask her if he should run for president.) Even with the benefit of hindsight, that didn't seem remarkable to him; that was just the way things were. How else would it have worked? "We're in love and she wanted us to stay together."

The move was a leap for both of you, I said.

"Well, Bar, she's never spoiled," he said. "And it's all worked out."

When World War II ended, he sped through college in two and a half years—still managing to graduate Phi Beta Kappa and to captain the baseball team and to be the last man tapped for Skull and Bones, the most elite spot in the university's most elite secret club.

Barbara Bush, meanwhile, played bridge, went to the movies with friends, worked half a day at the Yale Co-Op, and audited a course on American furniture and silver. She went to every Yale baseball game, sitting behind third base and faithfully keeping score for George, the first baseman. When she was pregnant with their first child, an anxious coach Ethan Allen finally asked her to move behind home plate, where she would be protected by a safety net. There, she sat in the special double-wide grandstand seat at Yale Field that had been installed to accommodate former president William Howard Taft, a Yalie known for his girth who had returned to teach after leaving the White House.

When the baby was born in 1946—named George Walker Bush, Georgie for short—Barbara Bush noted ruefully that he didn't weigh the sixty pounds she had gained during her pregnancy.

Now George Bush had an adoring wife and an adorable toddler and big ambitions. But to do what?

He had been struggling to decide what to do after graduating with a bachelor's degree in economics in 1948. George and Barbara discussed going into farming, as incongruous as that sounded even then. He applied for a management training job at Procter & Gamble but didn't get it. He thought about teaching. His faculty adviser thought he'd have a good shot at landing a Rhodes scholarship, but Bush worried about the money involved in spending a year in England, not to mention the delay in entering the business world, the real world. After three years in the Navy and at war, he was anxious to get on with the rest of his life. He didn't like the idea of joining the investment banking firm that Gampy Walker had formed. Too safe, and too dependent on the advantages of birth. "Doing well merely because I had the opportunity to attend the same debut parties as some of my customers does not appeal to me," he wrote a friend just before graduation.

In this way and others, his service in World War II and his harrowing rescue after being downed in the Pacific left an indelible imprint. "It was very important to George that he like his work," Barbara Bush said. "He told me he had thought about it a great deal while standing night watch on the submarine deck after being rescued. He had decided he did not want to work with intangibles; he wanted a product he could see and feel."

Not banking, then. Maybe oil.

Texas was a place where a man could make a fortune, and on his own. Well, perhaps not entirely on his own. George Bush accepted an offer from Dresser Industries, a holding company that owned several oil-related subsidiaries. CEO Neil Mallon was a family friend and became a mentor; Bush's third son would be his namesake. Bush's father, Prescott, had been on the Dresser board of directors since 1929. The job of equipment clerk with a Dresser subsidiary, the International Derrick and Equipment Company, Ideco for short, paid a magnificent $375 a month.

The job was in Odessa, Texas—a place so far away, so unknown, that it might as well have been the other Odessa, the one on the Black Sea. He told Barbara the news. "I've always wanted to live in Odessa, Texas," she declared.

For the generations that followed, deciding to make such a life-changing choice without consulting your spouse would seem inconceivable. Even by the standards of that day, her willingness to trail him across the country without a word of protest or caution was notable. He understood that. "Texas would be new and exciting for a while—hard on Bar perhaps—and heaven knows many girls would bitch like blazes about such a proposed move," Bush wrote his friend FitzGerald Bemiss, discussing the job offer. "Bar's different though, Gerry. She lives quite frankly for Georgie and myself. She is wholly unselfish, beautifully tolerant of my weaknesses and idiosyncrasies, and ready to faithfully follow any course I chose."

Sometimes, he had to remind himself to think about "whether I am considering her at all."

They shared a partnership, to be sure, but he was the one who would decide what to do and where to go in pursuit of his career. She was the one who would pack up their household and corral their growing family and make it work. Later, the women's movement would make Barbara Bush question for a time whether that was entirely fair, whether she had been shortchanged during what she called her "dormant" years. She would cite those questions as one factor behind a serious spate of depression.

At the time, though, it turned out that she really was delighted to live in Odessa.

Here's the irony: She moved to Texas to support her husband's bid for independence, but it was also a sort of declaration of independence for herself. On the East Coast, Barbara Bush had a critical mother in Rye and a forceful mother-in-law in Greenwich and a prettier sister down the road. Now, for the first time in her life, she was on her own. "She jumped in with both feet," said Susan Porter Rose, her White House chief of staff. First in Odessa and then again and again, she would embrace the new town, the new venture, the new adventure, the new network of friends.

"We were both from great big families, and I would have never grown up," Barbara Bush said later. "My sister had always picked out my clothes; my mother picked out my clothes; and I was perfectly willing to let Mrs. Bush, who I adore, make all my decisions." Now they would be living halfway across the country, not down the street, and that would no longer be an option. It would just be the two of them and Georgie, to be joined by the other children they planned to have as soon as they could.

There were ways in which Barbara Bush—blunt, funny, unpretentious, competitive, and less than impressed by old-school ties and new fashions—was a more natural fit in West Texas than she had been in her native New England. One observer said she grew to be like one of those cannot-be-denied matriarchs who ruled the ranch on the TV Western *Dallas*, say, or *The Big Valley*. "When you are a couple all grown up, nobody's son or daughter, nobody's shadow, you are you," she said.

In Texas, Barbara was Barbara.

"I was glad to get away, to move to Texas," she told me, even though she had no idea what was ahead. She had never met a Texan. For some reason, her stereotype of one was Jane Withers, the child actress not quite as famous as Shirley Temple in the 1930s and early 1940s. (Withers was actually from Georgia.) Decades later, Barbara Bush could still feel the heat and the dust, all of it. "We had exciting times," she told me. It was an adventure, just the three of them, George and Georgie and her.

Then she added something remarkable about that year in Odessa: "I can't really remember being unhappy there."

———— ————

George Bush loaded up the red two-door Studebaker his parents had given him as a college graduation present and headed for Texas. Barbara and Georgie, who was about to turn two years old, stayed behind at the big house at Kennebunkport with Bush's grandparents Gampy and Ganny Walker, until George could find a place for them to live.

That proved to be no easy task.

Their housing had been haphazard in the eight months after their wedding, when she followed him from Michigan to Maine to Virginia while his new Navy squadron, VT-153, trained for the expected invasion of Japan. Then President Harry Truman ordered atomic bombs dropped on Hiroshima and Nagasaki, and the war in the Pacific ended. Discharged from the Navy, Bush finally could head to Yale, which had been holding a spot for him since he was a junior at Andover. There, too, housing was jammed. In a Victorian house next to the university president's residence, divided into apartments for young families, they shared a kitchen and were grateful they had their own bathroom.

But nothing was quite as rustic as where they settled in Odessa, a blue-collar town in the middle of an oil boom. George Bush called to say that he had found "a sorry little house," but she was ready to join him, no matter what. "We stepped off the plane—after a twelve-hour flight in those days—to a whole new and very hot world," she would recall. "Odessa is flat as a pancake and as different from Rye, New York, as any place imaginable."

They moved into a two-room apartment on East Seventh Street with a shared Jack-and-Jill bathroom; the door on the neighbor's side could be locked while in use and was supposed to be unlocked when empty. When the original tenants on the other side moved out, a mother and daughter and young granddaughter moved in and began entertaining what Barbara Bush called "many gentlemen callers." The Bushes didn't raise moral objections but did protest when forgetful male visitors repeatedly locked them out of the bathroom.

It could have been worse, Barbara Bush said. Most of their neighbors on the unpaved road were still using outhouses. "We had the only bathroom on the street," shared or not, she told me. "The only refrigerator. We were very lucky."

She did have to get accustomed to smells of all sorts. Soon after they had moved in, she awoke with a start to the strong odor of gas. She frantically roused George and Georgie and the neighbors, urging them to flee the house before it blew up. "I thought we were being gassed," she said. "I woke up everybody in the neighborhood: 'Wake up! Wake up!'"

The danger, as it turned out, was only olfactory. The wind had shifted and she was smelling fumes from nearby oil-manufacturing plants, the old-timers told her. "I was used to it after a while," she said. Soon, they moved up, to an apartment on Seventeenth Street. "Still considered on the wrong side of the tracks, but we had our own bath," she said.

"Dearest Mommy + Daddy," she wrote to her parents on proper personalized stationery, grander than her housing. The stiff ecru paper was engraved with navy ink: "Barbara P. Bush, Box 807, Odessa, Texas." "Excitement ran high around here on Saturday," she told them in a letter saved in a box of her diaries at the George Bush H. W. Presidential Library. She sketched by hand a rough floor plan of the new place they had found. The railroad-style apartment had a living room, a kitchen, a bathroom, and a bedroom. "I went over on Friday night and looked through it + fell in love with it." Later, she recalled, "We lived in a duplex like the three bears. We slept in one room with three beds in a row."

Barbara's mother, Pauline Pierce, had been shipping care packages to Odessa with essentials she assumed weren't available there, things like cold cream and soap. "As far as my mother was concerned, we could have been living in Russia," Barbara Bush said. She finally wrote to inform her mother that her adopted town "had big, beautiful supermarkets, which Rye did not have at the time."

After almost a year in Odessa, the Bushes packed up the Studebaker again and drove to California for another year of apprenticeship at Dresser companies. He worked as an assemblyman at Pacific Pumps and then as a salesman of drilling bits for Security Engineers Company; he was constantly on the road. "We lived in a motel in Whittier, the beautiful Pierpont Inn in Ventura, a rented House in Bakersfield, and finally came to rest in an apartment in Compton," Barbara Bush said.

Then George Bush came home early from work on a September day in 1949 with crushing news.

He had gotten a call from Rye. Barbara's parents had been on their way to the train station. Marvin was driving; Pauline was sipping coffee from one of the English bone china cups she treasured. She put it on the seat between them. When he noticed it was about to spill on her, he reached out to steady the cup and lost control of the car. "Auto left road and struck a tree," the police report said. It careened down an embankment and crashed into a tree and a stone wall.

Pauline's head struck the windshield; she was dead of a fractured skull before the rescuers could arrive. Marvin was hospitalized with four broken ribs. A few months earlier, Barbara had seen her family in Cleveland, at brother Jimmy Pierce's wedding to Margie Dyer. Now Barbara was six months pregnant. Worried that the trip would be too arduous for her, Marvin Pierce told his daughter not to come back for her mother's funeral, so she didn't.

Soon after the memorial service, Marvin Pierce wrote an emotional letter to his children—a letter Barbara lost track of for decades. The letter, to his "Dearest Kids," was found again in 2017 in the papers of Don Rhodes, a longtime family aide, who died in 2011. (The Bushes' wedding certificate was found in the same folder.) The letter "is so loving and so sweet about her," Barbara said when she showed it to me. "They were a great couple."

"I think I have myself well enough in hand now to write this letter," Marvin Pierce wrote in his strong, slanted handwriting. He had been overwhelmed by the outpouring from friends and acquaintances, he told them. Three hundred people had sent flowers, and another three hundred had sent letters or telegrams. Eleanor Roosevelt was one of them; he had met her when he was publisher of *McCall's*. "Last weekend we must have had 150 people call on us each day which, while it is a fine thing to keep your mind off things, [it is] a drain not only upon one's depleted energies but also upon one's liquor supplies," he noted wryly. He said he was giving Barbara "the big diamond pin that mother loved so much." Sister Martha would get a ring that she had given her mother, and her mink coat; brother Jim a diamond pin and earrings; brother Scott his mother's pearls.

"I hope all of us can train ourselves to smile when I think of that wonderful woman, your mother," Marvin Pierce wrote. "I must confess that [at] this very moment I write through my tears."

Barbara Bush's feelings toward her mother were knotty. Pauline had doted on her older daughter, leaving her younger daughter with lifelong insecurities about herself. They had an almost visceral reaction to each other; Barbara Bush called it "a chemical thing." But for her mother to die so suddenly was a shock, and the decision not to make the trip to New York for the funeral left another layer of angst. Now the conflicts between them would never be resolved.

"What a lonely, miserable time that was," Barbara Bush said.

The new baby was born on December 20, 1949. She and George wanted to name her Pauline Pierce Bush, in honor of Barbara's mother. But the other grandmother, the practical Dorothy Walker Bush, noted that the child would go through life being teased as "P. P. Bush." They settled on Pauline Robinson Bush instead.

George Bush brought mother and daughter home from the hospital on Christmas Day. They decided to call her Robin.

George Bush was transferred back to West Texas, this time to Midland— just twenty miles down the road from Odessa, but a step up in status. In the hierarchy of West Texas towns, Odessa was known as a blue-collar town dominated by workers; Midland was home to some of their bosses, including any number of Ivy League immigrants from back east. Housing was still a challenge. They lived at Kingsway Courts and then at the aptly named George's Courts, a motel on Main Street.

Finally they managed to buy their first house, on East Maple Street, in a development known as Easter Egg Row.

It was akin to Levittown on Long Island and other cookie-cutter communities that sprouted after World War II to meet the demands of a flood of former servicemen and their young families. These houses had identical floor plans—847 square feet, with a carport and a concrete slab for a patio—but they were painted different bright colors. The Bush house was light blue. It cost $7,500. Just about everybody in the neighborhood was a transplant from somewhere else, drawn by the oil boom.

"We all had been uprooted; we all had young children; and we were all having a lot of fun," Barbara Bush remembered. "The women joined the Midland Service League, and the men played touch football in the Martini Bowl. We all worked in the Little Theater and the YMCA and volunteered at the hospital. Most of us were active in church; George was an elder, and we both taught Sunday School at the First Presbyterian Church. We took turns having cookouts on our tiny patios or in backyards and watching each other's children."

Bessie and Bill Liedtke lived nearby; he had moved to Midland from Oklahoma; she was from Austin. Bill's brother, Hugh, was in the neighborhood as well, with his wife, Betty. The Liedtke brothers would become business partners and lifelong friends with the Bushes.

"We had four kids and they had four or five kids, and actually our kids all knew each other," Bessie Liedtke told me. Now age ninety-two, she lived near the Bushes in Houston; she and Barbara would get together with friends for lunch at the Bayou Club on the first Monday of the month. (They called it the 1925 Club; one requirement for membership was a birthdate in that year.) "Midland was crowded and everybody was kind of in their having-baby age."

That presented some challenges when they were trying to elect someone with the free time to serve as president of the Midland Service League, she recalled. "Somebody said, 'We need a president,' and they said, 'Well, she's pregnant. She's pregnant.' Finally, they said, 'Who's not pregnant?' And I don't think but two or three hands went up in this group of women. But that was what you did back in those days," she went on. "You just didn't have any money, but you had babies."

Barbara Bush would use remarkably similar language. "In our time it was different, you married and had children," she said years later. "It was what you did. And we did, too."

The Bushes were eager to have more children after Georgie, and fast, but Barbara then suffered a miscarriage. They were living in Odessa. "Bar is still not quite up to par," Bush wrote his mother. "I know that her disappointment over this miscarriage was large. As I told you before we both are sort of hoping that we will have another child before too long. Bar thinks about it a lot, and foolishly worries too much. I don't like to have her upset."

Robin was born a year later, when Georgie was three.

By now, George Bush was ready to go into business on his own. He left Dresser and formed Bush-Overbey Oil Development, Inc., in partnership with his neighbor across the street, John Overbey, and the help of some financing from his uncle Herbie Walker. Three years later, they joined forces with the Liedtke brothers. Hugh Liedtke thought they could have more impact with a company name that began with the beginning or the end of the alphabet, with an "A" or a "Z." So they named their new company "Zapata," after a Marlon Brando movie, *Viva Zapata!*, that was playing in Midland at the time.

The Bushes moved into a bigger house in Midland, on West Ohio Street. Barbara was pregnant again, this time with Jeb. "It was truly an exciting time, a life filled with risk and hope," she wrote in her memoir. "Life seemed almost too good to be true."

She would turn out to be right, grievously so. A few weeks after Jeb came home from the hospital, Robin was diagnosed with leukemia, and nothing else would matter for a time.

George and Barbara had more children, of course. After Jeb, three more would be born in the space of just four years: Neil and Marvin in Midland, and Doro after the move to Houston. In what became a family joke, Neil and Marvin would express relief that they had been born before their little sister arrived. "They kept having boys until they finally got another girl," Neil Bush told me with good humor. Deliberately? "Well, they stopped after Doro," he noted. "Marvin and I were on the bubble, I think."

Not so, Barbara Bush told me. She had hoped to have an even bigger family. "I would have liked one more," another child after Doro, she said, still a bit wistful after all these years. "Two girls would have been nice."

———

George Bush was often on the road; Barbara Bush was always in charge at home. She described it as a time "of long days and short years, of diapers, runny noses, earaches, more Little League games than you could believe possible, tonsils, and those unscheduled races to the hospital emergency room, Sunday school and church, of hours of urging homework, short chubby arms around your neck and sticky kisses."

Not to mention the occasional resentment about the division of duties. Sometimes she had the "feeling that I'd never, ever be able to have fun again; and coping with the feeling that George Bush, in his excitement of starting a small company and traveling around the world, was having a lot of fun," she said years later. "I went through that like thousands of other women. The problem was that I didn't know they were going through it too."

She once made an observation, either wry or irked or both: "In a marriage, where one is so willing to take on responsibility, and the other so willing to keep the bathrooms clean... that's the way you get treated."

Barbara Bush gained a reputation in Midland as one of those supermoms, the commander in chief of her brood.

"I remember Mother being the Cub Scout den mother," George W. Bush told me, "driving us to the Monahans Sand Hills where we got on garbage lids and surfed, or I vividly remember us going to Carlsbad Caverns." She drilled him on his French lessons as they drove to Big Spring for his orthodontist appointments. "I can still picture us riding through the desert with me repeating, 'Ferme la bouche...ouvre la fenetre,'" he said. (That translates as "Close your mouth...open the window.")

Neil Bush recalled the elaborate gift bags she created for his eighth or ninth birthday party in Midland. She tied each of them to kite string that she wound through the pine trees in a small wood; following them to the prize would be a bit of an adventure for his friends. When he was diagnosed with dyslexia and was struggling to read, she spent years helping him learn, trying one approach after another.

It was often left to her to handle the inevitable family emergencies. When Jeb was twelve years old and walking "peculiarly," she took him in for an appointment. After an examination, the doctor warned it might be a rare bone disease, surely a jolting reminder of daughter Robin's dire diagnosis and of brother Scott's childhood malady. "George was away, so my friends held my hand," she said. Fortunately, "it turned out to be only an infection in his heel." Jeb told me his mother never let on to him that there might be something to worry about.

The elder George Bush was revered by his wife and his children, then and later. He invented the concept of "quality time," Jeb Bush said—but it was a necessary design because his time with his children was so often a scarce resource. "Even when we were growing up in Houston, Dad wasn't home at night to play catch," he said. "Mom was always the one to hand out the goodies and the discipline. In a sense, it was a matriarchal family."

"Somebody has to take care of the nest," Barbara Bush said, "and that's me."

Growing up, George W. Bush was the child most likely to test the rules. "Georgie has grown up to be a near-man, talks dirty once in a while and occasionally swears, aged 4-½," his father wrote to a friend with obvious pride. "He lives in his cowboy clothes." In middle school, he would pilfer his mother's cigarettes; he was caught smoking in an alleyway by the school's football coach and in Kennebunkport by his paternal grandparents. At those times, his father would quietly express his disappointment. His mother would yell.

"She could get hot, and because we had such similar personalities, I knew how to light her fuse," George W. Bush said. "I would smart off, and she would let me have it."

One summer in Maine when he was a teenager, his mother announced that she and his father were taking him out to dinner. "I said, 'Uh-oh,'" George W. Bush told me, sensing trouble ahead. They went to the Grist Mill Inn. "Before the menu even arrived, Mother says, she blurted— she's a blurter—'You smoke! I discovered an ashtray under your bed, and you smoke!' Kind of emotional. And Dad looked at her and said, 'So do you.' That was the end of the conversation."

Whatever their conflicts, Barbara and her oldest son were also exceptionally close.

One day when he was home on a break from Andover, she called him into her bedroom, her voice urgent. His father was on the road; she needed him to drive her to the hospital. She was hemorrhaging. She had just suffered a miscarriage. The housekeeper, Paula Rendon, handed George W. a jar in which she had put the fetus, in case the doctor might want to see it for some medical reason.

"I remember thinking: *There was a human life, a little brother or sister,*" George W. said. At the hospital, he paced the hallway nervously. ("Don't worry, honey," an older woman assured him, "your wife will be just fine.") Barbara Bush had to spend the night at the hospital, and he returned the next day to bring her home. He told her they needed to talk about this, about whether she really should be having more children— surely an unusual exchange between a teenage boy and his mother.

"Dad gets his energy from his family, and the family was so well organized because of Mom's steadfast, watchful eye on us," Neil Bush told me. "She did all of that work while freeing him up to pursue his ambitions and to succeed the way he did." Jeb Bush said: "Mom was the street cop."

Only later did the family give Barbara Bush the moniker the Enforcer, but it was a role she filled almost from the start, out of necessity. Who else was around to do it? She became the unmistakable matriarch of a sprawling family that included five rambunctious children and an ambitious husband.

———★———

Chapter Seven

How Hard Could It Be?

George Bush sometimes hadn't conferred with his wife before making big decisions, but for whatever reason he did before taking his first step into politics. Republican elders in Houston asked him to consider taking over leadership of the Harris County GOP. Sure, Barbara replied. How hard could it be?

"In February 1962, just before Doro and I left to visit Mom and Dad Bush for a week in Florida, George asked me how I'd feel if he became chairman of the Republican Party of Harris County," Barbara Bush recalled. "He said he really wanted to do it, and I said fine. So off Doro and I went for a great little vacation, and when we got back, George was in the meanest political battle of his life."

In a precursor of the conflicts that would follow him in politics, Bush found himself in a fight between establishment Republicans and hard-liners to his right—in this case, members of the extremist John Birch Society. Later, when he was running for president, he would face skepticism from Christian evangelicals who were emerging as a force in the GOP. A New Englander, an Episcopalian, and a Yalie, Bush was viewed with suspicion by some despite espousing conservative policies on the economy and a hawkish stance on foreign policy. He may have been a conservative Goldwater Republican by ideology, but he was a moderate Rockefeller Republican by heritage and manner, and on some cultural issues.

"It was ugly," Barbara Bush said. She had assumed he was being appointed as chairman, not that he had to campaign for it. He set out to stump in every one of the county's 210 precincts. She usually went along with him, needlepointing and listening. She hadn't had a particular interest in politics before, but attending the precinct meetings was one way she could spend time by his side, and help him.

"I never even thought about it," she told me. "Just, if he was going to do it, I was there." Her only complaint about their early days in Houston had been that they were rarely together, between his business travel and the demands of their five children. That caused her "some pain and jealousy," she said. "I just didn't think there was enough time for us."

She knew he had a political itch, and she wasn't surprised when he wanted to run for county chairman. He had been thinking about politics for years, especially after his father was elected to the Senate from Connecticut in 1953. His aspirations were high from the start. "I'd like to be President," he wrote to a potential primary rival in 1966. "The chances are slight, but please don't limit me."

Barbara Bush herself became a target for the John Birchers who saw conspiracies everywhere. In 1964, when George Bush sought the nomination to challenge Democratic senator Ralph Yarborough, a campaign flyer arrived in the mail with what was portrayed as an explosive revelation: Barbara Bush was the daughter of the president of the McCall Corporation, which published *Redbook*. That was factual enough, but it went on to describe the staid women's magazine as a tool of communism. Another flyer described her as "an heiress who spent all her time on the Cape"—a moniker not exactly designed to endear her to the voters of Texas, though in fact she wasn't an heiress and had never been to Cape Cod.

Bush won the Harris County chairmanship in 1962 and the Senate nomination in 1964, though he lost the general election to Yarborough in the Democratic landslide that followed the assassination of President John F. Kennedy. As county chairman, Bush filed a lawsuit challenging Texas's congressional redistricting; that court case quickly rebounded to the benefit of his party and himself. In 1966, he was elected to the House to represent a newly drawn GOP-leaning district in Houston.

George and Barbara and their three younger children prepared to move to Washington. Son George W. was enrolled at Yale, and Jeb stayed with friends in Houston to finish the ninth grade. When they pulled up to their new house—bought sight unseen from a retiring senator and family friend, Milward Simpson of Wyoming—the piano didn't fit and the rooms seemed cold and tiny. There had been a snowstorm. Bush invited the moving men to spend the night at the house, which sent Barbara rushing to a nearby Sears before it closed to buy sheets for the beds.

The next morning, January 4, 1967, she was up at 4 a.m. to unpack boxes. Then she headed out the door to begin two days of briefings for incoming Republican congressmen and their wives.

It was, she said, "exciting, overwhelming, intimidating, interesting, exhausting."

The networking skills that had made Barbara Bush a force among the young families in Midland were the ones she now deployed in Washington. "I mean, that's me," she said with a shrug.

The Bushes had hosted a regular Sunday barbecue in West Texas that drew neighbors, friends, coworkers, and strays. Now they started the same weekly tradition in Spring Valley, their new neighborhood in DC. She became best friends with neighbor Andy Stewart, the wife of Supreme Court justice Potter Stewart. She was a tennis partner of Sandra Day O'Connor, a lawyer who would become the first woman on the high court. Republican speechwriter William Safire and his wife, Helene, were regulars at the Sunday lunches, although later, as a columnist for the *New York Times*, he would blast Bush as president, at a cost of their friendship.

When Nixon aide Patrick Buchanan moved into the neighborhood in 1974, the first knock on the door was from George and Barbara Bush and their dog, C. Fred, delivering a bottle of champagne to welcome them. Their sociable gesture didn't stop Buchanan from challenging Bush for the Republican presidential nomination in 1992, though. "That was kind of a breach," Buchanan told me in an understatement.

Years later, when Bush was president, some of the friendships Barbara had helped forge among both Republicans and Democrats during those Sunday cookouts served him well. "He had some great friends in the House, really," said Andy Card, who would become a deputy White House chief of staff and a cabinet member during his administration. "And Barbara Bush was the reason most of them were good friends."

When Bush ran for reelection in 1968, Texas Democrats didn't bother to field a candidate against him. But he had his eye on being more than a junior congressman in the minority party. Representative William Steiger, a Wisconsin Republican elected in Bush's class, organized a quiet campaign to urge Nixon to choose Bush as his running mate in 1968. When Nixon picked Maryland governor Spiro Agnew instead, Bush set out to collect some political chits during the fall campaign. "Since George was unopposed in 1968, he worked hard for the Nixon–Agnew ticket," Barbara Bush said. "I sat in Washington with the children, biting my nails while George traveled all over the country campaigning."

George Bush would court Richard Nixon and be rewarded for it.

In 1970, Nixon was among those urging Bush to give up his safe House seat to run against Yarborough; the Democratic senator was a nettlesome critic of the president. Nixon promised Bush a soft landing if he needed it, which he did, in part because Lloyd Bentsen unexpectedly challenged Yarborough for the Democratic nomination. Instead of facing Yarborough, a liberal with a long voting record ripe with targets, Bush found himself running in the general election against the more centrist Bentsen. Bush lost. (He would have revenge of a sort down the road, when he won the White House in 1988 against the Democratic ticket of Michael Dukakis and Bentsen.)

"George was very disappointed. He always had wanted to be in the Senate, especially since the days his father had served there," Barbara

Bush said. As they were leaving the Shamrock Hilton Hotel in Houston on Election Night, after Bush had addressed supporters, eleven-year-old Doro burst into tears. "I'll be the only girl in the fifth grade whose daddy doesn't have a job," she sobbed. Her parents tried to reassure her, but the next morning Barbara Bush cut short a tennis game with friends because she couldn't stop weeping herself.

"Now the big question for us was: What next?" she said.

Nixon came through. He offered Bush a job in the White House; Bush expressed interest in the United Nations instead, and the president agreed. Barbara had never traveled outside the United States before, but she plunged into the round of diplomatic events at the UN with enthusiasm. "I was born to the job: I love people and adore eating," she joked. She said, "When George was at the United Nations, I felt as if I were being treated to a trip around the world every night, only I didn't have to pack."

She also began to volunteer one morning a week at Memorial Sloan Kettering Hospital, where Robin had been treated nearly two decades earlier. But in what may have been a sign of the grief she still carried, she made a point of working with the adult patients, not the children.

During the 1972 campaign, Bush again stumped for the Republican ticket. When Nixon won a second term, Bush hoped to land the number two job at the State Department, but Nixon had the chairmanship of the Republican National Committee in mind. As George Bush left to meet with the president at Camp David, Barbara Bush urged him to decline the RNC job if that was what Nixon proposed. "I just felt it would be a terrible experience," she said. "Party politics are dog-eat-dog."

That was the job Nixon offered; Bush was reluctant. In a letter to Nixon the next day, Bush noted his wife's reservations that the new job would be seen as a step down. "She is convinced that all our friends in Congress, in public life, in God knows where—will say, 'George screwed it up at the U.N. and the President has loyally found a suitable spot,'" Bush wrote. But he told Nixon he would take the post. "So my initial 'no' has changed after a sleepless night to a happy 'yes.' The shock has worn off, and Barbara will see that it makes sense. And besides, she's your biggest fan. So I'm ready."

In fact, Barbara Bush was hardly Nixon's "biggest fan." He had helped her husband's political career, she acknowledged, "but he was not lovable." He was an awkward man who never seemed to remember her name, despite all the receiving lines and receptions where they had met. But she called Pat Nixon "a great lady." In an interview with me, she asked, "Was she a drinker at one time?" Those were the rumors, I said. "I don't blame her," she declared. "If I'd been married to Nixon, I would have taken to the bottle, too."

~ · ~

They faced the developments and disruptions that mark the lives of just about every family.

Barbara's father, Marvin Pierce, died in 1969; his children had never warmed to his second wife, Willa, though she would become a responsibility for them. George Bush's father, Prescott, died in 1972. Jeb Bush became the first of their children to get married, returning from a student-exchange program in Mexico with a young woman, Columba, who didn't speak English. Jeb didn't ask his parents' permission, but his mother did insist on meeting Columba before the small wedding ceremony took place in 1974.

"I was very nervous!" Columba Bush told me, and she was not sure what to expect. "[Barbara] was very welcoming and put me at ease."

And there was this: Barbara Bush decided to stop dyeing her hair.

The decision was made for convenience, after a hair-coloring mishap and a general sense that her husband didn't care or even notice what color her hair was. A decade later, her appearance would become a source of whispered concern during Bush's first presidential campaign; some advisers worried her matronly looks undercut his message that he represented a new generation of leaders. Eventually, her cloud of snowy white hair would define her public persona. The headline over her section in an exhibit on First Ladies, mounted in her son's presidential library in 2018: "Everyone's Grandmother."

It became an urban myth that her hair turned white almost overnight after Robin died, a case study in the way journalists can repeat an error without checking until it becomes widely accepted as fact.

The first time this assertion appeared in print seems to be a *Los Angeles Times* story about the new First Lady published on November 20, 1988. "Their daughter, Robin, died of leukemia at the age of 4. Barbara, then 30, 'nearly fell apart,' she has said and friends recall that her hair turned white virtually overnight," the story read. (In fact, Robin was three when she died, and her mother was twenty-eight.) A *New York Times* story a few months later, on January 15, 1989, repeated the error that Robin was four and picked up the sentence about her hair verbatim, albeit without credit: "Friends recall that her hair turned white virtually overnight."

After that, it was repeatedly stated as fact.

"That's baloney," Barbara Bush told me, although she noted with exasperation that she "read this all the time." It was years after Robin died, when she was thirty-five, that she saw the first signs of gray and began to dye her hair. But she liked to swim laps in the pool for exercise, and the combination of chlorine with hair coloring was sometimes catastrophic. "It turned green in the chlorine," she recalled. "The children will tell you, 'Oh, she had orange hair once' and 'She had green hair.'"

The last straw was when she tried a rinse called "Fabulous Fawn" just before heading out on a campaign trip in Texas during the Senate race in 1970. "Well, as the day got hotter, and when the air-conditioning quit working on the plane, 'Fabulous Fawn' began to trickle down my back." That was the last time she colored her hair. She decided to let nature take its course. Let other people worry about how it looked.

"What you see is what you get," she said years later. "People who worry about their hair all the time, frankly, are boring."

George Bush was on a trip to California in August 1974 when reports began circulating that President Nixon had decided to resign.

The mushrooming Watergate scandal had made the RNC post even more treacherous than Barbara Bush had feared when he agreed to take it in January 1973. As Republican Party chairman, Bush had been cast as one of Nixon's defenders, arguing against "hounding" Nixon out of office. Secret White House tapes would show an eager-to-please Bush flattering the embattled president. At the height of the scandal, on the day H. R. Haldeman and John Ehrlichman were forced to resign, Bush phoned Nixon. "I really was proud of you and, by golly, I know it was tough," he told him.

Then the "smoking gun" tape was released on August 5, 1974. It showed Nixon trying to use the CIA to convince the FBI not to investigate the Watergate break-in, citing national security concerns. The president's impeachment was all but guaranteed, and there was political peril for his defenders. Bush was in California for a Republican fund-raiser. On August 7, he drafted a letter to the president urging him to resign. Then he caught a red-eye flight back to Washington.

On August 8, Nixon did decide to resign. Now another president would give Bush a place to land. Bush had hopes, once again, to be picked for the vice presidency, but Gerald Ford chose former New York governor Nelson Rockefeller instead. Ford had an ambassadorship in mind; they discussed London and Paris and finally agreed on Beijing, then known as Peking. Because the United States didn't yet have full diplomatic relations with the People's Republic of China, Bush was named chief of the US Liaison Office, not ambassador.

George Bush's rise in the dozen years since he ran for Harris County Republican chairman had been dizzying; he was building a résumé that would position him to be a credible candidate for president himself. Now he was on his way to serve as the top US diplomat in China.

Barbara Bush would call their year in Beijing the best of times. Not since the early years of their marriage had it been the two of them, away from parents and children. As it turned out, though, the China posting would also test their marriage. When they returned to the United States a year later for Bush to take over leadership of an embattled CIA, she fell into darkness. It would be the worst of times.

Chapter Eight

—⋆—

Darkness

They had lived for just over a year in China, a remote posting during that pre-Internet age and almost a tonic after George Bush's difficult tenure as Republican National Committee chairman during the Watergate scandal. They were out bicycling in Beijing on a Saturday in November 1975 when an urgent telegram from Secretary of State Henry Kissinger arrived at the US Liaison Office. The unexpected message: President Gerald Ford wanted George Bush to head the CIA.

Both of them were surprised and wary.

"I remember Camp David," Barbara Bush cautioned her husband. Three years earlier, Bush, then the US ambassador to the United Nations, had been called to the presidential retreat by Richard Nixon and asked to head the Republican National Committee. The partisan position would cast Bush as a leading defender of the White House during a growing scandal that ultimately would force Nixon to resign. Now Ford was asking Bush to leave his post as US envoy to China to take over a spy agency being battered by congressional hearings into allegations of incompetence and malfeasance. The CIA job, like the RNC post, was more likely to hurt than help his ambitions for higher office.

Barbara was more willing to say no to a president than her husband was. She had advised him against taking the RNC job—defending Nixon during Watergate could have undermined Bush's own political future—and she cautioned him against accepting the CIA job this time. He would acknowledge her reluctance when President Ford visited China the next month after Chinese vice-premier Deng Xiaoping alluded to the political implications. "You have given him a post that is not considered to be very good," Deng said in a private meeting, sparking laughter. Bush replied, "You're talking like my wife, Mr. Vice-Premier."

Despite her reluctance, and his, Bush sent a return telegram accepting the job the day after it was offered, on Sunday. On Monday, Ford announced it as part of a broader personnel shuffle. The Bushes prepared to head home.

Back in Washington, George Bush plunged into the demands of his new post, but Barbara Bush found herself falling into the worst personal crisis she had faced since daughter Robin had died more than two decades earlier. Overwhelmed by pain and loneliness, she contemplated suicide. She would pull over to the side of the road until the impulse to plow into a tree or drive into the path of an oncoming car had passed.

"I felt terrible," she told me years later. "I would pull over and park so I wouldn't go hit a tree. I mean, I really felt that depressed." She went on, "I really wasn't brave enough to do that, but that's why I pulled over, so I wouldn't do that, or I wouldn't run into another car."

She hid her depression from their children and her friends, from nearly everyone except her husband. He encouraged her to seek professional help, which only deepened her gloom. "I swore to myself I would not burden him," she wrote in her memoirs in 1994. "Then he would come home, and I would tell him all about it. Night after night George held me weeping in his arms while I tried to explain my feelings. I almost wonder why he didn't leave me."

After the crisis passed, she blamed a toxic combination of factors for the darkness.

For one, she had been involved in her husband's work since he had run to be chairman of the Harris County Republican Committee back in Houston. She had been his partner during his days in Congress and at the United Nations and in China. Now the demands for secrecy at the

CIA prevented him from telling her much about what he was doing. "I couldn't share, because the truth is, I can't keep a secret," she told me. "You tell me a secret, I'll keep it for about a day, maybe a day and a half."

Other factors may have contributed as well. In retrospect, she thought the onset of menopause might have caused a hormonal imbalance. She also had an empty nest at home, her children away at school or starting careers. Doro, the youngest and still in high school, was away at the Connecticut boarding school she'd been enrolled in when they left for China.

What's more, the women's movement prompted Barbara Bush to question for a time the value of her contributions as a wife, mother, and homemaker. "I thought that was a fourth ingredient into it, besides the no-sharing the job, the children gone, the menopause," she said. "I thought the women's movement, at that time—it isn't so true anymore— sort of made women who stayed at home feel inadequate."

In retrospect, some of those close to her speculated to me that there might have been another reason for Barbara Bush's depression as well. Her name was Jennifer Fitzgerald. She was seven years younger than Barbara and divorced, small and blond with average looks, fiercely protective of George Bush and prickly to others. He hired her to move to China as his special assistant and then follow him to the CIA as his executive assistant. She would work by his side at government and campaign jobs for more than a decade.

Allegations that they had an affair would erupt during the 1988 and 1992 presidential campaigns. Both Bush and Fitzgerald would consistently deny them. So would Barbara Bush.

However, a woman who shared a friend's beach house with Fitzgerald said her housemate had begun what was at least a flirtatious relationship with Bush when he was chairman of the Republican National Committee. At the time, Fitzgerald was an assistant to Dean Burch, who headed the Federal Communications Commission and then became a White House adviser to Presidents Nixon and Ford. Burch, Bush's good friend and mentor, had introduced him to Fitzgerald.

Bush would call the beach house in Ocean City, Maryland, at least once a day and sometimes more often during the summer of 1973 or 1974. In that era before cell phones, he would ring the landline and whoever was nearby would pick up the receiver. Bush would identify himself by name and ask to speak to Fitzgerald. Her giggly manner and their whispered conversations made it so clear that the calls were personal, not professional, that others in the house wondered why he wasn't bothering to use a pseudonym.

When Bush was leaving Washington for China in the fall of 1974, he hired Fitzgerald to join him, although she had no particular experience in foreign policy. "I am looking forward to Jennifer Fitzgerald coming over to be my secretary," Bush wrote on October 21, 1974, part of the first entry in his China diary. "I think there is a lot to be said to having a buffer between the State Department and the ambassador."

A week before Fitzgerald was to arrive in Beijing on December 5, 1974, Barbara Bush abruptly returned to the United States. She managed to snag a seat on an Air Force plane carrying Secretary of State Henry Kissinger, who had been making a diplomatic visit to China accompanied by his wife and children. In her 1994 memoirs, Barbara would write that her departure from China had been "planned for months," but there were signs at the time that it was precipitous, and even a time of crisis for the couple.

"I asked if there was extra room on the plane," Bush wrote in his diary on November 28, 1974, Thanksgiving Day. "[Deputy White House national security adviser Brent] Scowcroft first wired there was none. Then Kissinger invited her. Then the day of the departure they told me there was a little flap in the States about Kissinger's kids and wife and that the press was insisting that they pay. And Karen Jenkins [a Kissinger aide] thought it would be better if I paid. So I, a little sore about it, wrote out a check for sixteen hundred dollars to the U.S. Air Force and said, 'Now you tell them I paid in advance,' for approximately the first class trip which she said they were being charged at to go one way from Peking to Washington."

He noted with annoyance that they could have saved a considerable amount of money if Barbara had waited a few days to take a commercial flight. "Ironically Bar had gotten round trip flight Peking-New York-Peking—$967. What a massive financial whipping. She could have stayed here four days longer and then done that. *C'est la guerre!*"

But she didn't wait.

"Barbara boarded the plane with the Kissinger group and headed off for the first Christmas we will be apart in 30 years," Bush wrote. It was the longest stretch that George and Barbara Bush would ever spend apart during their marriage, and it was the only time that they wouldn't be together over the Christmas holidays. George Bush's mother, the person whose counsel he heeded the most, arranged to visit her son for three weeks, arriving on December 18 with her sister-in-law.

"I miss you more than tongue can tell," George Bush wrote Barbara in a letter dated December 22, 1974, quoting a cherished family phrase that had been coined by Robin, "but maybe these little gaps are good cause they teach me that I could never live without you." Whatever the reason for their separation, Barbara returned to China early the next year, in 1975.

Jennifer Fitzgerald may have been a private heartache then. She would later become a political headache, and a persistent one.

⌒ ⌣

As Barbara Bush struggled to deal with her depression, she once tried to tell her doctor how she felt. At an appointment in 1976 for a physical, he asked her how she was, and she began to cry. But he didn't understand the depth of her despondency. "You didn't say anything; I just thought you were tired," he told her later. She replied, "Well, I was tired, but tired of hurting."

Even to her own children, she kept up an uncomplaining front. She later called that the lesson of her "stoic New England self-control and Texas toughness." Doro Bush Koch would recall how much time her mother had spent in her room with the door shut during those days.

"Maybe I should have picked up on this warning signal, but the truth is, it wasn't until Mom's 1994 memoirs came out that my brothers and I learned she had suffered from depression during that CIA period," Doro said. "We had no idea."

Actually, Neil Bush did have an idea, although he didn't fully understand what was going on until later. He recalled a conversation they had one day, just the two of them, when he was home from college. Even years later, the memory made his eyes well with tears.

"I remember Mom saying after all the kids had grown up how she felt like she had done nothing in her life," Neil told me in an interview at his small Houston office. "But she had raised five kids...She'd supported a husband who had been moving around and had done all these amazing things, and couldn't have done it without her. For her to see some of her peers working and engaged in activities outside of the house kind of gave her a sense of worthlessness. Which looking back on it, it's like, how in the world could she have ever thought that? But it was real to her."

Neil didn't realize at the time that his mother was clinically depressed. "I'm only aware in looking back on it," he said. "I had no clue that it was that serious. But that's where this memory came rushing back, hearing her disclose that she had that problem."

Her vulnerability was at odds with her image as confident and resilient—as someone more likely to intimidate others than to be intimidated by them, or by life. Her younger brother, Scott Pierce, and his wife, Janice, visited the Bushes in Washington during this time and realized she was having a tough patch. "George came back as the head of the CIA, and it was the first time in her life with him that she couldn't talk to him about what he's doing," Scott Pierce told me in an interview at his Florida home. "She felt closed out of his life," Janice Pierce added.

That said, it is a sign of how firmly her persona of strength was set that even decades later her brother questioned the depth of her depression, and dismissed the notion that she really might have taken her own life. "It was a very temporary thing," Scott Pierce declared. "Committing suicide? She wouldn't." Janice Pierce agreed with him: "That wouldn't be in her makeup."

But Barbara Bush did think about it. For months, she couldn't shake the blues. "My 'code' told me that you should not think about self, but others," she said. "And yet, there I was, wallowing in self-pity. I knew it was wrong but couldn't seem to pull out of it." She began to volunteer again at the Washington Home for Incurables, a hospital for the seriously ill, later renamed the Washington Home and Community Hospices. That seemed to help restore her spirits.

She finally realized that her depression was lifting, although she couldn't pinpoint precisely when it went away, or why.

She mentioned her struggle with depression in a dinner speech in 1991, although the only news coverage it attracted was a throwaway mention at the end of a story in the *Washington Times*. Utah senator Orrin Hatch had visited the White House to ask her to speak at a fund-raiser for the National Foundation for Depressive Illness. She almost never did such events for anything other than her chosen causes such as literacy and cancer, she told him, but in this case she made an exception. And she kept the commitment, even though the black-tie gala ended up being held during the closing hours of the First Gulf War.

She started by thanking her hosts for letting her speak before dinner so she could return to the White House. "These are troubled times, and I just feel I should be with George," she said, according to a typewritten text in the Bush Library archives. She arrived back at the Oval Office in time to watch her husband announce that he was calling for a cease-fire.

In her speech, she had described the dilemma of a woman with depression in terms that sounded personal. "Will someone with the best of intentions tell her to 'snap out of it'... or 'get hold of yourself'?" she asked. "Will the people closest to her reproach her for feeling sorry for herself...or not counting her blessings? And how will she feel about herself? Guilty...Ashamed...Desperate?"

Some see depression as a failure of willpower or moral character, she said. "And that's what I thought, too, back in 1975, when I had my own six- to eight-month encounter with depression...I was very lucky—it did pass, and it never returned. But while it lasted, it was awful."

Barbara Bush's experience made her more empathetic and less judgmental toward people who were facing emotional problems. "I used to think that you could control your emotions, that you just needed to think of others and not yourself," she said. But afterward, "I also realize you cannot handle everything alone. And when things go out of control, you should seek help." She would see that quandary up close again when one of her granddaughters struggled with drug abuse and mental illness; then, she would encourage professional help, and she would express compassion, not blame, when her granddaughter stumbled.

Later, there were those close to the Bush family who would wonder how the future for all of them might have changed if the story had turned out a different way, if she had committed suicide during her darkest days. In that alternate universe, the repercussions could have reshaped the lives of her husband and children, with implications even for American history. Mary Kate Cary, a documentary filmmaker who was a White House speechwriter for President Bush, saw parallels to *It's a Wonderful Life*. The 1946 movie, a Christmas perennial, contemplates how the small town of Bedford Falls would have been different if protagonist George Bailey had never been born.

"Would George Bush have run for president as a widower?" Cary asked. "Probably not. Would George W. have run for office? Would Jeb have run for office? I think it would have totally changed the dynamic of that family if she had gone through with it." She noted Barbara Bush's central role in her family and her decades of work on behalf of literacy. "I don't think she has any idea of the ripple effect of her life and how many people she's affected in a positive way. Thank God she was strong enough to overcome the pain."

Chapter Nine

——⋆——

"What Are We Going to
Do About Bar?"

Barbara Bush was there, but she mostly listened.

Late in the summer of 1978, George Bush gathered a handful of confidants at Kennebunkport for an early political strategy session. They included Bill Steiger, a Wisconsin congressman and a fellow member of the Republican class first elected in 1966 (he would drop dead of a heart attack by the end of the year, at age forty) and Dean Burch, a former RNC chairman and White House aide to Nixon and Ford, who would be a mentor and ally.

And, most important of all, James A. Baker III. He already was Bush's friend and tennis partner. Then and for the rest of their careers, Baker would become Bush's campaign mastermind, confidant, and consigliere, as well as a respected policymaker in his own right. They met when Baker was a rising young lawyer in Houston and Bush, six years his senior, was a rising young oilman. Both got involved in the Texas GOP during the days when Republicans were beginning to assert themselves in a state that had been dominated by Democrats for decades. Their lives would be inextricably intertwined as both rose to the pinnacles of power—Bush to the presidency, Baker to lead the Treasury Department for Reagan and the State Department for Bush.

"Strategy and timing were debated," Barbara Bush recalled. "It was decided that if George was going to make the run, he must step up his travel and start lining up teams in every state." He would follow Carter's 1976 model, the template for long shots. It relied on shoe leather over name recognition, on the meticulous cultivation of grassroots support, especially in the states with early contests. By the time he formally announced his candidacy at the National Press Club in Washington on May 1, 1979, Bush already had visited forty-two states over the previous eight months.

Barbara's role in this new endeavor wasn't entirely clear, to her or to others. Bush's advisers weren't sure how much of a political asset she would be. She was outspoken and blunt. Bush once told a top aide that the problem with a strong wife is that she could make her husband look weak in comparison. Barbara Bush sometimes worried about that too. There were also concerns about her appearance. Bush looked younger than he was; she looked older than she was. Voters sometimes assumed she was Bush's mother, not his wife. That was painful for her, and it was at odds with the campaign's efforts to contrast his youth with Reagan's age. By Inauguration Day, Reagan would be sixty-nine, the oldest president elected up to that point; Bush would be fifty-six.

"Mrs. Bush, people say your husband is a man of the eighties and you're a woman of the forties. What do you say to that?" Jane Pauley demanded in an interview during the campaign on NBC's *Today* show. Barbara Bush found the question devastating. "Why didn't she just slap me in the face?" she wrote in her memoirs. "I was speechless and heartsick." She managed one of her signature rejoinders: "Oh, you mean people think I look forty? Neat."

Her outspoken sister-in-law, Nancy Ellis, told Barbara that she had been the subject of a family discussion at a dinner that hadn't included her. The topic: "What are we going to do about Bar?" With a campaign ahead, they considered whether they should urge her to lose weight, to color her hair, to wear more fashionable clothes.

Barbara felt humiliated. It was an unwelcome echo of her mother's childhood critique of her weight, of the unflattering comparisons with her chic sister. "They discussed how to make me snappier," Barbara Bush wrote in her diary. "I know it was meant to be helpful, but I wept quietly alone until George told me that was absolutely crazy." He reassured her, but the suggestion stung, and she didn't forget it.

"I tell you the truth, it hurts," she said eight years later, the snub still on her mind. "When George was first going to run for president, a member of our family said, what are we going to do about Barbara? I said, funny, it doesn't bother George Bush."

As usual, she used self-deprecating humor as a shield. A profile in the *Cincinnati Enquirer* said a friend had asked her if she would mind watching her husband age during the presidency, as presidents do. "I said, 'Hot dog! I'd love to watch him age,'" she replied. "'Then he'll look like me.'"

She was dispatched to speak at ladies' teas and Republican clubs, tracking her itinerary in a fawn-colored leather appointment book that was battered by the end of the campaign. Her name was engraved in gold and a "George Bush for President" sticker was plastered on the cover. No other wife of a candidate was pursuing such a grueling routine, and on her own. She had to insist to campaign planners that they schedule her to spend one week a month traveling with her husband, just to have a chance to see him.

One night, George and Barbara ran into each other in the Des Moines airport, each headed to a different flight, neither aware that the other was nearby. "I look at Bar's schedule and I think it is too intense, too tough," Bush wrote in his diary. "She doesn't get home enough. We've overdone it."

"She worked like hell for her husband to get the nomination," Peter Teeley recalled. He had gotten to know Jim Baker when both worked on Gerald Ford's presidential campaign in 1976, but he was new to the Bushes when he became George Bush's press secretary. He was struck by Barbara Bush's sharp instincts. At one point, she questioned why they were going to Kennebunkport; wouldn't that reinforce Bush's image as an elitist? "I thought, *This person has a mind of her own and is going to say what she thinks*," Teeley said.

Even so, the Bush campaign did little to spotlight her—a contrast, say, to the way Bob Dole's campaign was featuring Elizabeth Dole. A voter might well be uncertain about just who Bush's wife was. Only two of seven TV ads Bush aired during the primaries showed Barbara, and in neither ad was she identified as his wife. On the cover of one campaign brochure was a photo that showed her standing just behind him, but it wasn't clear whether she was an enamored supporter or something more. Another brochure ran through his résumé and managed to give thumbnail descriptions of his positions on twenty-three issues, from agriculture to welfare reform, but never mentioned that he was married, or to whom.

The men who were running things—and they were all men, all the strategists who mattered—underestimated her appeal and discounted her contribution. Barbara Bush didn't recognize her value, either.

George Bush wasn't the most obvious contender for the White House in 1980. The only elections he had won were two races for the US House in a Republican-leaning district in Houston. He had lost two Senate contests in Texas. He had agreed to chair the Republican National Committee during Watergate, a role that entailed defending the disgraced Richard Nixon. He had taken over the CIA after a time of scandal; heading a secret intelligence agency wasn't typically a stepping-stone to higher office.

What he did have, though, was drive. Even Jimmy Carter, who knew something about that trait, suggested Bush was destined to run for the Oval Office. The two men had an odd exchange during the transition from Ford's White House to the Carter administration. Bush had gone to Plains, Georgia, to deliver an intelligence briefing to the president-elect, the third time he had briefed Carter since the former governor had become the presumptive Democratic nominee. When one of the CIA officers in the session said a particular issue would require action around 1985, Carter interrupted. "I don't need to worry about that," he said. "By then George will be president and he can take care of it."

Carter, half smiling, then nodded at Walter Mondale, the vice president–elect, who was sitting across the room. He added, "Either George or Fritz Mondale there." (As it turned out, in 1985 Ronald Reagan would be president, Bush would be his vice president, and Mondale their vanquished 1984 Democratic rival.)

George Bush had told the new president he was willing to stay on as director of the CIA, but Jimmy Carter wasn't interested. Barbara Bush found a house for them in Houston, on Indian Trail in the Tanglewood neighborhood. George Bush signed off on the purchase without even seeing it. She was happy about heading home. He was not.

It was the first time in a decade that George Bush wasn't in public office as a member of Congress or the cabinet or the diplomatic corps. He was suffering from "withdrawal symptoms," he wrote an old friend, "as tense as a coiled spring." The chitchat at the country club and the C-suite— he had signed on to chair the executive committee at First International Bank—didn't interest him, not after being immersed in intelligence affairs and foreign policy and even the business of the House Ways and Means Committee. He turned down an offer from H. Ross Perot to run his oil business in Houston. "I just get bored silly about whose daughter is a Pi Phi or even bored about who's banging old Joe's wife," he said. "I don't want to slip into that 3 or 4 martini late late dinner rich social thing."

Barbara recognized his restlessness. "I wonder if George will ever be happy at home again?" she wondered in her diary.

Then he found his next mission. Within weeks after Carter's inauguration, in early 1977, Bush began telling a few close friends that he wanted to run for president in 1980. Ford had been defeated, and the leading Republican contender was Reagan, who could be vulnerable on grounds of age and ideology. There would be a big field, and Bush wanted to be in it. His résumé would be his calling card. His campaign slogan—"A president we won't have to train"—was designed as a dig at both Carter and Reagan, former governors with no Washington experience.

"The peripatetic Bushes, Barbara Pierce and CIA husband, George, are 'once again thinking about a new direction,'" the Smith College alumnae magazine reported in February 1977, with no hint about where that new direction might lead. "We have our 1st grandbaby who lives in texas and are so lucky to have 5 contributing children," Barbara wrote in the section for class notes.

Three decades earlier, George had simply announced to his wife that they were moving to a new life in Texas. This time, again, Bush didn't consult her before deciding to run for president. Both of them still viewed such big decisions as his to make. "Look, George Bush never even exactly came right out and asked me to marry him. And he never came right out and told me he was thinking of running," Barbara Bush told a reporter in August 1979. "But I could see the way he was going." If she had wanted to raise objections, she said, "I would have told him."

Early in the campaign, Jennifer Fitzgerald emerged as a strain within the staff, though gossip about her wouldn't erupt in public until after the 1980 election. Other staffers found her rude and secretive, a negative force at the center of a lean campaign team that needed to be collaborative and nimble. Her influence seemed inexplicable to them, but Bush insisted on keeping her close despite the complications she created in her role as his gatekeeper.

He resisted even when the complaint came from Baker, his close friend and campaign manager. Baker already had the mien of a wise man and heavyweight credentials; he had run Ford's campaign during the general election in 1976. No one other than the candidate himself was considered more crucial to the long-shot campaign's chances of success.

Baker gave Bush an ultimatum: Either Jennifer Fitzgerald was going to leave the campaign or he would. To Baker's reported astonishment, Bush said he would have to think about it. Only the next morning did he tell Baker that Fitzgerald would be leaving the Houston campaign headquarters. She was moved to a fund-raising post in New York.

⌒ ⌣

Barbara Bush had no trouble extolling George Bush's qualities as a person or embracing his policy positions on the economy and foreign policy and defense. But she did struggle with one issue: abortion.

In 1980, George Bush tried to navigate a position down the middle. He opposed abortion but also opposed passing a constitutional amendment to ban it. He was against federal funding for abortion in general but supported exceptions in cases of rape, incest, or to preserve the health of the mother. When Ronald Reagan picked him as his running mate, though, Bush promised to support the GOP platform, which endorsed a constitutional amendment that would overturn the 1973 Roe v. Wade decision. By 1988, when Bush was the presidential nominee, the GOP platform was even more strongly pro-life. It asserted that "the unborn child has a fundamental individual right to life which cannot be infringed."

On cultural issues, Barbara Bush often found herself at odds with Republican orthodoxy and the GOP's increasingly conservative tilt on cultural issues. "In all our years of campaigning, abortion was the toughest issue for me," she said later.

During that first presidential campaign, she tried to sort out her views on abortion, to figure out where she stood. On four ruled sheets of paper, undated but tucked into a folder with her diary entries and letters from 1980, she wrote out by hand what she believed and why. She never disclosed this paper or discussed the reasoning she outlined in it. It was in effect a conversation with herself. The notes provide a window into how seriously she took the issue, and how she saw it as a moral question. Her deliberations might astonish cynics who assume that the calculations of those in the public eye are always political.

The memo to herself might be the reason she never wavered on the issue. She was determined not to create problems for George Bush during his political career by openly disagreeing with him, but she also wouldn't agree with him, not on this. She would keep her mouth shut. "The elected person's opinion is the one the public has the right to know," she said.

As was the case regarding so many other big questions, her experience with the life and death of daughter Robin helped shape her views.

"Thoughts on abortion," she wrote across the top of the first page, underlining the words. Then she tried to crystallize the issue in her mind.

"When does the soul enter the body is the #1 question," she wrote. "<u>Not</u> when does life begin, as life begins in a flower or an animal with the first cell. So the question is does the life begin (soul entering the body) at conception or at the moment the first breath is taken? If the answer to that question is at conception, then abortion is murder. If the answer to that question is the moment the first breath is taken, then abortion is not murder."

She decided that Robin had answered that question for her.

"What does Barbara Bush feel about abortion," she wrote, referring to herself in the third person as she tried to think through the issue. Then she answered the question she had posed.

"Judging from both the birth and death of Robin Bush, I have decided that that almost religious experience, that thin line between birth, the first breath that she took, was when the soul, the spirit, that special thing that separates man or woman from animals + plants entered her little body. I was conscious at her birth and I was with her at her death. (As was G.B.) An even stronger impression remains with me of that moment, 27 years ago [when she died]. Of course, extreme grief, but that has softened. I vividly remember that split second, that thin line between breathing and not breathing, the complete knowledge that her soul had left and only the body remained."

Robin's soul had entered her body at the moment of her birth, her mother decided, and it had left at the instant of her death.

"What do I feel about abortion?" Barbara Bush continued in her distinctive handwriting, bold and clear, with no words crossed out or rewritten.

"Having decided that the first breath is when the soul enters the body, I believe in Federally funded abortion. Why should the rich be allowed to afford abortions and the poor not?" She said she could support limits on the timing of abortions—"12 weeks, the law says"—but she wrote it was "not a Presidential issue," underlining "not" twice. "Abortion is personal, between mother fathers and Dr."

She considered what public policies might make sense. "Education is the answer," she wrote. "I believe that we must give people goals in life for them to work for—Teach them the price you must pay for being promiscuous."

Along the side margin of the last page, she wrote, "Needs lots more thought."

~ ~

At the beginning, Barbara Bush didn't relish speaking in public. She had to brace herself to do it. She devised a forty-minute slideshow of photographs she had taken in China; she would talk about their adventures in a destination too exotic for most Americans at the time to imagine visiting. She developed other techniques, too, including a bit of legerdemain to manage the political imperative to remember names.

She would teach the small trick to the local volunteers who drove her from one event to another. In New Hampshire, that was Kathleen Gregg, who had just married into a political family. Her father-in-law was a former governor and Bush supporter, her husband a future senator and governor. Starting in 1978, when she was twenty-eight, she began accompanying Barbara Bush during her frequent visits to the state, site of the first presidential primary.

"She'd say, 'I'm going to walk in, and if you could help me with names,'" Kathy Gregg told me decades later in an interview at their New Hampshire home, laughing at the memory. Her husband, Judd Gregg, was sitting by her side. "'Now, if I give someone a great big kiss, that means I don't know their name.' So she'd work the room and you could see, you know, 'Hi, John. Hi, Cindy. Hi, Susan.' And then, all of a sudden, big kiss. Well, that meant that she didn't know Marilyn's name." That was a sign the assistant was supposed to discreetly step in and help.

Barbara Bush was relentless when it came to promoting George Bush. In the weeks before the New Hampshire primary in 1980, the *Boston Globe* had decided to leave coverage of a news conference Bush was holding to the wire services. "We heard footsteps and a steely-eyed woman walked into the paper's office at the Massachusetts Capitol and inquired who was in charge here," recalled Walter Robinson, then the statehouse bureau chief. It was Barbara Bush, and she wasn't taking no for an answer. "She said, 'In thirty minutes, George Bush is having a press conference at the Parker House. Get your notebook.'"

Robinson and one of the reporters on his staff, Larry Collins, dutifully trailed her back to the hotel a block away. "I was actually a little intimidated," Robinson said; following her seemed to be a smarter course than protesting. Collins ended up filing a story about it for the *Globe*, a particularly important outlet because of its sizable circulation in southern New Hampshire.

The Bush campaign was a family affair, and one that whetted the interest of George W. and Jeb to pursue politics as careers. George W. already had run for a House seat in Texas in 1978. Now he was pursuing a business career, but he spent the final weeks before the caucuses stumping in Iowa. "I loved every minute of the retail politics," he said. The campaign was an introduction to campaigning for Jeb, who had moved back from Venezuela, where he worked for the international office of a Texas bank. A fluent Spanish speaker, he spent six months running the campaign in Puerto Rico, which was holding its first presidential primary; Bush won. An introvert by nature, Jeb was pushed out of his comfort zone; it was there that he discovered he liked the energy of person-to-person campaigning.

Neil worked in the New Hampshire campaign, living in Nashua; that's where he met his first wife, Sharon. Marvin, a senior at the University of Virginia, took a year off school to work in Iowa. Doro, an undergraduate at Boston College, enrolled in a typing class to gain skills she could use at the Massachusetts state campaign headquarters.

In the opening Iowa caucuses, all the effort, all the travel, paid off. To the amazement of the political establishment, and to front-runner Ronald Reagan and his team, George Bush won. "Our suite/room was a mad house," Barbara Bush wrote the next day in her diary. "How sweet it is—how sweet it is!!"

They headed on to a roller-coaster schedule in New Hampshire. But a few weeks later, Reagan trounced Bush in that primary, winning by more than two to one. A debate in Nashua, scheduled to be between the two of them, was a disaster for Bush when four other contenders showed up and elbowed their way onstage. Bush seemed petty and peevish in trying to exclude them. "George looked like the heavy," Barbara admitted. She told a friend that Reagan had used the moment brilliantly. He demanded that the others be allowed to participate.

Bush would have some victories in the primaries that followed, but he would have more defeats, and Reagan emerged as the all-but-certain nominee. Bush wanted to stay in until the end, until the final June 3 primaries in California and elsewhere. Baker and others warned that he should avoid the scars that might preclude him from being considered by Reagan as a running mate. But when reporters asked if he would consider accepting the number two spot, Bush had scornfully invoked the famous declaration of Civil War general William Tecumseh Sherman in 1884—"I will not accept if nominated and will not serve if elected"— and told them, "Take Sherman and cube it."

Jeb Bush, for one, argued that his father should go out in "an Alamo-style campaign finish, with guns blazing, until the ammo ran out."

Bush finally huddled at his house in Houston with the advisers whose opinions he valued most: Jim Baker, Victor Gold, Pete Teeley, and Bob Mosbacher. Barbara was there too.

"It was like a hundred degrees, and humid," Teeley remembered. They sat in the sunroom at the rear of the house and debated back and forth. Camped out in the front lawn were local reporters and photographers, including a twenty-four-year-old correspondent for KXAS-TV named Karen Parfitt. After her marriage, she would be known as Karen Hughes, and eventually became one of George W. Bush's most trusted advisers during his presidential campaigns and administration.

That day, though, she was just one more member of the press scrum, hanging out in the heat and waiting to see if the local presidential candidate was about to hang it up. She had never met any of the Bushes before. "It was brutal and you're melting, and she comes out and brings us iced drinks," Hughes recalled. "I vividly remember thinking, *This has got to be the worst time of her life, and here she is bringing us [drinks], you know, because she was worried about how hot it was.*"

George Bush wasn't quite ready to make a decision; he wanted to sleep on it. His inner circle agreed to meet again the next morning. As Teeley was leaving, he warned the Bushes to steer clear of the news crews until a final decision had been made.

The next morning, when Teeley and Baker arrived, there were television cameras strewn on the front lawn but no photographers or reporters in sight. When he got back to the sunroom, he discovered where they had gone. "The whole press corps is in the swimming pool with the Bushes. She's carrying around lemonade for people to drink. I said, 'What's going on?' She said, 'It's hot as hell out there. We invited them to come in.'"

Once the reporters had been ejected from the backyard, the discussion resumed. Baker and others told Bush he could no longer win the nomination, and by staying in he could divide the Republican Party and make it harder for Reagan to win in November. What's more, he could poison whatever chance he might have of being chosen as Reagan's running mate. Bush still wanted to stay in. "It was a tough decision," Barbara wrote in her diary.

She had a skeptical eye toward Baker's full motives too. "I may have been mad at Jimmy Baker at that time, for saying that he wanted to get out," she told me years later. "We knew we couldn't win; he knew it," she said of her husband. "He just wanted to stay in so the people who worked for him had a chance" to win delegate races and attend the national convention.

"I think Baker's point was, if you want to be considered for vice president—" I began.

"Baker wanted to be considered as chief of staff" in a Reagan White House, she broke in. "He ran for that."

Reluctantly, Bush agreed to withdraw.

Within days, Barbara Bush mailed a leftover campaign postcard to her friend Elsie Hillman. It was printed with the slogan "George Bush: A President We Won't Have to Train." "Boo-hoo!" Barbara wrote. "All over—but wasn't too fun. Do you think it was right, not finishing?"

She had fretted in her diary about what might be ahead if her competitive husband failed in the campaign he had been waging for years, and after coming so tantalizingly close to success. "I feel we are very near the end of this long quest—Will I be able to cope with the letdown George will feel," she wrote. "Will I be enough?"

"Will I be enough?"

As it turned out, though, the campaign wasn't over.

Chapter Ten

—★—

The Frost That Never Thawed

Nancy Reagan was nowhere to be seen.

It was the morning after Ronald Reagan's surprise announcement to the Republican National Convention that he was choosing George Bush as his running mate. On the stage of Detroit's Joe Louis Arena hours earlier, Nancy Reagan couldn't hide her dismay. "She looked like a little girl who had just lost her favorite Raggedy Ann doll: sad, disappointed, almost crushed," a *Washington Post* reporter wrote. Nevada senator Paul Laxalt, the Reagan campaign chairman, wrapped his arm around her shoulders to comfort her.

Laxalt would have been her preference for Reagan's running mate. He was a trusted friend, but he was also another western conservative who would have done little to broaden the national appeal of the GOP ticket. "At the time, I didn't like George Bush," Nancy acknowledged later. The wounds from the primary battles—when Bush questioned her Ronnie's age and competence—were still fresh. So was her assessment that Bush looked feckless during that pivotal New Hampshire debate in February. He had floundered when four other Republican contenders showed up and demanded to participate. Reagan had seized the moment. "I am paying for this microphone, Mr. Green!" he famously declared, though the moderator's last name was actually Breen.

In Detroit, the Bushes took the half-mile drive down East Jefferson

Avenue from the Pontchartrain Hotel, where they were staying, to have breakfast with the Reagans at their hotel at the Renaissance Center. In the Reagans' suite on the sixty-ninth floor, with its panoramic view of the Detroit River, the governor and his top aides waited in the living room to greet them.

The awkward moment was eased a bit by Barbara Bush's directness. "Governor, let me promise you one thing: We're going to work our tails off for you," she told him as they walked in. In their brief phone conversation the night before, George Bush had signaled to Reagan that he was willing to align himself with the pro-life stance of the presidential nominee and of the conservative Christians who were a rising force in the GOP. Bush was also prepared to defend the supply-side policies he had derided during the primaries as "voodoo economics."

Barbara Bush's opening declaration was designed to reassure Reagan and his team that she wasn't going to create any complications for them, either.

Just the day before, at a luncheon in honor of Betty Ford and Nancy Reagan hosted by the National Federation of Republican Women, Barbara had arrived sporting a pro-choice button. She had refused to discuss her support for abortion rights during the primaries, but with her husband's political ambitions apparently vanquished, she felt free to make her own stance on the controversial issue clear again.

That burst of liberty was over almost before it began. With her husband unexpectedly joining Reagan's ticket, Barbara Bush didn't abandon her pro-choice views. But she once again stopped talking about them. The pro-choice button she had worn at midday had vanished from public view by the end of the night. While many assumed she still supported abortion rights—an accurate assumption that some moderate and liberal Republicans found reassuring—she would rebuff attempts by reporters and activists to engage publicly on the issue again until she published her White House memoirs fourteen years later.

Ronald Reagan wasn't enthusiastic about choosing Bush, but it became the necessary political move. That said, he would be won over by the deference and loyalty his vice president and his wife would show. But Nancy Reagan was another matter entirely.

That Thursday morning in the Detroit Plaza Hotel suite, she lingered in the bedroom before making an entrance into the living room, a frosty beginning to a relationship that would never thaw. "The bitter campaigns of Iowa and New Hampshire were still fresh in my memory," she said of that first meeting in Detroit. She eventually would reach a sort of accommodation with George Bush, although she could never be counted as a reliable ally.

But Nancy Reagan's antipathy for Barbara Bush, hidden from public view, created grievances behind the scenes that would persist for the rest of their lives.

Decades later, some of Barbara Bush's heat toward Nancy Reagan had cooled, but she hadn't forgotten their friction. "She really hated us," she mused in an interview with me. "I don't know why, but she really hated us."

The two women had met for the first time in 1968, pleasantly enough, at the Republican National Convention in Miami Beach. Richard Nixon easily won the nomination that summer, but Reagan, then in his first term as governor of California, already was the favorite of some delegates and a rising force in the GOP. Bush was a first-term congressman from Texas who had harbored long-shot ambitions of being chosen as Nixon's running mate. In the convention hall, Barbara walked over to introduce herself. "I found them both very attractive," she wrote in a letter to George Walker, a Bush cousin who was then serving in Vietnam. "She is tiny and really a very lovely natural beauty."

Four years later, at festivities for Nixon's second inaugural in 1973, the Reagans and Bushes met again. Then in his second gubernatorial term and a conservative hero, Reagan and his wife were among those toasting Bush at a glittering Washington dinner hosted, remarkably enough, by H. Ross Perot. The billionaire businessman was honoring three Texans including Bush, who had just left his post as US ambassador to the United Nations to chair the Republican National Committee.

The other honorees were White House adviser Anne Armstrong and deputy defense secretary Bill Clements, later governor of Texas. At the time, Perot and Bush were friendly enough, though they were never close and would later become bitter foes.

By the 1980 campaign, however, Reagan and Bush were rivals. Reagan was the front-runner for the GOP nomination, Bush the upstart challenger, and Nancy and Barbara combatants on the front lines. Reagan's team portrayed Bush as a squishy moderate with a long résumé but few achievements. Bush's allies depicted Reagan as too old and too conservative to win the White House. The campaign slogan described Bush as "a president we won't have to train." That was a not-so-subtle suggestion that Reagan, who had never worked in Washington, couldn't say the same.

Once he had won the Republican nomination, even the affable Reagan had some trouble getting past the scars from the primaries. In his mind, that debate in Nashua had branded Bush as a lightweight who couldn't stand up under pressure. The Reagans were annoyed that he had stayed in the race after it was clear Reagan was going to be the nominee. They worried that would make it harder to unify the GOP and win the White House.

When the convention opened, Reagan still hadn't chosen his running mate, and Bush still hadn't given up hope it might be him. When Bush was backstage that Wednesday night, about to go out to deliver his big speech, he was told that Reagan had finally made a decision: Former president Gerald Ford was going on the ticket, an unprecedented pairing. Bush felt as though he had been punched in the stomach. He delivered his prepared remarks, then walked the few blocks back to the Hotel Pontchartrain with son Jeb.

They stopped in the hotel bar to drink a beer before heading upstairs to the Bushes' suite, where several cases of beer had been brought in for an end-of-the-campaign party.

"It was like a funeral," Barbara Bush said. Jeb was particularly upset. "It's not fair," he told his parents in the bedroom. Barbara suggested they just pack up and leave town, but Bush rejected that idea. "We came to this convention to leave politics with style and we are going to do it," he told her.

He was no happier about the turn of events than they were. He took off his shoes, changed into a T-shirt, and opened another beer.

Then everything changed.

At 11:38 p.m., as they were watching the convention on TV, waiting for Reagan and Ford to arrive onstage, the phone rang. The negotiations with Ford had collapsed after he suggested in an interview with CBS anchor Walter Cronkite that the two men would have a "copresidency." James Baker picked up the line, then handed it to Bush. Reagan asked him to be his running mate; Bush accepted. Once the Reagan team had announced the news, he and Barbara stepped into the hallway to speak to a half dozen reporters who had been hanging around to write what they had assumed would be his political obituary.

She was beaming. He was grinning, almost goofy, and he wasn't wearing socks. "To be very candid with you," he told them, "I thought it was going the other way."

Ronald Reagan had reluctantly accepted his strategists' calculations that none of the other options for running mate—New York representative Jack Kemp, Tennessee senator Howard Baker, former Treasury secretary Bill Simon, former defense secretary Donald Rumsfeld, and Laxalt among them—made as much political sense as Bush did.

Nancy Reagan was unpersuaded. Like Barbara Bush, she was fiercely protective of her husband, and more likely than he was to carry a grudge.

George Bush acknowledged as much decades later, in a short and carefully phrased foreword to *Lady in Red: An Intimate Portrait of Nancy Reagan*, written by Sheila Tate. Tate had served as press secretary for Nancy Reagan in the White House and then as press secretary for George Bush during his 1988 campaign. Introducing the book, which was published in 2018, Bush managed to strike a seemingly positive tone about Nancy Reagan while never actually saying he liked her. He called her "a complicated person."

"Nancy Reagan was truly one of the most loyal and protective spouses I have ever met in my ninety-three years," he wrote, an assessment likely to be shared by anyone who had met or tangled with her. "My dear friend Ronald Reagan could not have asked for a better partner. No matter the issue—politics, world affairs, inside White House gamesmanship—Nancy had his back."

For Barbara, though, Nancy became a nemesis.

They were so alike, and so different.

Indeed, the two women were distantly related, although there are no signs that either of them ever realized it. Their common ancestors were Edward and Margaret Marvin, a sixteenth-century couple from Essex, England. The Marvins' son Matthew, Nancy's direct ancestor through her biological father, immigrated to America in 1635 or 1636. His brother Reinhold, Barbara's direct ancestor through her father, followed about a year later. That made the two women tenth cousins.

Even without that obscure connection, Nancy Davis and Barbara Pierce could have been sisters. Both were born in hospitals in Manhattan, and almost exactly four years apart, in 1921 and 1925. (As an adult, Nancy routinely shaved two years off her age, making the two seem even closer.) Both would ruefully remember themselves as chubby little girls. Both were no better than middling students at private all-girl high schools—Nancy at the Chicago Latin School for Girls, Barbara at Ashley Hall in South Carolina. Both attended Smith College, one of the elite Seven Sisters schools in New England, though their paths never crossed on campus. Nancy graduated from Smith in the spring of 1943; Barbara arrived at the Massachusetts school that fall.

Both married men they adored—Barbara at age nineteen, dropping out of college when she did; Nancy at age thirty, after pursuing an acting career in Hollywood. And both served as unswerving defenders of and true believers in their husbands. During the long political journeys that took Reagan and Bush to the White House, Nancy and Barbara each emerged as a trusted sounding board, an influential adviser, and, at times, a feared enforcer.

And both stood on the same side of a generational divide and the limitations of its expectations for women—that a political wife should never appear to be too powerful, too pushy. That traditional definition didn't really fit either of them, though both avoided openly defying it.

Somehow, too, each managed to feel superior to, and also threatened by, the other.

Nancy Reagan's personal insecurities were legendary and understandable after a childhood that did little to foster a sense of stability. Her parents had separated by the time she was two. They divorced a few years later, at a time when divorce was rare, because her father wanted to remarry. Her colorful and ambitious mother, Edith Luckett, parked the toddler with an aunt and uncle in the Washington suburb of Bethesda, Maryland, while she tried to break into the theater world. When Nancy was seven—her legal name then was Anne Frances Robbins—her mother married a wealthy Chicago neurosurgeon, Loyal Davis. When his stepdaughter was in high school, the austere Dr. Davis agreed to adopt her, and she legally changed her name to Nancy Davis.

While Barbara Pierce's childhood had challenges of its own, she had clear advantages that Nancy Davis didn't. Barbara was raised in a stable family, anchored in an affluent New York City suburb, surrounded by siblings and particularly close to her father. There was never any question about what her name would be. She was part of a New England aristocracy that dated its direct ancestry to the *Mayflower* and had no doubts about its rank in society and in the world, even when the bank accounts were stretched thin. She was comfortable in her skin and certain of her place.

The Bushes called themselves Texans, but they were by birth charter members of the eastern establishment. They were the definition of the New England WASP, that privileged class of white Anglo-Saxon Protestants. When George Bush won his first congressional election, the young couple bought the Washington house of a retiring senator, a family friend, sight unseen. His father welcomed his son and daughter-in-law to town with a black-tie dinner at the 1925 F Street Club—perhaps the most quietly exclusive enclave in the capital, favored by presidents and top officials from the State Department and the CIA.

The Reagans, in contrast, were outsiders from the other coast. Even after he had won the presidency, some in the Georgetown set dismissed Reagan as a right-winger, and as an actor playing a role—"an amiable dunce," Clark Clifford, an adviser to four presidents over four decades, said at a tony dinner party. His comment was immortalized in a front-page story in the *Wall Street Journal.*

Nancy was disdainful of Barbara for her sturdy figure, her matronly clothes, and her blunt manner. To Nancy's amazement, Barbara didn't bother to dye her white hair, wear much makeup beyond a slash of lipstick, or worry about the wrinkles that lined her face. But Nancy also was envious of Barbara's self-confidence, her social standing, and her close-knit family, attributes that hit Nancy at some of her greatest vulnerabilities. "I think she just was insecure," Barbara Bush told me.

Barbara was disdainful of Nancy as brittle and shallow, and as a mother who had failed to forge a close or even functional relationship with her children. In Barbara's book, that came close to being an original sin. But she also admired Nancy's slender figure, the grace with which she wore stylish fashions, and the open devotion she commanded from an adoring husband. While George loved nothing more than being surrounded by as many people as possible, Ronnie favored evenings at home alone with Nancy. Barbara would have liked to share more of those with George, and for him to want to have them.

And there was the legacy of Barbara's mother, who put such a premium on appearance and style, on beautiful things and social status. In her priorities and pleasures, Nancy may have had more in common with Pauline Pierce than Barbara did. Was Nancy, like Barbara's sister, Martha, the sort of daughter that her mother would have preferred to have?

—— ﹏ ——

The morning after the 1980 Republican National Convention ended, reporters peppered Barbara Bush with questions about reports of animosity between the Reagans and the Bushes. "George Bush is going to be a great, pleasant surprise to Governor Reagan, because George is so supportive, and he's a team player, and he doesn't backbite," she said in one of a series of interviews in her hotel suite as Reagan and Bush held private meetings. When the reporter asked why that would be a surprise to Reagan—wasn't that a sign there were suspicions?—Barbara was quick to demur. "None of us really know each other yet," she replied. "We're sort of like new dogs, sniffing each other out."

"We're sort of like new dogs, sniffing each other out."

That plainspoken image was vintage Barbara Bush, and just the sort of comment that appalled Nancy Reagan. "Nancy was so formal and had this standard of what a First Lady should be," said Charlie Black, a Republican strategist who worked for Reagan that year and Bush in later campaigns. Barbara "could be, let's say, irreverent." Which was just the point a reporter raised: "Is your 'earthy directness' the reason Nancy Reagan doesn't like you?"

"Why, that's silly," Barbara Bush replied. "We've only met twice. And from what I've seen of Nancy so far, I like her and she likes me. Furthermore, I think she's ravishingly beautiful. When we were with them, I could hardly take my eyes off her...and she's been just darling to us. If anything, I think she's just shy."

"People say there is a big difference between you and Mrs. Reagan," the reporter persisted. "Can you describe the difference?"

"Why, yes," Barbara replied, then used a bit of hyperbole in describing herself. "Nancy is a size four, and I'm a size forty-four."

That was the script Barbara Bush would follow for the next eight years, in the undefined and often thankless role of Second Lady: Deny there's a problem and deflect the suggestion that there is with self-deprecating humor. On this, as in most things, Barbara Bush was more concerned with defending her husband's political interests than she was with protecting her own feelings or polishing her image.

When the convention ended, the Reagans escorted their new running mate and his wife to the vice presidential nominee's hometown for a photo op and a rally. But the Bushes' Houston home had sat unoccupied while they were on the road for the campaign and its aftermath. Jack Steel, a neighbor and confidant, offered to help. "Jack Steel got the Bayou Club to make lunch, got the cleaners to come in and clean the house," Barbara Bush told me, still grateful years later. "He did everything, and we came home to a house we hadn't lived in for three months, totally ready."

Also on the campaign plane were Reagan's daughter, Maureen; his son, Michael; and Michael's son Cameron. The two-year-old boy "did everything but climb up the walls," Barbara remembered, eyes rolling. It was one of the few times Reagan had spent time with his grandson, a family distance Barbara found shocking and inexplicable. George Bush took the toddler into a playroom stocked with toys for their visiting grandchildren. As Barbara Bush was saying grace before the meal, Cameron stormed back into the dining room, pulling a clattering toy behind him.

Nancy seemed more nonplussed by the interruption than her hosts were. "Don't worry," Barbara told her. "This happens all the time."

During the three and a half months of campaigning that followed, Nancy Reagan and Barbara Bush joined forces without their husbands along just once, at a stop in Baltimore in September. They "whisked through the Inner Harbor and were gone almost as quickly as they came," the Associated Press reporter wrote. A wire-service photo of their brief news conference showed Nancy speaking, Barbara dutifully standing just behind her.

Barbara would tally the exhausting statistics of her travel in that month alone: stops in 37 cities in 16 states over 27 days of campaigning.

On Election Day, the Republican ticket carried forty-four states. Ronald Reagan and George Bush had ousted Jimmy Carter and Walter

Mondale in a landslide, and the Bushes were headed back to Washington. "In May, we had bowed out of politics forever," Barbara Bush said. "Six months later, I was the wife of the vice president–elect of the United States of America."

— —

Victory did nothing to ease the tensions between Nancy Reagan and Barbara Bush.

Almost immediately, there was the crisis of the coats. At her husband's urging, Barbara Bush had gone to New York to splurge on designer clothes for the inaugural events ahead. "George told me to go to New York and buy," she told me, "because he kept reading how frumpy I was. It didn't do much good, but he said, 'Just go to New York.'" She bought clothes from designers Bill Blass, Adele Simpson, and Diane Dickinson, choosing a purple dress and red coat for the inauguration.

Until, that is, Nancy sent a message. "The word came that just said, 'I'm going to wear red,' and I thought, *Oh, my gosh*," Barbara Bush told me. She understood that it was an order for her to wear a coat of some other color, regardless of what she had planned. "I wasn't stupid," she said.

She wore a new blue coat instead, saving the red coat for occasions Nancy Reagan wouldn't be attending. Indeed, she so carefully avoided "Nancy Reagan red" at joint appearances from then on that a bright "Barbara Bush blue" became her signature color. After she became First Lady herself, Barbara Bush began to wear red more often again, her wardrobe choices no longer hostage to Nancy Reagan's edicts. (The double-breasted coat she wears on the cover of this book is a defiant red.)

George and Barbara Bush found themselves frustrated and flummoxed about why relations with Nancy Reagan continued to be so problematic, especially since their interactions with President Reagan were cordial. In their view, they did everything they could to accommodate her. Barbara blamed the coat snafu on her own cluelessness, not the prickly sensitivities of the First Lady. "Thank heavens Nancy Reagan slipped the word to me that she was wearing red," she insisted. "In my excitement I had forgotten that I was not the 'mother of the bride' and never thought to ask!"

Everything Barbara Bush did seemed to annoy Nancy Reagan. Not even Reagan's White House chief of staff Jim Baker, one of George Bush's closest friends from Houston and his former campaign chairman, could smooth things over. Baker repeatedly found himself caught in the middle. "It put me in one hell of a tough spot," he told me.

In another early sign of what was ahead, Nancy Reagan relayed a blunt message to the Bushes through mutual friends. William Wilson, a Los Angeles businessman and member of Reagan's kitchen cabinet, was on the board of Pennzoil; Hugh Liedtke, a Texas oilman and former business partner of George Bush, was the company's chairman. Wilson sent Liedtke a letter written in a crude but clear code that said "the top lady"—that would be Nancy—wanted him to tell his friends that they should keep a lower profile in the press. Nancy referred to the Bushes disparagingly as "the Shrubs." Barbara never saw the letter, but Hugh's wife, Betty, one of her closest friends from their Midland days, did. "That wasn't very nice," Barbara Bush told me. "I didn't get into the news, but it was George, I think, she didn't want to get into the news."

"It burned me up, and it burned Barbara up," George Bush told historian Jon Meacham. "We couldn't back down if we hadn't backed forward. We hadn't done anything. Hadn't done a damn thing. And I was very careful about that, always."

It was true that Bush hadn't abandoned his hopes of one day winning the presidency, but he was careful not to challenge Reagan, not to distance himself from the president, and not to upstage him, at least until Reagan's second term was halfway over and Bush's 1988 campaign had begun. He was so sensitive about respecting Reagan's primacy that when he rushed back from a trip to Texas after Reagan had been shot by a would-be assassin, the vice president overruled aides who suggested his helicopter land on the South Lawn. That was the privilege of presidents, he told them.

On that day, March 30, 1981, Barbara Bush had attended two events with Nancy Reagan, a reception for the Washington Performing Arts Society and a luncheon with cabinet wives for the National Trust for Historic Preservation. She was back at the vice president's residence when news of the shooting at the Washington Hilton broke. "My heart ached so for Nancy," she said, but she recognized that Nancy wouldn't want her to rush to her side. "I knew that the best thing I could do for her was to stay away; what she needed was a best friend."

Again and again, Barbara Bush said, she lowered her profile and took pains to defer to Nancy. Faced with what she saw as exasperating demands and disparagement, Barbara Bush would limit her venting mostly to her husband and her diary. "I tried very, very hard, truthfully," she told me.

At one point, Lee and Walter Annenberg, who were friends of the Bushes and the Reagans, tried to figure out why Nancy had such a visceral dislike of Barbara. A mutual friend relayed their thoughts to the vice president. "Nancy does not like Barbara," Bush then dictated to his diary. "She feels that Barbara has the very things that she, Nancy, doesn't have, and that she'll never be in Barbara's class...Bar has sensed it for a long time. Barbara is so generous, so kind, so unselfish, and frankly I think Nancy Reagan is jealous of her."

"I think it was a class thing," said conservative writer George Will, who regularly met with President Reagan at the White House and had lunch with Nancy Reagan at the Jockey Club. He was not a fan of Bush, as he made clear in his syndicated column, once memorably likening the vice president to a "lap dog." (Insiders suspected he was channeling Nancy's view with that.) Nancy felt Barbara looked down on her, he said, that she viewed Nancy as not in her league. Nancy wasn't the only one who felt that Barbara Bush could be imperious at times. Several senior staffers from the Bush White House and campaigns told me they revered the Bushes but also joked that they were forever seen as "the help."

In his 2003 satirical book, *Lies and the Lying Liars Who Tell Them: A*

Fair and Balanced Look at the Right, comedian Al Franken wrote a chapter titled "I Meet Former First Lady Barbara Bush and It Doesn't Go Well." It chronicled his efforts to engage her in conversation when they were seated across the aisle from each other during a flight to Washington, DC, from Houston in January 2000. Franken, who was later elected to the US Senate from Minnesota, said she repeatedly responded with a preemptive dismissal: "I'm through with you." He initially assumed that was "a hilarious bit of playacting" but eventually concluded she actually was ordering him to pipe down and leave her alone.

The Bushes insisted they were noncombatants in a war Nancy Reagan was waging against them. Still, Nancy Reagan had reason to suspect that she was the occasional target of Barbara Bush's sharp tongue.

Lou Cannon, a White House correspondent for the *Washington Post* and the reporter with the deepest sources in the Reagan White House, was covering a vice presidential trip to New Hampshire in 1986. Barbara Bush, who could be a gifted mimic, came to the back of the small plane to chat with the handful of reporters aboard, as she sometimes did. "She did some imitations of Nancy that were funny but they were also cutting," Cannon recalled. "It was like watching a person saying things they shouldn't say."

None of the reporters wrote about it, but few episodes that tantalizing were likely to stay secret for long. A few weeks later, Nancy Reagan asked Cannon, "Were you on that plane, Lou?"

"I said I was, but I refused to get into that thing with the wives, and she knew that," Cannon told me. "She didn't press me. She knew damn well what happened on that plane."

When Kitty Kelley's tell-all biography of Nancy Reagan was published in 1991, gossip columns reported that Barbara Bush, then First Lady, was reading it with apparent relish, albeit with the cover masked by a jacket borrowed from some less provocative book. When Kelley's tell-all book about the Bushes was published in 2004, it reported that Nancy Reagan had delighted in dishing the details of George Bush's alleged marital infidelities.

For Nancy Reagan, there were other sources of resentment. "A lot of Reagan people think that George Bush wouldn't have become president without Ronald Reagan, and that wasn't ever quite appropriately credited," said Mark Weinberg, a White House press aide who regularly accompanied the Reagans to Camp David on weekends and became close to them. Nancy Reagan smoldered when she heard Bush in his acceptance speech at the 1988 Republican National Convention promise a "kinder and gentler" America. "Kinder and gentler than whom?" she asked pointedly.

And there was this: Barbara had been collecting friends and allies in Washington from the time her husband was a member of Congress to his days as Republican chairman. She had the comfort and support of an expansive and trusted network. But Nancy's small circle of confidants was centered in California. She often felt lonely and embattled in the White House, especially when she was criticized in news stories about commissioning new White House china or borrowing designer dresses or inserting herself into controversies over her husband's schedule or staffers. The same characteristics that had burnished her status in Los Angeles—her exquisite clothes, her taste for the finer things, her celebrity friends—became a source of derision in Washington.

From Nancy's point of view, that may have been the most exasperating thing of all. No matter what she did, she always seemed to get negative stories while Barbara Bush always seemed to get positive ones. That was "one big difference," Sheila Tate said. "Barbara was so good with the press. Nancy was very wary of the press."

"I think Mrs. Reagan felt that Mrs. Bush got a much fairer shake, a more generous shake—less critique, less criticism," Mark Weinberg said. Barbara Bush "got off the hook for things in a way that she never did. That bothered her a lot. Fundamentally, she just didn't think that was fair. And sometimes she would express that. She felt like, my God, if whatever I do is wrong, whatever she does is right."

Both women wielded influence with their husbands behind the

scenes, for instance, but those close to Nancy complained that she was more likely to be portrayed as meddling and shrewish.

"Barbara Bush was just as devoted to her husband, just as calculating and loyal," George Will said, "but she never got the reputation that Nancy had to live with, that Nancy was (a) a cold and calculating operator, but also (b) a kind of parvenu with the clothes and the china and all the rest, whereas no one, probably for class reasons, suspected that of Barbara Bush."

Nancy Reagan never disparaged Barbara Bush in front of the East Wing staff, Tate said. "The one thing I've got to say about Nancy Reagan, and I don't care what you think, she never gossiped to her staff, never, never," Tate told me.

But Nancy Reagan did unload to friends—perhaps not realizing that Barbara Bush's formidable network often was relaying what Nancy was saying back to her. "Friend after friend would report that at small dinner parties in NYC she would say, 'I don't know why the press lets Barbara Bush get away with designer clothes,'" Barbara wrote in her diary, adding, "I wonder if it ever occurred to her that George Bush paid for my clothes."

Barbara Bush described efforts to avoid inciting Nancy Reagan's ire that verged on the comic.

In September 1983, George and Barbara Bush were attending a reception at the White House for the presidents of historically black colleges. "I had gotten the word that of course, Mrs. Bush, you are welcome to go, but Mrs. Reagan won't be there," she wrote in her diary. "I said fine, feeling a little uncomfortable about it."

When they arrived at the reception, a White House aide told her she wouldn't be onstage. "I said, that's perfectly all right, I'll just stand in the back," she replied. That didn't sit well with the vice president's domestic policy adviser, Steven Rhodes, who was apparently unaware of the risks of allowing a White House spotlight to fall on the Second Lady. He came up to her and announced he had arranged for her to stand onstage.

She refused. "I said don't be ridiculous, if Mrs. Reagan is not there, of course I am not going to stand on the stage . . . We have not pushed ourselves up on the stage and I certainly don't want to start it now." She told Rhodes, "You butt out of this."

"Then they said Mrs. Reagan was coming, so once again I was up on the stage," she said. When the Reagans arrived, she recalled, the two women kissed.

— ⁀ ⌣

Nancy Reagan seemed determined to include the Bushes at White House social events only when she had no other choice.

Protocol required that the vice president and his spouse be included at state dinners, so they were. But during their eight years of residency at 1600 Pennsylvania Avenue, the Reagans invited the Bushes upstairs to the private family quarters of the White House only a time or two before Bush had been elected to the presidency himself. They never invited the Bushes to accompany them to Camp David. And the Bushes didn't receive one of the most sought-after invitations of Reagan's presidency, to a glittering White House dinner in honor of the Prince and Princess of Wales on November 9, 1985.

Documents in the Reagan Library archives track Nancy Reagan's apparent determination to make sure they were excluded.

The first draft of the invitation list, dated October 2, 1985, shows the names of Vice President and Mrs. Bush on the second line, just below the Reagans themselves. But the Bushes' names have been crossed out with the slash of a black pen. Also scratched out on the paper were plans for the Bushes to greet guests in the Red Room while President and Mrs. Reagan welcomed Prince Charles and Princess Diana at the North Portico.

There was no indication who made the changes, but the universe of those empowered to do so wouldn't extend much past the president and the First Lady.

On a second draft of the plans for the dinner, dated one day later, on

October 3, the Bushes' names don't appear on the guest list. But below the approved names is a section labeled "Suggested additions"; Vice President and Mrs. Bush are at the top of that category. Some of the others listed below them have been marked by hand to add to the guest list; the Bushes aren't.

On a third draft of dinner plans, dated October 7, the Bushes again appear at the top of the list of "Suggested additions." Once again, their names were slashed out by pen. When deputy White House chief of staff Michael Deaver cautioned Nancy Reagan against excluding the vice president and his wife from the dinner, saying it would be a breach of protocol, she reportedly responded, "Just watch me."

That night, Princess Di arrived resplendent in a midnight-blue velvet dress and pearl choker; Nancy greeted her in the beaded white Galanos gown she had worn at the inaugural balls earlier in the year. Legendary soprano Leontyne Price sang in the East Room after dinner. On the dance floor, actor John Travolta twirled Princess Di. Nancy's interior designer, Ted Graber, and her pal Betsy Bloomingdale were invited, along with an astronaut, a ballerina, an artist, an architect, the commissioner of baseball, and her stepdaughter Maureen—but not the vice president and his wife.

A year later, there was a similar drama behind the scenes over whether the Bushes would receive another prime invitation, to President Reagan's seventy-fifth birthday party.

Lee Verstandig, who had a short and troubled stint as Nancy Reagan's chief of staff, described his almost farcical efforts to include the Bushes in the president's birthday party in 1986. The invitation list he presented to Nancy Reagan for review included them, but when Verstandig showed it to her, the First Lady picked up a pen and with a dramatic flair crossed out their names. He took credit for slipping the Bushes back onto the guest list, on the grounds that it was the appropriate thing to do, although it's not clear whether his boss realized he had done that. Years later, he told me his only concern that evening was in a "subtle" way limiting "the visibility of the Bushes" onstage during the celebration.

Coincidentally or not, Verstandig announced his resignation from the First Lady's staff on the day of the birthday party, February 7, 1986. He had been on the job just twenty-four days.

~ ~ ~

George Bush had been waiting, and waiting, for an endorsement from the president he had served for nearly eight years. President Reagan had declined to support any candidate during the Republican primaries, and the White House resisted entreaties from the Bush team for an endorsement after Bush had won enough contests that his nomination seemed assured. Only when the final challenger, televangelist Pat Robertson, had folded his campaign did the president agree.

"This was irritating as no Vice President had ever been more loyal or saved a President from more problems and the President had not really come out swinging for him even though he was the nominee," Barbara wrote in her diary. "Well George came home that afternoon and said that he had seen Ron's speech and that it gave him a rousing endorsement." The president had written the words in his own hand, with plans to declare his support that night at the President's Dinner, a black-tie GOP fund-raiser.

But when the long-awaited moment came, those weren't the words that Reagan read from the teleprompter. In a three-sentence statement, he simply recited Bush's résumé and then said, "I'm going to work as hard as I can to make Vice President George Bush the next president of the United States." Not only was his embrace less than effusive; he also inexplicably mispronounced Bush's name the first time he said it. (He made it rhyme with "rush.")

The puzzled reaction in the ballroom that night and the headlines in the newspapers the next morning raised so many questions that White House spokesman Marlin Fitzwater felt compelled to release a written statement insisting that the president was in fact "enthusiastic" about Bush's candidacy.

When the Bush team tried to find out what happened, they identified a familiar villain. "We later learned that Nancy took it out as 'this was Ron's night,'" Barbara Bush wrote. They assumed that Nancy was manipulating her affable husband, although it was never clear whether Ronald Reagan was aware of what she was doing, or why, or how aggravating her behavior was to the Bushes.

For the Bush forces, another politically important embrace by the popular president was scheduled a few months later, in August 1988, when Reagan agreed to join Bush at a campaign rally in Los Angeles. The event was sponsored by the Bush campaign, not by the White House. Even so, Nancy Reagan felt free to issue orders to Barbara Bush.

"We were campaigning full swing across the country and I got a message from SPR [Chief of Staff Susan Porter Rose] that Mrs. Reagan had sent a message that I should not attend a rally in Los Angeles where Ron was finally joining George as SHE WOULD NOT BE THERE," Barbara Bush wrote in her diary, her outrage visible in her use of all caps. "So what?! My husband was running for president, for heaven's sake."

Nancy Reagan was in the Reagans' suite upstairs at the Century Plaza Hotel that night, where the rally was being held. She didn't come downstairs to attend it.

Barbara Bush did—her most deliberate act of defiance in eight years.

George Bush kept struggling to understand, and to defuse, the acrimony.

He hired Sheila Tate, who was close to Nancy, as his press secretary for the 1988 campaign. "By the way, my wife is 100 percent supportive of this," he told Tate when he offered her the job. She took the peculiar comment as a reference to reports of tension between Barbara and Nancy, although she said she hadn't been aware of any problems while she was in the White House. When *Air Force Two* landed at the first stop of the first campaign trip Tate took with Bush, the vice president signaled her to join him in his car. "Come ride in my limo with me," he said. Then he immediately asked: "Why was Nancy so mean to my wife?"

In November 2017, I asked Bush if he ever figured out a satisfactory answer to that question. "Why was Nancy Reagan so mean to Barbara?" I asked when we met in his office in Houston. The former president, battling vascular parkinsonism, could understand and respond to questions, although speaking more than a few words at a time was difficult.

"I don't know," he said finally. "I don't know."

After the 1988 election, Barbara Bush would be in a position to exact a small measure of revenge—though George Bush would have to win the presidency first, and that proved to be no easy task.

Chapter Eleven

—✶—

Triumph

The night had been a catastrophe, and the mood on *Air Force Two* was close to panic.

The 1988 presidential campaign was supposed to be the triumphant culmination of George Bush's decades in politics—*the White House finally in sight!*—but he had just smashed into a roadblock almost before it had begun. In the campaign eight years earlier, an upset victory in the Iowa caucuses had launched him as a national figure. Now he had been humiliated with a third-place finish in the Iowa Straw Poll, a meaningless exercise except for what it exposed as his weakness. The thumping was an invitation to predators, to Bob Dole and Jack Kemp and others, that the nomination could be wrested from him.

As the plane headed back to Washington, George Bush tried to calm his top strategist, Lee Atwater, a tightly wound operative from South Carolina given to explosion even when things were going well. It was Barbara Bush who summoned Rich Bond, an Atwater deputy who had organized Iowa for Bush in 1980, to the front cabin.

"Rich, when are you going back to Iowa?" she asked, her message unmistakable. She had picked up her needlepointing, as she often did when she was bored or stressed. But Bond didn't see the embroidery as comforting or kindly. Years later, in a conversation with me, he would liken it to the menacing scenes in Charles Dickens's *A Tale of Two Cities* when Madame Defarge would encode in her knitting the names of those to be sent to the guillotine.

"Tomorrow," he said.

And he did.

Barbara Bush had taken up needlepointing when George Bush took up politics. During his first campaign, to be Harris County Republican chairman, she began needlepointing to avoid being driven to distraction during the endless rounds of precinct meetings where he would make his case to GOP loyalists, asking for their support. She nearly always went along for the ride, to hear his speech and watch his back. Doing the meticulous stitching while she listened kept her hands busy and her mind centered. (Decades later, she would recommend it to frazzled new mothers.)

For some, it also reinforced the perception that she was little more than a spouse on the sidelines, safely ignored. By now, the strategists on the plane knew better than that. She listened more than she talked, at least in meetings. But as George Bush rose in politics, her confidence grew, and so did his confidence in her. By the time he ran for president a second time, Bush had come to appreciate his wife's advice in ways he hadn't before. He increasingly relied on her not only for moral support but also for insights about how things were going and who could be trusted. When she spoke, he listened, so his aides did too.

Even her offspring saw her in a new light. "One very good thing came out of that campaign" in 1980, she later said. "The children treated me like an adult for the first time. Before that, they asked me all the 'peanut butter and jelly' questions and George all the 'steak and potato' questions. Then they discovered I could campaign with the best of them."

This time, top aides heard the message she delivered—get back to work, now—while they tried to figure out what had gone wrong and how to fix it.

The campaign was in its early stages. The Iowa Straw Poll was held on September 12, 1987, before Bush had even formally announced his candidacy. He was the front-runner, but not a commanding enough one to ward off challenges from a string of Republican rivals, Kansas senator Bob Dole and New York congressman Jack Kemp and televangelist Pat Robertson among them. Bush should have been the favorite in Iowa, given his triumph in the 1980 caucuses. Then, he had bested even Ronald Reagan before having his hat handed to him in the New Hampshire primary that followed.

But on this night, the vice president and his high-powered team had watched with alarm as lieutenants for Dole and Robertson marched their troops into the Hilton Coliseum, on the campus of Iowa State University in Ames. The Iowa Straw Poll was a signal of which challenger was worth watching and whether the front-runner had feet of clay. Atwater and Bond had climbed to the last row of the highest tier to get the widest possible vantage point.

"Where are our people?" Atwater demanded. Bond didn't have an answer. This time around, Bush had a state organization laced with the Republican establishment, but Robertson had the energy of an emerging army of Christian conservatives, many of them new to politics. Dole, the senator from Kansas, tapped suspicion that this Connecticut-Yankee-turned-oilman couldn't really understand the plight of family farmers. By the end of the evening, Bush had taken a shellacking, finishing behind both Robertson and Dole.

Any air of invincibility around Bush's bid for president had been punctured.

—◡ ◡—

Barbara Bush commanded respect, affection, and fear among many of her husband's closest aides. She usually saved her blunt advice for the end of the day, for his ears only. But at key moments during this crucial campaign, she spoke up in ways that would play a major part in the biggest political victory of Bush's life, his election to the White House in 1988.

Few in the public realized the role she was filling. They saw a down-to-earth matron in sensible shoes. "She had the prematurely white hair, like I do, and was a little on the heavy side and therefore had the grandmotherly appearance, so people viewed her that way," Fred Malek told me. He ran the 1988 Republican National Convention for Bush and was manager of his reelection campaign in 1992. "She was a great grandmother, but she was also sharp as a tack, witty, sharp, and could wield that dagger effectively if she wanted to."

As soon as the 1984 campaign was over, Bush had spent time over the Christmas holidays studying a memo from Lee Atwater about the election four years away. It wasn't too early to start planning. In March 1985, Bush revamped his vice presidential staff to get ready. A month later, he invited his most trusted aides and closest family members to meet at the presidential retreat at Camp David, a plum locale President and Mrs. Reagan had rarely offered, and never when they were going to be there.

On one side of the broad conference table that morning were the Bushes' five grown children—George W., Jeb, Neil, Marvin, and Doro—as well as George's sister, Nancy Ellis, and his three brothers, Prescott, Jonathan, and Bucky. That was a statement of the important role the family would play in this campaign, as they had in the last one, in 1980. Since then, his children had deepened their political experience.

George W., then working in the oil business in Texas, would move to Washington to play a central role as adviser and enforcer in the campaign; his parents wanted him to keep an eye on Atwater, a brilliant tactician but one with sharp edges. Jeb, a real estate developer and entrepreneur in South Florida, had been elected chairman of the Dade County Republican Party; he would be appointed Florida secretary of commerce in 1987 but resign in 1988 to campaign for his father. At the 1988 Republican National Convention, Jeb would be a delegate from Florida; Neil would be a delegate from Colorado. Marvin and Doro would sometimes be deployed as surrogate speakers.

On the other side of the table at Camp David were the hired hands: Craig Fuller, chief of staff of the vice president's office; Marlin Fitzwater, the official spokesman; Robert Teeter, the pollster; and Atwater. The elder George Bush went around the table making introductions, then opened the floor to questions.

"What are you going to do for my dad?" George W. Bush demanded.

The swagger of the vice president's oldest son wasn't what Fitzwater, new to the staff, noticed first. He was struck more by the quiet authority of his wife. "This was my first suspicion that Barbara Bush runs this show," he told me. "She didn't say much, but they all defer to her and she was taking notes on everything."

He thought to himself: *My word, what is this woman all about?*

Barbara Bush was a traditional figure who bridged a transformational time. She looked like a throwback to Mamie Eisenhower and Bess Truman, unfashionable and unthreatening. "I think I'm half Eleanor, half Bess," Barbara Bush once said. Like Eleanor Roosevelt, she had opinions and sometimes expressed them. Like Bess Truman, she was perfectly comfortable standing to the side, out of the spotlight. Her successor, Hillary Rodham Clinton, would adopt a very different model, reflecting a new generation.

"Barbara is the memory bank," said Lud Ashley, the Ohio congressman who had been George Bush's classmate at Yale. "George will get ticked off at somebody and then forget about it. Barbara remembers." Ashley said Barbara exhibited the life lessons learned from her father, a college football star. "Her brothers were linemen, taught to hit hard, to play both sides off. That was also part of Barbara's personality." George was raised to trust people, he said, but Barbara "doesn't mind impugning motives. He's more ready to take people at face value. It's just not in his nature to see beneath the surface. It is in hers."

Her antennae were sharper than her husband's to spot the motives of others, and her memory was longer for political slights and offenses. She was his most trusted barometer on just how far he should go, an especially critical quality during a campaign that would cross old boundaries of attack. She had helped build and maintain a remarkable network of friends and associates, including a Christmas-card list of thousands that became political legend. She recognized a social revolution that was reshaping attitudes toward women's roles, but she also sensed a wariness among voters toward a political wife who was too outspoken, too powerful.

Hillary Clinton would test that line. Barbara Bush would not.

In 1980, the campaign hadn't put her in the spotlight, although she was almost constantly on the road, stumping for her husband. Even now, strategists weren't sure how much of an asset she would be. Questions about her appearance came up again, picking at a scab from the campaign eight years earlier. Some strategists also worried about her sharp tongue.

"People were nervous about her because she's so unpredictable," Fitzwater said. "She didn't suffer fools, so you always had this kind of fear that she was going to tell off somebody."

Indeed, she had done just that during the 1984 campaign, when the Reagan-Bush ticket was running for reelection. News stories raised questions about just how tough Bush was, while Democratic rival Geraldine Ferraro was portrayed as a groundbreaker; the Queens congresswoman was the first woman nominated for national office by a major party. "There seemed to be a double standard: one for her and one for George," Barbara Bush griped privately. After the first time she met Ferraro in person, at the annual Italian-American Dinner in Washington, she wrote sarcastically in her diary, "It was good to see that she didn't have wings and a halo and her feet were on the ground."

Then, in one of the presidential debates, Democratic presidential nominee Walter Mondale needled Ronald Reagan about the impact of the 1981 tax bill, saying it benefited the wealthy, not workers. Mondale singled out Bush, calling him "one of the wealthiest Americans" and someone who had reported paying 12.8 percent in taxes. "That meant he paid a lower percent in taxes than the janitor who cleaned up his office or the chauffeur who drives him to work," Mondale said. (Of course, a Secret Service agent drove Bush to work, as Mondale, a former vice president himself, knew. But he had made his point.)

That "really had burned me up," Barbara Bush said. She read that Geraldine Ferraro and her husband, real estate developer John Zaccaro, had assets of at least $4 million. That made them wealthier than the Bushes. The next morning, on their way to New York for the annual

Columbus Day parade, she was still fuming when she went to the back of *Air Force Two* to chat with the two wire-service reporters on board, Ira Allen of United Press International and Terence Hunt of the Associated Press. "Well, you're not exactly paupers," Hunt teased.

Barbara Bush shot back that she and her husband had never tried to hide their wealth, unlike that "four-million-dollar—I can't say it, but it rhymes with rich." The plane was ready to take off, and she walked back to the front cabin.

The two reporters debated what to do about the comment. Neither had been running a tape recorder, and they realized that Barbara Bush probably assumed she was speaking off the record. Allen argued that unwritten rule couldn't apply here. "Something like that could not be off the record," he told me. "You just called your husband's opponent a bitch." What's more, the campaign had been edging up to that dig. Press Secretary Pete Teeley already had called Ferraro "bitchy." Later, after the vice presidential debate with Ferraro, Bush would tell an audience of longshoremen that he had tried "to kick a little ass last night."

When the story about her comment moved on the wires, Barbara Bush called her husband in a panic. "What am I going to do?" she asked him. "I'm in terrible trouble; the press is at the airplane waiting for me to get off." At that moment, Bush was in a car with Richard Moore, a friend and former Nixon aide; Bush later would appoint him ambassador to Ireland. Bush conferred with Moore, who had an idea. "Dick said, 'It's Halloween; you got it made.'"

When she got off the plane, she apologized—and insisted that the word she had in mind was "witch."

Decades later, Barbara Bush told me she thought she had been talking to the reporters off the record, but she didn't offer that as an excuse. "I should have known better," she said. "Nothing's off the record." At the time, she was distressed by the furor she raised; she called Geraldine Ferraro and apologized. There was speculation that the remark was a calculated attempt to get under Ferraro's skin or to dent her image among voters. Not so, Barbara Bush said. "I just said it to be mean," she said. "Stupid."

The original jab and her clever recovery made those words nearly immortal. Her children teasingly dubbed her the poet laureate of the family. "For several years I thought it would be engraved on my tombstone," she said.

~ ~

Jim Baker understood power, and he recognized Barbara's influence. There were times when he tried to enlist her as an ally.

After leading the 1984 reelection campaign for Ronald Reagan, Baker moved from serving as chief of staff in the Reagan White House to Treasury secretary in his cabinet. But there was no doubt that Baker would serve a major role in the 1988 campaign for his old friend from Texas. In September 1985, as Treasury secretary, Baker spoke at an annual Republican conference on Mackinac Island in Michigan. In a bid for national attention, Michigan Republicans had moved up their caucuses, and the initial voting for the state's precinct delegates was scheduled to start in August 1986.

Baker was alarmed by what he saw: Jack Kemp's fledgling campaign was out in force. "There were campaign flyers on every chair," Baker told me in an interview in his handsome Houston law office, his consternation clear decades later. "I came back from that and I called George...I said, 'You need to get Barbara over here. I want to tell you both something.'"

Baker wanted Barbara Bush there to help him persuade her husband to heed a message he didn't want to hear. At that point, Bush hadn't declared that he was going to run, though Baker was certain he would.

"The three of us sat there and I said, 'This guy's running. He's geared up. You need to start focusing on your campaign.'" Kemp already was lining up support; others were going to follow. Baker was counting on Barbara to second the need to get moving, something Bush was reluctant to do. "He had this uncanny ability to pigeonhole things, okay? Governing was one thing; campaigning was something else. She would be influential on that. She would be looking out after his best interest. It

ORIGINS

General James Pierce, Barbara Bush's great-great-grandfather, was a leading figure in Sharpsville, Pennsylvania, and an entrepreneur of the Industrial Age who amassed a fortune, only to have it squandered by his five sons. (*Pierce Genealogy: Being the Record of the Posterity of Thomas Pierce . . .,* by Frederic Beech Pierce)

The *Pittsburgh Post-Gazette* wrote about the violent brawl that erupted in 1884 between Barbara Pierce Bush's great-grandfather and his brother over control of the Sharpsville Railroad. Their family feuds contributed to the Pierce family's financial downfall. (Courtesy of the *Pittsburgh Post-Gazette*)

THE FIGHTING PIERCES.

Hard Blows Exchanged by the Sharpsville Railroad Belligerents.

Special to the Commercial Gazette.

ERIE, PA. May 14.—The feeling which has existed for some time between the New York, Pennsylvania & Ohio railroad and the Sharpsville railroad people over the construction of a track by the former to the Pierce, Kelly & Co. furnaces terminated in another outbreak to-day. The New York, Pennsylvania & Ohio employes, led by Jonas J. Pierce, a half owner in the furnaces, proceeded to put down the side track to the plant to-day, and, while so engaged, were set upon by the Sharpsville railroad employes led by Wallace Pierce, its President, and brother of Jonas J. Pierce. Wallace Pierce attacked his brother Jonas, striking him a brutal blow in the face. James Pierce, son of Jonas Pierce, came to his father's rescue and vanquished his pugnacious uncle by knocking him down with a stone. A general riot was imminent, but cool heads and police interference brought about a parley which prevented further bloodshed. More trouble is anticipated.

Marvin Pierce, who would become Barbara Pierce Bush's father, as a baby on the shoulder of his maternal grandfather, Jerome Marvin. The boy and his mother and sister would move in with his maternal grandparents in Dayton for a time as his father struggled to earn a living. (George Bush Presidential Library and Museum)

The Miami University of Ohio yearbook from 1916 shows Marvin Pierce, Barbara Pierce Bush's father, in football gear. He was a star athlete at the school and a mentor of Earl "Red" Blaik, who would become a renowned football coach at West Point. (Image courtesy of the Walter Havighurst Special Collections and University Archives, Miami University Libraries, Oxford, OH)

A campaign poster for James E. Robinson, Barbara Bush's maternal grandfather, who was elected to the Ohio Supreme Court. As a lawyer and county prosecutor, he took on cases to protect battered women, sometimes raising the ire of powerful local men. (Ohio History Connection)

REPUBLICAN NOMINEES
FOR SUPREME COURT OF OHIO

JAMES E. ROBINSON   REYNOLDS R. KINKADE

ON THE JUDICIAL BALLOT
PLACE YOUR "X" BEFORE THESE NAMES

Mexico Lures Four · Widowed Grandmothers

Columbus, O., Nov. 29.—(U.P.) —Four widowed grandmothers— all more than 60 years old—left for Mexico today in a trailer. "We think life begins at 60," said gray-haired Mrs. James E. Robinson. The others, Mrs. John M. Stanley, Mrs. Mary Albright and Mrs. Walter Houston, all nodded their agreement.

A United Press story from the *Indianapolis Star* about the adventures of Lulu Dell Flickinger Robinson, Barbara Bush's maternal grandmother. In 1939, she embarked on a road trip to Mexico and Canada with three other widows over the age of sixty, a feat considered so astonishing at the time that it attracted press attention. (Courtesy of the *Indianapolis Star*)

CHILDHOOD

Barbara Bush as a baby. She was the third of four children, and easy to overlook in a family where her siblings seemed to have either more prospects or more problems. (George Bush Presidential Library and Museum)

Portrait of Barbara Pierce Bush's mother, Pauline Robinson Pierce (far left), with her four children (from left to right): Jimmy, Scott, Barbara, and Martha. As an adult, Barbara would characterize Jimmy as "Peck's bad boy," Scott as "the best," and Martha as "the pretty one." She called herself "the little fat one." (George Bush Presidential Library and Museum)

LOVE AND MARRIAGE

When George Bush asked for a photograph of Barbara Pierce, this is the one her mother gave him, showing her with her dog Sandy. He carried it during World War II, to the chagrin of Barbara, who thought she looked like a child in it. (George Bush Presidential Library and Museum)

George Bush in the Avenger aircraft he flew in combat during World War II. He named it after Barbara, the girl back home he worried might "fluff" him off and ditch him for someone else. (George Bush Presidential Library and Museum)

The first dance by George and Barbara Bush after their wedding in 1945; she is wearing the veil that her mother-in-law had worn at her wedding in 1921. (George Bush Presidential Library and Museum)

Photo of the young family of George and Barbara, including George W. on the horse, and Robin on her father's shoulder. (George Bush Presidential Library and Museum)

Barbara with her daughter Robin, whose death from leukemia at age three would reverberate through her parents' lives. (George Bush Presidential Library and Museum)

A copy of the pastel portrait of Robin Bush that Barbara Bush would display in the Bush homes for the rest of her life. (George Bush Presidential Library and Museum)

POLITICS

Portrait of the Bushes in front of the US Capitol during George Bush's tenure in the House of Representatives. From left, Jeb, Marvin, George Bush, Doro, Barbara Bush, Neil, and George W. (George Bush Presidential Library and Museum)

George Bush and Barbara Bush ride bikes in Beijing's Tiananmen Square during his stint as the US envoy to China. She would remember the yearlong posting as the best of times, although it was followed by a devastating personal crisis. (George Bush Presidential Library and Museum)

George Bush as CIA director testifying before Congress, with aide Jennifer Fitzgerald to his left and Barbara Bush just behind him. During his presidential campaigns in 1988 and 1992, Bush would face persistent rumors about his relationship with Fitzgerald. (Photo by Wally McNamee/CORBIS/Corbis via Getty Images)

One of a series of photographs taken for a Bush family Christmas card in the 1970s; a more formal version of the picture was chosen for the card. Barbara Bush's massive Christmas card list would become a legendary tool to boost the political careers of her husband and sons. From left, Marvin, George Bush, Doro, Neil, Jeb, George W., and Barbara Bush. (George Bush Presidential Library and Museum)

Barbara Bush visits campaign headquarters in New York in February 1980. She campaigned indefatigably for George Bush during his first bid for the White House, although some campaign strategists worried that her matronly appearance might undercut his image as the leader of a new generation. (Photo by Frank Leonardo/*New York Post* Archives/© NYP Holdings, Inc. via Getty Images)

The only campaign appearance that Barbara Bush and Nancy Reagan made together during the 1980 campaign without their husbands was at the Inner Harbor in Baltimore. The relationship between the two women would always be fraught, finally ending in an explosive confrontation after both had left the White House. (AP Photo/ William A. Smith)

After the 1980 Republican National Convention in Detroit, presidential nominee Ronald Reagan and Nancy Reagan accompanied the Bushes home to Houston. The first campaign stop of the 1980 GOP ticket was at the Houston Galleria shopping mall. (AP Photo/*Houston Chronicle*, Curtis McGee)

The first draft of the guest list for the glittering dinner at the White House honoring the Prince and Princess of Wales on November 9, 1985. When told she couldn't cross off the Bushes' names, Nancy Reagan reportedly replied, "Just watch me."

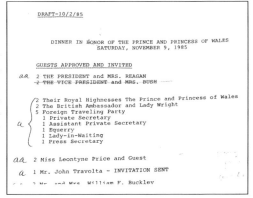

DRAFT-10/2/85

DINNER IN HONOR OF THE PRINCE AND PRINCESS OF WALES
SATURDAY, NOVEMBER 9, 1985

GUESTS APPROVED AND INVITED

aa   2 THE PRESIDENT and MRS. REAGAN
~~2 THE VICE PRESIDENT and MRS. BUSH~~

2 Their Royal Highnesses The Prince and Princess of Wales
2 The British Ambassador and Lady Wright
5 Foreign Traveling Party
1 Private Secretary
1 Assistant Private Secretary
1 Equerry
1 Lady-in-Waiting
1 Press Secretary

aa   2 Miss Leontyne Price and Guest

a   1 Mr. John Travolta - INVITATION SENT

  2 Mr. and Mrs. William F. Buckley

Barbara Bush helps build signs during a stop in Louisville at the Jefferson County Republican headquarters on September 8, 1988. During her husband's presidential campaign in 1988, her role would expand both as a surrogate speaker and as a trusted adviser behind the scenes. (AP Photo/Mike Fisher)

FIRST LADY

George Bush is sworn in as the forty-first president of the United States on January 20, 1989, as Barbara Bush holds the George Washington Inaugural Bible. The Bible had been used by George Washington for the first presidential swearing-in. It was the bicentennial year of Washington's inauguration. (AP Photo/Bob Daugherty)

President Bush and Barbara Bush at an inaugural ball in 1989. Her dress, now on display at the Smithsonian's National Museum of American History, was designed by Arnold Scaasi. She also wore her trademark faux pearls and shoes that cost $29. By the end of the evening, her feet hurt and she regretted having tried to save money. (George Bush Presidential Library and Museum)

The photo of Barbara Bush holding Donovan, a baby with AIDS being cared for at Grandma's House, helped battle the stigma against people suffering from HIV/AIDS. Barbara Bush would play a crucial role in encouraging her husband to address the HIV/AIDS crisis. (AP Photo/Dennis Cook)

To: The Leubsdorf Family - Carl and Susan - We loved having Ben and Will - you all at our favorite place! Warmly - Barbara Bush and Millie

The author and her family with Barbara Bush and dog Millie. At the picnic for White House reporters at Kennebunkport in 1990, Barbara Bush challenged her to explain why she was working outside the home when her children were young. (White House photo, provided by the author)

would be harder for him to say, 'No, I've got to be vice president' to the two of us."

Their conversation had immediate consequences. Within days, the nascent Bush campaign raised its head. Aides put out word that a Michigan steering committee was about to be named, and that a staffer from the Fund for America's Future, Bush's political action committee, would be deployed to organize the state. "We got tired of getting our face bloody and not hitting back," Ellen Conaway, the PAC's Midwest director, told a reporter.

Barbara Bush hadn't been particularly enthusiastic about another presidential campaign. She complained to herself that it had started the day after her husband was sworn in for a second term as vice president. A year later, she confided a surprising reservation in her diary. "George is obviously the most qualified person for the job," she wrote then. "Do I want him to run? Absolutely not!"

Later, she said she didn't feel that way very often. She was ready, as she had been from the start, to follow George Bush wherever he wanted to go. "I would love to come or go or whatever you say," she had written him at age sixteen when he invited her to his senior prom at Andover. That attitude would be strained during their long marriage, but it would never be broken.

And she never stopped watching his back.

Frank Fahrenkopf, picked by Reagan to chair the Republican National Committee, was regularly invited to the vice president's residence for small dinners with elected officials and financial contributors and activists, seated around three or four small round tables. He usually served as the host of one of the tables, but when he entered the dining room one evening in late 1984, his place card put him next to Barbara Bush. He was sure that was a sign of, well, something. Not necessarily something good.

"I said to myself, 'Hmm, this is interesting,'" Fahrenkopf told me years later. "And we got the dessert, and then she turns to me and she says, 'Mr. Chairman,' and...a chill just ran right up my sleeve. She said,

'I'd like to talk to you in the library.'" Once away from the others, she came right to the point. "'Do you know that in the last—I think it was six, could have been seven—issues of *First Monday*, there were no pictures of George?'"

First Monday was a glossy monthly magazine published by the RNC. The articles consisted mostly of partisan cheerleading. What made it important wasn't the quality of the content or the size of the circulation, which was about one million. It was that its readers were the sort of Republican regulars who were likely to walk precincts, show up for straw polls, and vote in primaries.

"I said, 'Bar, that can't be right.'" Check it, she told him, and call her in the morning. "So I get in the car. I call [RNC communications director William] Greener. I said, 'Billy boy, you get me the last dozen issues of *First Monday*. Have them on my desk. I'll be there at seven tomorrow morning.'"

To Fahrenkopf's chagrin, he found that after an interview with Bush was published in the January/February 1984 edition of *First Monday*, the vice president hadn't been mentioned in its pages for the rest of the year. "I called her and said, 'Barbara, you're right; I'm sorry, and we'll make up for it.'"

That he did. In the next issue, in January 1985, Bush's photo was on the cover of *First Monday*, and there were two other photos of him inside the magazine. He was mentioned ten times in connection with Reagan and the reelection victory—especially notable since there had been no similar references to him in the magazine during 1984, the election year. In the February 1985 issue, there were four photos of Bush.

In one of them, Bush was pictured with Reagan, and Barbara.

The presidential primaries were crowded in both parties in 1988.

The Democratic field was a proving ground for many of those who would define the party for decades: Tennessee senator Al Gore, who would become Bill Clinton's vice president four years later, and who would one day have a showdown with Bush's son for the White House. Delaware senator Joe Biden, who would serve as Barack Obama's vice president for two terms. Missouri representative Dick Gephardt, who would be the majority leader of the House through most of Bush's presidency. In the end, Massachusetts governor Michael Dukakis won the nomination.

At the start, though, Colorado senator Gary Hart was considered the strongest early prospect, since he had come close to defeating Walter Mondale for the nomination four years earlier. This time, a scandal would upend Hart's campaign and unnerve Bush's advisers.

The standards were changing when it came to covering the personal lives of candidates and presidents. Only decades later did historians detail romances kept largely secret at the time between Franklin D. Roosevelt and Lucy Mercer Rutherfurd, who was with him when he died in Warm Springs, Georgia; between Dwight Eisenhower and Kay Summersby, his chauffeur and secretary in Europe during World War II; and between Lyndon Johnson and Alice Glass, the wife of a major supporter. John F. Kennedy's sexual exploits were known by some White House reporters but not widely written about until years after his death.

Now the rules about what news was fit to print were being rewritten in the aftermath of a *Miami Herald* investigation in 1987 of allegations of womanizing against Hart. The story about his alleged liaison with Donna Rice prompted Hart, who was married, to suspend his presidential campaign. Two weeks later, a photograph published in the *National Enquirer* undercut his denials of a fling. It showed Rice, a South Carolina beauty-pageant winner, perched on his lap and holding his hand. He was sitting on a dock wearing a T-shirt that read "Monkey Business Crew." The *Monkey Business* was the name of the yacht they and others had taken to Bimini before he had announced his presidential campaign.

The furor effectively ended Hart's national political prospects and his hopes of running for the White House in 1988.

For George Bush, rumors about his relationships with several women had been fodder for Washington gossip for years. In 1981, when he was vice president, a bizarre allegation that he had been shot in the predawn hours as he was leaving the Capitol Hill home of a woman he knew was roundly denied and never substantiated. It caused enough of a furor, though, that the *Washington Post* dissected it in a front-page story anyway. The headline read, "Anatomy of a Washington Rumor: False Tale Takes Life of Its Own, Swiftly Spreads—Then Collapses."

The next year, stories about Jennifer Fitzgerald and her influence over Bush would fuel a new round of speculation and innuendo that was never entirely put to rest. She had been working for him, or in jobs he helped find for her, since he hired her to move to China as his assistant in 1974. Campaign manager Jim Baker had banished her from Bush's Houston headquarters in the 1980 campaign. But when Bush was elected vice president, she returned as the gatekeeper who sat just outside his office door in the White House.

"The Power Behind Bush" was the headline on a story about Fitzgerald in 1982 by Ann Devroy, a respected White House correspondent who then worked for the Gannett News Service and later for the *Washington Post*. When Deputy Chief of Staff Rich Bond, a key staffer in the 1980 campaign, told Bush that he couldn't work with Fitzgerald anymore, it was Bond who ended up out the door. The story said Fitzgerald had "almost unlimited influence" with the vice president; it quoted Chief of Staff Dan Murphy as saying she had "a special status" with Bush. *Time* magazine published a similar suggestive story a few weeks later.

Aboard *Air Force Two*, en route to Florida for a speech to AFL-CIO leaders, Chase Untermeyer, Bush's executive assistant, called back to the White House to get a copy of the *Time* story, which had just been published. He gave a copy to Barbara Bush. The two of them then had what he called "an intense private conversation" about it.

"Despite occasional rudeness from Jennifer, Barbara says they get along because they have to," Untermeyer wrote in his diary, then referred to her by her initials. "BPB has 'spies' who tell her what's going on, because she (and others) know Jennifer isn't going to tell them. But like all the other conversations I've ever had with anyone, Barbara and

I were stuck with what to do about the problem. I predicted that it will take a 'cataclysm'—an embarrassment to the VP or Jennifer worse than an unfavorable story in *Time*—to force her departure. Both of us agree that the word best describing Jennifer's relation to the world of Bush is 'pathos.' "

"My own opinion is that Jennifer really does hurt George," Barbara Bush wrote in her own diary soon after the stories were published by Gannett and *Time*, but "his eyes really glaze over when you mention her name. She is just what he wants, he says and says the hell with it all."

Bush refused to remove Fitzgerald from his staff despite persistent rumors about their personal relationship and complaints from higher-ranking aides about her brusque manner. In 1983, a trusted senior adviser thought the allegations about Jennifer Fitzgerald were on the verge of boiling over, of becoming a story that would be impossible to squelch. Decades later, he described to me his uncomfortable visit to see Bush at the vice president's residence, to warn him. The two were seated on the veranda when Barbara Bush came by. She asked what they were discussing.

Bush said, "We're talking about Jennifer." Barbara Bush looked at the adviser and said, "George has a blind eye regarding Jennifer."

All that helps explain why Bush's team watched Gary Hart and the *Monkey Business* coverage with concern. They worried that it might provide an opening for reporters to write about the whispers around Bush. By now, Bush had relieved some of the staff tensions by transferring Fitzgerald to his Capitol Hill office, part of a shake-up to put things in place for the presidential campaign ahead. She was sidelined from his day-to-day operations, albeit still on his staff.

After the Hart story broke, Atwater began to get calls from reporters about the scuttlebutt around the vice president. A frantic Atwater went to media adviser Roger Ailes. Ailes went to Bush. "They haven't got shit" to support allegations of an affair with Fitzgerald, Bush assured him. But in his diary, Bush worried about "a whole new rash of rumors on the sex front." *Newsweek* and *U.S. News & World Report* already had published gossipy items.

The Bush team—including Barbara—suspected Bob Dole's campaign of stoking the story.

Bush finally called Dole and asked him to stop his aides from spreading the rumors, and Dole agreed. But the *New York Post* got wind of the call and wrote about it, enraging Bush and sparking a whole new round of stories. Two *Newsweek* staffers, Howard Fineman and Evan Thomas, asked Atwater about the rumors. Atwater went to George W. Bush, and the younger Bush went to his father. "They're just not true," he told his son. George W. Bush then called the journalists and declared, "The answer to the Big A question is N-O"—the "A" standing for adultery.

Barbara Bush worried that the quotable denial might provide a peg for journalists to write more stories. *Newsweek* ran a brief item, headlined "Bush and the 'Big A Question,'" that reported "the nation's political-rumor mill" had been "rattled with talk of an impending GOP sex scandal." Still, the furor did die down, at least for a time.

Whether the allegations were true or not, the stories were "agony" for his family and humiliating for his wife, Bush knew. "She was telling me that her friends all had heard these ugly rumors," he dictated to his diary in the fall of 1987. "Someone had called from Connecticut to say, 'I'd heard your marriage was on the rocks.'"

In public, Barbara Bush rejected the gossip as ridiculous and outrageous, as part of "the ugliness" of politics. When a reporter for the *Houston Post* noted that the Bush family had a "brush" with that ugliness, she replied, "It wasn't just a brush. It was a large fat smear and I didn't like it one bit." Then she added, "I'm just not going to bother with something that didn't happen." In the privacy of her diaries, Barbara Bush expressed no doubts about her husband's faithfulness, although she acknowledged what a divisive figure Jennifer Fitzgerald was on his staff, and how difficult she could be.

The allegations of an extramarital relationship would have been problematic for any politician, especially for a man who had burnished his reputation as a devoted husband and father. Dealing with the allegations would have been painful for any spouse, especially for a woman who revered her husband and had devoted her adult life to raising their family and boosting his career.

Barbara Bush's steadiness was crucial not only for George Bush's family life but also for his political future. Her dismissal of the rumors as untrue and her depiction of their marriage as unshaken, and unshakable, were essential in containing the story. Several of Bush's aides who weren't sure whether to believe his denials told me they decided to take their cue from Barbara Bush. "There was nobody who worked for George Bush that she didn't know everything about," one of them told me. "I think that influenced a lot of us to say, 'Look, this is Barbara's problem. She's living with him, living with this, so...'"

After all, Barbara and George Bush had weathered worse than rumors of infidelity. Their marriage had endured the death of their daughter.

As it turned out, it was a different *Newsweek* story that caused more serious political damage.

Bush formally announced his presidential candidacy on October 13, 1987, on a platform in the atrium of the Hyatt Regency Hotel in Houston. A high school band played "The Yellow Rose of Texas." Red, white, and blue balloons were poised to drop from the ceiling. But the festive spirit was undercut by the new issue of the magazine. The cover photo of Bush on his cherished speedboat was flattering, but the headline wasn't: "Fighting the 'Wimp Factor.'" The campaign had given the magazine insider access in hopes of getting a favorable profile. But the story declared that Bush "suffers from a potentially crippling handicap, a perception that he isn't strong enough or tough enough for the challenges of the Oval Office."

"It was a cheap shot," Barbara Bush fumed.

Amid all the tumult, Bush also had one other thing on his mind. On the October day in 1987 that he announced he would run for president, the election that would cap his career, Bush thought about the daughter he had lost. "Bar looks beautiful," he wrote in his diary, then added, "Thirty-four years ago today, Robin died."

⁓ ⌣

The Iowa caucuses turned out to be a lost cause.

The disaster at the straw poll provided a warning of trouble ahead, but not a path to avoid it. The only question was how bad the loss would be and how much damage it would cause. This campaign was different, and harder, Barbara Bush thought, because her husband had a full-time job in addition to being a candidate. In December 1987, in the final weeks of campaigning before the caucuses, their presence was demanded in Washington, where Soviet leader Mikhail Gorbachev was arriving for his first visit to the United States.

Gorbachev had a face "like Daddy's, smiling eyes and teeth of iron," Barbara Bush recorded in her diary, a shrewd assessment. Then she added sourly, "The Doles were not there, probably in New Hampshire or Iowa blasting George."

An old scandal also became a new problem for the campaign.

Reagan had been ensnared in the Iran-Contra affair, the revelation that his administration had sold arms to Iran and funneled the profits to the Nicaraguan Contras. The story broke in November 1985; a special commission and congressional investigations were completed in 1987. But questions over Bush's role persisted. In an interview on CBS before Reagan's State of the Union address in January 1988, anchor Dan Rather pressed the vice president about what he had known, and what he had done. "How would you like it if I judged your whole career by those seven minutes when you walked off the set in New York?" Bush shot back, a reference to an embarrassing incident from Rather's past. (Roger Ailes had suggested the possible rejoinder with him before the interview, to use if things got tough.)

"It was just plain ugly," Barbara Bush wrote in her memoir. She didn't have any problem with her husband punching back, though. "George forgives to a fault," she wrote. "But you can just take so much."

Her attitude would prove crucial to Bush's comeback that year.

Bush's strategists calculated that Pat Robertson wasn't an existential threat; they figured he might carry the Iowa caucuses but could never go the distance to win the Republican nomination. But Dole could. The day before the Iowa contest, George Bush worried about what was about to happen. "It's my hope that if we get wiped out here that it just doesn't bounce back too much in other states," he wrote in his diary. "Also, I'd hate to come in third, with Dole first. I wouldn't mind being third if Robertson beats out Dole."

The next day, it was Bush's worst nightmare: Dole first, Robertson second, Bush a distant third. He received thirteen thousand fewer votes than he had in 1980. "What a difference eight years make," Barbara Bush said. "We could understand Bob Dole's victory; he was 'the farmer's senator.' He also is a tough opponent...However, Pat Robertson's second place finish to our third was a shock...

"The plane trip to New Hampshire was awful." For a time, she would campaign hard but refuse to watch television news shows or read the newspapers.

There were just eight days between the contests in Iowa and New Hampshire, eight days to avoid a second defeat that might well undermine Bush's political future. Dole was on the rise. Ailes argued that Bush had to bring him down, fast and hard. Ailes, who would later build Fox News into a conservative force, cut a TV spot that was more hatchet than scalpel. Titled "Senator Straddle," the ad showed two faces of Dole separated by the word "STRADDLED" as it ticked through issues from nuclear arms control to oil import fees.

"Bob Dole straddles, and he just won't promise not to raise taxes," the narrator intoned ominously. "And you know what that means."

Ailes screened it for the Bush team. Craig Fuller and Bob Teeter were squeamish. Was it fair? Was it presidential? Bush said it was too harsh to use. For one thing, he knew that governing might demand that a responsible leader raise taxes, although that was a campaign promise he would later make, then break. John Sununu, the blustery New Hampshire governor who was his state chairman, had Bush campaigning on a furious schedule, calling in to every local radio show and shaking hands at every McDonald's and Dunkin' Donuts they could reach. As Primary Day approached, Bush huddled with his top advisers again in his hotel room. Teeter presented the latest tracking polls, which showed Bush up one day, down the next.

Ailes renewed his case for the TV spot. "Look, this is not really a negative ad," he argued. "This is a factual ad." They watched it as Ailes went through one assertion after another: "There is a fact; there is a fact; there is a fact."

"I don't want to attack Bob Dole," Bush said. Sununu chimed in. "This is a state where people are used to having facts delivered to them, sometimes in tough ways," he said, noting that an ad he had aired in his gubernatorial race showed his opponent's nose growing like Pinocchio's. "It's not a shock to people here."

Bush looked at his wife. "I don't think it's so bad, George," she said.

That exchange—"*I don't think it's so bad, George*"—in effect gave a reluctant Bush permission to air the ad, despite his misgivings that it might go too far, play too rough. If Barbara thought it was acceptable, then it was. On that decision may have hinged not only Bush's New Hampshire campaign but the political career that would follow.

If Bush hadn't aired the ad, there is no guarantee that he would have defeated Dole in New Hampshire. If he had lost in New Hampshire, the Republican campaign would have headed to the Super Tuesday contests across the South with Bush a two-time loser and Dole the candidate with momentum. That was precisely Dole's strategy. His pollster, Richard Wirthlin, a veteran of Reagan's campaigns, had figured from the start that the Kansas senator was almost certain to win the nomination if he carried both opening contests. And that he was almost certain to fall short if he didn't.

There is at least an argument to be made that without airing the ad, Bush might never have been president. And some of Bush's closest aides believe that he would not have agreed to air the ad without Barbara Bush's assent. "I don't think he wanted to run what he thought was a nasty ad [if it was one] that she didn't want run," Sununu told me. She was, he noted, "a little more feisty" than her husband.

Andy Card was running the New Hampshire campaign for Bush. He told me that Barbara Bush's advice was crucial, then and later. "She had rough edges," he said, edges that her husband didn't have. "He was predisposed not to belittle anybody—to a fault, you know? And she would toughen him up."

The vitriol in the "Senator Straddle" ad pales in comparison to the slashing negative attacks leveled in subsequent presidential campaigns, among them debunked allegations that Barack Obama was born in Kenya, for instance, and false assertions that John McCain had fathered a biracial child out of wedlock. But the 1988 campaign did represent a sort of turning point in what was seen as acceptable for a mainstream contender. Two ads aired on Bush's behalf—the "Senator Straddle" ad against Dole during the primary, and a Willie Horton ad against Dukakis in the general election—proved just how well negative ads could work.

"It was so unlike him," Barbara Bush told me, recalling how reluctant her husband had been to air the "Senator Straddle" ad. She agreed that she was more likely than he was to see an attack as fair game, and as necessary. At age ninety-two, she couldn't remember precisely what she had said at that crucial meeting in New Hampshire decades earlier, but she said the recollections of others sounded credible. "I can see myself saying that," she said.

There was a reason she was particularly open to launching an attack on Dole, she told me. "Every rumor that started, started from his campaign," she said of the Kansas senator, including the gossip that had flared months earlier about George Bush and other women. "I mean, the bad affairs and everything. They were really dirty. So I was ready for..."

She didn't finish the sentence.

The ad succeeded in getting under Dole's skin. On the night of the primary, in an interview that showed Dole and Bush side by side on a split screen, NBC anchor Tom Brokaw asked if they had anything to say to each other. "I wish him well, and I'll see him in the South," Bush said. Dole snapped, "Tell him to stop lying about my record."

Bush won the New Hampshire primary over Dole by 9 percentage points, 38 percent to 29 percent, a solid victory that steadied his campaign and put him on a glide path to the Republican presidential nomination. Robertson faded to a distant fifth. "Tonight, I somehow feel that I have a lot in common with Mark Twain," Bush told cheering supporters. "Reports of my death were greatly exaggerated."

On the Democratic side, Michael Dukakis won the New Hampshire primary. The next month, on March 8, 1988, both Bush and Dukakis largely swept their parties' Super Tuesday contests across the South.

The race in November was going to be Bush versus Dukakis.

At the Republican National Convention that summer in New Orleans, George Bush would make the best speech of his life, a deft reintroduction to voters. Barbara Bush would make the most personal speech of her life.

She was not yet the enormously popular figure and political asset that she would be four years later. Then, at the 1992 convention in Houston, her appearance would command more attention and more applause. This time, she wasn't even one of the evening's featured speakers. Many in the crowd in the Louisiana Superdome didn't bother to quiet the general hubbub during the seven minutes she spoke. But as I sat in the press stands of the convention hall, writing a story for *Newsday* about something else, the intimacy of her words and the emotion she conveyed made me stop what I was doing to listen. I didn't write a story about her speech then, but I never forgot about it, either.

They were the most private remarks Barbara Bush would ever deliver in such a public arena. She noted in passing her husband's résumé, the stints in Congress and at the United Nations and the CIA and the vice presidency. Then she turned to the tragedy that had beset their family, making herself exposed and vulnerable in a way she rarely allowed.

"The hardest thing we ever faced together was the loss of a child," she said, her voice thickening as she worked to keep her emotions in check.

Watching from the family box, son Neil wiped away a tear. "I was very strong over the months we were trying to save her—at least, I thought I was. Maybe I was just pretending. But when she was gone, I fell apart. But George wouldn't let me retreat into my grief. He held me in his arms and he made me share it and accept that his sorrow was as great as my own. He simply wouldn't allow my grief to divide us apart, push us apart, which is what happens so often when there's a loss like that.

"For as long as I live, I will respect and appreciate my husband for the strength of his understanding."

Two weeks before Election Day in 1988, the *Washington Post* calculated that Barbara Bush already had campaigned in 92 cities in 29 states, given 184 interviews and held 13 news conferences, delivered scores of speeches, and traveled more than 50,000 miles, sometimes with her husband and sometimes without him.

Nothing loomed as more crucial to the outcome of Election Day than the task of defining Dukakis as something other than the pragmatic governor many voters saw him to be. On that front, as in the primary campaign against Bob Dole, Barbara Bush would once again be a decisive voice.

History favored Dukakis. No sitting vice president since Martin Van Buren in 1836 had won the White House. In May, a Gallup poll showed Bush trailing Dukakis by double digits, a sobering 54 percent to 38 percent. One-third of the so-called Reagan Democrats who had voted for the Republican ticket four years earlier were inclined to support Dukakis this time.

That said, in two focus groups of Reagan Democrats, convened by the Bush campaign in Paramus, New Jersey, the voters didn't have a clear sense of either candidate, and they didn't like what they heard that evening about Dukakis. As governor, he had vetoed a bill requiring public school teachers to lead students in the Pledge of Allegiance. During his tenure, a convicted murderer named Willie Horton, who had gotten a weekend furlough from a Massachusetts prison, had kidnapped and raped a woman, and pistol-whipped her fiancé. Al Gore had raised the prison-furlough issue against Dukakis during one of the Democratic primary debates, but it hadn't gotten traction.

When Bush convened his top advisers at the family retreat in Kennebunkport over the Memorial Day weekend, Roger Ailes pushed again to air attack ads. Bush worried it would make them look desperate. Ailes told him, "We *are* desperate." Bush knew that was true. He dictated to his diary that Bob Teeter's briefing had left him with a "semipanic feeling about being behind in the polls."

The next month, in June, Bush's strategists were still trying to convince him to toughen the attack, to portray the furlough program as an outrage and the governor who allowed it as soft on crime. "We were 17 points down, but nobody knew anything about Dukakis," recalled Charlie Black, who had been the chief strategist for Jack Kemp's campaign in the primaries but was now advising the Bush team. Atwater, Teeter, Ailes, and Black met with Bush in a suite at the Jefferson Hotel to go through the campaign's latest polling. Their conclusion: The negatives on Dukakis could be driven up, but only if Bush hit him in both TV ads and speeches.

Atwater had urged Black to go to the session with Bush. "You're more persuasive," he told him. George and Barbara Bush knew the campaign needed Atwater's manic energy and razor-edged instincts, but he realized they were sometimes wary of his judgment. Bush was furious when he discovered Atwater had defied his instructions by giving a campaign slot in California to political provocateur Roger Stone, a former business partner of Atwater and Black, who later worked for Donald Trump. "Are there no lengths to which we will not sink?" Bush demanded in a confrontation on *Air Force Two* that has not been reported before. He ordered that Stone be fired.

Black was smoother, with a more reassuring mien. At the meeting, he listened more than he talked.

"I finally just said, 'You know, Mr. Vice President, this guy's out there lying about all his great accomplishments in Massachusetts and about your positions. We're not asking you to lie. We're asking you to tell the truth about him. And we'll try to make it as polite as possible," Black told me. "And he didn't like it."

Barbara Bush was persuaded first. "She had tougher political instincts than he did," Black said. That was important, because by now Bush trusted her more than anyone else. "I think she was sort of a conscience for him about what they believe and things that were within the rules and maybe something that was not within the rules."

Charlie Black didn't remember Barbara Bush's precise words, but he remembered her meaning. "She said something like, 'This won't violate your rules, George.'" That was enough. The decision was made, the road cleared. "Then we launched off, and you know the rest of the story."

That month, Bush began using Willie Horton's name in speeches. In the fall, his campaign aired an ad that didn't use Horton's name but cited his case. Over a video of both black and white prisoners moving through a revolving door, the narrator said Dukakis's "revolving-door prison policy gave weekend furloughs to first-degree murderers" who had then "committed other crimes like kidnapping and rape."

"Now Michael Dukakis says he wants to do for America what he's done for Massachusetts," the ad said. "America can't afford that risk."

More inflammatory was an ad produced by an independent group, albeit one with ties to the Bush camp. Larry McCarthy had worked for Ailes for six years, until 1987. Now he produced a spot that showed a glowering mugshot of Willie Horton, an African American. While out on furlough, the ad said, Horton "fled, kidnapped a young couple, stabbing the man and repeatedly raping his girlfriend."

"Weekend prison passes," the narrator said. "Dukakis on crime."

The ad brought accusations of racism. Jim Baker, Bush's campaign chairman, denounced it and called on the group to take it down. The criticism stung George Bush. "Now you keep reading that it's the worst campaign in history—the ugliest, the meanest," he dictated to his diary in mid-October. "The media was not about to define Michael Dukakis, and a lot of them are liberals; and not only are they not about to define him, they come to his defense."

Barbara Bush was defiant.

In her diary, she recounted the Willie Horton saga without apology or regret. "George used this heinous incident to illustrate that Dukakis was not tough enough on crime," she wrote. "Then a pro-George independent committee—not our campaign—decided to turn the example into a campaign ad, using the image of a sinister-looking Willie Horton, who was black, as the focus. We got blamed for dirty politics and racism. Baloney. The ad was not ours, and the truth of the matter is, Willie Horton should not have been out of prison."

Just weeks before Election Day in 1988, the allegations of a Bush affair flared again. Speculation that the *Washington Post* had a story in the works was so feverish that it was blamed for a drop in the stock market. *Post* editors took the unusual step of denying that they were getting ready to publish such a story. "Ugly," Barbara Bush wrote in her diary that day. "How do you defend against that which isnt, wasnt and never will be?"

The next day, one of Dukakis's political aides fanned the rumors. "I wasn't on the stock market yesterday but I understood they got a little concerned that George Bush was going to the White House with somebody other than Barbara," Deputy Field Director Donna Brazile told reporters. "George Bush owes it to the American people to 'fess up."

Dukakis apologized to Bush and Brazile resigned from the campaign.

Coincidentally, Barbara Bush already had accepted invitations to appear on TV shows that morning. She had been dreading questions about her relationship with Nancy Reagan. Now she had a bigger problem. George Bush asked Baker to call her and talk through it. "Jimmy said I should just tell the truth and say, 'This is absurd. There is absolutely no basis for that rumor and I am not going to dignify it with an answer.'"

That was precisely the script she followed.

On *Live with Regis and Kathie Lee*, host Regis Philbin began by saying,

"It's a tough question—" and Barbara Bush interrupted, "Then don't ask it. It's such an absurd rumor that I'm not going to dignify it with an answer." She took the same tack throughout that difficult day. "I'm not going to dignify something so ugly," she said. She labeled the reports "absurd, ridiculous, outrageous." She declared, "I'm not going to talk about it."

That night, her sarcastic sense of humor had returned. "Jim Baker was right it all faded away," she wrote in her diary, adding in all caps, "(THAT'S A JOKE>IT BUGGED US UNTIL THE END OF THE CAMPAIGN.)"

Fortunately for her, the end of the campaign was just weeks away. Bush swamped Dukakis by nearly 8 percentage points, carrying forty states—a landslide.

"We went to bed sort of in shock," Barbara Bush wrote in her diary. "I mean, George is going to be the 41st President of the United States. Hard to believe. Think of all the people who should be here and who would be so proud and say, 'I knew it all the time!!!'" She mentioned the men who had seen promise in Bush and helped him: Oilman Neil Mallon. His father, Prescott Bush. Her father, Marvin Pierce.

She didn't mention her role in her husband's rise to the White House. Neither did he when he spoke to reporters and supporters the next morning. But in reality, it was not his victory alone. It was also hers.

Two days before the election, as the polls signaled a big victory ahead, campaign press secretary Sheila Tate told George Bush, "You know you're going to win." He replied, "I don't know that. I do know that if I win, people are going to fall madly in love with Barbara Bush." Tate decided to pass the compliment on to Barbara Bush. "I told her and she went, puh-puh," puffs of air that didn't even form words, dismissing the notion as ridiculous.

It would turn out to be true.

Chapter Twelve

——⋆——

First at Last

The day before George Bush was inaugurated as president, Barbara Bush stood onstage at the Kennedy Center and made fun of herself. "I want you to watch me all week and remember," she teased at a luncheon honoring the new First Lady. She opened her jacket to show the custom lining and pivoted with an exaggerated model's pose. "Notice the hair, the makeup, the designer clothes, and remember. You may never see it again." Everyone laughed.

Barbara Bush didn't mention Nancy Reagan by name, but she understood the comparisons that would be drawn with the meticulously groomed woman who was back at the White House, packing her designer clothes for the flight home to California. Nancy Reagan understood, too, and seethed. That may have been one reason she would include a not-so-subtle dig at Barbara Bush's fashion sense in the memoirs she would publish a few months later.

After eight years of dysfunctional family drama and palace intrigue from the White House residence, Barbara Bush presented herself as America's grandmother, comforting and comfortable, although in fact that was just one dimension of her complicated persona. At the Kennedy Center tribute, her entire brood turned out—her children and their spouses and all ten grandchildren. The closeness of their clan was another contrast with the Reagans. Noelle Bush, then eleven, appeared onstage with the Mora Arriaga mariachi band to play "Deep in the Heart of Texas" on her accordion.

"Goodbye, First Fashion Plate," the New York Post proclaimed. "Hello, First Grandmother."

She did nothing to discourage the commentary that things were going to be different. "A Down-to-Earth Tenant for an Exclusive Address" was the headline on the front page of the New York Times the Sunday before the inauguration. "The irreverent 63-year-old—as steadfast as Mother Courage and as spirited as Auntie Mame—makes it plain that the new First Lady will offer a striking contrast to the departing one," the story said.

America loved it, and her. Even decades later, only Jacqueline Kennedy scored favorable ratings as high as Barbara Bush did among First Ladies—higher than Nancy Reagan's by double digits. (Nancy Reagan set records in the other direction, with the highest disapproval ratings of any First Lady who had served up until her tenure.) "My mail tells me a lot of fat, white-haired, wrinkled ladies are tickled pink," Barbara Bush said. She credited her willingness to spotlight her flaws. "I think it makes them feel better about themselves."

And she was getting a lot of mail. In those days before social media, she received more than thirty thousand letters in the first one hundred days of the new administration. Each year in the White House, she would average about one hundred thousand pieces of mail.

"As a woman of a certain age, I am awed by her self-confident acceptance of the life cycle," author Doris Willens wrote in a laudatory op-ed, describing herself as a Dukakis voter who was nonetheless delighted by Barbara Bush's emergence. "Not for Mrs. Bush the beauty salon coverup of her white hair, nor the anorexic embrace of the 'can never be too rich or too thin' doctrine. It can't have been easy, this wife's path [to] the White House. Many a snide Oedipal joke followed the Bushes on the campaign trail."

Now the girl who had been stuck in the middle and easy to overlook, overshadowed by her prettier sister and never particularly diligent in school, would become a fixture on Gallup's list of the most admired women in the world. She would be mentioned by at least some of the Americans polled every year for the next quarter century.

For eight years, she had toed a line that Nancy Reagan had drawn, keeping her head down and her words measured, obeying the edict that she leave center stage to Nancy. Now Barbara Bush finally was free to be, well, herself.

There was one particular way the new First Lady was determined to behave differently from her predecessor: in her attitude toward the Second Lady.

"I will not treat her as Nancy Reagan has treated me," she vowed in her diary during preparations for the inauguration. Barbara Bush was never close to Marilyn Quayle. She would sometimes liken her to Hillary Clinton, and not in a good way—as a demanding woman who didn't always put her husband's career first. That surely reflected their generational divide. But she made a point of including Vice President Dan Quayle and his wife in big events such as the Kennedy Center Honors, and she allowed the Quayles to designate some guests to be invited to state dinners. That was a courtesy Nancy Reagan hadn't extended to the Bushes.

On her way out the door, Nancy Reagan insisted she had no advice for Barbara Bush, although she sniffed that the job was considerably more difficult than being Second Lady. "It is something you are never prepared for and you can never get used to," she said. She acknowledged having "mixed feelings" about leaving the White House. A *Saturday Night Live* sketch that aired the day after the inauguration speculated just how reluctant her departure was; it depicted Barbara Bush being forced to enlist two Secret Service agents to pick Nancy up and carry her out of the family quarters as she upended the furniture, trying to hold on.

Barbara Bush would leave her own down-to-earth stamp on state dinners, the gilded evenings that reflect a First Lady's style. The Bushes held twenty-eight of the official black-tie dinners honoring foreign heads of government or state in four years, according to records maintained by the White House Historical Association. (The Reagans hosted fifty-nine of the dinners in eight years.) She made them a little less glittering and a bit more relaxed than Nancy Reagan had—not quite the Sunday cookouts she was famous for hosting when her husband was a rising oilman in Midland and a new member of Congress in Washington, but with a nod in that direction.

Barbara Bush was more hands-off than Nancy Reagan had been about the details. The flower arrangements and the table settings and the intricacies of the presentation, things that had so engaged her mother for events at the Apawamis Club in Rye, had never really interested her. "I am willing to turn it over to someone else," she said. "I trust the chef and the flower lady and Laurie Firestone," the social secretary. She told them to keep doing whatever they had done before. "If I don't like it, I'll let them know," she said. "Nancy Reagan was a perfectionist, and I am not."

Gone were the tasting dinners Nancy Reagan had held to critique each course of the elaborate meals, an exacting routine that had been the source of dread for the kitchen staff. Barbara Bush told the chef she needed to sample only the main course beforehand. "She said, 'You people know what you're doing,'" White House chef John Moeller recalled gratefully years later.

The Bushes began by holding a trio of state dinners in a span of fifteen days. The diplomatic hat trick was designed to navigate the delicate politics of the Middle East. Three months after moving into the White House, in April 1989, they honored first Egyptian president Hosni Mubarak, then Israeli prime minister Yitzhak Shamir, then Jordan's King Hussein.

Sometimes things would go awry during the evening, though that didn't seem to unnerve Barbara Bush. As always, she was unflappable. If that approach had worked for lively barbecues in their backyard, why not for elegant dinners in the State Dining Room? "What does it matter as long as people are having a good time?" she said with a shrug after mistakenly leading her husband into a state dinner honoring Pakistani prime minister Benazir Bhutto without giving the Marine Band time to strike up "Hail to the Chief," as protocol dictated.

There was the time the kitchen was marinating duck for the Jordanian state dinner when Queen Noor sent word that she preferred white meat. Laurie Firestone called the First Lady and asked if they should change the menu. "I said absolutely not," Barbara Bush recalled. "After all, the queen was, in truth, just an American girl [Lisa Halaby] who married a king, and she certainly would understand." The king, she reported afterward, "wolfed down" the duck.

Or the incident at the state dinner for Russian president Boris Yeltsin in June 1992. She was seated to his left; she made a point of putting a pretty and lively woman as the dinner companion to his right. During dinner, Yeltsin leaned over and said through an interpreter, "Barbara, I don't know the protocol, but what should I do if a woman has her foot on my foot?" She assumed it was the other woman; she wasn't sure what to advise. Then Yeltsin lifted up his foot—with Barbara's foot perched on top of it. She had unknowingly been grinding her foot on his. "He then told me that in Russia that meant the woman loved the man," she said. "I quickly told him that was not true in our country."

A more serious faux pas loomed at the state dinner for Mexican president Carlos Salinas in October 1989. Left to his own devices, the White House pastry chef had prepared a dessert that was listed on the menu as "Mexican Fantasy." The platters featured an elaborate adobe house constructed of edible sweets, filled with ice cream and surrounded by a fence and flowers. Leaning against the wall of the house was a candy Mexican boy taking a siesta with a sombrero over his eyes—an ethnic stereotype that risked offending the honoree, and, by the way, a detail that a tasting dinner might have caught beforehand.

Laurie Firestone, standing in the doorway, recognized the problematic figures as waiters were about to make a dramatic entrance into the

State Dining Room with the dessert course. She plucked off the sleeping boys as each platter was carried by.

~ ~

As George Bush began laying the groundwork for his first presidential bid, for the Republican nomination in 1980, Barbara Bush had pondered what she should adopt as her "cause."

She knew reporters and voters were sure to ask what her agenda would be if George Bush succeeded in winning the White House. Presidential spouses from Abigail Adams to Edith Wilson to Eleanor Roosevelt had exerted considerable influence, sometimes in public and sometimes in private. But in recent decades, First Ladies were expected to designate some signature issue. Lady Bird Johnson, a fellow Texan and a friend who had focused on beautifying the nation's highways and cities when she was in the White House, encouraged Barbara Bush to see the role as an opportunity. The White House would offer her a bully pulpit, the former First Lady told her, and she should use it on behalf of something close to her heart.

During the summer of 1979, Barbara Bush would turn that question over in her mind as she jogged in Memorial Park. She regularly used the park in their Houston neighborhood to exercise and to walk her dogs. One possibility was her volunteer work at hospitals—at New York's Sloan Kettering, where Robin had been treated, and at the Washington Home for Incurables, which admitted patients who had little hope of recovery, including many who couldn't pay. She had helped raise money for cancer research too. But she was looking for something with a broader reach.

"I've got to have a cause, and I want a cause that…will not cost money for the government, and is not controversial, and will help more people," she told me decades later, detailing the checklist she had in mind. "I would go to Memorial Park and run and I'd think, *Gosh, I should do teenage pregnancies*, or, *Gosh, I should do drugs*. And then it came to me: If more people could read and write and understand, those things would be taken care of. That was what made me decide."

Barbara Bush was an inveterate reader herself, especially of popular fiction by female authors. (In her memoirs, she made a point of mentioning some of her favorites, among them Maeve Binchy, Deborah Crombie, Sandra Dallas, Elizabeth George, Tami Hoag, Elizabeth Jane Howard, P. D. James, Anne Perry, Rosamunde Pilcher, and Judith Rossner.) She had always read books to her children when they were small. When son Neil was diagnosed with dyslexia in the second grade, she spent years working with him as he struggled to learn to read.

Beyond that, though, she had no special expertise in literacy and no particular perspective on education policy. She felt momentary panic when she arrived at an early campaign event, at Cardinal Stritch College in Milwaukee, to find that a roundtable of academics had been gathered to hear her literacy plan. She didn't have one, not yet. In what she called "one of my very few brilliant moments," she turned to them and said, "All right, before I tell you what I think, do you mind telling me now what you'd do with literacy?"

By the time the professors had finished talking, she had gotten a reprieve: Her time was up and she had to leave for her next event.

What followed from her decision in the park were decades of commitment to the issue of adult illiteracy—for eight years as Second Lady, for four years as First Lady, and for the rest of her life. In 1989, her chief of staff, Susan Porter Rose, had surprised and delighted her by laying the groundwork to establish the Barbara Bush Foundation for Family Literacy, designed as a platform for her to use whether or not her husband became president. When he did win the White House, she was instrumental in the enactment of the National Literacy Act of 1991 and the establishment of the National Institute of Literacy. She raised millions of dollars, highlighted local programs, honored volunteers and new readers, and pushed governors and CEOs and Hollywood to pay attention.

And presidents.

George Bush's record in the White House on this front reflected his wife's influence. After she weighed in, he reversed his administration's initial opposition to the literacy act. He signed the Adult Education Act, which increased federal funding for adult literacy, and established the Even Start program, which funded intergenerational literacy efforts. He convened an education summit with governors that set national education goals, a step that helped propel the fledgling charter school movement. The White House twice hosted National Literacy Honors ceremonies, nationally televised from the East Room.

All that had more to do with Barbara Bush than her husband, said Lamar Alexander, who served as education secretary in Bush's cabinet. He had been governor of Tennessee and was later elected to the Senate. "George H. W. Bush's legacy, interests, his skills were almost entirely in foreign affairs," Alexander told me in an interview in his Senate office. "It helped to have a First Lady whose passion was education." He ranked last in the cabinet, the secretary of what was then the newest department, and one that many Republicans had opposed creating. Her interest magnified his voice.

Years later, George W. Bush's presidency would show threads of his mother's agenda as well. During the 2000 campaign, the Texas governor identified education as one of his top priorities, and the No Child Left Behind legislation was one of the first major bills he signed as president. Laura Bush, a former school librarian, also focused on education and reading. She worked with the Library of Congress to establish the National Book Festival.

For son Jeb Bush, too, education would be a central issue in his campaigns for governor of Florida. He was an advocate of charter schools and for Common Core, even after his support became a target of attack when he ran for president in 2016. The 2010 program, developed by the National Governors Association and state school officers, established standards for what elementary and high school students should have learned at the end of each grade, including literacy skills.

Those who had been working on adult illiteracy, most in the form of local programs, many of which were run by volunteers, said the spotlight

Barbara Bush provided was transformative. "It was a hidden secret in this country until she elevated it," said Sharon Darling, founder of one of the nation's leading literacy organizations, the National Center for Families Learning, based in Louisville. "We always needed the visibility. She gave us the visibility."

What struck some was that she was drawn primarily not to children who were learning to read but to adults who had missed their chance, many of them living on the margins of society, a fair number of them immigrants.

"It wasn't cutesy little kids—not that she had anything against kids— but she picked up a cause that nobody else was paying attention to," recalled Benita Somerfield, who had worked in the New York publishing world before becoming the first executive director of the Barbara Bush Foundation. "The adults who were not literate are not little and cute, for the most part. She went to homeless shelters; she went to prisons; she went all over the place."

After George Bush was sworn in as vice president, Barbara Bush began holding regular breakfasts at their official residence, at the Naval Observatory, with administration officials, literacy experts, researchers, and advocates. Secretary of Education William Bennett sometimes joined them. "You just felt like you were going to a neighbor's house for coffee; that's how she always made you feel," Sharon Darling said. They would talk about what was working and how to encourage effective programs. She treated them with the familiarity of friends. "I would sit down on the couch, and when I'd get up she'd say, 'Fluff the pillows,'" she recalled with a laugh. "'Fluff the pillows, Sharon, because they get all mashed up.'"

Barbara Bush's office and her small staff became a clearinghouse for information about literacy, inside the government and out.

She calculated that as Second Lady she had participated in 537 literacy events and another 435 related to volunteerism, a remarkable pace. National reporters paid little attention to her visits to community literacy programs, but local reporters often did. She wrote a lighthearted book from the point of view of her dog, titled *C. Fred's Story*, and donated the modest proceeds to two literacy groups.

When she became First Lady, she had a bigger megaphone, and she used it.

Barbara Bush visited scores of literacy programs, in school basements and homeless shelters and food banks. She helped convince GM, Motorola, and other corporations to donate funds or start literacy programs. She convened meetings of governors' wives—among them Hillary Rodham Clinton of Arkansas—and hosted a Sunday evening radio show called *Mrs. Bush's Story Time*. Tapes of her reading children's stories aloud were packaged with a book titled *Barbara Bush's Family Reading Tips* and sold at retail stores. She worked with the Public Broadcasting System and Capital Cities/ABC to sponsor Project Literacy US, which provided programs and public-service announcements promoting adult literacy.

"It's part of the drug problem, part of ignorance and AIDS, part of homelessness and alienation," she declared in 1990 in her commencement address at the University of Pennsylvania, celebrating its 250th anniversary. She cited Benjamin Franklin, who had founded the school. "When Ben Franklin was dining in Paris, one of his companions posed the question: 'What condition of man most deserves pity?' Each guest proposed an example. When Franklin's turn came, he offered: 'a lonesome man on a rainy day who does not know how to read.'"

To be sure, other First Ladies have promoted causes to significant effect. Eleanor Roosevelt spoke out in the 1930s and 1940s on behalf of African Americans, women, and refugees, among other minority and disenfranchised groups. Hillary Clinton delivered a classic address on women's rights at the United Nations conference on women in Beijing in 1995. Laura Bush supported the rights of women in Afghanistan. Michelle Obama urged American kids to eat healthier diets and exercise more.

But since Eleanor Roosevelt, no modern First Lady had been more persistent on behalf of a cause—devoting more time or raising more money—than Barbara Bush was on literacy. "There were a lot of other splashy things she could have done," said Sharon Darling. "She always said, 'No, I'm talking about people who can't read and their children.' She was always so clear on the focus and the mission."

Barbara Bush generally insisted that she stayed out of her husband's official business, but she did weigh in when the Bush administration initially opposed the National Literacy Act. It was being championed by Illinois senator Paul Simon, who had convened the first congressional hearings focused on illiteracy. He spotted the First Lady as a potential ally, called her office, and invited her to breakfast. President Bush noticed it on her schedule.

"One day, George came in and said, 'What are you doing with him for breakfast, a Democrat?'" Barbara Bush told me. "I said, 'He's very interested in literacy, George.'" Did she then play a role in turning around the White House position on the bill? "I certainly did," she said. She didn't bother to lobby White House aides or cabinet members. She went straight to the president. "I encouraged," she said.

When the president signed the bill, he turned to Simon. The senator said, "I think Barbara ought to get the pen, Mr. President." The pen would be put on display at the Bush Library in the exhibit devoted to her.

At dozens of local events, Barbara Bush praised the adults who had finally learned to read and the volunteers who had helped them.

Sometimes she did more than praise. At a literacy event in Kentucky, a woman had been chosen to talk about how she finally had learned to read, and what it meant to her. But she kept her hand over her mouth, embarrassed about her teeth, marred by a lifetime lack of care. After she returned to Washington, Barbara Bush asked her aide, Peggy Swift, to get the woman's address. She sent the woman a personal check, for $200 or so, with a note saying she should use the money to get her teeth fixed.

The woman sent back a photo of her after the dental work had been done, smiling proudly. "Thank you," she wrote. "That just did so much for me."

Barbara Bush wrote another book, this time adopting the persona of her new spaniel, Millie. In a sign of the First Lady's rising visibility and popularity, it debuted at the top of the *New York Times* best-seller list. The profits, which would total more than $1 million, were designated for the Barbara Bush Foundation. Millie purportedly decided to do that "not because of its name, but because Millie is a very good mother herself, and she knows that parents are children's first and most important teachers," Barbara Bush said. "Although she prefers chasing squirrels, Millie knows that reading is essential to the welfare of Americans."

"I do think I've made a difference, and I think it's an important one," she told me in an interview during the final months of her life. "In fact, I think most of our problems would be better if more people could read, write, and understand." That had been her point from the start, when she started thinking about what cause to adopt while jogging in Memorial Park.

During the conversation, she mentioned that Houston Methodist Hospital was naming the atrium in a new tower after her and her husband. She had no shortage of other namesakes in various cities. There was the Barbara Bush Children's Hospital at the Maine Medical Center in Portland. Middle school students attended a school named after her in Irving, Texas. So did elementary school children in Mesa, Arizona, and in three Texas cities, Woodlands, Grand Prairie, and Houston. That school was just fourteen miles from her house, where we were sitting.

"Of all the things named after you," I asked, "which is your favorite?"

"They're naming a Literacy Plaza after me," she replied immediately, perking up. The design for the outdoor space would connect Houston City Hall with the historic Julia Ideson library building. "It's going to be a children's reading place, and an adult reading place, and it's going to have a huge screen, and they're going to do movies and operas and plays and put chairs out. They're going to have cafeterias. It's going to be very exciting." She said she had told the organizers, "I'm trying to stay alive until you name it."

The name had been announced, but the construction had made little progress when she died in April 2018. On the day she died, it was little more than an open space marked by a makeshift plastic banner tied to a fence: "The Barbara Bush Literacy Plaza." The next week, the Houston City Council approved nearly $400,000 to finish the job.

~ ~

Just how much enduring impact Barbara Bush had on adult illiteracy is hard to gauge.

The last national literacy study done by the Department of Education, in 2003, showed literacy actually declining from 1992 to 2003, the result of a mix of factors. A doctoral dissertation completed at Texas A&M in 2010 about the work of the Barbara Bush Foundation raised questions about her premise that literacy was an effective way to address societal problems such as homelessness, poverty, and teenage pregnancy. "According to a large amount of scholarly research and ethnographic studies, literacy is not necessarily the answer to all the problems of the world," Brandi Davis Westmoreland concluded. "Literacy instruction may result in increased literacy, but entrenched social problems still remain."

Lamar Alexander argued that looking at metrics was the wrong way to assess Barbara Bush's legacy on literacy. "Our country works family by family, school by school, community by community," he said. "I'm sure you could find individuals in the adult literacy program who could say, 'She inspired me to help this man learn to read.'" Her focus had a ripple effect across the country, he said. "When the First Lady said, 'My passion is literacy,' that made it more important."

When her foundation celebrated its twenty-fifth anniversary in 2014, Barbara Bush turned over leadership of the organization to her children Doro Bush Koch and Jeb Bush, and she encouraged them to try new approaches. Since its founding, the foundation had focused on offering grants to help finance new literacy programs or support existing ones. Now it moved toward tapping new technologies to help adults wherever they were, even if they were unable or unwilling to attend lessons in a church basement or at a community center.

"No matter how efficient you are in measuring the success of these mostly tiny programs, it wasn't scalable," Jeb Bush told me. His goal was to figure out ways to interact not with thousands of adults who needed help but with millions of them, "to figure out an environment where they could do this without shame, without being embarrassed." With an app, "the theory is you could put this on a device and people could do it as they go about their business."

In 2015, to mark her ninetieth birthday, the foundation launched a $7 million adult literacy XPRIZE, a competition aimed at creating a mobile app that could improve adult literacy within twelve months. In June 2018, two months after her death, five finalist teams were chosen. She had been following it closely. "She never lost interest," said Jean Becker, George Bush's chief of staff. "She never gave up."

Chapter Thirteen

—⭑—

Grandma's House

In the 1980s, fear of AIDS was rampant and politicians' attitudes toward gay rights were wary at best.

Presidents treated the topic like a political hand grenade. At a question-and-answer forum in Peoria in 1976, a Bradley University student asked President Gerald Ford about discrimination against gay people. In what may have been the first public remarks by a sitting president on the topic, Ford's response was convoluted and equivocal. "I have always tried to be an understanding person as far as people are concerned who are different than myself," he said. "That doesn't mean that I agree with or would concur in what is done by them or their position in society."

He said he didn't have "a pat answer under these very difficult circumstances."

First Lady Betty Ford would support gay rights, but only after she had left the White House, when she also became active in the fight against AIDS. In her memoir, published in 1979, she called singer Anita Bryant's antigay crusade "ill-considered" and said people shouldn't lose their jobs because of their sexual preference. "On the other hand," she continued, "I'm not sure I'd want my small children being taught by gay teachers."

During the 1976 campaign, Jimmy Carter became the first major-party candidate for president to declare that he opposed all forms of discrimination based on sexual orientation. But he also refused to put a gay rights plank in the Democratic platform, and as president he said same-sex ties weren't "a normal interrelationship." During his reelection campaign four years later, he wouldn't commit to signing an executive order banning employment discrimination against gay men and lesbians.

Ronald Reagan had gay friends in Hollywood, and in 1980 he won a straw poll of gay Republicans in California. But he didn't embrace their support. His response was to blast the gay rights movement itself as objectionable. "My criticism is that [it] isn't just asking for civil rights; it's asking for recognition and acceptance of an alternative lifestyle which I do not believe society can condone, nor can I," he declared.

As president, Reagan kept silent about the emerging crisis of HIV/AIDS for years, even as it became an epidemic on his watch, an omission that would stain his legacy.

Although AIDS was identified in 1981, during the first year of his tenure, Reagan didn't mention it publicly until 1985. By then, more than five thousand Americans had died of the disease. His administration resisted calls to allocate funds to AIDS research—the early money was designated at Congress's initiative—and the Reagan Department of Justice in 1986 decided that an employer could fire workers who were thought to have AIDS if other employees were worried about infection. At White House briefings in 1982, 1983, and 1984, press secretary Larry Speakes dismissed questions about the "gay plague" by joking about it.

In private, George Bush joked about AIDS too. In 1987, Elsie Hillman, a family friend and prominent Pennsylvania Republican, asked him to deliver the commencement address the following year at the Kiski School, a boys' boarding school near Pittsburgh. "Kiski? 1988?" he responded in a letter he typed himself, one that she preserved with her papers. He listed all the catastrophes that could befall him before then, from the Iran-Contra scandal to the disease that was then considered a death sentence. "What with [Gary] Hart, Contras, Aids, and jock itch I might not even be alive in the spring of '88," he wrote.

Bush seemed leery of speaking out forcefully on an issue that would

not only put him at odds with Reagan but also risk straining his relationship with the religious right, a rising force in the GOP. Some conservative Christians already viewed him as suspiciously moderate on cultural
issues. He supported Reagan's veto in 1987 of the Civil Rights Restora-
tion Act, legislation that was designed to reinstate federal protections
against discrimination for gays and others.

On another issue, abortion rights, Barbara Bush had shown caution.
From the moment Reagan tapped George Bush as his running mate in
1980 until Bush's presidency was over, she simply refused to discuss her
pro-choice views for fear of creating political problems for her husband.
But she took a different course when it came to the HIV/AIDS crisis
and the battle against discrimination. On that, she lobbied her husband
in private and made it clear in public just where she stood, even when it
drew fire.

In 1987, when a reporter for the *Atlanta Journal-Constitution* asked
Barbara Bush how she influenced her husband on policy, she replied,
"I go home and tell George about seeing babies with AIDS and soup
kitchens." Earlier that year, at her urging, George Bush had visited an
AIDS research lab, apparently the first time a major-party presidential
candidate had done so, and met with an AIDS patient at a moment some
feared any contact risked infection. In June 1988, sending a message in
the weeks leading up to the GOP convention that would nominate her
husband for president, she publicly agreed to cosponsor an AIDS benefit
in Dallas being held the next year.

She encouraged her husband to endorse legislation to bar discrimination and ensure confidentiality for AIDS patients, a recommendation
by the presidential AIDS commission that the Reagan White House
had ignored. The 1988 GOP platform called for more research into the
disease and compassion for those who had it, saying they "should be
encouraged...to remain on the job or in school as long as they are func-
tionally capable." The Bush team beat back a deliberately provocative
amendment to require AIDS testing for airline pilots, school bus drivers,
and others who worked in public transportation.

That said, George Bush didn't mention AIDS in his nationally tele-vised convention speech accepting the nomination, a more significant statement of his priorities than the Republican platform. His operatives reassured conservative columnists that the plank encouraging AIDS patients to remain in school or on the job as long as possible was no more than an "accidental endorsement" of nondiscrimination.

Onto this politically treacherous landscape stepped Barbara Bush.

"She never championed, but she was putting herself out there," said Kristan King Nevins, who became Barbara Bush's aide after the Bushes had left the White House. Nevins, who went on to work at the CIA and on Capitol Hill, speculated that Barbara Bush may have deliber-ately selected the uncontroversial cause of literacy as First Lady with the thought it could give her cover to also pursue a more controversial one below the radar. "I do know that she said, 'I want to pick something that is not going to cause problems for my husband,'" Nevins told me, "but I don't know if she had in the back of her mind, 'Then I could do this.'"

The impact she had was "monumental," Nevins said. Through the simplest actions—cradling a baby, attending a funeral, lighting a candle, writing a letter—Barbara Bush challenged public attitudes about gays and HIV/AIDS.

Her granddaughter and namesake heard about that legacy when Bar-bara Bush died in 2018. The younger Barbara Pierce Bush helped found the Global Health Corps, a nonprofit organization that recruited profes-sionals to work on international health issues, including HIV/AIDS. "I work with a ton of AIDS activists and a lot of people living with AIDS that were those that marched in the street in the '80s and '90s to make sure that they could get the drugs they needed," she told me. "I had so many that emailed me about their memory of my grandmother going to the AIDS home for children living with AIDS. Then one said so beau-tifully, he said, 'Your grandmother showed other people that we were fighting a disease, not people.'"

At the time, the elder Barbara Bush's determination on the issue was neither touted by her nor fully recognized by others. But it was quietly revolutionary.

"She didn't need to yell at anyone," said Edward E. McNally, a White House speechwriter who drafted a landmark address on AIDS for President Bush that she had encouraged. "She understood the weight of her role and her words."

On this, she forged a partnership with Burton Lee III, who had joined the administration as Bush's White House physician. He was an oncologist at New York's Memorial Sloan Kettering Cancer Center, where Robin had been treated for leukemia. Like Bush, Lee was an alumnus of Andover and Yale, and he was a friend of Bush's brother Jonathan. Through his connections with Bush, Lee had been appointed by Reagan in 1987 to the President's Commission on the HIV Epidemic.

Earlier in his career, Lee had been dismayed by the discrimination he witnessed against the cancer patients he treated, bias based more on fear and ignorance than on medicine. Now he saw much more brutal discrimination against those with HIV/AIDS.

Barbara Bush had no history of inclusive attitudes about homosexuality. Indeed, she and George had hurriedly announced their engagement when she was at Smith College to counter a rumor being spread by a classmate that Barbara was a lesbian. When she was Second Lady, she complained that obituaries for Connecticut representative Stewart McKinney, a friend, had reported, accurately, that he died of AIDS; she worried that disclosure would make things harder for his wife and children. As First Lady, when she walked offstage after a visit to the Whitman-Walker Health clinic, she told an aide how uncomfortable she felt when one of the HIV/AIDS patients began to talk about his lover.

When she delivered the commencement address at the University of Pennsylvania in 1990, a friend had to explain that the pink triangle some graduates had put on their caps meant they were gay. In her diary, she wrote not about the morality of their sexual orientation but about her fear that they were inviting problems. "I would have been so sad for my children [if they] had done that" because it could mean "a life of discrimination," she wrote.

But when Barbara Bush saw the stigma that HIV/AIDS patients faced, she recognized the parallels with one of the most painful experiences of her life. She never forgot what happened when her three-year-old daughter, being treated for leukemia, came home to Midland from Sloan Kettering for one last visit. "When Robin got sick, people avoided us like the plague," she told me decades later, her voice marked more by sorrow than anger. "Even my close friends." In this, as in so many things, the death of Robin reverberated.

In Washington, a local housing organization called TERRIFIC, Inc., had run into a brick wall in 1987 when it tried to open a group home for abandoned babies and young children who had been diagnosed with the virus that causes AIDS. No landlord would rent to them. They ended up having to buy a house, a five-bedroom Victorian in the Logan Circle neighborhood. They kept the address secret, for fear the building or its young residents might become targets. They named it Grandma's House, but they didn't dare erect a sign in front. It was hard to get workers to do the most fundamental tasks, such as installing phones, because of fears that they could catch AIDS simply by walking through the door.

Then, during the first one hundred days of the new administration, Barbara Bush's aide, Julie Cooke, called Grandma's House. Could the First Lady visit?

During the transition from the Reagan administration to the Bush administration, staffers in the president-elect's public affairs office had raised $700 to give as a charitable contribution during Christmas in the spirit of Bush's "thousand points of light" initiative. They decided to donate the money to Grandma's House, a gift that was never publicized. Jeffrey Vogt, who would work in the public liaison office of the new White House, delivered the contribution in person. Debbie Tate, president of the group, wrote a thank-you letter dated February 1, 1989, that ended with an invitation: "It is also our desire that our First Lady, Mrs. Barbara Bush would consider visiting TERRIFIC, Inc.'s Grandma's House."

David Demarest, who had been director of the public affairs office during the transition and was now the White House communications director, relayed the invitation to Susan Porter Rose, the East Wing chief of staff. The next month, on March 22, 1989, Barbara Bush arrived at Grandma's House accompanied by Burt Lee and Julie Cooke and a clutch of reporters and photographers.

Debbie Tate and Joan McCarley, cofounders of the group home, weren't sure what to expect.

"She didn't come like she had a script or like it was a performance," Tate recalled. Barbara Bush played with three of the children on the first floor and then went upstairs to the bedroom of an infant too sick to be brought downstairs. Donovan began whimpering in his crib, and Tate picked him up. "Debbie and Joan, you're providing great care and services, but give me that baby!" Barbara Bush demanded. "You don't know what you are doing." She cradled Donovan with the confidence of experience, and he quieted down.

The photograph of that moment, taken by Dennis Cook of the Associated Press, became iconic. It was remarkable precisely because it was so ordinary. Barbara Bush held a sweet-faced baby against her shoulder, her face pressed against his flushed cheek and her hand stroking his back. His eyes are closed; his mouth is open; his body is at ease. Even the colors of their clothing seem harmonious, and very American: She is wearing a bright red outfit; he has on a white terry onesie with navy blue stripes at his neck and wrist.

Donovan would die not long afterward.

That day, without saying a word, Barbara Bush had made her point. It was safe to hold a baby infected with HIV, or to hug an adult who had AIDS, or to go to school or work alongside someone with the disease. "Burt Lee told me, you know, it isn't catching; you can't be in the room with someone and catch it," Barbara Bush told me, dismissing the notion that she had displayed political courage. "And he said, 'It's fine. You can go.'"

When Barbara Bush died three decades later, Tate and McCarley were still at the helm of TERRIFIC, Inc., and Grandma's House was still caring for children with HIV/AIDS. The First Lady's visit had an instant effect, they said, and they were still grateful. "It was providential, I would say, because it was at a time there was a need to shock the conscience of the nation so they would know you could not get the AIDS virus by holding or touching," Tate recalled. McCarley said the First Lady had "impacted the whole world." They got calls from around the globe about caring for infants with HIV/AIDS.

"What joy it must have given every little child with HIV who suddenly had more playmates in April...than they had in March," said Tom Rosshirt, who was then a junior aide on Capitol Hill and would later become a speechwriter for President Bill Clinton. Three years before her visit, he had watched his brother Matt die of AIDS.

At Grandma's House, Debbie Tate had gotten permission from the White House to invite several adults who had HIV/AIDS and were living elsewhere to meet privately with Barbara Bush during her visit. One of them was Lou Tesconi, a lawyer who as a volunteer at a local AIDS organization had helped provide care and comfort for Matt Rosshirt during his illness. Soon after Matt died, Lou began studies to become a Catholic priest. Within a year, he had been diagnosed with AIDS himself and kicked out of the seminary. He then founded a Catholic lay ministry in Washington, Damien Ministries, to help people with AIDS.

"Mrs. Bush, it is a fantastic thing that you are holding these babies with AIDS," Tesconi, then thirty-nine, told the First Lady in the private meeting, a conversation he recounted to Tom Rosshirt afterward. "But the country sees them as innocent and the rest of us with AIDS as guilty. The whole suffering AIDS community needs a collective embrace from you today."

Tesconi told Rosshirt he had been speaking metaphorically. Barbara Bush in her memoirs didn't see it as a metaphor. She remembers him saying, "Will you give me a hug?" Both agreed on this: She stood up, walked over to Tesconi, and embraced him.

At a news conference that followed, she made a point of hugging him again, for the cameras.

Two years later, when Tesconi was in the hospital and near death, Rosshirt called the White House and asked for the First Lady's office. He reached press secretary Anna Perez, who immediately recognized Tesconi's name. Rosshirt told her that his friend would be comforted by a letter from Barbara Bush. Tesconi had told him that he wasn't afraid of dying, but he was afraid of dying alone. In the final days of his life, he would treasure the letter that soon arrived from the First Lady. A hand-written note from her at the end of the letter told him that he had made an impact, that his life had mattered.

A year after visiting Grandma's House, Barbara Bush and Burton Lee flew to Indianapolis to attend the funeral of Ryan White, a young hemophiliac who had contracted AIDS after a blood transfusion. The boy and his mother had fought a landmark battle in the courts to force his public school to allow him to attend classes, sparking a furious national debate. When Ryan was diagnosed in December 1984, his doctors had told him he had six months to live, but he survived for another five years, dying one month before his high school graduation.

Just before the service began at the Second Presbyterian Church, the First Lady slipped out of the holding room the Secret Service had set up for her off the sanctuary and found the waiting room where Ryan's mother was sitting. She told her about Robin, one mother in mourning to another. "She had lost a little girl to cancer, and I'd not known that," Jeanne White-Ginder recalled years later. "It felt like I was close to her heart."

The next month, Barbara Bush placed a candle in every window of the White House facing Pennsylvania Avenue and lit them at dusk, participating in a worldwide candlelight vigil to keep alive the memory of those who had died of AIDS.

Barbara Bush's efforts to focus attention on the HIV/AIDS

crisis would echo through two presidencies. She pressed George Bush to endorse antidiscrimination legislation and to increase funding for research. A generation later, her son George W. Bush would launch PEPFAR, the President's Emergency Plan for AIDS Relief. The initiative, one of the most affirmative aspects of his legacy, has been credited with saving millions of lives in Africa.

"She was an activist in her own way," George W. Bush told me, saying he saw a thread with his own activism on AIDS in Africa. "Parents serve as an example, and I was very proud of Mother when she hugged the AIDS baby. She busted stigma and the stereotype of coldhearted Republicans" by using the bully pulpit. "I'm confident it affected me."

The HIV/AIDS issue also provides an example of her hidden hand in the West Wing.

While ACT UP and other activist groups protested that George H. W. Bush wasn't doing nearly enough to address HIV/AIDS, some of the president's most conservative allies complained that he was going much too far. At the time, efforts to ban discrimination against gay men and lesbians alarmed some evangelical leaders. They argued that homosexuality was an offense against God, forbidden in the Bible and more deserving of condemnation than legal protection.

In March 1990, Bush decided to deliver a speech on AIDS, his first major attempt to address the subject. He would call for the National Institutes of Health and the Centers for Disease Control to go "on a wartime footing" to combat the disease.

Speechwriter Edward McNally got the assignment to write the remarks. A few days later, he received an envelope through interoffice mail that contained a set of well-worn cassette tapes with the audio version of *And the Band Played On*, a scathing account by Randy Shilts of how officials and institutions had failed to respond to the AIDS crisis in the 1980s. It had been sent by Barbara Bush. He had never received anything from her before about a speech.

"The clear message to me was, 'The First Lady wants this speech to sing,'" McNally told me years later. He drafted remarks that were intimate and personal. It apparently would be the only time during his presidency that George Bush would mention Robin by name in his public remarks.

"When our own daughter was dying of leukemia, we asked the doctor the same question every HIV family must ask—why, why this was happening to our beautiful little girl?" Bush said in the speech. He had seen friends die of AIDS, he went on. "There is only one way to deal with an individual who is sick: with dignity, compassion, care, confidentiality, and without discrimination."

The next month, Bush signed legislation that required the attorney general to collect statistics on hate crimes motivated by sexual orientation as well as by religion, race, and ethnicity. Among those invited to attend the bill signing were leaders of the Gay and Lesbian Task Force and of a group called Parents and Friends of Lesbians and Gays, known as PFLAG.

A week later, Richard Land, executive director of the Southern Baptist Convention's Christian Life Commission, wrote the president a letter complaining that leaders of gay rights organizations had been invited, saying the White House "should not be giving its sanction and implicit approval to such groups." House Republican whip Newt Gingrich objected, too, telling influential columnists Bob Novak and Rowland Evans that "any appearance of the president's sanctioning homosexual life styles with the same civil rights protection afforded race and gender is 'insane.'"

After the bill signing, Doug Wead, an Assembly of God minister who had been hired onto the White House staff in part as a liaison to evangelicals, wrote an apologetic letter on White House stationery to conservative Christian leaders. He told them that the invitation to the gay rights groups had come not from the president but from his aides. "Quite frankly, the president's staff did not serve him well," he wrote.

Then Barbara Bush wrote a letter of her own.

On May 10, 1990, she responded to a request she had first received months earlier from the founder of the DC Metro chapter of PFLAG, who had asked her to "speak kind words to some 24 million gay Americans and their families" and to "educate the public with facts about homosexuals." Paulette Goodman had seen news accounts of Barbara Bush visiting AIDS patients. "When I saw that, I thought to myself, *She's a caring lady*," Goodman told me years later. "I wrote to her as one mother to another."

A staffer had acknowledged the letter, but at the bill-signing ceremony, Goodman hand-delivered another copy to make sure Barbara Bush herself saw it. She gave it to a White House staffer, along with a packet of pamphlets from the group.

"I appreciate so much your...encouraging me to help change attitudes," Barbara Bush responded in a letter, written on White House stationery and signed "warmly." "I firmly believe that we cannot tolerate discrimination against any individuals or groups in our country. Such treatment always brings with it pain and perpetuates hate and intolerance."

As she surely expected—indeed, as was presumably her point—PFLAG immediately passed on a copy of the letter to the Associated Press. The lead to the AP story, distributed around the world: "A letter Barbara Bush sent to a support group will help parents of homosexual men and lesbians accept their children, the group's leader said Tuesday."

"I realized it was not for my eyes only," Paulette Goodman said. The letter was just two paragraphs long, but some activists credit it as the first endorsement of equal rights for gay men and lesbians ever issued from the White House. Goodman later contributed the original of the letter to the Rainbow History Project, an effort to record and preserve LGBT history in Washington.

By the end of that summer, Wead was ordered by Deputy Chief of Staff Andy Card to resign from the White House, "sooner than later."

"Doug was wearing his welcome out," Card told me, and the letter disavowing the White House invitations to gay rights groups was "the tipping point." "Barbara Bush definitely had some angst," Card said. But in cases like that, she typically wouldn't demand that someone be fired. "She wouldn't say, 'We've got to get rid of him,'" Card said. Instead, she would ask pointedly, "Do you really think he's serving the president well?"

That wasn't the end of it. In 1992, when George Bush was seeking reelection, conservative commentator Patrick Buchanan mounted a damaging challenge for the Republican nomination based in large part on social issues. In his speech to the GOP convention in Bush's hometown of Houston that summer, Buchanan declared that there was a "cultural war...for the soul of America" under way, citing "abortion on demand," allowing women to serve in combat roles in the military, and "homosexual rights."

The Astrodome reverberated with chants of "family rights forever, gay rights never."

— ⌣ —

A quarter century later, in 2007 or so, Barbara Bush and Kristan King Nevins were driving to an airport in Maine when the former First Lady mentioned something she had read that morning in a newspaper about the debate over same-sex marriage. At the time, just one state, Massachusetts, sanctioned gay unions; it would not be until 2015 that a US Supreme Court decision would make them legal across the country. In the story, a politician had quoted a slogan favored by conservative Christians who opposed gay marriage: "God made Adam and Eve, not Adam and Steve."

"How do we know?" Barbara Bush mused to Nevins. "I think God's okay with Adam and Steve."

In 1994, during the publicity tour for her memoir, Barbara Bush had signaled her acceptance of gay families with children. It was a time when same-sex couples often were barred from adopting children and gay parents were at risk of losing custody fights. She told NPR's *Fresh Air*, "We may have different families now, different setups, but family is what's important." Host Terry Gross noted that there was "a lot of debate over what 'family values' means, and who is defining what a family is."

"We, we may not be able to define it, but we know what it is," Barbara Bush responded. "We've got to get back to caring for our children."

Even in her tenth decade, she was open to changing her mind on cultural issues.

In the fall of 2015, as the Bushes were preparing to leave Maine to return to Texas for the season, historians Jon Meacham and Timothy Naftali visited them. "I am not sure how Tim got here or who he is," Barbara Bush, then ninety years old, wrote in her diary later that day, but she clearly enjoyed their conversation. (Naftali was a New York University professor and former director of the Richard Nixon Presidential Library and Museum.)

"He and I had an interesting discussion about sex," she wrote. She was upset that the Obama White House had made a point of announcing that they had hired the first openly trans person, for a post in the Office of Presidential Personnel, and that they had hired an openly gay person as well. There were no such announcements when the White House hired a heterosexual, she noted. Over lunch at a restaurant in Goose Rocks, Barbara Bush and Tim Naftali discussed gender-reassignment surgery, Caitlyn Jenner, and drag queens.

Naftali told her that he was gay ("I suspected that," she noted in her diary), and that as a gay man he was "thrilled" that the president was making a point that a person like him could be hired by the White House, and openly. "I ended up being persuaded in my mind that after years of hiding this may be a good thing," she concluded. "Nobody wants to be born Gay or Transgender. They have been misunderstood for years. He won the argument."

She now saw the issue from another person's point of view. "There are a world of folks born transgender who are quiet and lonely," she wrote in her diary. "How sad to be in the wrong body."

Chapter Fourteen

—✦—

The Reckoning

In public, she was breezy. In private, she was fuming.

Dozens of invitations had begun arriving soon after Barbara Bush moved into the White House, asking the First Lady to deliver commencement addresses in the spring of 1990. She wanted to accept a mix that included different sorts of schools and different regions of the country. She chose Saint Louis University, a Catholic school in Missouri; Southwest Community College in Cumberland, Kentucky, in Appalachia's Harlan County; and Wellesley College, one of the Seven Sisters schools in Massachusetts. She accepted invitations from two public high schools that were effectively local for her, Kennebunkport High School in Maine and Dunbar High School in Washington, DC. At the request of friend and philanthropist Walter Annenberg, she later added the University of Pennsylvania, an Ivy League school celebrating the 250th anniversary of its founding. (She agreed to step in when Czechoslovakian president Vaclav Havel belatedly declined.)

Her chief of staff, Susan Porter Rose, "hadn't been enthusiastic about accepting Wellesley," Barbara Bush wrote in her diary in April 1990, in an aside that suggested she wished she had listened to that advice. Rose had a feeling that the elite all-women school with strong feminist roots—witness that the student speaker for the class of 1969 had been one Hillary Rodham—might not be a friendly venue. She turned out to be right. Students at Wellesley would launch a protest that cast Barbara Bush in the center of a national debate over the lives of women in America.

There had been a hint of controversy a year earlier, in September 1989, when Barbara Bush's alma mater, Smith, awarded her an honorary degree at its fall convocation. Some students grumbled about whether that was appropriate. "There MUST be a better way to get a Smithie in the White House," said a campus T-shirt that sported photos of Nancy Reagan and Barbara Bush. She laughed when she saw it.

At Wellesley, where the objections gained more traction, the protesting students saw it as a healthy exchange over an important issue. To Barbara Bush, it felt more like an attack on the path she had chosen. She feared the firestorm would reinforce one of the perceptions she hated most, that she was an anachronism in a world that had moved on, that the contributions she had made were neither recognized nor respected.

"I'm willing to say she was mad," said White House press secretary Marlin Fitzwater, who was close to the First Lady. "It was sort of humiliating," East Wing aide Julie Cooke told me. "It was humiliating to all of us."

Novelist Alice Walker had been the first choice for graduation speaker in a vote by Wellesley seniors among seventy-six possibilities, and she had accepted. But Walker begged off after an earthquake in Northern California in October 1989 damaged her Oakland home and demanded her attention. In late December, the president of Wellesley, Nannerl O. Keohane, sent a request to Barbara Bush, not mentioning that she was the second choice.

"Each year the Senior Class at Wellesley chooses its Commencement speaker by popular vote of the Class," she wrote. "I am delighted to write to tell you that the Class of 1990 at Wellesley has enthusiastically chosen you to address them on June 1." She said the First Lady's "dedication to volunteerism" and her commitment to literacy struck a "resonant chord" at Wellesley. "The students are eager and welcoming," she assured her.

When Wellesley announced Barbara Bush would speak at graduation, though, that didn't exactly describe the reaction from some of them.

"It struck me as tremendously incongruous to tell us for four years that we should be recognized on our own merits and then invite someone on the eve of our graduation who was in the public eye because of who she was married to, regardless of how lovely she was as a human being," Peggy Reid, one of the graduates, told me years later. "Would the Harvard Class of 1990 invite Margaret Thatcher's husband to be their commencement speaker? That's so obviously absurd. So why wasn't it absurd for us to invite the president's spouse?"

Reid and a friend, Susana Rosario Cardenas, got on the phone that night to talk. "We were all wondering, why is it that the college had invited a woman who was being recognized due to her marriage to her husband?" Cardenas told me. "We thought there may be a few others who think similarly, and we came up with the idea of a petition."

They drafted language, discussed it with friends, printed out a copy for each of the dorms, and set up a table in the student center to solicit signatures. Of the 600 graduating seniors, 150 signed it. The tone was tough.

"We are outraged by this choice and feel it is important to make ourselves heard immediately," it read. "Wellesley teaches us that we will be rewarded on the basis of our own merit, not on that of a spouse. To honor Barbara Bush as a commencement speaker is to honor a woman who has gained recognition through the achievements of her husband, which contradicts what we have been taught over the last four years at Wellesley. Regardless of her political affiliation, we feel that she does not successfully exemplify the qualities that Wellesley seeks to instill in us."

While it would be "discourteous" to withdraw the invitation, the petition went on, it proposed adding "an additional speaker who would more aptly reflect the self-affirming qualities of a Wellesley graduate."

At Wellesley that spring, the petition drive prompted a story in the college newspaper, the *Wellesley News*. A stringer for the Associated Press filed a short story that went out on the wire. Two days later, the *Boston Globe* ran a follow-up article on the front page with a quote from the White House press secretary. That story may have gotten particular attention because it happened to be published the day after the Boston Marathon, along with the race results.

"It seems to me that a truly educated person would be able to recognize achievement whether in a classroom or in or out of marriage," Marlin Fitzwater retorted. Cardenas, one of the protest organizers, was quoted as saying, "If she hadn't been married to this guy who happens to be president we never would have heard of her."

Then: a deluge, much of it taking offense on Barbara Bush's behalf. More than seven thousand articles were published in magazines and newspapers around the world, according to an academic study published five years later. Cardenas had to move out of her dorm room and into a friend's apartment in Cambridge to get away from phone calls, some of them abusive, and finish her senior thesis. Years later, Reid had kept a box of the mail that poured in, some of it encouraging, some of it outraged.

A headline in the *Atlanta Journal-Constitution*: "Wellesley Women a Bunch of Snobs." The *Denver Post* called the protesters "snobbish little brats" and "wet-nosed upstarts." Columnists from conservative Cal Thomas to liberal Ellen Goodman enumerated the contributions Barbara Bush had made to public life. Senator Barbara Mikulski of Maryland, a Democrat, called President Bush to say how offended she was, offering to help. Former president Richard Nixon called Barbara Bush. "You tell those girls to go to the devil," he advised.

At Wellesley, Nan Keohane was hearing about it too. "Some alumnae thought it was ungracious and wrongheaded," she told me. "They thought the students were behaving in a very inappropriate fashion." She herself didn't have any problem with the debate, though she called it "the resistance" rather than a protest, noting, "Nobody was walking around with signs."

A reporter asked George Bush about it at a White House news

conference in early May. "Mr. President, do you believe that there is any, any merit to their argument that Mrs. Bush's accomplishments are largely related to her marriage to yourself?" Ellen Warren of Knight-Ridder newspapers asked. "I can't have any argument with that," Bush responded, smiling, to cautionary "oohs" in the briefing room.

Warren followed up: Was he offended by the students' objections to having her speak at their graduation? Yes, Bush said. While being First Lady had provided her with a platform, "I think that these young women can have a lot to learn from Barbara Bush and from her unselfishness, and from her advocacy of literacy and of being a good mother and a lot of other things," he said. "She's not trying to be something she's not. The American people love her 'cause she's something she is, and stands for something."

Bush was blunter in his diary. He derided the protesters as "elitist kids."

In public, Barbara Bush was gracious when asked about the controversy. The protesting students "were very reasonable," she said at a luncheon with reporters. "They're twenty-one years old and they're looking at life from that perspective." She noted that it had been her choice to live her "fabulously exciting, interesting, involved life."

"In my day, they probably would have been considered different," she said. "In their day, I'm considered different. Vive la différence."

In private, though, she felt embattled and hurt. "The darn Wellesley flap has taken on a life of its own," she wrote in her diary two weeks before the speech. "There are more editorials, more talk shows, etc. It is putting too much pressure on." She groused: "I have to remind myself that THEY invited me. I sometimes feel as though they think I invited myself."

Aides said later that she was more nervous about this speech than about any other she would give. She was adamant that she wasn't going to recast her message in the face of the protests. "I did not want to complain, explain, or apologize in any way," she told her staff. She was irked when a news story reported that a White House staffer had asked a dean at Wellesley what the students wanted to hear. That wasn't the point, she said; they were going to hear what she wanted to say.

Indeed, the speeches she delivered at St. Louis University and at the University of Pennsylvania in May included much of the same language she used at Wellesley in June, although they got much less attention. Her core message wasn't a response to the Wellesley protests. The initial drafts were written before the petition was being circulated, before the controversy flared.

She had met in the spring with her staffers and a West Wing speechwriter, Edward McNally, to discuss the commencement addresses. She and McNally had met when he was just out of Yale and working on the Bush presidential campaign in 1980. Assigned to Florida, he had acted as her advance man and driver when she campaigned there before an important straw poll.

At the meeting, she wondered aloud about just how much commencement addresses mattered. Who even remembered the speeches from their graduations?

McNally raised his hand. He didn't remember the commencement speech when he graduated from Yale, he said, but he did remember a professor's remarks at a ceremony marking his law school graduation at Notre Dame. Fernand "Tex" Dutile, voted teacher of the year by the class of 1982, was one of a half dozen speakers in the chapel that day. McNally paraphrased Dutile's words: He hoped the school had done a good job of teaching them about adherence to the Constitution and the rule of law. But at the end of their lives, he went on, they wouldn't regret not having gained one more client or argued one more case, but they might regret time not spent with a husband or a friend or a parent.

"I love that," Barbara Bush said. She asked McNally to call Dutile for approval to echo his construction and content. He did, and Dutile agreed. The language was tweaked, and she changed one key word.

They would be perhaps the most memorable words she would ever speak.

The protests and the debate they sparked over women's roles in the

United States created such a furor that all three major broadcast networks decided to carry the graduation speech live—the first time that had happened for a First Lady. Anchors and analysts were watching to provide the sort of commentary usually reserved for presidential addresses. It was the most media attention Wellesley had ever gotten.

Superpower politics became part of the Wellesley address too. After Barbara Bush had agreed to speak at the graduation but before it had been announced, the United States and the Soviet Union scheduled a summit between Bush and Soviet president Mikhail Gorbachev in Washington that overlapped with the commencement. Gorbachev's wife, Raisa, an influential adviser to her husband in a way that was groundbreaking on their home turf, would be traveling with him.

After checking with the Wellesley president, Barbara Bush wrote a note to Raisa Gorbachev; Foreign Secretary Eduard Shevardnadze carried it to Moscow. It invited Raisa to join her at Wellesley and deliver remarks to the graduates as well. Raisa eventually accepted. Bringing her wasn't a response to the protest—the invitation was extended before there was any sign of that—though later it would seem like a master stroke.

The morning of graduation, Barbara Bush and Raisa Gorbachev boarded an Air Force plane to fly to Boston from Washington.

— ⁓

Barbara Bush began, as usual, with self-deprecation.

"Now I know your first choice for today—guess how I know?—was Alice Walker, known for *The Color Purple*," she told the crowd of five thousand gathered on Severance Green. "Instead you got me—known for the color of my hair!" To her relief, that got a laugh. She felt a little less nervous.

George Bush had done some final editing, nixing an opening joke that involved him and Gorbachev. He was worried the Soviet leader might take offense. "Before we left, Mikhail told me personally that he foresees a new era of peace and harmony," the draft of Barbara Bush's speech had read. "I told him that I was also confident of continued warm relations between the United States and the Soviet Union. He said, 'Yes [Barbara]—but I was referring to you and Wellesley!' "

She didn't use the joke, although Bush had included a version of it in his toast at a state dinner for Gorbachev the night before. He noted the opening that day of their high-stakes summit. "And tomorrow, Mr. President, comes the moment that so many have been waiting for, a day when expectations will be at a fever pitch," he said. "That's right, tomorrow Barbara and Raisa go to Wellesley College."

She ditched another opening joke in her text. "I told George I might as well face up to the fact that I was invited here only because of the popularity and prominence of the sweet soul who shares my bedroom at the White House," the draft read. "He said: They invited you to Wellesley because of Millie?!"

In a speech that lasted just eleven minutes, Barbara Bush urged the graduates to make three choices. The first was to believe in something larger than themselves, as she had with literacy. The second was to live their lives with joy—again, as she had.

"The third choice that must not be missed is to cherish your human connections: your relationships with family and friends," she went on. "For several years, you've had impressed upon you the importance to your career of dedication and hard work, and of course, that's true. But as important as your obligations as a doctor, lawyer, or business leader will be, you are a human being first and those human connections—with spouses, with children, with friends—are the most important investments you will ever make.

"At the end of your life, you will never regret not having passed one more test, not winning one more verdict, or not closing one more deal," she told them. "You will regret time not spent with a husband, a friend, or a parent."

An earlier draft had a different word in that last sentence. It had read, "You *may* regret time not spent with a husband, a friend, or a parent." Barbara Bush changed that to make it less conditional, more emphatic: "You *will* regret time not spent with a husband, a friend, or a parent."

Her remarks acknowledged that times were changing. "We are in a transitional period right now—fascinating and exhilarating times, learning to adjust to the changes and the choices we, men and women, are facing…Maybe we should adjust faster, maybe slower. But whatever the era, whatever the times, one thing will never change: Fathers and mothers, if you have children, they must come first. Your success as a family, our success as a society, depends *not* on what happens at the White House, but on what happens inside your house."

At the end, she tweaked a remark she had made at the other commencements, suggesting the day when a woman would be president. This time, she gave it a twist.

"And who knows?" she said. "Somewhere out in this audience may even be someone who will one day follow in my footsteps, and preside over the White House as the president's spouse." She paused. "I wish him well!"

That brought down the house. The response was so great that Raisa Gorbachev would note it in her memoir, although the subtlety of the turn in the punch line—"I wish *him* well!"—may have escaped translation. She recalled "the wave of applause evoked by Barbara's remark that she was sure that in that very auditorium somewhere, perhaps in the back row, [was] the future spouse of a future President of the United States— or the future President herself."

⌒‿⌒

The East Wing staff, aware of how nervous Barbara Bush had been about the speech, had prepared a banner to welcome her home, regardless of how it went. "A Job Wellesley Done," it proclaimed. When she got out of the car on the South Lawn of the White House and saw it, she nearly cried.

The reviews were glowing, the reverberations remarkable. *American Rhetoric* rated it as one of the top one hundred speeches of the twentieth century. At no. 45, it was ranked just below William Jennings Bryan's

"Flag of an Empire" address in 1900 and just above John Fitzgerald Kennedy's civil rights address in 1963. (The only other First Ladies on the list were Hillary Rodham Clinton, for her 1995 speech at the UN women's conference in Beijing; and Eleanor Roosevelt, for two speeches in 1948 about the Universal Declaration of Human Rights.) Some analysts argued that Barbara Bush's remarks represented a cultural watershed, setting a marker about enduring priorities at a time when many women and men were struggling to sort out a changing world.

In her speech, Barbara Bush didn't dismiss the value or appeal of careers, but she admonished women and men to put a priority on human relationships and, especially, children. At a time of a cultural clash over the role of women, her down-to-earth manner, her lack of defensiveness, and her humor enabled her to address life's balancing act in a way that respected combatants on both sides.

She noted that one of Wellesley's long traditions had seniors compete in a hoop race down Tupelo Lane, with the winner destined to be the first to get married. In the 1980s, that had been revised to hold that the graduate who managed to roll a large hoop across the finish line first would be the first in the class to become a CEO or a millionaire.

"Both those stereotypes show too little tolerance," Barbara Bush said. She suggested that instead the winner be destined to be "the first to realize her dream, not society's dream—her personal dream." Indeed, that was a change the college would soon make, with the winner of the hoop race said to be "the first to achieve happiness and success, whatever that means to her."

Some of the protesters thought Barbara Bush had missed their point. About a third of the graduates wore purple armbands to symbolize their request that she "take a definite and vocal stand on critical issues that shape the lives of women in the United States," among them family and medical leave, equal pay, and reproductive rights. They thought the heated reaction of some of those who jumped to her defense inadvertently reinforced the argument they were making—that women challenging society's assumptions often were excoriated for speaking up, for making trouble. In a blistering *Boston Globe* column, Mike Barnicle had mocked the protesters as "girls (oops) female persons" and called Wellesley students "a pack of whining, unshaved feminists" who could make men at Boston College "appreciate the virtue of celibacy."

The protesters had T-shirts made with a slogan that combined some of the slurs that had been hurled their way. "We are women of the WURST kind," the T-shirt declared, an acronym they created for "Whiny Unshaved Radical Spinster Tartlettes."

"The point was we thought we had struck a chord in terms of these questions we had about women's roles and how we need to grapple with all these expectations, and all these women coming of political age, and what this meant for our future," Cardenas said. She was taken aback when she read Barbara Bush's 1994 memoir; she wrote that she was bothered that one of the protesters was from a South American country. "I thought she showed very bad taste criticizing the wife of the president of her host country," Barbara Bush said.

Though she didn't cite a name, that clearly was a reference to Cardenas, who was from Peru. "I thought, I mean, yes, I'm from Peru; why would that make a difference?" Cardenas said years later.

By then, she was working at the Inter-American Development Bank in Washington, with two teenage children. She didn't regret the protest, but she did see it from a somewhat different perspective. "When I was twenty-one I was quicker at judging people," she said; she and the other protesters assumed they knew who Barbara Bush was. "Since it's a two-way street, perhaps she also thought she knew us," she added. With the benefit of time, she said, "you learn not to judge people so quickly."

Peggy Reid didn't regret the protest, either, but she noted that during her life she had occasionally worked part-time and volunteered as she had reared her children. "As we get older, we all kind of go through all those phases," she told me. "You realize there is no perfect balance and you probably [learn] to have sympathy and empathy and respect for your sisters, no matter what."

Two months after she had delivered the speech at Wellesley, Barbara Bush delivered a similar message to an audience of one: me.

In August 1990, as a White House correspondent for *Newsday*, I brought my children to the annual family picnic the Bushes generously hosted for the reporters on duty in Kennebunkport. My two young sons were resisting my efforts to wrangle them when she walked over, wearing a broad-brimmed straw hat and a disapproving expression.

"How can you work when you have young children?" she demanded. It was clear that my stammered response was less than persuasive. (In fairness, I wasn't trying to be persuasive. I was trying to back out of her line of fire.) She told me, approvingly, that her daughter and her daughters-in-law were all staying home to rear their children. After the picnic, she graciously autographed a White House photograph from the day that showed her and her famous dog, Millie, with my family. She signed it to "The Leubsdorfs," the name of my husband.

A quarter century later, when I was interviewing her for this book, Barbara Bush took a different tone about the next generation. "All my married grandchildren, women, are working, and they have children," she told me with pride. "They're bringing up—except for one—they're bringing up very nice children." That "except for one" reference was a joke. She had just been complaining about the rambunctiousness of one of her great-granddaughters, a toddler, who had visited a few days earlier. That child's mother, she noted with a smile, was the only mother in that generation of the family who *wasn't* working outside the home.

I asked if she had counseled her granddaughters to think twice about working while their children were small—the point she once had made with me, although I didn't remind her of that. "No, I wouldn't think of it," she insisted. Indeed, Jenna Bush Hager told me her grandmother had encouraged her to agree to take on a bigger role at NBC's *Today* show even though her two daughters were very young. (That said, a granddaughter-in-law recounted a conversation she had with Barbara Bush that was almost identical to the one I had decades earlier.) Barbara Bush told me that she did give her granddaughters some other advice, though. "I counseled them to have more children," she said.

⁓ ⁓

Barbara Bush's views of the feminist movement that caught fire during the 1960s and 1970s, a movement that reexamined assumptions about women and opened opportunities for them, were complicated and sometimes critical. She believed mothers had an imperative to put their children first, ahead of any career, and she wasn't shy about expressing that opinion, as she did with me.

But during her husband's rise in politics, her growing confidence and expanding role mirrored the rising prospects for women generally, though she often operated out of public view. When TV host Charlie Rose noted in a 1994 interview that she was "not just a little dutiful wife over here, taking care of the children," she broke in: "There aren't dutiful wives anymore."

Consider the intersections of her life with the seismic changes affecting women in America.

The constitutional amendment giving women the right to vote was ratified just five years before Barbara Pierce was born in 1925. When she was a teenager, millions of women were entering the workforce for the first time to replace men who had been deployed overseas during World War II; she rode her bike from Rye to Port Chester one summer during the war to work in a nuts-and-bolts factory. The landmark book of the women's movement, *The Feminine Mystique*, was published in 1963; author Betty Friedan based the book on a survey she had taken of her Smith College class of 1942. Coincidentally, Barbara had entered Smith College a year later, in 1943.

Friedan's book focused on women very much like Barbara Bush—smart, well-educated, and capable—who had dropped out of college, or chosen not to use the college educations they completed, in favor of caring for their husbands and children. For some, that just wasn't enough. Friedan labeled their frustration "the problem that has no name."

Barbara Bush insisted that she felt no such frustration. She told me she had never read *The Feminine Mystique*, and that she never would. Her favorite book was a nineteenth-century romantic classic by Jane Austen. "I'm a *Pride and Prejudice* girl," she said.

She bristled at any suggestion that she might have regrets. ABC White House correspondent Ann Compton once introduced her at a Kennedy Center town hall forum by saying, "She sacrificed her college education to marry, she says, the first boy she ever kissed." Backstage afterward, Barbara Bush, then the wife of the vice president, upbraided Compton. "I never sacrificed anything; I made a choice," she told her. "That's what women's rights are all about, the right to choose."

In some ways, Barbara Bush walked the walk of feminism: She was competent and confident; she had strong opinions and wasn't afraid to express them; she supported the career aspirations of her granddaughters as well as her grandsons; she thought women should be free to choose what path they took. She had endorsed the Equal Rights Amendment and abortion rights when those were fierce controversies in the Republican Party, although she ducked those issues when they began creating complications for her husband's political career.

That said, she didn't talk the talk. She refused to call herself a feminist. She complained that George Bush faced a double standard when he ran against Geraldine Ferraro for vice president in 1984, and George W. Bush faced the same uneven playing field when he ran against Texas governor Ann Richards ten years later. "Certainly it's harder campaigning against a woman," she said. "They play by women's rules, and hit like a man."

In February 2018, in the last of five interviews I had with her during the final months of her life, her ambivalence toward the word and the movement was apparent.

"Do I believe in equal rights for women? Yes," she told me. "But I wouldn't put myself as a feminist, no . . . No, I believe we got the vote, we can do anything we want. But I'm not a feminist." What about the term did she reject? "Well, because I'm not going to get out and crusade for it. Don't you think feminists have to crusade?"

Not necessarily, I replied. We went around and around.

"You're being really slippery on the whole feminist thing," I finally said in surrender.

"Yes," she agreed, smiling. "Very slippery."

Her reluctance may have reflected a residue of resentment at what she saw as the movement's ridicule of women like her who had chosen to be wives and mothers first. Attitudes denigrating the contribution of home-makers had changed since the Wellesley furor in 1990, I said. She wasn't so sure. "It maybe still is that way," she replied.

During her husband's political career, she had been wounded when her appearance and her choices were mocked in ways that would be seen today as offensive and outrageous.

During the campaign year of 1988, she was repeatedly portrayed on NBC's *Saturday Night Live* by comedian Phil Hartman in drag. "Tell me, are you proud of your son?" the Barbara Bush character was asked during one skit. She replied, "He is not my son. He is my husband." The imperious interviewer turned to the audience and said, "Well, she looks so much older, I hardly think it's *my* faux pas."

On another *Saturday Night Live* skit that year, Hartman portrayed a frumpy Barbara Bush as comedian Jan Hooks depicted a stylish Eliza-beth Dole. In what purported to be a joint appearance on a TV show, the interviewer enumerated Dole's impressive education and governmental career. "Heavens, do they ever call you Wonder Woman?" she gushed, then turned to Bush and said in a patronizing tone, "Now, Barbara, I understand you've written a book about the family cocker spaniel and you're working on a rug." (That was her current needlepointing project, which took eight years to complete.)

Decades later, as we talked in the living room of her Houston home, Barbara Bush dismissed my question about whether that demeaning depiction had been hurtful. "Oh, that's okay," she said, adding, "You're sitting on the rug."

—— ——

Almost three decades after the Wellesley speech, in 2006, Barbara Bush seethed after another college commencement, this one at the George Washington University. She and former president George Bush each delivered remarks, and each received an honorary degree. Her speech, she told her diary, had been "really funny" ("if I say so my self") and pivoted to a serious note at the end.

"All of this to tell you that I was really hurt, well maybe mad, at least upset by my citation," she went on. "It was 3 or 4 minutes long and never said one thing that I had done for others...Literacy, hospital boards, anything. I was a house wife and a mother, a saint who sacrificed her life for her husband and children."

The citation mentioned Barbara Bush's father, her husband, her children, her humor, and her famous lack of cooking skills. It made no reference to anything else she had done over the previous eighty-one years of her life. "Like Abigail Adams, you remind us of the pleasures of a long marriage and the importance of family," university president Stephen Joel Trachtenberg had concluded. "You never let us forget that the hand that rocks the cradle is the hand that rules the world."

"I had not realized that I was a women's libber, but I am now," Barbara Bush wrote afterward, venting to her diary. "Of course I love that part of my life, but I love the other side, too."

Chapter Fifteen

Détente

Barbara Bush sat in the Green Room watching Nancy Reagan and Raisa Gorbachev go to war, ever so politely, over tea.

Soviet leader Mikhail Gorbachev was making his first visit to the United States in December 1987 amid excitement about the prospect of negotiating an end to the Cold War. Nancy and Raisa had met once before, at the opening Reagan-Gorbachev summit in Geneva two years earlier. Their relationship had been frosty from the start. Barbara Bush said the mutual antagonism was hard to miss. "It was what I call a 'chemical thing,' plus a cultural difference," she said. The greeting at the White House was a second chance to get along, perhaps, as their husbands headed into historic meetings on arms control.

It was a heady time, full of possibility and risk. The superpower confrontation that had defined the globe since World War II seemed poised for seismic changes that could reduce the threat of nuclear annihilation. At this summit, the conservative American president and the reformist Soviet leader would sign the Intermediate-Range Nuclear Forces Treaty, the INF, curtailing short-range and intermediate-range missiles and their launchers. They had held talks in Reykjavik, Iceland, a year earlier about an even broader proposal to limit nuclear weapons.

In her diary, dictated as she walked Millie around the grounds at the vice president's residence, Barbara Bush noted with amusement some of the similarities between the two reigning First Ladies. It was three days after the Gorbachevs had arrived in town. "I don't know how old" Raisa is, she said, "but think the paper said fifty-three or fifty-five. That's funny, for we really don't know if Nancy Reagan is sixty-five or sixty-seven and she won't tell. I guess Raisa won't tell either."

The White House tea, on December 8, 1987, had gotten off to a rocky start.

"We couldn't understand why you didn't come to Iceland," Raisa Gorbachev began, picking at a scab. Nancy Reagan hadn't attended the Reykjavik summit in 1986 because the initial plan had been for the leaders to meet without their spouses in attendance; Nancy suspected Raisa was trying to one-up her when she announced at the last minute that she would be there. "But I thought that only men were going—" Nancy Reagan started to say. Raisa Gorbachev interrupted her, that time and then repeatedly. She launched into a series of comparisons designed to cast Russia in the best light and the United States in the worst—asserting that there were no homeless people in Russia, for instance. Inexplicably, she began to discuss the American Civil War and the history of slavery in the United States. Russia, she noted, had freed its serfs in 1861.

Helena Shultz, the wife of Secretary of State George Shultz, leaned over and whispered to Barbara, "Nancy doesn't like this conversation." Barbara whispered back, "Who would?" It was like watching a slow-motion train wreck. Finally Nancy Reagan, her irritation barely masked, tried to end it. "I'm afraid that I am keeping you from your schedule," she said, a signal that it was time for her to go. Raisa Gorbachev didn't take the hint. "Oh, that's all right," she responded.

"They just never clicked," George Shultz said later, a statement that defined diplomatic understatement. Nancy Reagan was more blunt. "Who does that dame think she is?" she had demanded after the official dinner on the first night of the Geneva summit.

Mikhail Gorbachev took umbrage on his wife's behalf to the depiction of her as difficult. "American newspapers gossiped about an alleged 'cold war' between the First Ladies," he wrote in his 1996 memoir.

Raisa "did not 'wage war' with anyone—in fact she did a lot for mutual understanding and goodwill." He noted, pointedly, that "Raisa Maksimovna and Nancy Reagan are very different persons, both from their life experiences and professional interests. Nancy is an actress, Raisa an academic."

During the Washington visit, there was a flap between Raisa Gorbachev and Barbara Bush, too, a deliberate snub that was kept under wraps.

The Soviet Embassy had suggested that Barbara Bush take Raisa Gorbachev on a tour of the National Gallery of Art during her visit to Washington. Barbara was happy to do that, but White House staffers, alert to Nancy Reagan's concern that Barbara Bush never be allowed to upstage her, nixed the idea that she would be Raisa's escort there. "It was made clear that this would not be looked upon favorably," said Craig Fuller, then the vice president's chief of staff. Instead, Barbara made arrangements to have breakfast with Raisa at the Soviet Embassy, an encounter that wouldn't draw news coverage.

"I was supposed to take her someplace—I've forgotten where— and somebody in the White House didn't like that very much, so they canceled that," Barbara Bush told me years later. "I was to go there for breakfast with her. Well, I sat there and waited and she never came. She was paying me back for not taking her to the whatever-it-was…

"I sat right there at the embassy and waited the whole time," she recalled, until aides indicated she might as well leave. There was no breakfast. There was no explanation, no apology. She decided not to make a stink over it, at that time or later. She didn't mention it in her memoirs. "I just acted like that hadn't happened," she told me.

Their disparate reactions crystallized a crucial difference between Nancy Reagan and Barbara Bush. Facing an affront, Nancy took offense. Facing an affront, Barbara made a decision to let it go. That didn't mean she wasn't annoyed. In interviews with me and notations in her diaries, she made it clear that she found Raisa Gorbachev exasperating at times. But she did what she had done before, in a variety of circumstances, political and personal. She submerged her own feelings in the interests of her husband's career and, in this case, in the nation's interests as well.

"She understood where the president was at that time, in terms of the end of the Cold War and the relationship with Gorbachev, and she was determined to be a positive force for him in those discussions," Marlin Fitzwater, who served as White House press secretary for both Ronald Reagan and George Bush, told me. "And that would guide her relationship with Raisa."

That evening, the Bushes were designated to escort the Gorbachevs to Andrews Air Force Base for their departure for Moscow. The two men were in one limousine, the two women in another. On the drive down Suitland Parkway in Maryland, Barbara and Raisa had a remarkable exchange that would set the stage for the close relationship they would develop over time.

Raisa Gorbachev, as usual, lacked a light touch.

"She had been well briefed on me and had me down as a housewife," Barbara Bush wrote in her diary the next day. "She asked me if we ever served pies? I said that we did and she then gave me her recipe for blueberry pie: 'You take a cup of flour, a cup of cream and a cup of blueberries and mix 'em up and you have a pie.' Even I know that will not make a pie."

Rather than debate baked goods, Barbara Bush decided to change the subject. "I put my hand on her knee and said, 'Mrs. G., I am not a great cook. I can feed fifty, but no one would ever rave over my food. Tell me about your average day.'"

What followed was "the darndest conversation," Barbara Bush said. Speaking through an interpreter, they became as candid as confidantes.

Barbara Bush noted that Nancy Reagan had undergone surgery for breast cancer a month earlier. She didn't say so explicitly, but the failure of Raisa Gorbachev to express concern and sympathy had been seen by the American side as insensitive. Raisa replied that she knew about it, but in her country "they would not talk about it and the doctor would be in trouble for mentioning it." It was "very difficult" for a woman to have a breast removed, she said. In the United States, Barbara Bush replied, it would have been difficult for the First Lady to disappear from public view for surgery and not have the press demand to know where she was.

That led to a discussion about the news media's right to know about the personal lives of public figures. Raisa mentioned Gary Hart, the Colorado senator and Democratic presidential hopeful who a few months earlier had been entangled in a furor over his personal behavior. Barbara Bush, who had her own grievances against reporters, found herself defending their role. "We get so angry with the press for their probing personal questions but would die for their right to ask them," she finally declared.

Raisa Gorbachev asked, "What if the First Lady had an abortion?" Barbara Bush responded that the First Lady wouldn't have an abortion, and that "breast cancer and an abortion were certainly two very different things." She called Nancy Reagan "courageous" for being open about her battle with breast cancer, saying she had saved lives by encouraging other women to have mammograms.

The discussion that began with an ersatz recipe for blueberry pie had veered to cover breast cancer, abortion, scandal, the right to privacy, the role of the press in a free society, and a defense of Nancy Reagan—all before they pulled up on the tarmac at Andrews. "We arrived at the airport before we could pursue this anymore," Barbara Bush said. But they would talk again, many times, and at historic moments.

Barbara Bush didn't have a background in foreign policy; she had never even traveled abroad as a tourist. The first time she needed a passport was when her husband became the US ambassador to the United Nations. The posting in New York served as on-the-job training for both of them. George Bush's background in foreign affairs was so thin that even friends had wondered if he was right for the UN post. But she had approached the foreign dignitaries who suddenly surrounded her with the same energy and discipline that had made her the original soccer mom of Midland.

When Bush was UN ambassador and then vice president and president, Barbara Bush didn't pretend to offer advice on foreign policy or national security strategy. But she did have sharp insights on people and their motives, and she set out to forge ties that might prove helpful, then or later. She helped cultivate a friendlier relationship with French president François Mitterrand, who had never gotten along with President Reagan; that would pay dividends during the First Gulf War. She opened the family's retreat in Kennebunkport, Maine, to visits not only by Mitterrand but also by the leaders of Canada, Great Britain, Denmark, Japan, Jordan, Saudi Arabia, and Israel, and she welcomed their spouses and children too. At a perilous moment in Moscow, her instincts helped her avoid a misstep that might have sent a dangerous message.

The role of spouses in diplomacy can be subtle and easy to discount, but there are times they make a difference, often without drawing attention. Some of the leaders involved at the top ranks in negotiations to end the Cold War give Barbara Bush credit for helping in ways the public never saw.

West German chancellor Helmut Kohl was one of those. The national security archives of the West German government, now declassified, make it clear that Kohl believed Barbara Bush was making a difference, especially in contrast to Nancy Reagan. In a telephone conversation between Kohl and Gorbachev in 1989, the Soviet leader complained that Bush was stalling on scheduling another summit. Kohl assured him that Bush and Secretary of State James Baker were working in good faith and could be trusted. And he diplomatically broached the difference between Barbara Bush and her predecessor as First Lady.

"In addition, another factor comes into play that does not appear to have anything to do with politics," Kohl said, according to the contemporaneous account, translated from the German. "The wife of Bush contributed greatly to the calming. It was not always like that in the White House. He understood this, GS [General Secretary] Gorbachev offered.

The Chancellor noted that Barbara Bush was a mother and grandmother and would advocate for moderate politics and was not keen on stirring the pot."

Later, in a separate phone conversation with President Bush, Kohl relayed that both the Soviet leader and his wife had a positive view of Barbara Bush and her impact; they were diplomatic about Nancy Reagan. "The Chancellor's impression from several hours of conversation was that Gorbachev very clearly and palpably hoped for good contact with Bush," the account reads. "He held hope that this would be more possible with Bush than was the case with President Reagan. He was supported very strongly in this position by Mrs. Gorbachev. She spoke very nicely of Barbara, but avoided saying anything about other women."

As the leader of West Germany, and the person who would become the first chancellor of a reunified Germany in 1990, Helmut Kohl was at the center of the delicate negotiations. He was also attuned to interpersonal dynamics. "Helmut was the best retail politician of the G-7 members," Brian Mulroney, then the prime minister of Canada, told me. "He would have a particular sensitivity to the importance of events like Barbara Bush and her impact on Raisa. This would go right over the heads of most of them, but not Helmut."

Like Kohl, Mulroney saw Barbara Bush's hidden role as important.

"If you understand there was no person in the world with greater influence on Gorbachev than Raisa, then you can see the magic in what Barbara was doing," he said. "I remember many incidents where Barbara went out of her way to always pay special attention to Raisa, and show her the deference of a quite long-serving First Lady by the time Barbara came in, and to treat her with great respect and indications of affection."

In some ways, he said, the two couples were a matched pair: "They were two very influential leaders with two very influential wives."

To be clear, the relationship between First Ladies didn't determine the negotiations between their husbands. The antagonism between Nancy Reagan and Raisa Gorbachev didn't prevent Ronald Reagan and Mikhail Gorbachev from striking historic accords to reduce nuclear weapons and move toward an end of Cold War tensions. The efforts by Barbara Bush to forge a more cordial relationship with Raisa Gorbachev weren't responsible for the progress that Mikhail Gorbachev and George Bush made.

But those personal tiffs and ties weren't irrelevant, either. They were particularly important to Gorbachev, a man who put great stock in whether he could trust the rival with whom he was dealing. And one of the ways in which he represented a new style of Soviet leader was this: He relied on the counsel of his wife.

"If the First Ladies are on pretty good terms and trusting terms, if you will, then it's much more likely that the husbands will be—pillow talk and all that," Jim Baker, who served as White House chief of staff for Reagan and secretary of state for Bush, told me. "Bush and Gorbachev developed a very strong rapport, even though we had to tell Mikhail a couple of times, 'Hey, don't do [that]' . . . But it obviously helped tremendously to have a good relationship between the wives."

Barbara Bush and Raisa Gorbachev never became true friends, at least not in any nondiplomatic definition.

"Friends? Well, that's a big word," Barbara Bush replied drily when I asked. "I wouldn't put her down as my great friend, but I got along with her better than Nancy did. That was so stupid." Barbara Bush viewed Nancy Reagan's open irritation with Raisa as stupid not because she didn't understand it, but because it wasn't helpful to the larger goals of her husband and the country.

Raisa Gorbachev could be hard to like. She was inclined to launch into lectures on the ways communism was superior to capitalism. She didn't have much of a sense of humor. Building a relationship with her wasn't easy, and it didn't happen by accident. It was a deliberate act of will by Barbara Bush. She wrote a letter to her brother Scott Pierce before the Gorbachevs were scheduled to arrive in Washington in 1990, which would be the first time she met with them as First Lady: "One thing I can promise you. I am going to love her in spite of anything she does or does not do."

"I have the warmest feelings and great respect for Mrs. George Bush," Raisa Gorbachev would write a year later in her memoir. "I am impressed by her natural and direct manner with people." When Barbara Bush died, Mikhail Gorbachev noted the bonds that had grown between the two women. "She immediately developed a warm relationship with Raisa, they communicated easily and at ease," he said. "Barbara did a lot to build trust and friendship between us."

~ ~

The Gorbachevs' visit to the United States in June 1990 coincided with Barbara Bush's commencement address at Wellesley College. With the approval of the school's president, she had invited Raisa Gorbachev to accompany her to the women's college in Massachusetts and deliver remarks as well. After some back-and-forth, the Soviet officials who were planning the visit accepted. The White House offered to help draft her remarks; the Russians declined.

On the flight to Boston that day, Barbara Bush told Raisa Gorbachev she was going to go over her speech one more time. Raisa interrupted, apparently surprised. "Barbara, are we both supposed to be giving a speech?" Barbara was flabbergasted. Raisa pulled out a tiny piece of paper and began to write notes. Barbara asked the interpreter if it was true this was a surprise. Didn't she have a speech prepared?

The interpreter smiled, patted his pocket, and pulled out the translation of Raisa's remarks, ready to go.

At the commencement, Raisa Gorbachev's speech received a friendly reception. She talked about the importance of perestroika, her husband's economic and political reforms, and she recalled fondly her own graduation from Moscow University. "Being young is a marvelous time, a time of actions and expectations, of being confident of one's abilities, and sure that everything is still ahead," she declared, speaking through a translator. "I wish that all your dreams of the future come true."

Afterward, the two First Ladies went to Boston Common to meet with a group of elementary school students at the famous *Make Way for Ducklings* sculpture, based on the children's book by Robert McCloskey. Reporters asked how they were getting on. Barbara Bush said, "Just fine. We are having a great time." To be precise, she responded in eight words. When they asked Raisa the same question, "she gave the same answer, but took hours," Barbara Bush later joked. "George would say that she is the kind of person you ask the time and they tell you how to build the clock."

The Bushes also took the Gorbachevs to the presidential retreat at Camp David, an invitation with a special cachet. Barbara and Raisa changed into casual clothes to take a walk, but Raisa returned wearing very high heels, insisting that they were her walking shoes and rejecting Barbara's offer to loan her something more appropriate. Barbara then suggested they tour the camp in a golf cart. Even so, Raisa's feet were raw and blistered by the time they returned.

During that day, Barbara Bush's feelings toward Raisa Gorbachev changed. Beforehand, "I dreaded [having] the whole day alone with her," she wrote in her diary, but to her surprise she found her to be "very appealing and warm." She felt empathy. "Think about it the very first Russian wife of a president to be in the public eye," she wrote. "She has no staff...in fact no real role. She is a pioneer."

In Raisa, Barbara saw a proud woman who was struggling to figure out a role unfamiliar to her and new to the Russian people, uncertain about what clothes to wear, and sensitive to slights. She also saw a wife who had the ear of her husband, a man who in some ways had the future of the world in his hands.

As they chatted, Raisa told Barbara she had been deeply hurt by Nancy Reagan's memoir, *My Turn*, published the previous year, which depicted Raisa as rude and didactic. "I felt very disloyal when I told Raisa that it was a dreadful book and nobody would even admit reading it," Barbara wrote in her diary, adding in parentheses, "(George would kill me if he knew that I did that, but it was a dreadful book and nobody would even admit reading it.)"

In her memoirs, she offered a redacted version of that story for public consumption, gliding over her candid review of Nancy's book. "She once asked me why Nancy Reagan didn't like her," she wrote. "I said that I was sure that Nancy did like her. She said that she had read otherwise in Nancy's book. I was hard put to answer, but she almost answered her own question by saying that she did not know our customs and that she was trying to learn. She did dominate the conversation, but maybe she thought that was what she was supposed to do. Who knows?"

For whatever reason, Raisa Gorbachev felt she could ask Barbara Bush anything.

That afternoon at Camp David, the two women and Barbara's twenty-four-year-old assistant, Peggy Swift, sat and chatted. Raisa, who had a grown daughter of her own back in Moscow, quizzed Peggy about her life. She lived in an apartment with several girlfriends, Peggy told her; the Gorbachevs' daughter lived with her parents. Raisa asked what she did when she left work at night. Then she asked if she could go through Peggy's purse to see what she carried with her.

Peggy, startled, agreed to the unusual request. "I had a couple different lipsticks and different stuff and she couldn't understand why I'd have a Revlon, a L'Oréal, a Chanel—the fact that I had a choice of a bunch of different lipsticks and that at my age that I was living somewhere, not with my parents," she said. Raisa told her, "We don't have choices. When we walk into a drugstore we have lipstick and what's there is there."

It was a rare concession by a woman who spent much of her public rhetoric proclaiming the superiority of the Soviet system. "Mrs. Bush really peeled off the layers," Peggy Swift White told me years later, "and I think Mrs. Gorbachev was comfortable around her."

Raisa, whose influential role with her husband had made her a target in Russia, quizzed Barbara about why Americans seemed to like her so much.

"I think she had been hurt by the criticism about her, and she asked me why I was so popular," Barbara recalled. "I told her, as honestly as I could, that I felt it was because I threatened no one—I was old, whiteheaded, and large. I also told her that I stayed out of my husband's affairs. We both agreed that we put our husbands first above all else."

In their mutual devotion to their husbands, and in their behind-the-scenes roles as candid advisers to them, Barbara Bush recognized similarities between her and Raisa Gorbachev. When they met for dinner in Houston in 1992, a few months after the Soviet Union had fallen, Gorbachev was being careful not to criticize Russian president Boris Yeltsin. "Then Raisa would speak up because she thought he was not being tough enough," Barbara wrote in her diary. "That reminds me of me sometimes."

"I think they were empathetically close more than temperamentally close," Andy Card, then the deputy White House chief of staff, told me. Despite the differences in their personalities, they understood what the other was going through. He described Barbara's unspoken message to Raisa as this: "You're having a tough time; your husband is in a big position; big changes going on in your lives, and I understand that…

"It's a big step you're taking, and I'm going to help you in the step."

When Iraqi troops invaded Kuwait on August 2, 1990, Barbara's relationship with Raisa was a helpful bridge as George Bush scrambled to forge an international coalition to expel them.

After Bush got the first CIA reports about what was happening, he called Brian Mulroney, a close friend and trusted ally. The Canadian prime minister agreed to make a secret trip to the White House to confer before Bush called the other G7 leaders to discuss what to do—a consultation that would not be revealed for nearly three decades. Mulroney's plane landed in Washington on August 6; he and Chief of Staff Stanley Hartt boarded a Marine helicopter and landed on the South Lawn of the White House. The prime minister pulled a baseball cap over his head and walked into the White House. No one noticed him.

The day before, returning from a weekend at Camp David, Bush had told reporters, "This will not stand, this aggression against Kuwait." But it wasn't clear exactly what the United States planned to do, or whether the rest of the world would join forces with Washington. That's what Bush wanted to talk about with Mulroney.

Just five people sat around the table in the private dining room of the White House: the president and the prime minister; Bush's national security adviser, Brent Scowcroft; Mulroney's chief of staff; and Barbara Bush. Secretary of State James Baker was traveling and unable to get back to Washington in time to join them. "This was, I can say, a very important meeting from America's point of view," Mulroney told me in an interview, the first time he had discussed the secret session for publication. "We had the president musing aloud as to what his options were and what his first steps should be, not as to mess things up."

They chewed over how to keep the Soviet Union from splitting a common front at the United Nations. "We were going for a coalition that involved Arabs for the first time taking on a fellow Arab state," Mulroney said. "My position was, 'George, look, Canada is going to support you 100 percent, all the way through, provided you seek a resolution from the Security Council approving this.'" Not everyone in the administration endorsed this approach, but Bush, Scowcroft, and Baker agreed. Mulroney saw it as an imperative: "He had the imprimatur of the United Nations, which mollified a lot of people in terms of the Arab coalition; it allowed them to dodge a number of bullets."

Barbara Bush "could see, frankly, the thoughtfulness of this," the prime minister recalled. "And she mentioned at the dinner that she would make it her business to be communicating with Raisa, to keep up their communication."

It was crucial to cultivate support from both Gorbachevs, he said. "If you had seen them together, Raisa and Mikhail together, and listened to them over a private dinner—she was the doctrinaire one. She was the flamethrower. And he always had to have her on his side. And so what Barbara did to mollify Raisa by treating her in a manner that Nancy had not, Barbara was rendering yeoman service to the cause."

They discussed how to line up key Western leaders. Mulroney suggested Bush call French president François Mitterrand and not mention that he already had conferred with his Canadian counterpart. "If Mitterrand thinks he's the first guy you're calling and you get him on your side, he will be your most loyal ally," Mulroney advised, "and he will be of enormous benefit to us at the United Nations when we go for our resolution, and in French-speaking Africa."

If Mitterrand arrived at his office at 9 a.m. Paris time the next morning, that would be 3 a.m. in Washington, Bush noted. "I said, 'Yeah, that's right,'" Mulroney recalled, "and Barbara said, 'George, do it.'"

Bush had a secure phone on a side table just next to him. He picked up the receiver and told the switchboard operator, "Wake me up at three in the morning. I want to talk to President Mitterrand—put me through" then. Mulroney said Mitterrand would realize it was the middle of the night in Washington, and he would appreciate the idea that he was the first leader the American president was calling. "Because of this," Mulroney said, "Mitterrand was the key and most loyal ally Bush had during the entire thing."

Mulroney was among several foreign leaders who recognized Barbara Bush as an influential voice with her husband. "They wanted to stay on her good side," National Security Adviser Brent Scowcroft told me in an interview. In the weeks after the invasion, the Bush administration was chilly to Jordan's King Hussein, who had ties to Saddam Hussein. Mulroney urged Bush to understand the quandary King Hussein faced in his volatile region, and to invite him to Kennebunkport as a gesture of warm relations.

"George wasn't very pleased with the suggestion," Mulroney recalled, but Barbara Bush turned out to be an ally. "He called me a couple of hours later, and said, 'Yeah, well, Brian, I've told Baker to arrange it. I talked to Barbara and she thought it was a good idea.'" Two weeks after the invasion, on August 16, 1990, King Hussein and his entourage arrived at Walker's Point at noon for a lobster lunch and consultations. Twenty minutes after the king's helicopter took off, a helicopter carrying Prince Saud al-Faisal of Saudi Arabia arrived for a two-hour meeting.

Those frantic days tested even the organizational abilities of Barbara Bush. George Bush's beloved uncle John Walker died that morning at the nearby Southern Maine Medical Center after suffering an aneurysm;

he was the surgeon they had called for advice in 1953 when they got the diagnosis that Robin had leukemia. Five of their grandchildren were staying at the house; to get them out of the way, Barbara sent them to the beach for the day with a picnic lunch. And after the Saudi entourage left, George and Barbara went to an evening fund-raiser for Richard Snelling, then running for governor of Vermont.

On the eve of the US-led invasion, Mulroney was back at the White House for another intimate dinner with the president, a few senior aides, and Barbara Bush. Derek Burney, then the Canadian ambassador to the United States, apologized to Mulroney as he escorted him to Andrews Air Force Base afterward. If he had realized the First Lady was going to be there, he said, he would have suggested Mulroney bring his wife, Mila.

"He said, 'No, never mind about that,'" Burney recalled. "He said, 'You know why she was there, Derek?' I said no. He said, 'She's the keeper of the flame.' I said, 'What do you mean?' He said, 'Derek, he's about to commit the United States to war. He wants the person in the room in whom he has the greatest trust to be there when he's making one of the most momentous decisions of his presidency.'"

The response to the Iraqi invasion of Kuwait—organizing a global coalition to expel Iraqi forces and convincing a divided Congress to support an authorization of use of force—consumed President Bush and his White House for months. "It was as if the whole world was holding its breath," Barbara Bush said at the end of 1990. She worried about the weight on her husband's shoulders and the danger ahead for American soldiers and others.

When he confided that the airstrikes would begin in twenty-four hours, she told her diary that she'd "like to go to bed and pull the covers over my head and stay there for six weeks, and then peek out and see if it is all over."

She was relieved when it was over—remarkably, in six weeks and a day—and after a ground war that lasted just one hundred hours. She reveled in the praise of her husband's steady leadership, and his record-setting approval ratings, though she acknowledged, "It won't last." And she was grateful when things seemed to get back to normal.

The White House had been closed to tourists since the air war began. "I miss the tourists," she wrote in her diary on February 8. "They bring the White House alive, they make it truly the People's House." She added, "I am surprised that I feel this way."

～ ～

A few months later, when the Bushes visited Moscow, Barbara Bush's sure-footedness prevented what could have been a diplomatic disaster.

On the trip in July 1991, Gorbachev was Bush's official host, but the leaders of the Soviet republics were also slated to meet with the American president. The Soviet Union still formally existed, with Gorbachev as its leader, but the republics were breaking away; the new order was still being sorted out. The new president of Russia, Boris Yeltsin, was particularly aggressive in asserting that his standing was equal to or even exceeding that of Gorbachev.

That afternoon, Barbara Bush and Raisa Gorbachev went to Novodevichy Park, where a replica of the *Make Way for Ducklings* sculpture was presented to the children of Moscow from the children of the United States. It was an exact copy of the sculpture the two women had visited in Boston Common a year earlier after addressing the Wellesley College commencement.

Then, at a dinner at the Kremlin, the two couples set up a receiving line in the ornate Hall of the Order of St. Vladimir. Naina Yeltsin, Boris's wife, had come through accompanied by the mayor of Moscow; there was no sign of her blustery husband until the reception was ending and the two couples were preparing to go into the dinner hall. Yeltsin had called Gorbachev the previous evening, asking if he could enter the dinner with him and Bush. Gorbachev had refused.

Now Yeltsin swept in, first trying to pose a photo of him planted between Bush and Gorbachev. Gorbachev refused to cooperate, keeping his back turned to the photographers in the press pool. Yeltsin then offered his arm to Barbara Bush. "As I am going to sit by you at dinner, please let me take you in," he said.

Barbara Bush paused, sensing a trap. "Is that really all right?" she asked. In his memoirs, Mikhail Gorbachev said she "exclaimed, astonished." Barbara Bush turned to Raisa Gorbachev and moved to place her in the middle, next to Yeltsin. The three walked in together to the Palace of Facets for the dinner.

The whole maneuver was over in a moment or two, but the scene was portentous enough that the reporters and photographers in the press pool could tell something, *something*, was happening, although they weren't sure just what. "During all this, Bush and Gorbachev were looking the other way and were engaged in a long and detailed conversation that seemed to be about the elaborate chandelier hanging above their heads," a *Wall Street Journal* reporter on the scene noted wryly.

At stake was not just a breach in protocol. "She basically made the point with her body: The United States is neutral in all of this; we are not choosing sides; you cannot rope me into choosing sides," Jeffrey A. Engel, author of *When the World Seemed New: George H. W. Bush and the End of the Cold War*, told me. The entire trip had been designed to send just that message. Her ability to recognize an unexpected land mine, and to step around it, required judgment and agility. If she had accepted Yeltsin's arm and walked into the hall, "it would have further undermined Gorbachev and his political standing as head of the Soviet Union," Engel said. "If she had done that, it would have exacerbated and catalyzed the decline."

In *A World Transformed*, a 1998 book he coauthored with Brent Scowcroft, Bush recalled the episode. "He attempted to escort Barbara to dinner, which would have been quite embarrassing to Gorbachev," he wrote, "but he was not successful." Bush didn't say why Yeltsin wasn't successful. Here's why: Yeltsin failed in his ploy because Barbara Bush recognized what he was trying to do, then pivoted to deny him that small victory.

"Bigger than life. He is outrageous," Barbara said of Yeltsin in her diary. "Thank heavens I didn't go in with him!"

To be sure, the decline in Gorbachev's political position was inexorable. A month later, a coup attempt placed the Gorbachevs in harm's way for four perilous days. It failed, but the dissolution of the Soviet Union and the end of Gorbachev's rule were approaching. He would announce his resignation in a nationally televised speech on December 25, 1991; the next day the Supreme Soviet declared that the Soviet Union had ceased to exist. Gorbachev handed over his office, and control of the Soviet nuclear codes, to Yeltsin. It would be Yeltsin honored by the Bushes at a State Dinner in the White House six months later, in June 1992.

During the uncertain days of the attempted coup in August 1991, Barbara Bush wrote Raisa Gorbachev a letter, expressing concern for her and her husband. "My heart goes out to our friends the Gorbachevs," Barbara wrote in her diary. There were rumors that Gorbachev was "undergoing treatment" or had been put on a ship in the Baltic or had been taken to a military base. "Is Raisa with him?" she worried. "I hope so because they are so devoted."

The coup attempt left a mark on the forceful Raisa Gorbachev, always so confident of her political views. "Raisa never seemed exactly the same," Barbara Bush wrote after seeing her again in 1994, at a conference of world leaders in Italy. "She seemed quieter and frailer." Raisa would die five years later of leukemia, the same disease that had taken Robin's life.

Chapter Sixteen

The Reluctant Campaign

Perhaps only Barbara Bush realized this: Her husband was seriously considering not running for a second term in 1992.

"For the last few months George has talked privately like a man who is not running for office," she wrote in her diary in May 1991. Both of them were anguished over the way son Neil had become the poster child for the financial abuses uncovered in the savings and loan scandal; he was among those being sued by federal regulators in connection with the collapse of a Colorado bank. "I know he has the children on his mind. He is consumed with worry about Neil and a guilty feeling. He knows that Neil never would have been in this trouble if he hadn't been the son of the president."

She had reservations of her own about waging yet another campaign, though she was careful not to betray much of her reluctance to him. While she had emerged as an increasingly influential voice, that was true even now. "I did wonder sometimes in the White House if it was worth awakening every day to the abuse that opponents and the press give the President," she said. But the decision about what to do, about whether to run, would be his. That had always been their way.

Public scrutiny spotlighted and sometimes exacerbated their private travails. Their daughter Doro had gone through a divorce in 1990, moving with her two young children back to Washington from Maine. While

Bush was vice president, their son Marvin was diagnosed with ulcerative colitis. The life-threatening autoimmune disorder forced removal of his colon. His mother blamed the stress of being in a public family under fire for contributing to his disease, although Marvin scoffed at that idea. And Barbara Bush was struggling with a serious health problem herself.

A month or two after the presidential inauguration in 1989, she began losing weight, eighteen pounds in all, sudden progress after a lifelong struggle. "I convinced myself it was because I was eating smaller portions and working so hard," she said. But she also was having trouble with her eyes. They were inflamed and bulging, and sometimes she was seeing double. Aboard *Air Force One* in February, heading back to Washington after a trip to China, she sat down beside White House physician Lawrence Mohr and described her symptoms.

Mohr immediately suspected Graves' disease, just from examining her eyes. For reasons unknown, her thyroid glands were producing too much of the hormone that regulates the body's metabolism. (Barbara Bush joked that the sobriquet "doesn't mean you'll go to the grave; it's named for the doctor who diagnosed the ailment." That would be Robert J. Graves, a nineteenth-century British physician.) The next day, at the White House, Mohr drew a sample of her blood to test. He consulted with specialists at Walter Reed Medical Center and the Mayo Clinic.

When the doctors told Barbara Bush their diagnosis, she was matter-of-fact. "It was like, 'What do we have to do?'" Mohr told me.

That question turned out to be hard to answer. A long process of trial and error never entirely eliminated the bothersome symptoms. They began treatment with a drug called methimazole to tamp down the thyroid's production of hormones. Then she went to Walter Reed Medical Center to drink a radioactive liquid, sipped through a straw, to destroy her thyroid. Her eye problems persisted, and they prescribed prednisone, an anti-inflammatory drug. While they tried to keep the dosage as low as possible, the powerful corticosteroid had troubling side effects. Finally, in January 1990, she underwent a ten-day treatment of having her eyes irradiated.

In public, she dismissed the notion that anything was seriously amiss. "She's just fine; piece of cake; never broke her stride," her press secretary, Anna Perez, breezily assured reporters after the treatment at Walter Reed with the radioactive substance.

That wasn't the whole story.

"She wasn't feeling great," Mohr recalled years later, in an interview at his home in Charleston, South Carolina, where he was teaching at the Medical University of South Carolina. "Her eyes were clearly bothering her. She had lost weight. She was feeling fatigued." More than a year after the diagnosis, in the summer of 1990, her eyes were still swollen and teary, and she was often seeing double. She was trying to wean herself off prednisone, a painful process. The steroid had weakened muscles in her right hip, forcing her to take physical therapy to strengthen them. "I confess I was in a lot of pain," she said.

While she almost never complained, her distress was impossible to hide from Sharon Darling, an ally in the literacy movement. "We visited a program, and it was way out in the boonies," Darling recalled. They were flying around North Carolina in an Air Force jet. "Her eyes were just killing her, just killing her, and yet she would stand there and let people flash pictures," Darling told me. "You know, everybody wanted their picture taken with Barbara Bush." She never declined to pose with them. Back on the plane, she would put cold compresses on her eyes. "She was in such agony."

Even after decades had passed, in the final months of her life, she was dealing with the disease's symptoms. "Mine affected my eyes to this very day," she told me at one interview. "I very often see you twice, not badly, just when I'm tired. And you're not bad-looking," she added, deploying humor to deflect any suggestion that she was fishing for sympathy.

In her memoirs, Barbara Bush expressed more concern about her dog's medical plight than her own. Her beloved Millie had developed a different autoimmune disorder, lupus. "That summer was a tough one for Millie, who had been limping and crying," she wrote. "At first her veterinarians thought she maybe had lead poisoning from the scraping of the paint off the White House walls. I was heartsick. It was obvious she was in pain, although she was, as always, undemanding and remained my shadow."

Then George Bush was diagnosed with Graves' disease too.

In May 1991, the president was jogging at Camp David when he found himself panting and unable to finish. The medical staff on duty gave him an EKG. His heartbeat was irregular, in fibrillation. Barbara had been swimming in the pool at the presidential retreat. She was hurriedly summoned and they boarded the *Marine One* helicopter for a short flight to the Bethesda Naval Hospital in Maryland.

"As I sat there, the most dreadful thoughts ran through my mind: *Dear God, this wonderful man must not die*," Barbara Bush recalled. He would stay overnight in a hospital suite as doctors worked to restore his heartbeat to its usual rhythm. He began to do some paperwork. "A little later, as he worked away, I thought: *Don't you dare die. I'll never forgive you.*"

Bush was treated with medication, and the doctors made plans to shock his heart back into rhythm the next morning if the drugs didn't work. That would require putting him under general anesthesia and invoking the Twenty-Fifth Amendment, temporarily shifting the powers of the presidency to Vice President Dan Quayle. Aides debated whether to announce that in advance; after conferring with Bush they did. (The procedure turned out not to be necessary. By morning, his heart was beating steadily again.)

The underlying problem was diagnosed as Graves' disease, the same disease his wife had, although the ailment affected them in different ways—his heart, her eyes. Like her, his treatment included drinking radioactive iodine. Doctors began drawing blood every day as they tried to carefully moderate his hormone levels. Too little would leave him lethargic; too much risked triggering his heart into fibrillation.

The oddity of both Barbara and George Bush being diagnosed with the same noncontagious disease while at the White House posed a medical mystery that was never authoritatively settled. The fact that both were under stress, perhaps coupled with a genetic predisposition for the disease, was the least conspiratorial medical explanation. Marvin's diagnosis in 1985 of ulcerative colitis was another indication of a possible genetic predisposition for autoimmune disorders in the family.

Still, some wondered if there had been an environmental trigger at the White House or in the vice president's residence, where they had lived for eight years. Or perhaps some aftereffect, innocent or nefarious, from their time in Beijing. Barbara Bush told me there were "all sorts of rumors about the Russians looking down on us." The Soviet Embassy was less than a mile from the vice president's residence, and built on higher ground. Had the Soviets been up to no good?

The water and air in the White House already were managed in ways to guard against contamination. The vice president's residence was built in 1893 for the superintendent of the US Naval Observatory and was obviously aging; Marilyn Quayle was concerned that the Bushes' ailments might signal some problem there. The water, the plumbing, the paint were tested; nothing notable was found. But there was never a full-fledged investigation into what might have contributed to both Bushes developing the same autoimmune disorder, and within fifteen months of each other, not to mention Millie's ailment.

Barbara Bush told me she was inclined to see it as just one of those weird coincidences in life. At the time, she reported that George W. Bush jokingly had called to say she "could end all the talk if his dad and I would just stop drinking out of Millie's bowl."

There was an unspoken reason some advisers weren't interested in unleashing an aggressive inquiry: They saw no percentage in focusing too much attention on Bush's diagnosis and in the process fanning concern about his stamina for a second term. "They didn't want people to think that they were going to elect a damaged president," John Sununu, then the White House chief of staff, later told me. "The campaign people were in mortal fear," White House press secretary Marlin Fitzwater said. In private, Fitzwater and some others close to Bush believed the disease was having a serious impact on the president and on his campaign.

"If they hadn't had Graves' disease, he would have been reelected, I think," Fred Malek, his campaign chairman, told me. "Nobody at that point recognized the depths of what that caused." He said the president "had the energy to get up in the morning and handle his in-box, but he didn't have the mental energy to initiate, to cause change." He found it difficult to respond aggressively to the country's economic challenges and to the political challenges presented by Clinton, whose campaign was emphasizing his youth, his vigor, and his empathy.

Bush realized something was wrong. He told Colin Powell, then chairman of the Joint Chiefs of Staff, that the medicine he was taking caused "a slowing down of the mental processes" for a time. During the campaign, "I saw a passive, sometimes detached George Bush," Powell said, not the vigorous leader he had been before.

Fitzwater, who was constantly by Bush's side, said incidents of fibrillation continued, sometimes leaving the president pale and tired. "He was sick," Fitzwater said. "He was a different person."

Barbara Bush's role was more central in the 1992 campaign than it had ever been before. At home, she was George Bush's emotional ballast, and at a time when he needed one. On the stump, she was his most popular surrogate, with a favorable rating higher than his. Four years earlier, some strategists had wondered how much of a political asset she would be. Now, he sometimes seemed to be trying to ride her coattails, mentioning her name at every opportunity.

Republican candidates down the ballot lobbied for her to campaign for them too. "Without counting the days, I know I slept more nights in a hotel room than in my own bed, spending day after day on the road," she said when the 1990 midterm elections were over.

Behind the scenes, as always, she kept an eye out for those she thought were giving her husband smart advice and those who weren't. "I used to watch her at dinners, and she didn't miss a thing," former Rupublican national chairman Clayton Yeutter said. "Her eyes were darting around the room, and you could tell she was sizing up this person, that person, and others too. Those Barbara Bush wheels were turning the whole time...and I'm sure all of that got fed back to the president in the bedroom that evening. She was probably his best people evaluator."

She was having second thoughts about Sununu, a powerhouse in the 1988 campaign. In a story that may be apocryphal, Sununu reportedly asked her why people took an instant dislike to him. "It saves time," she responded. His arrogance as White House chief of staff had left a trail of bad feeling. "I wish that John would realize that he just has to move on," she wrote in her diary in October 1991. "He is hurting the president." He would be out in December.

She complained that the campaign team lacked the sharp strategic voice that Lee Atwater had provided in 1988; he had died in 1991 of a brain tumor, just forty years old. George W. Bush was back in Dallas, now managing partner of the Texas Rangers, though he would often confer with his father. Jim Baker was otherwise engaged as secretary of state. To her dismay, Baker was less than enthusiastic about leaving the world of diplomacy to return to the blood sport of electoral politics. He wouldn't move back to the White House until August 1992.

To be fair, Bush himself was less than enthusiastic. He liked being president, but the hand-to-hand combat involved in political conflict now seemed small after the experience of leading a global coalition into an actual war. He put off those who urged him in the summer and fall of 1991 to appoint a campaign team, to get organized in key states, to more aggressively respond to voter anxiety about the economy.

To reassure nervous supporters in New Hampshire, the campaign dispatched Barbara Bush to register her husband for the first-in-the-nation primary just before the filing deadline.

On December 18, 1991, she flew to Concord on a snowy day, heading to the secretary of state's office in the Capitol for the ritual of registering and paying a $1,000 fee. Governor Judd Gregg welcomed her, and his wife, Kathleen, stood by her side. They had been Bush supporters since

1980; Kathy Gregg had been the junior aide assigned to travel with Barbara when she campaigned in the state then.

But now the political landscape in New Hampshire was as slippery as the back roads. The Granite State economy was faltering; the unemployment rate was 7.1 percent that December and would jump to 8.1 percent in January. Even allies worried that Bush didn't seem to recognize how anxious workers were feeling. A week earlier, conservative commentator Patrick Buchanan, a veteran of the Nixon and Reagan White House staffs, had announced he would challenge Bush for the Republican nomination.

When Governor Gregg introduced Barbara Bush to statehouse reporters that day, she cautioned them that she was not "the political member" of the team and said she would refer those sorts of questions to him. Not that anyone believed that, of course. And not that she did.

"Nobody suffers more than George over the economy, worries more about people who are hurting, and works harder to get something done about it," she declared. "And although I was warned by everybody that I shouldn't say this, I think I will anyway." There was a scattering of nervous laughter from the New Hampshire pols lined up behind her. "Although I don't do political things and I stay out of George's business, but for three years I've seen George present a growth package and ask the Congress to do something about it, and for three years they've done nothing."

The volley of questions that followed were versions of the first: How worried were she and her husband about the perception he was out of touch with the average American on the economy?

"As long as one person is out of a job and hurting, the president is going to be hurting," she replied, again attacking Congress for failing to pass his proposed capital-gains tax cut and economic enterprise zones. When she turned to leave, a reporter shouted a final question: "What do you say to Pat Buchanan who is challenging you now?"

She kept moving.

"Barbara Bush Fighting Mad in New Hampshire," the Associated Press account of the day was headlined. The story began: "For three years she's been a kinder and gentler first lady, literary crusader, best-selling author and everybody's favorite grandma. But with her husband down in the polls and derided as a Herbert Hoover by the Democrats, Barbara Bush brandished her political fists Wednesday in snowy New Hampshire."

The case she made for him turned out to be more coherent than the one he would make for himself a few weeks later during his first trip to New Hampshire for his reelection campaign. At every stop, he invoked her name. "I'm very sorry she's not here," he told the Rotary Club dinner in Portsmouth. "Everybody is talking about, 'Where's Barbara? We miss her very, very much.'" She was on his mind as he was leaving too. "I'm heading back to DC to see my dog and my wife," he said, then caught himself. "May I, with your permission, may I change the order? I just don't want to have any misunderstanding."

She had been plainspoken and direct during her New Hampshire visit. He was disjointed and frenetic during his. "Message: I care," he said at a town hall–style meeting in Exeter. "Don't cry for me, Argentina," he told a perplexed audience of insurance employees in Dover. He quoted lyrics from a song by the Nitty Gritty Dirt Band, mangling the group's name as the "Nitty Ditty Nitty Gritty Great Bird."

⌒ ⌒

By some measures, George Bush should have felt triumphant as he faced the 1992 campaign. He had led a military and diplomatic victory in Operation Desert Storm, which in February 1991 succeeded in driving Iraqi invaders out of Kuwait; his approval rating soared to a record-breaking 89 percent. By the end of 1991, in December, the Cold War that had defined geopolitics since the end of World War II effectively ended on his watch, and peacefully, when the Soviet Union dissolved.

But George Bush was anything but triumphant. He was embattled and often exhausted, struggling to manage the effects of Graves' disease.

Even history was against him. In 1988, Bush had been the first sitting vice president in a century to win the White House, propelled in part by Ronald Reagan's popularity. Now, after twelve straight years of Republican rule, many voters were eager for political change, and for generational change. On Election Day, Bush would be sixty-eight years old; Clinton would be forty-six, the same age as Bush's oldest son.

There were also broader trends in motion, and early signs of the political revolution that would enable Donald Trump to win the White House a quarter century later. In the Republican primary, Pat Buchanan would tap resentment over immigration, trade, and multiculturalism with a "pitchfork" challenge for the nomination. (Barbara Bush would accuse Buchanan of using racist code words.) In the general election, H. Ross Perot, with a populist message of his own, would demonstrate the power of a billionaire businessman to command the public stage, undeterred and even boastful about his lack of governmental experience.

Neither George Bush nor Barbara Bush could quite believe that Americans would choose Bill Clinton, a man who had dodged the draft and cheated on his wife, over him. In her diary, "I wrote over and over again that Bill Clinton did not have a chance," she would later admit.

But in some ways, Bush's greatest triumph—presiding over the end of the Cold War—made voters more comfortable with the prospect of electing the first president since World War II who lacked military experience, a candidate who promised to focus on health care and education and other concerns close to home.

George Bush didn't seem to recognize the anxieties many voters felt about their own lives, much less be able to propose solutions for them. Most Americans thought the nation was in an economic downturn; it was cold comfort for Bush when economists ruled a month after the election that the recession technically had ended in March 1991. Elsie Hillman, chairwoman of the Bush-Quayle campaign in Pennsylvania and a family friend, sent Republican national chairman Rich Bond a biting letter in February 1992 saying the talking points they had sent "did not address what the voters were saying." Bush's own statement "lacked sensitivity," she complained.

The president never hit an easy stride. "I've never been through a trial like this one," a discouraged George Bush wrote a friend. He seemed surprised that the accolades for his leadership on foreign policy weren't enough to persuade voters he deserved a second term.

Jim Baker had a bold idea to invigorate the flagging Bush campaign: Replace Dan Quayle on the ticket. He wanted to enlist Barbara Bush as an ally.

The former Indiana senator had been a problematic partner since Bush unexpectedly picked him as his running mate four years earlier. Quayle faced an early furor over his military service during the Vietnam era, and questions about his maturity and judgment had persisted. He didn't help himself inside the White House when he declared in a speech that Murphy Brown, a fictional character on a TV sitcom, was setting the wrong example by having a baby out of wedlock.

Barbara Bush was among those who thought the comment was ridiculous and the controversy that followed was unhelpful. "She just thought it was inappropriate," Press Secretary Marlin Fitzwater recalled. He would walk back Quayle's comments at the White House briefing the next day.

"In '92, we had to be seen as agents of change or we didn't have a shot," Baker told me in an interview at his Houston law firm decades later. Republicans had held the White House for a dozen years, and the sky-high approval ratings from the end of Desert Storm were beginning to sink. "They only way we could be seen to be agents of change, in my view, was to change the ticket."

Bush's campaign chairman, Robert Teeter, took private surveys that showed dumping Quayle would be a boost. Baker liked the idea of replacing him with Colin Powell, who as chairman of the Joint Chiefs of Staff had gained national prominence during the war. On the ticket, Powell would be a historic figure, the first African American nominated for national office by a major political party.

Baker talked to Bush, who said he simply couldn't be the one to push aside Quayle. The vice president had been loyal, and Bush more than anyone understood how difficult that could be at times. It seemed wrong for him to ask Quayle to step down—and Quayle was refusing to take the hint from others that it was time for him to offer.

"We kicked it around again at the campaign," Baker recalled. "I said, 'Well, maybe I can talk to the president about seeing if Barbara would do it.'" A suggestion from the president's spouse that Quayle put his own ambitions aside for the good of the president, of the party, of the country, would be difficult for him to reject. "I don't know anybody else, even W. [George W. Bush], that would have the influence on Quayle to convince him that he ought to help the president by doing that."

But when Baker went to Bush to suggest enlisting Barbara, the president rejected the idea. "No," he said. "That's still too close." It would be little different from Bush asking Quayle himself.

A few weeks before Labor Day in 1992, when the fall campaign sprint would begin, old rumors were revived by a new book.

A just-published biography of a Washington lobbyist included a provocative anecdote about George Bush dating to 1984, when he was vice president. A US ambassador had complained about being asked to arrange for Bush and Jennifer Fitzgerald to share a private cottage during an official visit to Geneva, the book said. The ambassador, who had died in 1986, told friends it was obvious that the pair were romantically involved. The *New York Post* splashed the story and the headline "The Bush Affair" on the front page.

Bush was in Kennebunkport, meeting with Yitzhak Rabin, who had become prime minister of Israel a month earlier. At a joint news conference with the two leaders, as Barbara Bush and the rest of the family stood to one side, Mary Tillotson of CNN asked the president about the report, saying she was raising the subject "because you've said that family values and character are likely to be important in the presidential campaign."

"I'm not going to take any sleazy questions like that from CNN," Bush snapped. "I'm not going to respond other than to say it is a lie."

Later in the day, in an interview on *Dateline NBC*, cohost Stone Phillips asked Bush if he had ever had an affair. "You're perpetuating the sleaze by even asking the question," the president told Phillips, threatening to end the interview.

Bill Clinton's campaign was watching closely. The Democratic challenger had been battered by allegations of his own extramarital affairs, splashed over the tabloids and covered in mainstream news outlets. "Why does the press shy away from investigating rumors about George Bush's extramarital life," Hillary Rodham Clinton demanded in an interview with Gail Sheehy for *Vanity Fair*, complaining there was a double standard. "I'm convinced part of it is that the establishment—regardless of party—sticks together. They're going to circle the wagons on Jennifer and all these other people."

Then and later, Bush's defenders described him as a principled man whose denials deserved to be believed. "There was no unfaithfulness" in his sister's marriage, Scott Pierce told me with some force while we were discussing Hillary Clinton, although I hadn't posed that question to him. One of Bush's old friends from Texas, Dan Gillcrist, told me that the rumors "really made me mad, because I knew that was bullshit." After serving as a traveling aide for Bush on political trips for years, starting in 1968, he saw Bush get overtures from plenty of women but rebuff them all. "I could not believe that he would be unfaithful," he said.

A member of the Bushes' inner circle, speaking on condition of anonymity, gave me a different account of their relationship.

When Dean Burch introduced George Bush to Jennifer Fitzgerald in the early 1970s, Bush was simply captivated, according to this source. Jennifer Fitzgerald was just seven years younger than Barbara Bush and not a striking beauty, but she was flirty and solicitous and focused completely on him. Their surreptitious romance would last for more than a dozen years, inexplicable to those around him and impossible for anyone to manage. A half dozen other sources told me that her presence created problems with other staffers at the CIA, the campaign, and the vice president's office. Several aides decided to leave rather than deal with her. The persistent rumors were humiliating for his wife. They fueled gossip that was politically perilous.

Despite all that, Bush for years was unwilling to distance himself from her.

When Bush reorganized his team in 1985 to set the stage for his 1988 presidential bid, Jennifer Fitzgerald was transferred to run his Senate office—still his aide, but no longer his gatekeeper. "I used to think she was terrible," Barbara Bush told Chase Untermeyer, who had been Bush's executive assistant. "Now I just feel sorry for her." Only when Bush had won the White House in 1988—and after one of his closest and most trusted friends pressed upon him that he had no other choice—did the president-elect agree to move her off his staff, according to the source, who was in a position to know.

Jennifer Fitzgerald was named deputy chief of protocol at the State Department, an appointment the *Washington Post* reported with snark, writing that she "has served president-elect George Bush in a variety of positions." She rarely made news again, except in 1990 when she was fined $648 for failing to accurately report on her customs form a silver fox fur cape and fur-lined raincoat she had brought into the United States after an official trip to Argentina for the inauguration of President Carlos Menem.

"I was very close to her for a while. And liked her," Bush told historian Jon Meacham years later, when he was working on his biography of Bush, titled *Destiny and Power*. "I knew she was difficult, and knew other people didn't like her. She was hard to work with for other people around her." Did they have an affair? "No," he said.

Jennifer Fitzgerald, living quietly in retirement in Florida, also denied it. "It simply didn't happen," she said. "I have nothing but the deepest respect and admiration for the entire Bush family."

⌒　⌒

By now, Barbara Bush was one of the most experienced pols in either campaign. This was the fourth national campaign that she had been personally involved in, including two when her husband was running for vice president. She could see that things weren't going well. "I am flabbergasted by this campaign," she vented in her diary on September 28, 1992, her frustration clear. "We are allowing the Clinton campaign and the press to walk all over us."

The Clinton camp had a tactical edge and an energy that the Bush team did not. Even the shifting styles of campaigning were an asset for the other side. Bill Clinton's willingness to field questions from young people on MTV and play the saxophone for Arsenio Hall fit the changing expectations for what candidates could and should do.

George Bush saw it all as dismayingly unpresidential. He mocked "weird talk shows." But Barbara Bush was among those who recognized that the landscape was changing. Four years earlier, she had provided a crucial voice urging him to air negative ads against Dole and Dukakis. Now she encouraged him to adapt to the demands of the new day, to connect with voters on TV shows where the questions were more likely to be offbeat and personal than focused on the federal budget or foreign alliances.

"Clinton's out there burning up the airwaves all the time, and she sort of encouraged him, he ought to go do it," strategist Charlie Black said. Campaign aides wanted him to go on the shows, but he was reluctant. Barbara Bush pushed him to agree to a proposal by CBS to let morning anchor Paula Zahn trail him in the White House one day. "Well, he didn't want to do that," Black recalled, but Barbara persuaded him. "He didn't want to be doing things that weren't presidential in stature," he recalled, but she reassured him, "You're going to act presidential wherever you are, whatever the medium is."

By the end of the campaign, he was waging his campaign on talk shows, much like rivals Clinton and Perot. During the week before the election alone, he made appearances on TV shows with Larry King, Bryant Gumbel, Katie Couric, Charlie Gibson, Harry Smith and Paula Zahn, Sam Donaldson, and David Frost. Not to mention appeals to sports fans on ESPN and country music enthusiasts on the Nashville Network.

In public, Barbara Bush was an upbeat and indefatigable campaigner. In private, she was preparing herself for defeat—worried that it would crush her husband, but not entirely unhappy about the prospect of heading home to Houston.

"This morning I am absolutely convinced that George is going to lose," she wrote in her diary on October 3, 1992, precisely one month before Election Day. "It is wrong, but all the press are printing such negative things. I will miss the White House life, but I can already feel a little splurge of excitement about going home to Neil and Sharon, friends, to play golf, and to setting up a home in Houston. I would die for my George, who has been a superb president and will go down in history as a great leader for the free world. The momentum is so strong against him."

A week later, she couldn't wait for the campaign to be over. "23 MORE DAYS TO GO!" she wrote on October 11, 1992. "This morning George said to me, 'The hill may be too high to climb.' I don't like to hear him say that, but I certainly have felt that he was going to lose. I have this terrible feeling that he is worrying about me. He needn't. Wherever he is, I will be happy. I will just hurt for him."

A few days later, a glance at his watch during a debate became a defining image of George Bush's political vulnerability.

As soon as Barbara Bush had arrived at the site of the second presidential debate, at the University of Richmond, in Virginia, she sensed trouble ahead. The Clinton team had requested a town hall–style debate, something the Presidential Commission on Debates hadn't sponsored before. The Bush negotiators agreed—a surprise to the other side, because the format fit Clinton's informal, I-feel-your-pain style of speaking, not Bush's more traditional manner.

"The spouses and families are brought in, and Barbara is sitting at the top of one of the bleachers," recalled Frank Fahrenkopf, the Republican cochairman of the debate commission and a former chairman of the Republican National Committee. The debate stage was set with three tall barstools. "I said, 'Barbara, Barbara, it's Frank,' and she turned around, and she glared at me. She said, 'Frank, this isn't *The Oprah Winfrey Show*. We're electing the president of the United States.'"

"And I said, 'This wasn't our idea to do this. Your people agreed to this.'" That was clearly news to her, and her face made it clear she didn't think it had been wise.

After debates in all of Bush's campaigns, the loyal Barbara Bush typically declared him the clear winner, no matter what. But even she admitted that wasn't true of this one. The Richmond debate "was the toughest for George," she acknowledged in her memoir. She thought the audience was stacked against them. "As far as we could tell, there were no businessmen or -women or any small businesses represented." She mocked the questioning; it seemed unfair to her too.

At one point, he looked at his watch—an instant metaphor that it was time for him to go.

"It was a funny set-up," she wrote in her diary, making it clear that "funny" didn't mean she found it humorous. "Carole Simpson, the moderator, asked George to answer first every time and then gave no rebuttal time. [In fact, Simpson rotated among the candidates in addressing questions first.] The questions were things like, 'Mr. President, do you care? Do you really care about people?' As George is not too great about tooting his own horn, he did not hit this one out of the ballpark and I think he knew it."

In the final stretch of the campaign, Bush's strategists began to see signs of a comeback. Then, four days before the election, special counsel Lawrence Walsh announced an additional indictment against former defense secretary Caspar Weinberger in connection with the Iran-Contra investigation. The scandal was revived in the headlines. Weeks after Election Day, a federal judge threw out the indictment, but the political damage had been done. (On Christmas Eve, Bush would pardon Weinberger.)

On his last campaign swing, Bush barnstormed from New Jersey to

Pennsylvania to Ohio to Kentucky to Louisiana and, finally, back to Houston. George W. Bush was aboard *Air Force One* too. The younger Bush hadn't been embedded at campaign headquarters, as he was in 1988, but from Dallas he had been a voice his father heeded. Campaign strategist Mary Matalin described him as "the No. 1 troubleshooter, the No. 1 political antenna, the No. 1 confidant of his father, the No. 1 problem-fixer."

"I tried to stay upbeat, but I had a sinking feeling that this good man would go down in defeat," George W. Bush said later. The next day in Houston, after looking at the early surveys of voters as they left polling places, he went to his parents' hotel suite at the Houstonian Hotel. "How's it going, son?" Bush asked him. "Not so good," he replied. "The exit polls are in, and it looks like you're going to lose." His father became very quiet.

Jim Baker talked to George Bush as he sat in the barber chair at the hotel that day. "It really shook him," Baker recalled. "It was hard. It was really hard on all of us, and particularly hard to lose to Clinton and to lose the way we did, with Ross Perot coming in there and getting 19 percent. We would have won without him. And we were moving on the last weekend before the vote."

There would be no comeback that weekend, and little suspense on Election Night. It wasn't even close. In the three-way race, Clinton won with 43 percent of the popular vote, carrying thirty-two states and the District of Columbia. Bush received just 37 percent of the vote, carrying eighteen states. And Perot received 19 percent of the vote, the largest share of the popular vote for an independent candidate since Teddy Roosevelt ran as a Progressive in 1912.

The president who had soared to the highest approval ratings in modern times had been ousted.

"He was 90 percent popular a short time before, but I sort of understood it," Barbara Bush told me, recalling that day. Republicans had held the White House for twelve years; the Cold War was over; domestic anxieties were on voters' minds. "It was okay," she said, then paused.

"Wasn't okay," she said, correcting herself. "In fact, it was very sad. Doro wept, I'm sure."

Doro Bush Koch remembered that night too. "We all gathered in Dad and Mom's suite to watch the returns," she said. "We were in the living room, and Mom was in the bedroom reading a romance novel. Things were not looking good at all, casting a pall over the room. Periodically, however, Mom would walk in the room and say, 'What's it like to drive a car?' And then walk back out. A few minutes later, she came in and asked, 'How do you buy an airplane ticket?'"

Like it or not, they were about to find out.

Chapter Seventeen

———*———

Evicted

They woke up at 5:30 that morning, just like always, even without set-ting an alarm. But there was no White House butler to ring that they were ready for coffee. The newspapers weren't delivered to their bed-room; they had go out and pick them up off the driveway. The dogs had to be walked and fed. Twenty-four hours earlier, George and Barbara Bush had awakened in the White House, and he had been the leader of the free world, at least until noon.

Now they were back home in Houston, following an eviction from the White House courtesy of Bill Clinton and the American voter.

Their final day at the White House had been fraught. Both braced themselves, trying to avoid breaking into tears as they said good-bye to the residence staffers and the grounds workers. "Well, this is the day," Barbara Bush recorded in her diary on the morning of January 20, 1993. "Both of us are ready. The news and TV programs are full of end of term stories about George, his successes and his failures, and 'The new begin-ning' by Clinton. All of this to be expected, but we need to get out of here."

Her pain was more than emotional. The day before, rushing to pack, she had rounded a corner into the West Sitting Room, slipped, and fell, colliding with the door molding. It was a bookend to a mishap almost precisely four years earlier, just before the inauguration in 1989. Then, she had tripped and cut her leg at the Texas Ball; the wound required a late-night trip to the Georgetown University Hospital emergency room and fourteen stitches. Now, closing the cut on her arm took eleven stitches by a doctor in the White House medical office. She was flummoxed when she tried to figure out how to wash her hair without getting her bandaged arm wet. Although, all things considered, that seemed to be the least of her problems.

The dawn had been clear, the day's events unfolding on a precise schedule. Suddenly, they were cast as the extras in someone else's show. The Oval Office, the horseshoe pit they had installed, even the bedroom was no longer theirs. "The awful moment arrived when the Clintons drove up to the house and somehow or other it was not as bad as I thought it would be," Barbara Bush said, taking a detached tone at a traumatic time. Both Bushes felt they were turning over the White House to a less honorable man, but they'd both had lifetimes of training in good manners. That helped.

"What did it feel like to welcome Clinton? I hear you were very gracious," George W. Bush later asked his father. George H. W. Bush replied, "I didn't have a choice."

Furniture and boxes already had been shipped to the house they were renting in Houston's Tanglewood neighborhood until their new home could be built on a lot nearby. (They had bought the lot in 1980, before they knew Reagan would put Bush on the GOP ticket and send them back to Washington for what turned out to be another dozen years.) Bush had joked that Barbara wanted to leave with the furniture. "He was right," she said. "Once we lost the election, I had tried to ignore the hurt and turned my mind toward Houston and a new life."

That was the advice she had given her family the morning after the election. "It's over," she told George W. Bush over an early cup of coffee, blunt as ever. "Get over it and move on with your lives."

After Bill Clinton and Al Gore had been sworn in, George and Barbara Bush boarded the Boeing 747 that he had used as president, joined by a handful of longtime staffers and close friends. Since he was no longer commander in chief, the plane wasn't designated as *Air Force One* for the flight home, that distinction now reserved for Clinton.

Both Bushes resented much of the news coverage of the campaign; they thought reporters had been biased against him. "I honestly believe that most of them wanted Bill Clinton to win," she said. Now they rejected requests to allow a press pool to accompany them as they left Washington. That was in contrast to the Reagans and the Carters and the Fords, all of whom had allowed a small group of reporters and photographers to cover their flights home, including in the aftermath of defeats for Carter and Ford. It was a rare case when the Bushes let hard feelings prompt them to reject a custom that was valued both by the journalists of the moment and by the historians who follow them.

Barbara Bush wasn't swayed. "The press complained bitterly to me that they were not being allowed to send a press pool," she said. "That amused me, and I told them that any one of them who had voted for George should speak up then or forever hold his peace. The silence was deafening."

When they landed at Ellington Airport in Houston, the Bushes were surprised and touched by the welcome. Hundreds of well-wishers greeted them at the airport, some holding up signs. A banner declared: "Houston Loves Barbara and George." Along the route to their new home, stores and motels had spelled out "WELCOME HOME" on their marquees. People stood along the roadside, some waving flags. Neil Bush's three children had lined the driveway of their rental house with yellow balloons and tacked up handmade signs across the doorway. Inside, friends had unpacked their boxes and filled the house with flowers.

"Everybody was so nice; I mean everybody," Barbara Bush told me, her eyes welling with the memory. "We were coming down the road. There was a truck and a couple standing by it, and they had a big sign that said, 'Welcome home, George and Barbara.'" The couple in the truck hardly could have realized that their goodwill gesture would nearly bring her to tears a quarter century later.

"I remember sensing a sadness," said grandson Pierce Bush, then a first grader and part of the family's welcoming committee. "It's sadness about something kind of magical coming to an end." He thought his grandfather was worried that he had let people down.

For the first time in his adult life, George Bush was waking up with neither a big job nor an aspiration for a big job in mind. Early in their marriage, Barbara had once told her new husband, "I can't wait for you to retire." He had replied that he couldn't think of anything worse.

What's more, they woke up that morning to an infuriating story in the newspaper, thanks to an old nemesis.

~ ~ ~

Nancy Reagan had made what seemed to the Bushes like yet another unprovoked assault. A *New York Times* column by Maureen Dowd and Frank Rich reported that during coverage of Clinton's inaugural parade, as the Bushes were flying to Texas, Nancy Reagan had called ABC News to deny an account of how she had treated the Bushes.

"It was the political equivalent of the hand-from-the-grave punchline of the Stephen King novel 'Carrie,'" the reporters wrote. Nancy Reagan had been trying to reach correspondent Barbara Walters to complain about something that had been said the day before. She was connected to anchor Peter Jennings on the air, then insisted that she talk with Walters. A bemused Jennings and David Brinkley, and a national television audience, sat by and listened.

"She insisted that, no matter what Barbara Bush said, she had given Mrs. Bush a full tour of the White House, including laundry chute, during the 1988 transition," the story said. "And she complained bitterly that the Bushes had never invited the Reagans back for a state dinner."

The Bushes were aghast. At the low point of their political lives, Nancy Reagan had made one more petty dig. "It was ugly," Barbara said. The next day, on January 22, 1993, Nancy tried to call her; Barbara made herself unavailable. But she picked up the phone when the White House operator called again, a day later, on January 23, and asked, wasn't she going to take Mrs. Reagan's call? Reluctantly, she did.

"She started out by saying that she knew that this was a hard time with packing boxes and all...but...and here I interrupted her and said that all was well," Barbara Bush recalled. "I told her that our friends and family had given us such a good welcome home and that they had pretty much unpacked for us, BUT that the thing that made it tough was having her say all those ugly things about me on the air. She said that she was just trying to explain. I asked her not to explain about me anymore."

The grievances of a decade, submerged for so long, finally erupted.

"I told her the press was outside my door yelling questions about her statements and that I was not answering, but that she had hurt me badly and I just could not understand it," Barbara Bush said. In fact, there were no reporters outside her door; that was a falsehood designed to give Nancy Reagan heartburn. Barbara reminded Nancy that they had invited the Reagans to the White House just ten days earlier, to present the Medal of Freedom to the former president—a ceremony that became maddening for the Bushes because of Nancy's machinations over the guest list, by the way.

Barbara was sure Nancy was calling for the same reason that she usually had reached out over the past twelve years: to make sure Barbara would back up Nancy's version of events, whether it was true or not, and to shield her from bad publicity of her own making. But Barbara was done with all that. Not again, she railed in her diary, punctuated by a trio of exclamation points: "Since I had said nothing and since I don't do that and since she had not thanked us for the reception, I just didn't feel like playing her game any more!!!"

Decades later, Barbara Bush told me the story with the energy of that moment. She may have been ninety-two years old and in the final stages of congestive heart failure, but she was still more than capable of getting steamed as she recounted their conversation from 1993.

"And we did have your wonderful husband to the White House," she remembered saying, "and don't you ever call me again!" Another phone line was ringing, Barbara informed Nancy. Then she hung up.

The confrontation was cathartic. "I have not talked to her since, but I certainly felt better," Barbara Bush wrote in her diary more than a year later. Nancy Reagan never called again—who would have dared?—and the two women never had another extended conversation, though they did see each other in passing at the funeral of former president Richard Nixon in April 1994.

There, Barbara Bush thought both Ronald and Nancy Reagan looked worn. "I was dreading seeing her, but she caring what people think gave me a kiss and we did not spend too much time together," she wrote afterward.

She added: "I better watch out I might get feeling sorry for her."

Barbara Bush knew how to go about setting up a new household. She had done that more than two dozen times during her long marriage, from a shotgun apartment in Odessa, in the Texas Oil Patch, to the grand US ambassador's residence in the Waldorf, near the United Nations. This time, she initially looked at some of the big houses near the Houstonian Hotel, where they had been staying for years during their visits to their home city. "It just wasn't us," she told me.

Instead, they built a house on the land they had bought back in 1980, a lot so narrow that skeptics had insisted they would never use it. It would have a big master bedroom and two guest bedrooms, an office for her, a small gym, a wrapping room, an elevator. "I wish that I had made the dining room bigger," she told me twenty-five years later. "We can get ten people in there. And I wish we had put a big bay window" in the living room. But all in all, she said, "it's just right."

Their new home was light-filled and unpretentious, its relatively small scale in contrast to the grand rooms they had been forced to vacate. In 2017, the house would be assessed at $2,035,705.

"Barbara is bustling—rental house...cozy and done," George Bush wrote to his longtime assistant, Patty Presock, on January 22, 1993, two days after arriving back in Houston. "New house—contracts signed, building starts tomorrow—Book contract, a major one, signed up and her computer is already digesting Chapter 1. Buying a car (Taurus, maybe Sable)—busy—and she's leaning forward."

He wasn't leaning forward, he admitted. "It's strange, it's very different," he told Presock. "I feel tired like I did after Robin died—and, yet, I've done nothing."

Barbara was establishing the household, refreshing connections with friends, focusing on the future. She quietly waived the Secret Service protection that was then a lifetime entitlement of former First Ladies; she wouldn't resume it until the 9/11 terror attacks in 2001. She drove herself around town in her new blue Mercury Sable wagon. "Look out, world," her husband joked. "Barbara is driving again."

George Bush would take longer to bounce back from his defeat. Only years later, when he was writing a book about his father, did George W. Bush realize how his parents had shielded their children from knowing how low George Bush was feeling. "It was surprising to me to learn that he took it really, really hard," he told me, adding, "They never wanted to burden their kids with their own burdens."

"It's hurt, hurt, hurt," George Bush wrote in his diary just after midnight on Election Night, "and I guess it's the pride, too."

The reality of his changed circumstances was impossible to miss. On Inauguration Day, after they landed in Houston and were driven to their new house with the customary police escort, Bush "got fidgety" and said to his friend and neighbor Jack Fitch, "Let's go to the office and see how they are coming along with the renovation." So they got back in the limousine, police cars in front and behind, for the two-mile drive to his new office. Some local reporters and TV crews were at the entrance; he did a few quick interviews on his way in.

About an hour later, though, when they came down to leave, there were no reporters in the lobby, no police escort in sight. In the parking garage across from the entrance, a single Lincoln Town Car and two Secret Service agents were waiting for them. "Then we joined the bumper-to-bumper business traffic going home for the evening," Jack Fitch recalled. They slowly made their way back home like any other commuter, nobody bothering to take a second look at them.

Bush's standing in public opinion polls was ticking up, but that was little solace. "Well, that's nice, that's very nice, but I didn't finish the job," he had recorded in his diary as he sat in the Oval Office one final time. He was sixty-eight years old, but he wasn't ready to retire, and he didn't like the fact that the decision of when to leave hadn't been his to make.

George Bush took responsibility for his defeat, though his allies had harsh assessments of Ross Perot and his independent candidacy, of special counsel Lawrence Walsh and his last-minute indictment on Iran-Contra, of Bush's own campaign operation, of reporters they thought were unfair.

In his paid speeches, George Bush began unleashing attacks on the news media so fierce that two former aides, Victor Gold and Sheila Tate, urged him to tone it down, saying the attacks were unseemly and out of character. Bush grudgingly agreed to do that, telling them he was starting a new 12-step program called PBA, which stood for Press Bashers Anonymous.

"Dear Vic, It's tough. Withdrawal is very tough," he wrote in a letter that he copied to Tate. Press Bashers Anonymous had been founded along the lines of Alcoholics Anonymous, he told them, and he described bashing the press as intoxicating. His audiences seemed to like it too. "I loved the roar of the crowd when I criticize...the opinionated, the self-appointed stars of TV," he wrote. It felt good "after all the years of saying 'thank you for that important question' when some bubble-headed reporter tried to stick it in my ear."

"I must say, it was much harder for him, imagine," Barbara Bush told me in an interview in the living room of her Houston home, recalling those days. George Bush, battling a form of Parkinson's disease, was wearing headphones and napping in front of a TV showing *Law & Order* reruns in the small adjoining den. "He wasn't grumpy. He just, you know, was restless."

They followed the pattern of a lifetime: When one of them was in trouble, the other stepped up. She had taken the lead in handling Robin's treatment for leukemia in 1953; he had been the strong one in the aftermath of their daughter's death. He had comforted her when she fell into a suicidal depression in 1976. Now, in 1993, after the worst defeat of his political life, she tried to pull him out of his funk.

"I am truly back," she wrote in her diary. "I, of course, have deep tinges of regret, but mostly for George. I have been so proud of him. He is not bitter, but just cannot seem to focus in on anything yet." She arranged social evenings with old friends in Houston and fishing weekends at friend Hugh Liedtke's house in Galveston, on the Gulf of Mexico. As she worked on her memoir, she would read him aloud diary passages from their past that seemed funny or poignant.

After eight years in the vice president's residence and four years at the White House, they began to adjust to life on their own. George Bush made his first foray to Sam's Club and returned with what his wife called "the world's biggest jar of spaghetti sauce"—which she accidentally knocked off the counter and smashed to pieces. "That was the night George and I made an amazing discovery: You can call out for pizza!" she said.

They also felt pressure to make money.

"I am looking at a car that costs $20,000," she wrote in her diary after a shopping trip that first weekend in Houston. "This will buy a small ford or Mercury Station wagon. In the old days that would have bought a Mercedes. George and I are shocked by the price of food! Wow. We went to the store on Saturday and spent $104 and had three bags full." (That kind of sensitivity to the angst some voters felt about the price of basic necessities might have been helpful in the campaign, when Bush was blasted for being out of touch.)

They had grown up amid affluence, to be sure, and Bush had sold his shares in Zapata, the oil business he helped found, for about $1 million in 1966, the year he ran successfully for the House of Representatives. Then, he wanted to avoid any appearance of conflicts of interest, and he knew he wanted a future in politics, not oil. Less than two years later, Zapata's stock price had doubled. "They made a ton of money, the Liedtke boys," Barbara Bush told me. "George got out early."

By the standards of most American households, they were well-to-do. But they had never been as wealthy as many assumed. For the lifestyle that they had lived and wanted to continue to live, and to be able to help out their children and grandchildren, they needed to build a bigger bank account. "We did not have a million dollars, let's put it that way," she told me. "Then a million dollars seemed like wham-o. But we did not have that at all."

During the years Bush was in office, the value of his investments hadn't kept up with the rate of inflation. When he left the White House, the $1.3 million in his blind trust had about half the purchasing power that his holdings had at the beginning of his political career. By then, much of their wealth was tied up in the family's Kennebunkport house, an asset that didn't generate income and one they would never consider unloading.

The details: In 1968, when he was a member of Congress, his net worth was $1.1 million, including $673,000 in stocks and other investments and $290,000 in real estate. In 1979, when he was running for president for the first time, his worth was $1,959,000. The next year, he bought a greater share of the Kennebunkport house from the Walker family. The purchase was a financial stretch for them; they sold their house in Houston.

As vice president, in 1983, his net worth was $2.1 million, including $879,000 in investments in his blind trust; the Walker's Point house was worth $950,000. As president, in 1991, his net worth was $3.7 million, including $1.3 million in the blind trust; the value of the Maine house had risen to $2.2 million.

After the election, in December 1992, their personal lawyer, Terri Lacy, joined them at Camp David to talk about the future. An expert on taxes and estate planning for the wealthy, she delivered a sobering message to Barbara. The federal government provides money for the office of former presidents, but not of First Ladies. Even so, Barbara Bush would have an influx of mail to deal with, and requests for public appearances, and more. Lacy had checked with the office of Betty Ford, who had moved out of the White House sixteen years earlier. Her postage expenses alone were still running $100 a month.

"I felt like crying," Barbara Bush said. "Everyone knew that I had never earned any money, as I had never seriously worked in the forty-eight years we had been married. So besides losing the election, now at sixty-eight years old I was going to have to make some money. I honestly thought Terri was slightly crazy."

Their personal finances were on George Bush's mind too. In their final weeks in the White House, after returning from the taping of NBC's annual *Christmas in Washington* show, they went for a walk on the South Lawn. With them were two couples they had invited to spend the night, Spike and Betsy Heminway and Kenneth and Linda Lay. (Ken Lay, the founder and CEO of Enron, would be convicted of securities fraud in a celebrated case in 2000.) A White House usher overheard the three men, walking ahead of the women, deep in conversation about what Bush was going to do next.

"I need to do something that'll make some money," Bush told them, "not a lot, just some."

He wanted to make money, but he didn't want to look like he was cashing in. Months after leaving the White House, Ronald Reagan had been blasted for delivering two speeches in Japan for the eye-popping payment of $2 million. The Bushes had cringed, both for the size of the paycheck and for the fact that it had come from foreign interests.

Now their perspective was a little different.

Steven Clemons had no ties to Bush, but he got a call from Japanese interests asking if he could facilitate a speaking package for Bush similar to the one Reagan had gotten: eight days and eight speeches for a multimillion-dollar paycheck. They called Clemons because he had helped arrange Richard Nixon's final trip to Japan and Korea; at the time he was executive director of the Japan America Society of Southern

California. He would later become executive director of the Nixon Center for Peace and Freedom. He looked up the phone number for the former president's office in Houston and dialed it. Bush's assistant answered; Clemons could hear George Bush in the background, still trying to figure out how phones worked. "Put him on hold," he could hear Bush saying. "Make him wait a minute."

To Clemons's surprise, Bush then picked up the line.

The former president was "definitely intrigued" by the offer, Clemons said. Bush called back after conferring with Barbara, who had counseled caution. "Barbara said we can do this but we're not going to do the price they want. We need to do a lot less and I only want to do one or two speeches, not eight," Bush told him. "Barbara doesn't want me to... do what Reagan did."

In the end, Bush didn't sign on to do the speeches in Japan, though he did deliver a lucrative early speech in Singapore. A year later, at Nixon's funeral, Clemons introduced himself to Barbara Bush in person and reminded her of the Japanese offer. "I'm so glad that didn't happen," she told him. They wanted to make some money, but not at the expense of his reputation. It was clear that her husband had relied on her advice.

There were other ways to increase their bottom line, including speeches in less controversial settings. George Bush delivered a speech that year to an Amway convention for $100,000, at that time thought to be the highest fee ever paid to a former president for a domestic speech. In that one night, he made half of what he had earned in a year as president. In 1994, he gave a total of 111 speeches and traveled to twenty-two foreign countries. Barbara Bush was amazed and delighted to discover that she could command up to $60,000 for a speech herself.

Their fears of struggling financially proved to be unfounded, even naive. They would amass enough assets after leaving the White House to finance a comfortable life for themselves, to loan money to some family members when they needed it, and to pay the college tuition costs of their grandchildren.

Unlike other modern presidents, Bush never wrote a memoir, though he did coauthor a book with former national security adviser Brent Scowcroft about the foreign policy challenges they had faced. While he was in office, Barbara Bush had produced two lighthearted books, one of them a best seller, from the points of view of her dogs. The profits from *C. Fred's Story* and *Millie's Book* had been designated for literacy organizations.

Not this time. She signed a contract with her longtime editor Lisa Drew for $2.3 million to produce a memoir in her own voice, the largest advance Macmillan had ever paid until then. The 575-page tome, based in large part on the diaries she had been keeping all those years, got mixed literary reviews when it was published in 1994, but it would hit the *New York Times* best-seller list for twenty weeks, including six weeks at number one.

Less successful was her stab at writing fiction. During her book tour, she had tea with best-selling mystery writer Mary Higgins Clark at the American Booksellers Association Convention in California. She missed writing, Barbara Bush told her. Try a novel, Mary Higgins Clark suggested: "She said that it was really easy."

As it turned out, Barbara Bush didn't find writing fiction easy, and she eventually gave up—though not before she had plotted a murder mystery that centered on two female roommates, one a flight attendant and the other a Secret Service agent. Given their busy Washington work schedules, they went to a "very discreet dating service" for help with their love lives. "All the men who dated the Secret Service agent ended up dead," she related later. "Guess who the jealous murderer was?"

Spoiler alert: It was the flight attendant.

～ ～

The publication of Barbara Bush's memoir in 1994 was one final occasion that would fuel Nancy Reagan's fears. How would she be portrayed?

She could hardly call and ask, given the conflagration that marked their last phone conversation. But Nancy sent word about her worries to Marlin Fitzwater, who had served as White House press secretary to Reagan and Bush, and remained close to both. Fitzwater called Jean Becker, who was Barbara Bush's research assistant and editor for the book; she later would become chief of staff for George Bush.

When Jean Becker relayed Nancy Reagan's query, Barbara Bush was sufficiently amused that she wrote a mock book chapter enumerating every slight and every snub, although she limited its readership to Becker's eyes only. Nancy had reason to be nervous. She had written about Barbara mostly in passing in her 1989 memoir, *My Turn*, but her one extended passage seemed designed to patronize, and to sting.

"First ladies have different styles," Nancy wrote, defending herself from the perception that she was obsessed with clothes. "But if you look back at some of my predecessors, you'll see that after a few months, even some of the first ladies who seemed not to care very much about fashion and appearance began to pay more attention to their hair and their clothing. As I write these words, this is happening with Barbara Bush. And it's only natural—once you find yourself representing the nation, on display and photographed all the time, not only throughout the United States but all over the world, you begin to dress more carefully. You realize that people *like* to see you in different clothes. They want to see you looking your best."

Five years later, in her memoir, Barbara Bush also mentioned Nancy Reagan mostly in passing. Her references were brief and positive, although a careful reader might pick up on her pique over the delay in getting a tour of the White House family quarters after the 1988 election. Nancy had invited her to tour her new home just nine days before the inauguration.

"On January 11 . . . she showed me everything, including the laundry rooms and upstairs kitchen after I asked," Barbara wrote. (The "after I asked" is the tell, along with the reference to the late date.) When she noted that she had converted the beauty parlor into a small office for herself and birthing room for her dog, she even added the context that Nancy repeatedly had demanded: "Pat Nixon had made it into the White House beauty parlor," Barbara Bush wrote. "And I know that it always irritated Nancy Reagan that she got 'the credit' for putting it in."

Nancy Reagan might have been reassured if she knew that Barbara Bush viewed *My Turn* as a model of what to avoid.

"Poor Nancy," she told me, her tone of voice not actually conveying sympathy. "I mean, why would you write a book and say *It's My Turn*? That's a little bit like someone who wrote *What Happened*," a reference to Hillary Clinton's account of why she lost the 2016 presidential campaign that just about everyone thought she would win.

"I mean, they're very similar: Blame it on someone else," Barbara Bush said. "Don't ever write a blame book," she advised me. For herself, she said, "I don't have anyone to blame."

"But you held your tongue about any number of people in your book," I noted.

"Good," she replied.

There were times when Barbara Bush didn't hold her tongue, of course. She sometimes prodded George Bush to take a tougher stance—to approve airing negative ads, for instance, or to be on guard about people's motives—and he sometimes urged her to take a softer one. At times, he would smooth her rough edges.

That happened when her younger brother, Scott, asked for help in supporting their stepmother. Their beloved father, Marvin Pierce, had married Willa Martin in 1952, three years after their mother was killed in an automobile crash. Marvin died in 1969; Willa would live for close to four decades more, until 2006. None of the Pierce children ever warmed to her, but Scott lived nearby and he felt a certain obligation to help support her after his father's death, especially as her eyesight began to fail.

When Scott retired in 1994, he reached out to Barbara. (Their older brother, Jimmy Pierce, an ardent outdoorsman who worked for outdoors and sports magazines, died in 1993. Their older sister, Martha Pierce Rafferty, would die in 1999.)

"I called up Bar," he told me. "I said, 'Bar, how'd you like to help me a little bit with Willa?'" She said no and hung up. "The phone rang about three minutes later. It was George. Says, 'Bar gave you the wrong answer.'" They began to chip in.

George Bush even moved to shield journalists from his wife's ire. *New York Times* columnist Maureen Dowd had accepted an invitation to attend a party celebrating the 2013 publication of *All the Best*, a collection of Bush's letters, at the Washington home of C. Boyden Gray, his former White House counsel. She was bringing Jill Abramson, then the paper's executive editor, in part because Abramson wanted to get a look at Gray's Georgetown mansion and the potbellied pig he kept there as a pet. Their names were on the guest list. When the two women arrived, Bush was standing in the main hallway and grabbed them.

"Bar will kill me if she sees the two of you!" he exclaimed. Maureen Dowd had written caustic columns about both presidents named Bush, though she had maintained a cordial relationship with him; Jill Abramson had written investigative stories when Bush was president about the business dealings of sons George W. Bush and Jeb Bush. The former president escorted them into a small anteroom, away from the other guests, to chat for a few minutes. Then they took the hint and slipped out of the party.

⌒‿⌒

In a turn that was almost Shakespearean, George Bush's crushing defeat in 1992 would open the door for George W. and Jeb to run for office themselves, and the sons' political victories would mend any damage that remained in their father's spirits.

Jeb had considered running for a Miami congressional district in 1986, but he decided to wait until he was more established and better able to support his family. He was interested in the 1994 governor's campaign in Florida, but he waited to see what happened in his father's reelection race first. "I was not going to run if my dad was president," he told me. "It was clear to me that it would be impossible, and unfair to him—put him in a precarious position as well. He had a job to do, and it would be a distraction."

George W. Bush had a similar view about running for governor in Texas. "Had Dad won in 1992, I doubt I would have run for office in 1994," he said, "and I almost certainly would not have become president."

Now both of them were free to cut their own course without the risk of disrupting their father's presidency. Their mother helped, behind the scenes and on the stump. Her famous Christmas card list and its thousands of names were tapped for fund-raising. The publicity tour for her memoir just happened to take place in the weeks leading up to Election Day in 1994. Of the eleven cities on her schedule, two were in Texas, in Houston and Dallas; and two were in Florida, in Sarasota and Miami. A reporter for the *St. Petersburg Times* asked if she thought her stop would boost her son.

"If it weren't a boost, I wouldn't have asked the book people to send me to Florida," she replied.

The results would be something of a surprise on Election Night. Jeb had always been the serious one, powering through the University of Texas at Austin in two and a half years and graduating Phi Beta Kappa and magna cum laude. He had married, started a family, and worked for a prominent Texas bank while George W. still seemed to be finding his way. But Jeb would narrowly lose in Florida, by 2 percentage points. (He would run again and win four years later.) George W. would win in Texas, decisively, by nearly 8 points.

Their parents had been in Florida the weekend before the election but they watched the returns from their home in Houston. "The joy is in Texas, but our hearts are in Florida," George Bush told reporters. In his suite at the Four Seasons Hotel in Austin, George W. Bush tried to find a quiet spot to take a call from his parents; he ended up ducking into the bathroom. He thought their pain over Jeb's defeat seemed to overwhelm their happiness for his victory.

Barbara Bush, for one, was amazed that he had won, and she was struck by how her son's future immediately seemed to overtake her husband's past.

"The day after the election I walked into the hairdresser, where I think I paid $35 for a haircut, and he stood there and said—regular haircutter—'I can't believe that I am cutting the hair of the mother of the future governor of Texas!'" she said two weeks after Election Day. "And I was like, well, how about the wife of the former president of the United States?

"When you're out, you're out."

Chapter Eighteen

—✶—

First Son

For better or worse, Barbara Bush and George W. Bush were exceptionally close and remarkably alike.

Physically, it was the resemblance between George H. W. Bush and George W. Bush that was uncanny. The side-by-side statues in the courtyard of the forty-third president's library in Dallas look like they could be depicting the same man at different stages of his life, rather than father and son. But in personality and humor and temperament, and temper, the younger Bush was more like his mother—a kinship that knit them together but also sparked conflicts as he was growing up and even as he served in the Oval Office.

First Ladies are scrutinized for what they can illuminate about the man in the Oval Office. (One day, a First Gentleman presumably will draw similar scrutiny for what he tells us about the woman in the Oval Office.) Their personas and their priorities, not to mention their clothing and their causes, are the subjects of curiosity, speculation, and analysis.

Even so, First Mothers do more to shape a president, from his values to his resilience to the way he relates to others. Psychological treatises have explored the fact that most modern presidents were reared by strong mothers; many had remote or absent fathers. Barack Obama's father moved back to Kenya, leaving his adventurous mother to raise him with the help of her parents. Bill Clinton's father was killed in a car accident three months before his son was born; his irrepressible mother was the formative figure in his life. Franklin D. Roosevelt's father died when he was eighteen; his mother was so close to her son that she moved to Cambridge to be nearby when he enrolled at Harvard. Richard Nixon worshipped his mother, calling her "a Quaker saint." George H. W. Bush was devoted to his mother, Dorothy Walker Bush, someone his wife once admiringly described as "the most competitive living human."

Barbara Bush saw much of herself reflected in her firstborn son, and he felt the same way. "I used to say I had my daddy's eyes and my mother's mouth, which is really true," George W. Bush once told me during an interview at his presidential library; he posed in front of the pair of statues. "We have the same sense of humor. We like to needle to show affection, and sometimes to make a point. We both have tempers that can flare rapidly. And we can be blunt, a trait that gets us in trouble from time to time."

"They're like the same person in a lot of ways," Pierce Bush, the son of Neil and Sharon, told me. "My grandmother and my uncle George's energy is very similar. It's very sharp. It's very quick. You have to be on your toes."

Barbara Bush acknowledged their similarities, though she cautioned that wasn't necessarily a good thing. "Unfortunately, that's true," she said. Why unfortunately? "Well, we both say terrible things," she replied.

Their connection, sometimes stretched but never broken, burnishes Barbara Bush's historic standing. Only she and founding mother Abigail Adams have been both the wife and mother of American presidents. But Abigail Adams died before John Quincy Adams was elected to the White House. She didn't play a role in her son's presidency. Barbara Bush did—a distinction she recognized. During the 2000 campaign, George W. Bush's first bid for the White House, a reporter shouted a question: What would it mean to her to join Abigail Adams?

"I don't think she was living," Barbara Bush replied. "I plan to be living."

"I was always impressed with the depth and longevity of the relationship," Dick Cheney told me in an interview in the small study of his home in suburban Washington. He served as defense secretary for the elder Bush and as vice president for the younger Bush. "She was very much a part of his life and the family. Always had the feeling that she was the strong, centered asset, with sometimes a biting sense of humor. But when I was with W., he was more like his mother than like his father. The personality he had developed over the years really tracked better with Barbara than it did with George."

Both were more combative than the elder George Bush.

In 1980, during George H. W. Bush's first bid for the presidency, a young Massachusetts legislator named Andy Card had driven the candidate back to Kennebunkport after a long day of campaigning in Massachusetts and New Hampshire. Bush popped into the house to go to the bathroom while Card unloaded the luggage. Later, Card would become a senior official in both Bush administrations. The first time he met George W. was that night, when he walked through the front door and straight into a shouting match between George W. Bush, then thirty-three, and his mother.

"Ugly words were being said," Card told me years later. "He is giving her lip; she's giving it right back to him. He's standing there with a Styrofoam cup, and he's spitting in it, 'cause he was chewing tobacco." Brown drool trailed down one side of his mouth. "She's giving it to him, and [saying], 'That's not the way to talk to me!'"

Then Barbara Bush noticed Card and turned on a dime. "Oh, Andy! It is so good to see you!" she declared.

～ ～

Barbara Bush and her oldest son would discuss the most profound matters of life.

As an adult, George W. became more serious about his religious beliefs. Evangelist Billy Graham and his family visited the Bush retreat in Kennebunkport in the summer of 1985, an encounter that George W. credited with putting him on a path to accepting Jesus Christ as his personal savior.

Over time, he was inclined to believe that only those who had done so could ascend to heaven. His mother disagreed; that view was too rigid, she told him. She offered to call Graham for his perspective. "I happen to agree with what George says about the interpretations of the New Testament, but I want to remind both of you, never play God," the famous preacher advised. Later, when the exchange became public during one of his gubernatorial campaigns, Bush would demur. "I believe God decides who goes to heaven," he would say, "not George W. Bush."

He turned thirty-nine the summer of his crucial encounter with Billy Graham at Walker's Point. A year later, he would stop drinking, a relief to his parents and to his wife, Laura.

When he was in his twenties, his parents had worried about the course their oldest son was on. It wasn't unusual for him to drink beer and bourbon and B&B liqueur, all at one sitting. He seemed more interested in having a good time than in settling down in his personal or his professional life. Those concerns were eased after he married Laura Welch in 1977, at age thirty-one. Their twin daughters were born in 1981; he was devoted to them. He stopped drinking cold turkey after an alcohol-fueled evening in 1986, just shy of his fortieth birthday and as his father was preparing for another bid for the presidency.

George W. and his mother would still sometimes clash.

She had started smoking at age eighteen, when she was a student at Ashley Hall, and finally managed to give it up when she was forty-two. She stopped smoking on New Year's Day 1968, her determination fueled by her husband's skepticism that she could do it. "For about six weeks I would wake up in a cold sweat," she remembered. She became so adamantly antismoking that George Bush warned her she was becoming "a bore" on the subject.

At the Republican National Convention in Houston in 1992, where Bush would be nominated for a second term in the White House, Press Secretary Marlin Fitzwater's desire to avoid Barbara Bush's ire fueled his search for a private place to enjoy a cigar. He spied an empty room at the end of a long hallway.

"I thought, 'Nobody's ever going to come back here,'" Fitzwater told me years later. "I lit up a cigar and no sooner had I got it lit up than George W. came walking down the hallway, and he said, 'Marlin, have you got an extra cigar?' I said, 'Sure.' So I gave him one of my cigars, and he lights up, and the two of us are standing there, huffing away, and all of a sudden...around the corner comes Mrs. Bush...

"The two of us, without saying a word to each other, did exactly the same thing: We tucked those cigars in our pockets," Fitzwater recalled. "She walks right up to us, and we're standing shoulder to shoulder, and she looks up and says, 'How's it going, boys?' And we both said, 'Fine.' And she kind of looked around and she said, 'Well, I better go.' She turned and left. Never cracked a smile."

As she was walking away, she delivered a parting shot: "Oh, by the way, boys," she said, "your pants are on fire."

George W. Bush had long had political ambitions. In 1978, he ran for an open House seat in West Texas, but he lost to Democrat Kent Hance. Two years later, his father was elected vice president, and the son's opening seemed to have passed, at least for the moment. Having the elder Bush in the White House didn't make it impossible for him to run, but his mother and others believed it made the political calculations more complicated.

That was on George W.'s mind at the Republican National Convention in New Orleans in 1988. In an interview with the *Houston Chronicle*, the biggest paper in Texas, he volunteered that he was more likely to succeed in politics if his father failed. "That is a strange thing to say, isn't it?" he said. "But if I were to think about running for office and he was president, it would be more difficult to establish my own identity. It probably would help me out more if he lost."

That said, he worked hard for his father's election in 1988, relocating to Washington for a time to be his eyes and ears during the campaign. A month after the election, he moved from Midland to Dallas, a stronger political base in the Lone Star State. He joined an investment group that bought the Texas Rangers, becoming the managing partner and public face of the team's ownership. And he asked an ally, Doug Wead, to prepare an analysis of how presidential children had fared in public life.

Back in Washington, Barbara Bush was a skeptic. In April 1989, at a White House luncheon with eight Washington reporters, she was asked if her son was positioning himself for a political campaign of his own in Texas. One of the reporters was the bureau chief of the *Dallas Morning News*, the dominant newspaper in her son's new hometown. "I'm rather hoping he won't because everything that happens bad with the administration is [going to be] young George's fault," she said. "I'm hoping, having bought the Rangers, he'll get so involved that he won't do it."

Message sent, and received, though that didn't guarantee it would be heeded. "For 42 years, she has given me her opinion," Bush responded when the *Morning News* reporter called him for comment. "I have listened to it—sometimes." He didn't run for governor in 1990, while his father was president. He waited until four years later, when his parents had moved home to Houston after his father's defeat.

Even then, his mother warned him that he couldn't win; she thought that Ann Richards, the colorful Democratic incumbent, was too popular to oust. ("That didn't discourage me in the least," George W. Bush told me.) She remained a skeptic until the end. "George is confident that he is going to win," she wrote in her diary in October 1994, weeks before the vote. "I don't think so."

He did win, an especially sweet victory for his mother since H. Ross Perot had endorsed Ann Richards. Barbara Bush held a grudge against Perot: She blamed his independent presidential candidacy, and the 19 percent of the vote he had pulled, for her husband's defeat in 1992. "You can say that he put his silver foot in his mouth," she said, smiling. That was a twist on the memorable line Richards had used in her 1988 Democratic National Convention keynote address to mock George Bush.

Speculation about whether George W. Bush would run for president began almost as soon as he was elected governor, and it intensified when he won a second term in 1998. "Mother, I'm really struggling with this," he told her as they walked into First United Methodist Church in downtown Austin on the morning of his second inauguration as governor. "She said, 'Make up your mind.' She didn't say, 'Run' or 'not run.' She said, 'Make up your mind.'"

At the service, the Reverend Mark Craig in his sermon described how God had summoned Moses to action. "Like Moses, we have the opportunity, each and every one of us, to do the right thing, and for the right reason." Barbara Bush leaned forward in her seat at the other end of the pew, caught her son's eye, and mouthed, "He is talking to you."

"It was kind of, as I recall, a liberating moment, because I kind of did make up my mind right then," George W. Bush told me. "Serendipitous, or maybe it was meant to be."

Barbara Bush says she found her sons' political campaigns more agonizing than those her husband had waged. "I guess it is a normal instinct to want to protect your children from being hurt," she said. The primary debates during George W. Bush's presidential campaign in 2000 were so painful that at times she couldn't bring herself to watch them, although she didn't admit that to him.

A Republican debate before the South Carolina primary "was such agony for me that I just could not watch," she recalled. "George did and kept calling, 'Bar, you must come and watch. He's doing a great job.' I just couldn't." She was working in her small office when the debate ended and the phone rang. It was George W. Bush, asking how he had done. "I lied: 'You were great!'" she said. "And quickly called George in the other room. I couldn't tell him that I hadn't watched."

During that campaign, she had to ask daughter Doro to explain the furor over something being shorthanded as "The Big C" question. What did the "C" mean? Cocaine, her daughter told her. George W. Bush was refusing to answer reporters' questions about rumors he had used cocaine in the past. Barbara Bush vented to friends in a letter. "I am sick of it, yell at the tube, and go into another room," she wrote. "My gut feeling is that he should not answer the question; not because he has or has NOT used drugs, but because what he did 25 years ago is not relevant now. Incidentally, nobody has come forward to say he did use cocaine, and I have not asked him, nor has his father." (George W. Bush never did publicly answer the question of whether he had ever used cocaine.)

George Bush had decided not to offer his sons political advice, but Barbara Bush said she couldn't make that promise, even if there were times they didn't want to listen to her. "I advise them a lot, but they don't—they just let it go in one ear and out the other," she said. When Jeb Bush was being inaugurated for his second term as governor of Florida, he described the process. "Now my mother, she doesn't usually wait for my call," he said. "She calls me."

At times, she served as a conduit between her sons and their father. In 1998, she told George Bush that George W. and Jeb were uneasy with campaign news coverage that praised them at his expense. He wrote them a letter reassuring them that they should feel free to go their own way, to establish their own identities. "Your mother tells me that both of you have mentioned to her your concerns about some of the political stories—the ones that seem to put me down and make me seem irrelevant—that contrast you favorably to a father who had no vision and who was but a placeholder in the broader scheme of things," he wrote.

"I have been reluctant to pass along advice," he went on. "But the advice is don't worry about it...No one will ever question your love of family—your devotion to your parents."

Even so, George Bush's feelings were hurt when it became clear that his son's campaign consultants wanted to limit his visibility at the Republican National Convention in Philadelphia in 2000, where George W. Bush would be nominated for president. A few months earlier, in April, strategist Karl Rove met over dinner in Austin with the Bushes and their chief of staff, Jean Becker. "He sort of intimated that we should not come to the convention other [than] to make the speech that a former President would normally give," Barbara Bush wrote in her diary. "He was worried about the picture. It should be the Presidential Candidate and the VP and their families."

They had been hoping and planning to sit in the family box through-out the convention, "to cheer him on as a mom and dad."

Rove realized it was a difficult conversation for them to hear, but he saw it as important for the political prospects of their son. "The objec-tive was to say, he needs to be seen as his own man," Rove told me years later. The younger Bush needed to be perceived "first as the governor of Texas and an aspirant for the presidency, and then as your son. There are so many good things about the Bush family that have put him in this place, but he can't be seen as 'mini-me.'"

The problem was "ironic because he's absolutely essential to his son's success. But if he had been too big, it would have been hurtful."

In her sons' campaigns, Barbara Bush headlined fund-raisers, cam-paigned in key states, and kept score. The year before the 2000 election, she raised more than $1.1 million for George W. Bush's campaign. After one primary debate in 1999, she wrote in her diary that she didn't "give a darn" about attacks by Gary Bauer and Steve Forbes, who had never been allies, but she complained about Dan Quayle and Lamar Alexan-der blasting her son. "The latter two really hurt," she wrote. "They are friends."

She did more than write in her diary. Lamar Alexander soon heard about her displeasure.

Alexander, a former Tennessee governor, had worked with Bar-bara Bush on literacy issues when he was education secretary in Bush's cabinet. He had waged a respectable bid for the Republican presiden-tial nomination in 1996 and decided to try again for the 2000 nomina-tion, which meant running against the son of his former boss. "I made a speech in '99 attacking George W. that by today's standard was very, very mild," Alexander recalled. He had questioned Bush's pitch that he was a "compassionate conservative," saying, "You don't beat Al Gore by trying to sound like Bill Clinton. People are tired of Bill Clinton's wea-sel words. If we want to win, we should give them straight, plain talk."

"Next thing I know, Howard Baker calls me," Alexander confided. Baker was the grand old man of Republican politics in the Volunteer

State, a former senator and White House chief of staff for Ronald Reagan. Baker and Barbara Bush knew each other from their time in Washington, and since then they had served together on the board of directors for the Mayo Clinic.

"What did you say about George W.?" Baker demanded. "Barbara called me."

"She didn't like it one bit that someone would even make mild criticism of her firstborn," Alexander said. He protested, "Howard, I'm running against him. We're both running for the same job." But it was already clear that Alexander wasn't getting traction against Bush. "I was doing so poorly by that time there was not much to say," he told me in an interview years later in his Senate office. "I just listened. I was out of the race within a few weeks."

She also served as her son's ready foil. "Speaking about Mother, I have learned that no matter how old you are or what your job is, you can never escape our mother," George W. said to laughter in the speech that began his presidential campaign in earnest. She was still giving him advice, he told the crowd at the Republican Midwestern Leadership Conference in Indianapolis, and the cowboys in Texas had told him he should listen to her.

Now that she was seventy-five years old, the old questions about how much of an asset she would be on the stump were settled. She was a big gun—a "silver-haired, pearl-draped howitzer," the New York Times said. A CBS News poll in 1999 found that 63 percent of Americans had a favorable opinion of Barbara Bush; only 3 percent had an unfavorable one.

Her final swing, just before Election Day, took her to Iowa, Minnesota, Pennsylvania, and Wisconsin, with three more states scheduled for the last day.

In the privacy of her diary, she expressed no more confidence that her son was going to prevail than she had six years earlier, when she had predicted he wouldn't be able to oust Ann Richards. "Miss Pessimistic (me) really doesn't think he is going to win," she wrote in mid-October. On Election Night, in the family's hotel suite, she sat on a sofa, needlepointing and listening through headphones to the audio version of a biography of the interior designer Sister Parish. When her son seemed to have won, she went back to her room, then returned when that outcome was in doubt. When it was clear that the election wouldn't be settled that night, she went to bed.

After a month of recounts and court challenges, George W. Bush did finally win the Electoral College vote, though he would trail Democrat Al Gore in the popular vote. Their son's victory for the White House was a sort of vindication for his parents, overwhelming any remaining bitter feelings from George Bush's defeat eight years earlier—and propelling both his mother and father even more firmly into the history books.

This time, Bill Clinton would be moving out of the White House and another President Bush moving in. The campaign and the recount had been "hard fought," Clinton recalled, "so relations between our two families were still somewhat strained on Inauguration Day" when the president-elect and his parents arrived at the White House before the ceremony on the West Front of the Capitol.

"Barbara seemed to be a happy and proud mother and was magnanimous in victory," Clinton told me. He was touched when she took a moment to talk to Chelsea Clinton, complimenting the twenty-year-old on how she had handled growing up in the public eye over the last eight years. Barbara Bush understood how difficult that could be.

On the night of September 10, 2001, George and Barbara Bush happened to be staying overnight at the White House; they were in town for meetings and a dinner. On the morning of September 11, they left early to fly to St. Paul, where both were slated to deliver speeches.

Then the bloodiest terror attacks in American history struck New York and Washington.

Their plane never made it to Minnesota, grounded in Milwaukee when air traffic control ordered planes across the country to land at the nearest airport. The former president and First Lady checked into a motel, took a walk on a public golf course across the highway, had dinner at a nearby Outback restaurant, and, like Americans everywhere, checked that others in their family were safe. The next morning, their son, the president, gave them special permission to be flown to Kennebunkport.

In Washington a few days later, they attended the prayer service at the National Cathedral, joining President George W. Bush and all his living predecessors. Later that month, they watched their son address a joint session of Congress. "I suddenly felt as though I had lost my son—he became yours, the nation's," Barbara wrote a friend. "I had a few selfish tears and tears of pride."

Eventually, though, after controversy over the Iraq War threatened to undermine his presidency, she began giving George W. Bush advice, including advice he didn't always want to hear.

George Bush had made a public vow not to offer unsolicited advice to his son, even when the issue was dealing with his old foe Saddam Hussein, and perhaps particularly when that was the case. "For the most part, I didn't seek Dad's advice on major issues," George W. Bush said. "He and I both understood that I had access to more and better informa- tion than he did." When George W. Bush called his parents, "mostly he called up and said 'hello' and 'how's your health?' and 'how's it going?'" Marlin Fitzwater told me. "He did not want any advice from his father, especially on Iraq, on the war."

His father "would just buy it; he played the game," keeping his coun- sel to himself, Fitzwater said. "But Barbara, if he asked her a question, she'd give him an answer."

In public, she heatedly defended him; so did his father. But in pri- vate, as the war dragged on and no weapons of mass destruction were found—they had been the rationale for the invasion—she worried about the course he was on and the voices he was heeding. Sometimes, her son chafed at her input. "I almost hate to admit this, but there were many times where I would say something to him and he would say, 'Have you been talking to my parents?'" Andy Card told me. "I would have said

FIRST LADY

George Bush, then president, and Barbara Bush share a private moment during the dedication of the Ronald Reagan Presidential Library in Simi Valley, California. (George Bush Presidential Library and Museum)

Barbara Bush at Wellesley College's commencement in 1990, with Raisa Gorbachev, wife of Soviet leader Mikhail Gorbachev. The choice of Barbara Bush as the commencement speaker prompted a protest by some of the graduating class and a nationwide debate over women's roles. (George Bush Presidential Library and Museum)

Barbara Bush and Raisa Gorbachev chat at a dacha during a state visit to the Soviet Union in 1991. Barbara Bush made a deliberate effort to develop a friendly relationship with Raisa Gorbachev, a step that foreign leaders say eased superpower negotiations. (George Bush Presidential Library and Museum)

George Bush and Barbara Bush together in the Oval Office, with Millie, Barbara's beloved English springer spaniel. (George Bush Presidential Library and Museum)

Barbara Bush reads *Brown Bear Brown Bear* to students at the Ferguson-Florissant School District in Florissant, Missouri. She championed the cause of adult literacy and founded the Barbara Bush Foundation for Family Literacy. (George Bush Presidential Library and Museum)

Barbara Bush sits on the floor in the White House residence with her grandchildren and watches *Frosty the Snowman*. Her progeny would later dub her "the Enforcer," a nickname that reflected her determination to keep them grounded. (George Bush Presidential Library and Museum)

Barbara Bush campaigns for her husband in Concord, New Hampshire, on February 17, 1992, as he was being challenged from the right by populist Pat Buchanan. (George Bush Presidential Library and Museum)

Barbara Bush talks to third-party candidate H. Ross Perot after the third presidential debate in 1992, in East Lansing, Michigan. She blamed Perot's candidacy in part for her husband's defeat for reelection. (George Bush Presidential Library and Museum)

Barbara Bush gives Hillary Clinton a tour of the White House family quarters on November 19, 1992, about two weeks after George Bush lost his bid for reelection. "I don't know how it happened, and I'm not over it yet," a candid Barbara Bush told her successor. (George Bush Presidential Library and Museum)

An awkward interaction of the living First Ladies at the First Ladies Celebration Gala, held on behalf of the United States Botanic Garden in Washington, DC, on May 11, 1994. Barbara Bush expressed admiration for Lady Bird Johnson and Betty Ford, but she sometimes found herself at odds with Nancy Reagan and Hillary Clinton. From left: Nancy Reagan, Lady Bird Johnson, Hillary Clinton, Rosalynn Carter, Betty Ford, and Barbara Bush. (Clinton Presidential Library)

AFTER THE WHITE HOUSE

Barbara Bush directs George Bush at a community service project in Philadelphia in April 1997. (*USA TODAY* Photo/ Robert Deutsch)

On the Election Night that wouldn't end in 2000, Barbara Bush joins her family at the Texas governor's mansion as results come in. From left, Texas governor George W. Bush, who would be declared the winner after a contentious recount in Florida; Jeb Bush, then the governor of Florida; and George H. W. Bush. (Photo by Brooks Kraft LLC/Sygma via Getty Images)

Barbara Bush accepts a challenge by *USA TODAY* photographer Robert Deutsch to stick out her tongue for the camera in 1994, when she was publicizing her memoirs. A decade later, in 2004, she defended granddaughter Jenna Bush when Jenna stuck out her tongue at news photographers in a picture that sparked controversy. (*USA TODAY* Photo/Robert Deutsch)

The closeness between Barbara Bush and her oldest son is apparent at an event to promote his plan to overhaul the Social Security system. Unlike her husband, she would often give her son advice when he was president, whether he wanted to hear it or not. (AP Photo/ Charles Dharapak)

George W. Bush had asked who had been the best First Lady in history, prompting Laura Bush and Barbara Bush to point to each other during the conference "America's First Ladies: An Enduring Vision," in Dallas on March 5, 2012. (AP Photo/LM Otero)

George and Barbara Bush admire the vista from their son's presidential library in Dallas at its dedication in 2013. Also present on the rooftop were President Barack Obama and Michelle Obama, former president Bill Clinton and Hillary Clinton, and George W. Bush. (Photo by Paul Morse/The George W. Bush Center)

The Bush family in Kennebunkport in 2015. (Courtesy of Evan Sisley/Office of George H. W. Bush)

Photo from Barbara and George Bush's seventy-first anniversary in 2016. When Barbara died in 2018, they had the longest marriage of any presidential couple in history. (Photo by Evan Sisley/Office of George H. W. Bush)

Barbara Bush, at age ninety, campaigns for her son Jeb in New Hampshire during the 2016 presidential primary. (Photo by Daniel Acker/Bloomberg via Getty Images)

For many years, friends who called themselves the 1925 Club had lunch on the first Monday of the month at the Bayou Club in Houston. From left to right: Barbara Bush, Ada Grundy, Bessie Liedtke, Barbara Riddell, and Helen Vietor. All were born in 1925 except Ada Grundy, who was born in 1924. (Author photo)

George and Barbara Bush hold hands during a concert for hurricane victims at the George Bush Presidential Library on October 22, 2017. She is wearing the star sapphire ring he gave her when they became engaged in 1943. (Photo by Pete Souza)

Author Susan Page with Barbara Bush in the Bushes' home in Houston at the first of five interviews for this book, conducted during the final six months of Barbara Bush's life. (Photo by Jim McGrath)

A photo taken before the memorial service for Barbara Bush in Houston went viral. It shows First Lady Melania Trump with George H. W. Bush, George W. and Laura Bush, Bill and Hillary Clinton, and Barack and Michelle Obama. (Photo by Paul Morse/Office of George H. W. Bush)

Barbara Bush's grandsons carry her coffin out of St. Martin's Episcopal Church in Houston. (*USA TODAY* Photo/Jasper Colt)

Barbara Bush's funeral in St. Martin's Episcopal Church in Houston. Barbara Bush had wondered whether enough people would want to attend to fill the huge sanctuary. They did. (*USA TODAY* Photo/Jack Gruber)

Kelly Yates, in College Station, Texas, was among thousands of mourners who lined the route of the motorcade carrying the body of Barbara Bush from the memorial service in Houston to the burial site at the Bush library on April 21, 2018. (AP Photo/Mark Humphrey)

Marshall Ramsey, a cartoonist for the *Clarion-Ledger* in Jackson, Mississippi, drew a cartoon when Barbara Bush died that showed Robin greeting her mother in heaven. Jenna Bush Hager, Barbara Bush's granddaughter, posted it on her Instagram page, and it went viral. (Marshall Ramsey/*The Clarion Ledger*/USA TODAY Network)

something that was critical, and evidently he had heard it from his parents, so he thought I'd been talking to the parents."

Barbara Bush didn't have an alternative strategic vision that she was urging him to follow. But she did worry that he wasn't willing to listen to his father or the foreign policy advisers he had relied on, among them former national security adviser Brent Scowcroft and former secretary of state James Baker. Both had warned in increasingly outspoken ways about the risks of a full-fledged invasion and then about the costs of doubling down on the war. Scowcroft wrote an op-ed in the *Wall Street Journal* seven months before the invasion headlined "Don't Attack Saddam." Bush was listening to his own team instead, including Defense Secretary Donald Rumsfeld, a longtime rival of his father, and Vice President Dick Cheney, who noted that the elder Bush's course had left Saddam in power.

Barbara Bush was incensed when George W. Bush pushed Scowcroft aside. He had been chairman of the President's Foreign Intelligence Advisory Board, giving him an influential platform to express his views, but at the end of 2004 he was not invited back on the panel. He told friends he had been "fired." She saw her son enmeshed in a controversial war that was driving down his approval rating and raising questions about his leadership.

"Barbara Bush is *allegedly* TICKED off at Dick Cheney, Karl Rove, Andy Card, nearly all of them—except Karen Hughes—for how her boy is faring in the hearts and minds of Americans," Steven Clemons, a foreign policy analyst with connections to Scowcroft and others, wrote in his Washington blog in December 2005. "The matriarch of the Bush clan is colder than the North Pole ice right now to those around her son who she thinks have undermined him."

Card would resign as White House chief of staff three months later. Rumsfeld was pushed out of the cabinet almost a year later, in November 2006. Cheney, whose influence waned in the final years of Bush's second term, told me he was never aware of any concerns about his advice that Bush was hearing from his mother.

She warned her son that Cheney was pushing him too far to the right. She thought the vice president had changed since undergoing heart bypass surgery. His outlook had darkened. (These exchanges were first reported in *The Last Republicans: Inside the Extraordinary Relationship Between George H. W. Bush and George W. Bush*, by Mark K. Updegrove, published in 2017.) "She'd say things like, 'Dick Cheney's changed,'" George W. Bush told me. "I'd say, 'What are you talking about?'" The decisions he was making were his, not Cheney's. "Mother, there's one president," he told her. "Just so you know, if you've got a problem with Dick Cheney, that means you've got a problem with me. And don't be blaming anybody else for the decisions I made. I made them all."

"He told me that," she said, and she got the message. After that, she was more likely to keep her counsel to herself, at least when it came to the war.

⁓ ⌣ ⌣

In some ways, George W. Bush's presidency would bear his mother's stamp.

Like his mother, he trusted his gut. He rarely agonized, even on tough calls. (As she had urged him when he was weighing whether to run for the White House: "Make up your mind.") Like her, he was blunt-spoken in ways that sometimes raised eyebrows; wife Laura flinched when he vowed to catch Iraqi leader Saddam Hussein "dead or alive." He was comfortable being around and relying on strong women. Karen Hughes had been his trusted adviser from his first campaign for governor; Condoleezza Rice was his national security adviser. He would appoint more women to the cabinet than any president before him.

"They were like mirror images in some ways, with a little bit of distortion," Karl Rove said of Barbara Bush and George W. Bush. Before Rove was the chief strategist for George W. Bush's two presidential campaigns, he had been a young special assistant to George H. W. Bush at the Republican National Committee. "They're both very direct. They have a great sense of humor. They're very smart. They're fiercely supportive of their families. But there's a candor between the two of them that's pretty powerful."

While some saw her candor as hurtful, Rove viewed it as essential—that is, "if you like knowing where you stand." With her son, he said, "she was the one who could speak real truths to Forty-Three."

It was rare for Barbara Bush to offer George W. Bush advice on what policy to follow; that hadn't really been her role with her husband's presidency, either. She rebuffed those who wanted her to lobby her son, even on causes close to her heart. When Sharon Darling, an ally in her campaign for adult literacy, asked her to encourage her son to renew funding of the Even Start program for family literacy, Barbara Bush snapped, "I'm not getting involved in policy in that way, and you know that."

But she did worry about whether her son's staff was serving him well, and she let him know when she thought they weren't. She saw some as manipulative or exploitative; she thought some of the neocons were pursuing an ideological agenda that wasn't necessarily in his best interest, or the best interest of the country. When Barbara Bush would call Andy Card, then the White House chief of staff, Card said her message was usually, "Don't mislead." She also would say, "Don't think you're bigger than you are," warning, "It's a privilege to work here; remember you don't have to work here."

Some of her son's advisers found her a forbidding figure, someone to be avoided. She could make a cutting remark designed to "knock you back on your heels," an aide said. When George W. introduced one of his speechwriters to her, saying he was working on a major address, she told the staffer, "Well, then we'll know who to blame." He didn't interpret the comment as an attempt at humor.

She twice created unwanted controversies for her son—once on the Iraq War, and once on Hurricane Katrina—with comments that were uncharacteristically tone-deaf. Both made her sound cold and elitist, the words of noblesse oblige, at odds with the down-to-earth and compassionate persona that had made so many Americans like and admire her.

In 2003, in the days before the Iraq War began, she said in a TV interview that she had decided not to be consumed with the fevered speculation about when the US-led invasion would begin. "He sits and listens and I read books, because I know perfectly well that, don't take offense, that 90 percent of what I hear on television is supposition, when we're talking about the news," she said. "But why should we hear about body bags, and deaths, and how many, what day it's going to happen, and how many this or what do you suppose? Or, I mean, it's, it's not relevant. So why should I waste my beautiful mind on something like that, and watch him suffer?"

She said she was responding to a question about whether she was watching for signs of strain in her son amid speculation about what was ahead, but her comment drew fire for seeming to dismiss concern about the US casualties that would follow.

Two years later, she seemed insensitive to the plight of those who had fled Hurricane Katrina.

"Almost everyone I've talked to says, 'We're going to move to Houston,'" she said after visiting displaced residents of Louisiana who were being temporarily housed in the Houston Astrodome. "What I'm hearing, which is sort of scary, is they all want to stay in Texas. Everyone is so overwhelmed by the hospitality. And so many of the people in the arena here, you know, were underprivileged anyway, so this, this is working very well for them."

She complained to friends that the furor over her words—"*this is working very well for them*"—was unfair. "I got taken out of context and was quoted as saying, 'They were all poverty stricken'...like they didn't matter," she wrote in her diary. "I did say that I was so proud of Houston and that all the people we talked to saw an opportunity to get a new life and had hope for the first time and wanted to stay in Houston."

She worried most that the controversy over her words "might hurt GWB," who had enough problems over Katrina without her adding to them.

Chapter Nineteen

—⋆—

A Second First Lady Named Bush

When George W. Bush became president, he was exasperated by the endless stories comparing him to his father, sometimes favorably and sometimes not. There were undoubtedly times Laura Bush felt the same way. It couldn't have been easy to have the formidable Barbara Bush as your mother-in-law, even before you succeeded her in a public role that had made her something of a national icon.

Barbara Bush was extroverted and outspoken, frank to a fault. Laura Bush was quieter and more reserved. Even Barbara's choice of clothing fit her personality, favoring polka dots and colorful prints that others didn't always see as flattering to her figure. Laura was petite, tailored, coiffed.

Their lives reflected their generations. Barbara Pierce had dropped out of Smith College at age nineteen to marry the first boy she ever kissed, and to become his supportive spouse for the seventy-three years that followed. Laura Welch graduated from Southern Methodist University, worked as a teacher and librarian, and didn't seem distressed when she celebrated her thirtieth birthday with no serious boyfriend in sight. Her sense of identity as a young adult hadn't been defined by a husband. She was less deferential to her mother-in-law than Barbara Bush had been to Dorothy Walker Bush. Among other things, Laura and Barbara sometimes clashed on discipline of the next generation, of the twins—Barbara's namesake and especially the free-spirited Jenna.

While she had chosen to become a teacher, a traditional field for women, "I never felt I was so traditional," Laura Bush said. "For instance, teaching in minority schools, you know, not marrying until my thirties. I felt I was in many ways very contemporary." In the 1970s, she joined a women's consciousness-raising group; she read *Sisterhood Is Powerful* and books by Betty Friedan and Germaine Greer.

Strains between mothers-in-law and daughters-in-law are hardly unknown, or even unusual. They are the stuff of TV sitcoms (think *Everybody Loves Raymond*), not to mention the Brothers Grimm, who included three tales about evil mothers-in-law in their first edition of nineteenth-century folklore. But the relationship between Barbara and Laura Bush played out on a public stage, and there was no template for them to follow. Abigail Adams hadn't lived to see the day her daughter-in-law Louisa Catherine Adams would become First Lady—although as it turned out, the Bush women would share some parallels with the Adamses.

After their tenures in the White House were over, Barbara and Laura Bush participated in a handful of joint interviews that displayed a bemused byplay and the occasional flash of family fission.

"There are a lot of myths about First Ladies and they're sort of a stereotype of every one, that you get stereotyped the minute you move in," Laura Bush said in a forum at the elder Bush's presidential library in 2011. "It doesn't matter what you do; that's your stereotype."

Even before Laura Bush had moved into the White House, moderator Richard Norton Smith noted, she was being portrayed as "the second coming of Mamie Eisenhower."

"First of all, let's be fair to Mamie Eisenhower," the historian said with a smile.

"Yeah, who's that an insult to?" Laura Bush said. "Me or her?"

"Insult to you," Barbara Bush jumped in.

"That was rhetorical," Laura Bush told her.

The two women didn't meet until George W. Bush brought Laura Welch home to tell his parents they were getting married, and soon.

Laura and George W. had met at a backyard barbecue in Midland in July 1977. Mutual friends Jan and Joey O'Neill had been trying to introduce them for two years. The attraction was immediate. They dated for just six or seven weeks before he proposed and she accepted. That weekend, George and Laura saw her parents in Midland. The next weekend, the newly engaged couple drove to Houston for the christening of two-month-old Noelle, the daughter of Jeb and Columba Bush, who were then living in Houston. At their small house, Laura met James and Susan Baker and then her future in-laws.

"They are perfect for each other!!!" Barbara Bush recorded in her diary. His parents had been worried about George W. Bush, who had just turned thirty-one, because of his propensity for drinking and his general lack of direction. Laura seemed to be a stabilizing influence—serious, sweet, and smart. "Mother was thrilled that I married Laura, and was very welcoming," George W. Bush recalled. Laura Welch thought it helped that she had grown up in Midland and gone to school with some of the boys who had been in the Cub Scout troop Barbara Bush once led. "I came with more recommendations than just her son," she told me with a laugh.

They didn't want to wait to get married, and they didn't want a fuss. After lunch that Sunday, the elder George Bush pulled out his pocket calendar and looked at his schedule for available weekends that fall. Laura was hoping the wedding wouldn't be on the weekend of her birthday, but that turned out to be when her prospective father-in-law was free. The date was set for November 5, one day after Laura's thirty-first birthday and just three weeks away. "There was no time even to order printed wedding invitations," Laura Bush said. "Mother and I addressed all of ours by hand."

George and Barbara Bush may have felt echoes of their own romance.

The attraction between them at that Christmas dance at the Greenwich Country Club in 1941 had also been instantaneous, their commitment to each other quick to follow. Their wedding had an improvisational air, too, because of World War II. Barbara and her mother had ordered engraved invitations, but they had to cross out the date and write in another when George's leave was delayed.

Even so, Laura found her early relationship with her mother-in-law puzzling. "When I married George, I had thought that I would be embraced by his mother every bit as much as he was embraced by mine," she said. "I had planned on being more a daughter than a daughter-in-law, but Barbara Bush had five children of her own. She was their defender first." They saw each other mostly during what Laura called "those harried Maine vacations," when the Bush clan invaded the compound at Walker's Point.

In Kennebunkport, Laura wasn't interested in participating in the water sports and competitions that were featured parts of the daily routine. "And what do you do?" Dorothy Walker Bush, Barbara Bush's mother-in-law, had asked Laura when she arrived. "I read, I smoke, and I admire," Laura replied, unintimidated. With that answer, "everybody sat back on their haunches with their mouths on the floor," Barbara Bush would recall. Laura's new brother-in-law Marvin joked that having her join the noisy family was as incongruous as Katharine Hepburn starring in *Animal House*.

"She is a darling even natured person," Barbara Bush wrote in her diary after Laura and George and their two toddlers visited Kennebunkport in the summer of 1983. "She reads a lot and is sort of interesting. Calls her babies dollies and talks to them all the time so the girls are very big talkers. George is very proud of them."

Laura, the only child of parents who adored her, was sometimes taken aback by Barbara's brusque manner. After the wedding, she had rarely gotten a personal call from her mother-in-law until a year later. George W. Bush had just lost a bid for a US House seat. Neil Bush, who had moved to Midland to help his brother's first campaign, had headed back to Houston and then off to graduate school.

"Bar wanted me to collect Neil's things, box them up, and ship them to Houston," Laura said. "With that, she was off the phone." She hadn't posed it as a request. "I had my marching orders, and I was fuming as I drove around locating Neil's things in the places he had stayed, as well as rounding up big boxes from the supermarket. There were no pack-and-ship stores back then. I gathered, folded, and boxed everything, and carted it all to the bus station, irritation washing over me."

A decade later, Laura and Barbara Bush would forge a closer relationship. George and Laura and their daughters moved to Washington so he could help with his father's 1988 presidential campaign. They rented a town house close to the vice president's residence. Every Sunday, they would walk over for a casual lunch. Laura and Bar would chat about books they were reading or take excursions to see an art exhibit that sounded interesting. "It was really a bonding experience for all of us," Laura would recall. "Until then, Bar and I certainly hadn't been close at all."

Away from the chaos of Kennebunkport and the conventions and the inaugurations—"those high-profile, high-pitched events where Gampy's political career was on the line"—Laura finally saw her mother-in-law as "a funny, warm woman and a mother who is devoted to her husband and her children."

Whatever their strains, they had this bond: Both loved George W. Bush. And both realized how many traits George W. and Barbara Bush shared. "Bush didn't have to marry his mother because he is his mother," a *Texas Monthly* profile quoted a mutual friend as saying.

"You have said he's, in temperament and personality, a lot like his mother," journalist Cokie Roberts said to Laura Bush at what was billed as Laura and Barbara's first joint interview, on ABC's *This Week*, in December 1999. The opening contest for the 2000 Republican presidential nomination, the Iowa caucuses, was just weeks away.

"Careful," Barbara Bush cautioned.

"That's right," Laura Bush replied.

"Careful," Barbara Bush repeated.

"Well, they're both feisty," Laura Bush went on, undeterred. "They both like to talk. They're funny. You know, I think there are a lot of characteristics that they share."

"And you said he's incorrigible?" Roberts asked.

"So's Bar," Laura Bush said.

"Exactly," Barbara Bush agreed. "I mean, I'm not going to argue with that."

—— ~ ——

Despite their differences, Barbara and Laura also shared some characteristics.

"They're both alike in that they were unbelievably strong defenders of their husbands," George W. Bush told me, ticking through similar traits. "They were both alike in that they protected their children. Laura is less irreverent than Mother could be"—although he agreed that Barbara Bush had set a high bar on that trait. He said both were "unbelievably nurturing," an attribute their husbands especially appreciated while they were in office. "They were both great First Ladies that way because the job of the presidency is tough, but it can be made a lot tougher if upstairs in the White House there was somebody who (a) didn't want to be there; two, was unbelievably critical all the time. Both of them were very supportive, not only publicly, but kind of calming privately."

Karl Rove, the top strategist in George W. Bush's two presidential campaigns and a deputy chief of staff in the Bush White House, saw parallels in three generations of Bush women, going back to Dorothy Walker Bush, the wife of Prescott Bush.

"You have Prescott, Forty-One, and Forty-Three, and what all of them have in common, every one of them married an exceptionally gifted, capable, and strong woman—every one of them," Rove told me. "Barbara is more outgoing than Laura, but both of them are incredibly perceptive. Both of them are really strong. Both of them are true partners to their husbands. Neither of their husbands has made a major decision, particularly with regard to their public life, without the support and encouragement and agreement of their spouse."

When George W. Bush became president in 2001, his father declared that he wasn't going to offer advice unless his son asked for it, a promise the elder George Bush kept even when he was worried the younger George Bush was headed off-track. But Barbara Bush sometimes weighed in with both the new president and the new First Lady. The time would come when each of them would push back.

For Laura Bush, that moment came sooner than it did for her husband.

Early in the new administration, Barbara Bush heard complaints about Laura Bush's top staffer. Andi Ball had been highly regarded as chief of staff of George W. Bush's gubernatorial office, but she was new to Washington, and she was struggling in the same role for the First Lady. Relations between the East Wing and the West Wing were fraying.

Barbara Bush sent word that Laura Bush should replace Andi Ball. Laura Bush sent word back that it wasn't her call to make. The message was clear, a boundary drawn.

At the beginning of George W. Bush's first term, there were sometimes tensions between the current First Lady and the former one, according to someone who had conversations about it with both the elder and the younger presidents Bush. But in the end, he said, "they came to a good place." Barbara Bush backed off—on official matters, if not family ones.

"If you know her at all, you know she would probably really love to give advice," Laura Bush said of her mother-in-law. But Barbara Bush was herself "the daughter-in-law of a very strong...mother-in-law and I think she knows that daughter-in-laws don't really want a lot of advice." After all, as a bride Barbara Bush had moved to Texas from New England, away from the realm of her husband's mother. She revered Dorothy Walker Bush, but she also wanted to cut her own path.

Barbara Bush told me that she realized Laura didn't need her advice. "She saw it for years, and she was the governor's wife," she said, adding, "She's much smarter than I am."

Laura Bush had a stronger sense of self, and a stiffer spine, than her reserved manner might indicate. When asked during the 2000 campaign whether as First Lady she would follow the role model set by Barbara Bush or Hillary Clinton, she replied, "I think I'll just be Laura Bush."

Her tenure in the White House, like that of her husband, was reshaped by the September 11 terrorist attacks on New York and Washington eight months after his inauguration, and by the long wars in Iraq and Afghanistan that followed. She adopted the cause of women and girls in Afghanistan while she was in the White House and continued it after she left. Working with the Librarian of Congress, she also helped establish the National Book Festival, similar to the Texas Book Festival she had founded when her husband was governor. But she was a less forceful and less quotable national figure than Barbara Bush, and her poll ratings were never as high as her mother-in-law's had been.

Any friction between the two women was more likely to be over personal matters than political ones.

Laura Bush didn't always appreciate her mother-in-law's sharp tongue. "People think she's a sweet, grandmotherly, Aunt Bea type," she told the White House Correspondents Dinner in a humorous speech in 2005. "She's actually more like Don Corleone."

"She was very, very strong; I think people know that. She had a strong personality," Laura Bush later told me. "She did say things that hurt people's feelings. Everyone I know has an example of something she said to them that they'll never forget—in a bad way," she said with a laugh. "On the other hand, people forgave her. You knew it was just that she didn't have a filter, in a way, and that none of it was meant in a mean way. She would point out things maybe that people didn't want to hear."

She added, "But I think in a lot of ways those things made her more lovable and, in a sense, pointed to her vulnerabilities," sometimes signaling her sensitivities about herself.

I asked Barbara Bush about a line in Laura Bush's 2010 memoir, *Spoken from the Heart*. She wrote that her mother-in-law had "managed to insult nearly all of my friends with one or another perfectly timed acerbic comment."

"Oh, only one friend," Barbara Bush responded dismissively. One of

Laura Bush's friends had written her to complain after Jenna Bush had been photographed sticking out her tongue at the press during the 2004 campaign. She should do something about her granddaughter's behavior, the friend said. "My answer was, '99 percent of America would like to stick their tongue out at the press.' Sorry. That hurt her friend's feelings."

Barbara Bush didn't mention the rest of the letter to me. "She ended with her own zinger," Jenna Bush recalled. Which was this: "If this woman were a true friend, she should support my mother and mind her own damn business."

While Barbara Bush defended her granddaughter on that occasion, at other times she raised concerns with her son and daughter-in-law that they weren't imposing strict enough discipline on their daughters. "Were there some moments of tension?" George W. Bush said. "Perhaps, particularly if Mother criticized our daughters, which she occasionally would do. And our daughters were very strong-willed young women, starting as very strong-willed young teenage women. Laura would, of course, always side with the girls, no matter what the conflict was."

It was "head-butting by strong-willed women," the former president said. "Look, the girls, when they were teens, they could ruffle feathers, and Mother's feathers could be easily ruffled."

Laura Bush said her mother-in-law was careful about not giving her unsolicited advice, although she felt less restraint with her other daughters-in-law. "When I did something that she didn't approve of, my mother-in-law would give me 'the look' or would just by her attitude show her displeasure," said Columba Bush, Jeb's wife. While it was always in the context of being in a loving family, she told me, "I could feel it."

Barbara Bush was even more outspoken toward the next generation. "She felt it was her responsibility and right as a grandmother to point out different things she wanted to point out to grandchildren," Laura Bush said, "and not always telling them things they wanted to hear."

Jenna and Barbara sometimes defied the house rules at Kennebunkport, and they gave the agents in their Secret Service details trouble, making it harder for them to do their jobs. Their grandmother told their parents they should rein them in—for instance, when the girls were cited for underage drinking in Austin in the summer of 2001, soon after their father had taken office. Their parents were more inclined to give the girls freedom, and they were disinclined to turn over parenting decisions to her.

"The thing that really bothered me or bothers me is the fact that the girls (especially Jenna) are rude to their Mo[m] and dad," Barbara Bush vented in her diary. She wrote a letter to her granddaughters, castigating them for behaving recklessly and urging them to think about the consequences for their father when they acted out. "I felt that someone had to make the girls think of someone other than themselves," she wrote.

She was anguished about sending the letter. "I suspect the girls will never like me again," she worried. But she did send it.

For the record, they may have been unhappy about the letter, but their affection wasn't broken for the woman Jenna would later describe as "my strong, impulsively hilarious grandmother."

— —

The only other pair of First Ladies with a mother-in-law/daughter-in-law relationship was Abigail Adams and Louisa Adams.

Abigail Adams was an influential adviser to husband John Adams and a force in the lives of her sons. Louisa Catherine Adams, the wife of John Quincy Adams, was shy, beautiful, and musical. The relationship between the two women was never easy. When she was traveling to meet her in-laws for the first time, Louisa felt a "sense of dread approximat[ing] that of a prisoner headed to the gallows." Afterward, she wrote pointedly that while John Adams liked her, "He was the only one."

Her mother-in-law had warned her son against "spoiled and weak" women, and it was clear she thought that description might apply to her daughter-in-law. She was pretty, Abigail said of Louisa, but was she an American? Louisa had been born in London, the daughter of an

American consul, a merchant married to an English woman. (Louisa Adams was the only First Lady to be born outside the United States or the Thirteen Colonies until 2017, when the Slovenian-born Melania Trump moved into the White House.)

Indeed, when Louisa visited the Adams home in Quincy, Massachusetts, she found it filled with provincial and eccentric characters. "Had I steped [*sic*] into Noah's Ark I do-not think I could have been more utterly astonished," she wrote.

Abigail Adams would become a modern feminist icon, in part for her memorable entreaty to her husband to "remember the ladies" when forging the new nation. But she believed her place was in the home, and when her husband was president she spent much of her time in Quincy. In a way, Louisa provided more of a feminist model, not only advising her husband but also seeking a public profile. She was a significant figure in Washington life for three decades, and "proved her mettle," Laura Bush wrote in the foreword to a collection of Louisa Adams's writings, published in 2014.

"Louisa quickly discovered that she had married into a family of strong-minded souls," Laura Bush wrote, words that could have applied to herself. "Where she was quiet and demure, raised to listen rather than speak, her in-laws were used to free-flowing political debates and strong-minded women. Her ever-practical mother-in-law considered Louisa a 'fine lady,' a phrase that Abigail Adams may not have meant as a compliment." But Louisa "found her own strengths."

Years after Abigail Adams died in 1818, Louisa's attitude toward her softened. "We did not understand one-another; and half of the enjoyment I might have possessed...was lost to me in the paltry rival jealousies of those, whose interest it was to deceive her," her daughter-in-law wrote. She said she had gained new insight after reading a collection of Abigail Adams's letters, published in 1840.

"We are struck by the vast and varied powers of her mind; the full benevolence of an excellent heart and the strength of her reasoning capacity—Full of energy, buoyant and elastic," she wrote in a remarkable ode to her mother-in-law. "We see her ever as the guiding Planet around which all revolved, performing their separate duties only by the impulse of her magnetic power, which diffused a mild and glowing radiance over all who moved within the sphere of her fascinating attraction."

Four months after Barbara Bush's death, Laura Bush mused about the force that her own mother-in-law had displayed.

"I admired that she was so natural," she said. "She didn't dye her hair and she wore pearls to cover the wrinkles on her neck, and I think that appealed to the American people. She was so self-deprecating," and so candid. "I think that sort of candor that Bar had led people to talk to her and to tell her things they might not have told other people, or admitted to other people. She made them feel they could do that."

Chapter Twenty

———★———

Dynasty

When George P. Bush graduated from the University of Texas Law School in 2003, he thought about running for office in Texas. He had the heritage: His father had just started his second term as governor of Florida. He shared a first and last name with two former presidents, his grandfather and his uncle, the three of them differentiated by their middle initials. His middle initial was "P," for "Prescott," which happened to be the name of his great-grandfather, who had been a US senator.

When he wanted advice, he went to his grandmother.

Don't do it, Barbara Bush told him. "Don't ride on a name," she said. "Don't ride on somebody else's coattails. Make a name for yourself. Have your own identity. Marry somebody great." He took her counsel. He didn't run, not yet. He got married and started a family. He joined a big law firm, Akin Gump Strauss Hauer & Feld LLP, then cofounded a real estate and private equity firm, and an investment firm focused on oil and gas. He enlisted in the US Navy Reserve as an intelligence officer, eventually serving in Afghanistan.

A decade later, at age thirty-eight, he was ready to run. He won statewide election as Texas land commissioner in 2014 and reelection in 2018. In the final months of her life, his grandmother followed the 2018 primary challenge by a Tea Party candidate with alacrity. "Hey, Pops, George P. is going to tell you about his race," she said when he visited his grandfather in the hospital. She urged George P., "Talk about the nasty things he's been saying about you on Twitter."

But a dynasty?

Barbara Pierce Bush reacted to the suggestion that she led a dynasty as though it were a dirty word. It dripped with entitlement, a signal that the next generation didn't need to work quite so hard. That was neither her view nor the message she tried to convey to George P. or the rest of her progeny. Don't ride on your name, she warned them. Have your own identity. And marry somebody great.

Many Americans saw Barbara as the nation's grandmother, white-haired and kindly, if also blunt. For the generation of seventeen Bush cousins, she actually *was* their grandmother; they saw her as someone who was demanding and commanding, if also loving. And not much of a cook, by the way, another reality at odds with the assumptions that outsiders made.

"One woman recently came up to me as I was boarding a flight and said, 'I always dreamed of having a grandmother like yours! She seems like the type of woman who bakes amazing cookies,'" Jenna Bush Hager said. "I laughed. I can honestly say that I have never tasted a cookie made by my grandmother. Or a cake, or a pie. I cannot remember Barbara Bush ever baking anything."

During summers in Kennebunkport, Barbara Bush didn't do much baking, but she did call the shots. "She was the boss," Pierce Bush, the son of Neil and Sharon, told me.

"It was on the back of every bedroom door—there's a list of chores that you have to do every day," Marshall, the daughter of Marvin and Margaret, told me. "It says, literally, 'These are the rules of Walker's Point: One, do not leave wet towels on the floor...Do not leave clothes on the floor. If you need to do laundry, either ask Paula if you're too young to know how to do it, or you do it. [Paula Rendon was the house-keeper.] Don't leave half-empty Coke cans.'" The issue of opened and unfinished sodas was a pet peeve, Marshall noted. "She hates that more than anything."

"We didn't have someone that cooked us breakfast—that was another thing that's on there. 'Breakfast is between 5:30 AM and 8:30 AM. If you miss it, too bad. Figure it out.'"

In many families, grandparents spoil their grandchildren, sometimes over the objections of their parents. In the Bush clan, Barbara Bush disciplined her grandchildren, sometimes over the objections of their parents. "When they were young, she helped teach them what was right and what was wrong," Columba Bush, married to Jeb and the mother of George P., Noelle, and Jebby, told me. "As they got older, she taught them to serve others and the importance of family."

Barbara Bush had the saccharine nickname of Ganny and she called her grandchildren "the Grands," but she showed the next generation the same steel spine she had displayed in rearing her own children. At times, that led to clashes and hurt feelings. There was no doubt about this: She set the rules at her house, and she enforced them.

The cousins could invite friends over when they were visiting in Maine, but they had to get permission first. "It's fine, bring whoever you want, but you have to ask," Marshall said. "I forgot to ask, so I got in trouble" when a friend showed up. "I was not allowed to have any guests for the rest of the summer." Lesson learned.

Another ironclad rule: Ask before you use her car. "My grandmother had just had double knee surgery, and she had one really specific rule: If you want to borrow her Smart Car, which was her new toy, you had to ask her permission," Pierce recalled. "Well, she was, like, sleeping, so I thought it'd be cool if Robert [Koch, his cousin] and I went to Dairy Queen." A frantic phone call from his father followed. "Pierce, where are you?" Neil Bush demanded. "Ganny's really mad because you did not ask for permission for the Smart Car." After Pierce hurried back, he got what he called "a lashing"—verbal, not physical, but stinging nonetheless.

Her ire wasn't manufactured. A decade later, Barbara Bush remembered the incident as clearly as Pierce did. "I was so damn mad at him when he took my car without asking," she told me.

Then there was the summer that Robert Koch, the son of Doro and Bobby, kept raiding the freezer that was stocked with ice cream bars. The unwritten rule was that each grandchild could have a Klondike bar after lunch. "They were kind of dissipating at a faster rate than normal," Robert recalled, "and that was due to me. And Ganny kind of gave me a warning, like, 'You're eating a few too many Klondike bars; you've got to slow it down.' And I would continue to sneak the Klondike bars until, finally, one day I went to sneak one—and there's a padlock on the freezer."

He called it "classic Gans."

In the privacy of her diaries, Barbara Bush gushed about her grandchildren in ways that might have surprised them—how beautiful this one looked, how sweet and smart this one was. There were times when she worried about whether their various parents were following the right course, were teaching the right values. This child needed more attention, she thought, and this one more discipline. She was outraged when a friend of Jebby told her that her grandson had been singled out by police officers for harassment, apparently because he was Hispanic; later, in an interview, she would tear up recalling the bigotry he and his brother had encountered.

And she anguished over Noelle, the daughter of Jeb and Columba, who struggled with substance abuse and mental illness. No other grandchild prompted more diary entries. Like many Americans who have faced similar family crises, Barbara Bush felt powerless to make things better, or to slay the demons that afflicted someone close to her. She had faced dark times of her own when she had battled depression. All she could do, she eventually concluded, was offer the granddaughter she affectionately called Nosy her love and pray for the best, so that's what she did.

In public, Barbara Bush might go a little easy on a grandchild caught in a tough patch. "She's gentler with people that I think really are going through more difficult times," Pierce Bush told me. "I don't hear the sharpness so much." But with others, she could be caustic in ways that left wounds. She could bring her daughter, Doro, and some of her grandchildren to tears when she nagged them about their weight, about needing to go on a diet. It was as though she couldn't stop herself from repeating the same sort of hurtful barbs that her mother had made to her.

When he was nineteen or twenty years old, Pierce concluded that her criticisms were in a way a peculiar compliment, because she thought they could take it, and that they were worth improving. "Somebody told me once, 'Your grandmother, she really gives it to people that she thinks can handle it,'" he said. "I realize that the things that she does and kind of the sharpness—it really is to the benefit of the person who's getting the needling." That said, he added, "It didn't make it easier when we were little kids." It was something they had to learn to weather, like it or not.

She was such a force that the family joked they felt her judgment even after she died.

Doro went shopping for a new dress for the memorial service, but after she chose one she found herself wondering, *Will Mom like this?* The dress had slits on the sleeves; she worried that was a fashion detail Barbara Bush wouldn't have favored. Doro went upstairs to her mother's bedroom, tried on the new dress, and looked at herself in the full-length mirror on the wall.

At that moment, the mirror fell off the wall and shattered. Fluke or not, Doro returned the dress to the store and bought another for her mother's funeral.

"I mean, she's just always been very loving and supportive, but tough for sure," granddaughter Marshall said. "She doesn't take much crap from people, as I'm sure you have very quickly learned. She just always expected all of us to be our best." Ellie LeBlond Sosa, Doro's daughter, called her grandmother "the rock of our family."

Barbara Bush seemed to see it as her mission to make sure no one got too comfortable, too self-satisfied—an attitude that had unnerved any number of White House staffers through two administrations. As young adults, Pierce had given cousin Jebby a tour of the new headquarters he had helped build for Big Brothers Big Sisters in Houston before they stopped by their grandparents' house. They were describing how impressive the $8 million building was when she spoke up. "She starts talking about how great George P. is doing and how great that is," Pierce recalled. He saw the praise of Jebby's older brother as calculated. "She's doing it as a way to put us back in our spots, but also to just make sure that we realize we need to be doing that, right?" That they needed to keep stepping up. That they shouldn't think they could rest on their laurels.

George P. wasn't exempt from her gibes. In 2000, at age twenty-four, he was working on his uncle's presidential campaign before entering law school. *People* magazine had rated him as fourth on a list of the one hundred most eligible bachelors, citing "his chiseled features, movie-star smile and hard-to-ignore moniker." He ranked just behind actor Matt Damon. His grandmother called, and not to congratulate him.

"What is the definition of 'eligible bachelor'?" she demanded. "You have no income and you're not nearly as cute as George Clooney." (Clooney was rated as the number one eligible bachelor on the list.)

During their first weekend in the White House, just after the inauguration in 1989, Barbara Bush noticed that granddaughters Jenna and Barbara hadn't shown up at the dining room table for a family meal. A butler mentioned that the seven-year-old twins had telephoned the kitchen and ordered two sandwiches to be delivered to the single-lane bowling alley downstairs. The elder Barbara Bush said they ordered peanut butter and jelly; the younger Barbara Bush said they ordered grilled cheese. But they both agreed on what happened next.

"We heard footsteps walking down the hallway and we think, 'It's going to be this grilled cheese!' And we're so excited about this wonderful new situation of a bowling alley in my grandparents' house," the younger Barbara Bush recalled. But it was not a friendly butler at the door. "My grandmother walked in and she was mad; she made it very clear that this was not a hotel and this was a home and it was not *our* home." She warned them never to pull a stunt like that again. "We never, ever did that again," the granddaughter said. "We learned our lesson immediately."

In the fall of 2017, ten of the seventeen Bush grandchildren gathered in College Station, Texas, to celebrate the twentieth anniversary of the dedication of the George H. W. Bush Presidential Library—the biggest gathering ever of the cousins for a public conversation. The panel discussion before a standing-room-only audience included George P. Bush (son of Jeb); Pierce Bush and Ashley Bush (children of Neil); Marshall Bush and Walker Bush (children of Marvin); and Sam LeBlond, Ellie LeBlond Sosa, Robert Koch, and Gigi Koch (children of Doro). In addition, Lizzie Andrews, Neil's stepdaughter, was there.

Barbara Bush listened from the front row in her scooter—laughing, shaking her head in mock outrage, and occasionally wiping away a tear. She would die six months later.

"From the very beginning, they called me one of their own grandchildren and this made me feel so special," said Lizzie, who was thirteen years old when her mother, Maria Andrews, married Neil Bush. It was less than a year after Neil's contentious divorce from his first wife, Sharon, and in the middle of George W. Bush's reelection campaign for president. The elder George Bush dubbed her "Lizard"—having a nickname was a sign of acceptance and affection—and Barbara Bush would insist that Lizzie sit next to her at dinner.

Grandson Sam LeBlond related a story from the private dinner the family had shared the night before. Barbara Bush had declared, "I have some relationship advice for everybody at the table." Sam was seated next to her. "Of course everyone perks up," he told the crowd in the auditorium. "You know, she's been married seventy-plus years. Then came her advice: 'If you're in a relationship, the man should be the disciplinarian.'"

While the audience looked puzzled, the cousins onstage erupted in laughter. They knew who the disciplinarian had been in her relationship, and it wasn't the man.

In an interview a few months after the library forum, Marshall credited the closeness of the cousins to their grandmother's influence.

"Ashley's in LA, I'm in Houston, Ellie's in Boston—I mean, everyone's all over the place. There's no reason that we should be as close as we are, but we are," Marshall said. Their friendships grew over years of family gatherings during Christmas holidays and Kennebunkport summers. "I think that they just wanted to make sure that we all spent time together, and I think, too, maybe, have a normal life outside of them being president. That was never who my grandparents were to any of us. They were always just our grandparents."

Being Barbara Bush's namesake hasn't always been easy.

"Such a big name for a little girl," the younger Barbara Pierce Bush told me. She grew up being teased by her classmates; Domino's assumed she was a prankster when she tried to order pizza for delivery. As a young adult, promoting the nonprofit Global Health Corps she had helped found, she arrived at a conference she'd been invited to address. "I was looking around trying to figure out who I should go connect with and a woman came up to me and she said, 'Oh, are you her intern?'" she recalled. "In my mind initially I thought, well, no, I don't have an intern here. Then I realized that they thought my grandmother was speaking there."

Her parents expressed sympathy about all that. If they had realized how famous the elder Barbara Bush would become, they would have chosen other names, Laura Bush once told Barbara and her sister, Jenna, who was named for Laura's mother. The twins were skeptical about that. Their grandmother was already the wife of the vice president when they were born, they noted. "Our point was, like, 'Mom, you knew.'"

Her grandmother's influence reverberated in the life of Barbara Pierce Bush beyond sharing a name. In 2003, while a student at Yale, she accompanied her father to Africa on a trip that launched PEPFAR, the President's Emergency Program for AIDS Relief, an initiative that in some ways echoed the elder Barbara Bush's efforts to address AIDS in the United States. In Uganda, the younger Barbara Bush was stunned by the human costs she saw. She changed her major, enrolled in health policy classes, and worked for a time at a children's hospital in Cape Town.

She helped launch a group modeled on Teach for America. The Global Health Corps recruited professionals with various backgrounds to work in the United States and abroad on health issues, among them HIV/AIDS. (The junior Barbara served as CEO for eight years, then in 2018 began moving away from day-to-day management of the group, though she remained on the board of directors.) "I mean seeing literally, like, thousands of people lining the street waiting for drugs that they needed to live, that we had in the United States, was something that was very hard for me to wrap my brain around," she said of that first trip to Africa. "The lack of justice in that."

Her grandmother had provided a role model on the imperative of trying to help others, she said. "We talked about service a lot, but not in a kind of big-picture macro way. It was more like, do what you can do to help others. It was very Golden Rule-ish in terms of treat others as yourself, and [we] talked a lot about humility and focusing on other people."

Near the end of her life, the elder Barbara Bush gave her namesake some unexpected advice. In November 2017, Barbara and Jenna were in Houston on a publicity tour for their joint memoir, *Sisters First: Stories from Our Wild and Wonderful Life*. The younger Barbara brought news that she had broken up with her boyfriend, a young man her grandmother had liked. "I just wasn't in love with him; I wasn't going to marry him," she told her. The elder Barbara told her she had done the right thing. She knew that her granddaughter's commitment to the Global Health Corps, which involved her constantly traveling for close to a decade, would have delayed and complicated opportunities for starting a family.

Still, her next comment was a surprise: "You know, you could always have a baby by yourself," her grandmother said. "You could adopt or you could just have a baby." (That same month, the younger Barbara was set up on a blind date with screenwriter Craig Coyne; they were married in October 2018, at Walker's Point.)

Barbara Bush was ninety-two years old and a great-grandmother several times over, but her outlook on her namesake's options when it came to having children turned out to be thoroughly modern. "She brought it up out of nowhere," her granddaughter said. "She said it as if giving me her blessing in some ways."

A dynasty is defined as a hereditary succession of rulers—the Tang dynasty, for instance, which ruled China for nearly three hundred years—or a family that wields influence through generations in the world of baseball or business, theater or crime. When it comes to politics, scholar Stephen Hess, author of *America's Political Dynasties: From Adams to Clinton*, devised a numerical scoring system.

He ruled that to reach dynasty status, a family had to record at least three generations in public office—a standard that excludes the Clintons, at least so far. Under his admittedly arbitrary system, being president or chief justice earned ten points for a family; vice president or Speaker of the House four points; senator or governor three points; representative two points; and cabinet member one point.

With that, at the time of Barbara Bush's death in 2018, her family ranked sixth on a list of the top ten family dynasties in American history. Only the Bushes and the top-ranked family, the Kennedys, had family members still running for elective office. On the list, in order: the Kennedys, the Roosevelts, the Rockefellers, the Harrisons, the Adamses, the Bushes, the Frelinghuysens, the Breckinridges, the Tafts, and the Bayards. (Dynastic or not, not all of these families continue to be household names.)

The Bush political dynasty began with Prescott Bush, George Bush's father, elected to the US Senate from Connecticut in 1952. Since then, the offices that family members have held include two presidencies, two governorships, one vice presidency, one Senate seat, and one

House seat. If the calculation were expanded to include distant relative Franklin Pierce, the joint Bush-Pierce family ranking would jump to third, behind only the Kennedys and the Roosevelts. Franklin Pierce— Barbara Bush's fourth cousin, four times removed—was twice elected to the House, once to the Senate, and once to the White House, in 1852.

In the rising generation, at the time of Barbara Bush's death, two members of the extended Bush clan were in elective office. George P. Bush had ambitions beyond Texas land commissioner; he has jokingly been called "Forty-Seven," as though destined to become the nation's forty-seventh president after his grandfather (the forty-first president) and his uncle (the forty-third president). Walker Stapleton, the second cousin of George P., was elected and reelected state treasurer of Colorado. He won the Republican nomination for governor in 2018 but lost the general election. (Stapleton's mother, Debbie Stapleton, is George Bush's first cousin.)

For George P. Bush and Walker Stapleton, the family affiliation proved to be a mixed blessing with the rise of Donald Trump as the face of the Republican Party. In the Colorado GOP primary in 2018, Stapleton's primary challenger tried to use the kinship as a weapon, blasting him as a member of "the Trump-hating Bush family network." Stapleton easily won the nomination anyway. In the Texas contest, Donald Trump Jr. withdrew from headlining a fund-raiser for George P. Bush, who had voted for Trump in 2016, after Bush's relatives criticized the immigration policies of Trump's father. (George P. Bush's father, Jeb, posted a negative tweet about the administration's treatment of undocumented immigrants crossing the border with children. His aunt Laura Bush wrote an op-ed in the *Washington Post* that called the Trump administration policy of separating immigrant children from their parents "cruel.")

When I asked Barbara Bush if she thought the family would one day field another president, she seemed uncertain. She also seemed unconcerned.

"That's a good question," she mused. "Now, I'm hesitant to answer that, 'cause I've been wrong every time. Probably not. I mean, I think probably not. I don't know." She said she had no idea whether any of her other grandchildren would join George P. in seeking elective office, though some of the cousins had speculated among themselves that others in their ranks might eventually run for office. "Maybe an in-law?" she suggested, perhaps a reference to Henry Hager, the husband of Jenna Bush Hager and the son of a former lieutenant governor in Virginia. "Many generations down, maybe," she said.

Defining the Bushes as a political dynasty may miss the point, though. The next generation of the Bush family are all children who grew up in comfortable circumstances and attended the best schools, with a last name that opened doors. That said, a remarkable number are involved in public service defined more broadly than winning an election. "There are a lot of ways to serve," she said, "and being president is not the only one."

"I wouldn't call it a dynasty," George W. Bush told me. "I'd call it a tradition." His mother rejected the word "dynasty," and the idea of it, "because it's arrogant, and it's inherited. You don't inherit anything like that; it's earned. She used to say, 'I'm so proud that my two sons represent 25 percent of the country,' or something like that. She was very proud of Jeb and me as governor. I don't think she viewed that as, 'What a beautiful stepping-stone to waving the dynastic banner.' The Bush shield just doesn't exist."

Although it could exist, he added, undercutting what might sound self-important with a joke—just as his mother so often did. "It's easy," he said of creating a Bush shield. "All you've got to do is use a bush, a rhododendron or something."

To be sure, there are threads through the family that reflect the elder George Bush's political ambitions. But more threads reflect the commitment he and Barbara Bush espoused to helping others in whatever way they could. As president, George H. W. Bush called it "a thousand points of light." His volunteer initiative with that name was the only program he specifically asked his successor, Bill Clinton, to preserve. As First Lady, Barbara Bush told her staff on their first day on the job that she wanted something on her schedule every day aimed at helping others.

She became the matriarch of a dynasty shaped in that image.

For some of the cousins, politics didn't sound as appealing for them as it did for their great-grandfather or their grandfather or their uncles. "A lot of us saw our grandparents get beat up, our uncle get beat up, Jeb get beat up, George P., you know," Marshall told me. "And I think a lot of us don't want to expose our children, our husbands, ourselves to that, but we do want to do something. We want to be able to help. That's definitely, I think, what our legacy, our dynasty is."

"I think this generation is fabulous," Barbara Bush told me, mentioning millennials in general and those in her family in particular. "I bet you'd find most young people doing 'Run for the Cure' or collecting for something or other." She singled out praise for those who enlist in the armed forces. "I mean, can you believe there's an all-volunteer Army fighting in a war that's not too popular, to put it mildly? I think they're amazing."

She had some personal experience with that, although she didn't mention it, nor did the family disclose it to the public. Her grandson Walker Bush, the son of Marvin and Margaret, joined the Marines and was deployed to Afghanistan. For years in his grandparents' home in Kennebunkport, at Walker's Point, the only family photo in the foyer was a framed 11-by-16-inch photograph of him in his dress blues. After his discharge, and dealing with some of the postcombat issues that many veterans have faced, he finished college at Texas Christian University in Fort Worth, graduating with a major in history in 2018.

Service was a lesson he learned from his grandparents, he said. They taught him to "do something for your fellow man and the people around you to leave this place you're in better than when you arrive."

George P. Bush said he was inspired to enlist in the US Navy Reserve after he watched his grandfather participate in the christening of the USS *George H. W. Bush*, honoring his service in World War II. The younger Bush also cited as inspiration his experience when he was twelve and spent a month during the summer living at the White House. His grandmother insisted that he volunteer once a week at a soup kitchen while he was there.

Pierce Bush was working for a private equity firm and planning to go to graduate school to earn an MBA when he volunteered for the Big Brothers program in 2009 and became the mentor to a boy named Jaylyn. Three years later, he left his finance career to work full-time at the non-profit, eventually becoming CEO of Big Brothers Big Sisters Lone Star. It was the largest volunteer mentor organization in the country, serving thousands of children across half the state of Texas. Jaylyn became close enough that he eventually called the elder Bushes Ganny and Gampy.

Granddaughter Lauren Pierce Bush, a model who married the son of designer Ralph Lauren, became an honorary student spokeswoman for the UN World Food Programme when she was at Princeton. Then she cofounded and became CEO of FEED Projects. The social business sells bags and other accessories, devoting the profits to provide meals to children around the world through partners including UNICEF and the UN World Food Programme.

Over the years, the Bush family has generated less flattering head-lines too.

Neil Bush faced lurid allegations of misbehavior during his divorce in 2003. Columba Bush was detained and fined by federal customs offi-cials in 1999 for lying about the clothing and jewelry she was bringing into the country after a trip to Paris. At age nineteen, Jenna and Barbara Bush were cited in Austin on misdemeanor charges of underage drink-ing. When he was a student at Rice University, George P. Bush was investigated for burglary and criminal mischief, but not charged, after he showed up at 4 a.m. at the Miami home of his former girlfriend. Jebby at age sixteen was picked up by police, but not charged, when he and a girlfriend were found having sex in a car parked in a Tallahassee mall parking lot; when he was twenty-one, Austin authorities picked him up for public drunkenness and resisting arrest.

In families that achieve power, prominence, or wealth, the gener-ation that comes next can struggle. Tales of divorce, drug abuse, and squandered opportunity by the children and grandchildren of the rich and famous are standard fodder for supermarket tabloids and their social media heirs. By that standard, the Bush progeny generally have pursued lives of purpose and have managed to hang together as a family. Many of them credit Barbara Bush for that.

"I was born in 1986; my grandfather was elected president two years later, and then my uncle became president when I was, like, fourteen or whatever," Pierce Bush said. "But none of us were really spoiled kids, right? And I think it's because of my grandmother. She would never let us rest on that."

What did Barbara Bush see as her legacy?

"The children, the grandchildren, the great-grandchildren," she told me. "Every one of them is doing a good cause—every single one of them. You can't beat that. They all work for a living. None of them come to us for money. I mean, that's pretty good."

Chapter Twenty-One

—✦—

"We've Had Enough Bushes"

Barbara Bush blamed Donald Trump for her heart attack.

It wasn't technically a heart attack, though she called it that. It was a crisis in her long battle with congestive heart failure and chronic pulmonary disease that hit her like a sledgehammer one day in June 2016. An ambulance was called to take her to the hospital; the two former presidents who had been at home with her that day trailed in a car driven by the Secret Service. The tumultuous presidential campaign in general and Donald Trump's ridicule of son Jeb Bush in particular had riled her. "Angst," she told me. Afterward, Jeb, whose presidential campaign was already history, urged her to let it go, to focus on herself and have faith in the country.

"There's just a lot of angst" among those distressed by President Trump's leadership, Jeb Bush told me, using the same word that his mother had used. "So I think one of the solutions is don't watch it; don't obsess."

"Jeb said, 'Mom, don't worry about things you can't do anything about,'" Barbara Bush recalled. "He's right. Just do good, make life better for someone else."

How did she think things were going in the United States in the Age of Trump?

"I'm trying not to think about it," she said as the first anniversary of

President Trump's election approached. "We're a strong country, and I think it will all work out." Even so, she was dismayed by the nation's divisions and by the direction of the party she had worked for, and for so long. Did she still consider herself a Republican? In an interview with me in October 2017, she answered that question yes. But when I asked her again four months later, in February 2018, she said, "I'd probably say no today."

That was a stunning acknowledgment. Barbara Bush had been one of the most recognizable faces of the Republican Party through two presidencies. She was the matriarch of one of the GOP's leading families. But with Trump's rise, she saw it as a party she could not continue to support, a party she no longer recognized—even as one of her grandsons was on the ballot as a Republican.

Her comment reflected the aftershocks of the earthquake that was the 2016 election.

For Jeb, speculation about the prospect that he could be a third President Bush had been circulating since he was elected and then reelected governor of Florida. In 2002, as he was poised to win a second term, a family friend teasingly referred to him as "Forty-Four"—that is, the forty-fourth president, destined to succeed his brother, George W., the forty-third. "I pray for 44 a lot, too!!" Elsie Hillman said in a letter to his mother. Barbara Bush replied, "I so hope you are praying for 43 also!!"

But amid early jockeying before the 2016 election, Barbara Bush was skeptical, and in public, about whether her second son should run for the White House.

"There are other people out there that are very qualified and we've had enough Bushes," Barbara Bush declared on NBC's *Today* show in April 2013 amid speculation about whether Jeb was going to run. (You might have thought she would feel a personal incentive to encourage him to try: He could burnish her place in the history books, if he won, by making her the only mother of two presidents.) "It's a great country. There are a lot of great families, and it's not just four families."

Anchor Matt Lauer asked, "Have you expressed that to him?"

Daughter-in-law Laura Bush and her twins, Jenna Bush Hager and Barbara Pierce Bush, who were also on the TV set, began to giggle.

"Well, *now*," Jenna and the younger Barbara said almost simultaneously.

"It's on the *Today* show," Laura noted.

"Surprise!" Jenna exclaimed.

Four years later, the elder Barbara Bush told me she hadn't planned to say that. "I never think ahead," she said. A journalist had asked a question; she answered it. She hadn't told her son what she thought beforehand; he hadn't asked. "Jeb is not a man who asks your opinion too much," she said. "Jeb is a man of very few words. He will send me an email: 'Mom, have I told you I loved you lately? I do. Jeb.' That's it. That's a long telegram from Jeb."

In this case, Jeb was watching. So was the rest of the family. Gathered in Dallas for the dedication of George W. Bush's presidential library, they saw the interview on a TV in a hotel suite. "Thanks, Mom," an exasperated Jeb Bush said to the TV screen as his brother Neil laughed.

"It's a point of view that I respect, but it's like, you know, I thought maybe she would tell me first—call me crazy," Jeb Bush told me several years later. When he caught up with his mother that day, he demanded, "What the hell is going on? I wasn't planning on dealing with this." Having your own mother—your famous mother, practically an American icon—publicly opposed to your campaign just might be problematic for a candidate. She told him, "Well, I promise I won't do it again."

A few months later, as Jeb Bush was moving closer to running, he happened to catch another interview with his mother, this time on C-SPAN. Her words sounded familiar. "I think this is a great American country, a great country, and if we can't find more than two or three families to run for higher office, that's silly," she said. "I think the Kennedys, Clintons, Bushes—there are just more families than that...

"I would hope that someone else would run, although there's no question in my mind that Jeb is the best-qualified person to run for president," she said. "But I hope he won't."

Jeb Bush got on the phone. "Mom, you promised you weren't going to say this again," he said, reenacting their conversation for me. "And she goes, 'I didn't say it.' I said, 'What do you mean you didn't say it? It's literally on television. I just saw it like twenty minutes ago.'" The cable network liked the quote so much that the clip was being featured as a tease for the program. "She goes, 'I didn't say it,' and she kind of hung up on me."

Later, she called back with an explanation. "I said that *before* the *Today* show interview," she told him; C-SPAN had delayed airing it as part of a series on First Ladies. So, technically, she had kept her promise.

She did begin to temper her language. "This country, which is such a great country, that there are more than three families," she said on *Fox and Friends* in March 2014. "But then I read *The Bully Pulpit*, I think by Doris Kearns Goodwin, and she points out that in 1700 there were only three families, so maybe it's okay." Jeb "is the best-qualified person in the country, there's no question about that," she added. "Put me down as saying that."

She was reluctant for Jeb to run, but not because she thought he wasn't up to the job. He had been the serious son. When he and George W. were young adults, nearly everyone viewed Jeb as more likely to be a future president. But she had seen how brutal presidential campaigns and the presidency could be. Her husband lost his bid for a second term, a crushing defeat. Her oldest son left the White House excoriated for pursuing a costly war in Iraq. Jeb would inherit all their baggage, all their enemies, she warned. She also sensed a dyspeptic mood in the country, a weariness with the political establishment that would disrupt his path.

Eventually, she campaigned for him. He asked because he was in trouble; he had lost the opening Iowa caucuses and was struggling for traction in New Hampshire. She agreed not only because she would do just about anything for her family but also because she was alarmed by Trump, the rival who was coming on strong for the nomination. She recorded an ad, sitting on a dark set, speaking straight to the camera. And she returned to New Hampshire, the state that had rescued the elder George Bush's presidential prospects in 1988, to campaign once again.

This time, she was ninety years old and using a walker. She pushed it through a New Hampshire snowstorm as she went from event to dinner to interview.

"I love my son, and I know that America needs him," she said in an interview three days before the primary on *CBS This Morning*, sitting side by side with him. "He's honest, dependable, loyal, relatively funny, good-looking"—she elbowed him good-naturedly—"but funny. He's got the same values that America seems to have lost. He's almost too polite. I don't advise him, but if I gave him advice, I would say, 'Why don't you interrupt like the other people do?' And he does not brag like some people we know."

She refused to say Trump's name, but there was no mistaking whom she meant. "I'm not getting into a spitting match with him," she said. "He can spit further than I can."

Anchor Norah O'Donnell noted that Trump had ridiculed Jeb Bush for deploying his mother in the campaign. "Just watched Jeb's ad where he desperately needed mommy to help him," Trump had tweeted. "Jeb—mom cannot help you with ISIS, the Chinese or with Putin."

"Putin endorsed him, for heaven's sake," Barbara Bush erupted. "Putin the killer! Putin the worst! He endorsed Trump! That's an endorsement you don't want."

Trump won the New Hampshire primary. Jeb Bush finished a disappointing fourth. When he did no better in the South Carolina primary eleven days later, he decided to end his campaign. He called his mother. "I just want to let you know I'm heading home," he told her. "I love you," she said. Nothing more.

~ ~

Barbara Bush's negative opinion of Donald Trump dated back decades.

"The real symbol of greed in the 80s," she wrote in her diary in January 1990. She had just read a news story about Trump addressing a Los Angeles charity gala, an awards dinner for Merv Griffin hosted by the American Friends of the Hebrew University and attended by Ronald and Nancy Reagan. Trump had needled the former president for the high-priced speeches he had delivered in Japan. "I see President and Mrs. Reagan in the audience. Did you have to pay them $2 million?"

A month later, she saved news clippings to show a friend about Trump's separation from his first wife, Ivana. Their divorce would be finalized in 1992. She noted that Ivana's allies were saying the $25 million settlement in the prenuptial agreement she had signed wasn't enough. "The Trumps are a new word, both of them," she wrote. "Trump now means Greed, selfishness and ugly. So sad."

Trump had made a weird overture to George Bush in 1988, when he was poised to clinch the Republican presidential nomination. The New York developer told campaign strategist Lee Atwater that he was available to be Bush's running mate. Writing in his diary, Bush dismissed the idea as "strange and unbelievable."

Now, more than a quarter century later, Barbara Bush couldn't quite imagine that Donald Trump was going to win the White House on his own. "I don't understand why people are for him," she said in one interview. In another, she expressed astonishment that women could support him. George Bush ended up voting for Hillary Clinton, the first time in his life that he had cast a ballot for a Democrat for president. Barbara Bush wrote in Jeb's name on the last day of early voting. "I could not vote for Trump or Clinton," she wrote in her diary.

The only member of the Bush family in political life who announced he was voting for Trump in 2016 was grandson George P. Bush, who had been elected Texas land commissioner two years earlier and had hopes of higher office. He served as Texas "Victory Chairman" for the entire Republican slate in 2016. He was trying to navigate these new waters in the GOP. "I thought that my values and the values of the party more closely aligned to him," he said of Trump, although they didn't agree on every issue. "That shows natural progression within a party to have these serious debates."

Barbara Bush's original judgment, made three and a half years earlier, seemed prescient. The country apparently did feel there had been enough Bushes, and enough Clintons, in high office. Jeb Bush lost the Republican nomination; Hillary Clinton won the Democratic nomination but lost the general election, trailing Trump in the Electoral College, though she carried the popular vote. "I think people didn't want anybody who was in office," Barbara Bush told me. "I think they wanted a whole new world."

The morning after the election, George H. W. Bush, honoring the traditions of the office, called the president-elect to offer his congratulations. Trump "was very nice," Barbara Bush wrote in her diary. "He said that George was a great president and he admired us both. He said Jeb was strong and a great man. He is trying...at this moment...to be conciliatory. He says he wants to represent all the people."

Two weeks later, she wrote a warm letter to Melania Trump, who was facing intense speculation about whether and when she would move to Washington from New York. Barbara Bush urged her to do whatever was best for her, and to protect her son, Barron. She knew the White House could be a lonely place, especially for a child. She gave her some advice, the same advice she had volunteered to Hillary Clinton in 1992, when the Clintons were preparing to move into the White House with an only child.

Dear Mrs. Trump,

The world thought I was writing this note to Bill Clinton. I am glad that I am not. I wanted to welcome you to the First Ladies very exclusive club. My children were older and therefore I did not have the problems you do. Whatever you decide to do is your business and yours alone.

Living in the White House is a joy and their only job is to make you happy.

If you decide to stay in NYC that will be fine also. When you come to the White House let your son bring a friend. That is my unasked for advice.

God Bless you,
Barbara Bush

Barbara Bush also wrote a personal note to Karen Pence on the Christmas card she sent her and her husband, Vice President–Elect Mike Pence, soon after the election. "I really wanted to write you earlier to tell you how much fun I had as the wife of the VP," she told her, adding, "It is a lovely house."

Sitting in the living room of that "lovely house," Karen Pence showed me the card, even the envelope saved. She had first visited the house and met Barbara Bush in 1988, when Mike Pence was making a bid for Congress and the Second Lady hosted a reception for the spouses of GOP challengers. A photo of that meeting was now in a frame, sitting on the grand piano. At the time, Barbara Bush had advised her to move to Washington if her husband won the election. (He didn't that time, but he did later, and Karen Pence then took her advice.)

Those weren't the letters Barbara Bush had expected to write after the 2016 election. She already had drafted a funny congratulatory letter to send to Bill Clinton—assuming, as almost everyone had, that he would be taking over the role of presidential spouse. "It said, 'Welcome to the First Ladies Club,'" she told me. "'We can't wait to initiate you.'" But she never mailed it.

"I woke up and discovered, to my horror, that Trump had won."

She didn't hide her horror from those close to her. After Trump was elected, a friend in Kennebunkport gave her a Trump countdown clock as a joke present. The red, white, and blue digital clock displayed how many days, hours, minutes, and seconds remained in President Trump's term. She parked it on the side table in her bedroom, next to the chair she would sit in to needlepoint or watch television.

She liked the countdown clock so much that when they returned to Houston that October, she brought it with her. It sat on her bedside table, where she could see it every day.

Chapter Twenty-Two

"Hit in the Solarplex"

Bill Clinton hadn't been just a rival. During the 1992 election, he was someone the Bushes saw as unworthy for the office of the presidency. Almost to the end of that campaign, George Bush refused to believe that the American people would choose Clinton, who had dodged the draft and faced allegations he had cheated on his wife. Bush's lack of respect for his opponent made the election outcome even more crushing.

Eight years later, the wounds were still raw. "I think George respects the presidency so, and if there's any disappointment, that's the disappointment," Barbara Bush said in an interview on ABC's *Good Morning America* in August 2000, as Clinton was close to completing his second term. Host Charles Gibson pressed her to explain what she meant. "It's that there is disrespect that's been brought upon the office in the last eight years?" he suggested. She agreed. "By an unnamed person," she said.

By then, Bush's son George W. was running for president against Clinton's vice president, Al Gore. The elder Bushes had accepted an invitation to a black-tie dinner honoring the two-hundred-year anniversary of the White House on November 9, 2000. It would be two days after the voting, and they assumed the election would be over, one way or the other. But it wasn't. The acrimonious battle over who had won Florida, and with it the Electoral College, was just beginning.

"My-oh-my it was a tense evening," Barbara Bush wrote in her diary. Her assessment of Clinton and his moral standing hadn't changed. She bristled when he quoted John Adams's prayer, inscribed on the mantel in the State Dining Room, that "none but honest and wise men ever rule under this roof." "What absolute nerve," she fumed. "He was impeached because he lied to the American public and the special prosecutor," she said of Clinton. "I have come to the conclusion that he really does not know right from wrong."

She noted the awkward collection of people gathered at the dinner in the East Room. Hillary Clinton had just won a Senate seat in New York. Chuck Robb, attending as the son-in-law of former president Lyndon Johnson, had just lost his Senate seat in Virginia. And the Bushes didn't know whether their son had won or lost the presidency. Or as she put it: "So there we were a winner (Hil), a loser (Chuck), and Mr. and Mrs. In between (GB and BPB.)"

As years passed, though, tensions with Clinton eased.

Two weeks after George W. Bush won a second term in 2004, the Bushes attended the dedication of Clinton's presidential library in Little Rock, Arkansas. George H. W. Bush delivered gracious remarks, calling Clinton "one of the most gifted American political figures in modern times," then adding to laughter, "Believe me, I learned that the hard way."

Afterward, during a tour of the library, George Bush offered some advice, former president to former president, in the sort of conversation only friends would have. He urged Clinton to consider designating an open area next to the library as his gravesite, and soon, to make it easier to manage his funeral arrangements.

"Aren't we a funny country?" Barbara Bush wrote in her diary. "We all go to each other's funerals and Library openings. At the funerals you can see people thinking like the cartoons with a bubble over their heads: 'I certainly wouldn't do it this way.' 'Oh, I hope this many people come to my funeral.' Or Worse 'This guy was a rotten lying mean guy and all these liars are saying these nice untrue things about him.'" She said

Clinton still wasn't respected by those in the exclusive club of former presidents, but she also noted that he was hard not to like.

The next month, a devastating tsunami hit Southeast Asia. An estimated 230,000 people died; damages totaled billions of dollars. White House chief of staff Andy Card suggested to President George W. Bush that he ask his father and Clinton to lead efforts to raise private money for relief. Both immediately agreed. In February, they left for a four-day trip that would take them to Thailand, Indonesia, Sri Lanka, and Maldives.

"He leaves on Thursday for the Far East—he and Bill—the odd couple," Barbara Bush wrote a friend just before they left. "He truly likes working with him. We'll see after 17 hours of a plane ride on a cargo plane." She said her husband told her that Clinton "never stops talking evidently."

Their flight accommodations turned out to be more luxurious than a cargo plane. The Air Force 757 had a stateroom, but just one of them, and with one bed. The sleeping protocol was complicated: Both men were former presidents. Bush was eighty by now, Clinton fifty-eight. But Clinton had recently undergone quadruple bypass surgery. Clinton insisted that Bush take the bed. Clinton sat in the main cabin and taught Bush's chief of staff, Jean Becker, how to play a card game called Oh Hell. Later during the long flight, he stretched out on the floor with a pillow and a blanket to sleep.

In the end, the two former presidents raised $100 million for tsunami relief. They paired up for TV ads and interviews. They greeted fans together at the Super Bowl and played golf with pro Greg Norman at a charity tournament. Later, in joint fund-raising efforts after damaging hurricanes in the United States, they would raise more than $129 million in relief funds for victims of Hurricane Katrina and $2.7 million for victims of Hurricane Ike.

At the annual Gridiron Club Dinner in Washington that spring, George W. Bush got laughs from a white-tie audience of journalists and officialdom when he joked that Clinton, recovering from follow-up surgery, "woke up surrounded by his loved ones: Hillary, Chelsea... my dad."

Barbara Bush took longer for Clinton to win over than her husband. She always had a sharper eye for people's motives than he did. She thought that cultivating a friendship gave Clinton a patina of respectability after surviving impeachment and scandal. Republican friends called to complain that Bush was giving Clinton credibility. Not to mention that Clinton took mulligans in golf—a fundamental character flaw, in her book—and had a general history of cutting corners.

When talk show host Larry King asked her that spring whether she liked Clinton, she seemed uncharacteristically flummoxed. She gave both possible responses: yes and no.

"Yes, all right," she said. "Yes, no, I like him."

"You don't like him, though?" he persisted.

"No, I think he's—"

George Bush interrupted, rescuing her before she could detonate a political land mine. "She hasn't been around him, though," he said.

Barbara Bush recognized how much George Bush enjoyed Clinton's company and attention, and she saw how much Clinton seemed to care about her husband too. She might roll her eyes when talking about Clinton, but she grew to appreciate the friendship that he built with her husband.

"Bill Clinton came by in the afternoon," Barbara Bush wrote in her diary in September 2014, from Kennebunkport. "He still knows more about everything. He has a memory of a horse (if a horse has a memory) and seems to know something about every thing. He says as he grows older he cares more about the country than politics. He would like to see Jeb run so no matter who wins the country would have a leader."

That was based on the conventional political wisdom that the 2016 race might well end up being a Bush-Clinton reprise, this time between Jeb Bush and Hillary Clinton.

"Doro says that is B.S.," Barbara went on. "Funny, but Bill cares about George."

Before a Kennedy Center tribute to George Bush in 2011, a fund-raiser for his Points of Light initiative, twenty-seven members of the Bush clan gathered in the greenroom for a family photo. Clinton, who was slated to speak at the event, was standing nearby. George W. Bush and Neil Bush urged him to join them in the picture, granting him honorary sibling status. "Brother of another mother!" Neil shouted. "Get in here!" Clinton, beaming, stood in the back row, near some of the grandchildren.

"Dad has this amazing relationship with Bill Clinton," Neil Bush told me. "But Mom doesn't have the same affection for Bill. She still remembers how Bill beat Dad...He apparently cheats in golf and did things that Mom doesn't particularly like. But it shows that Dad has this forgiving, amazing nature that is welcoming...and Mom is much more black and white."

A few days before we talked, Neil had dinner in New York City with his daughter and son-in-law, Lauren Pierce Bush and David Lauren, and their friends Chelsea Clinton and Marc Mezvinsky. "I told Chelsea, 'Your dad's been so great to my dad.' And she said, 'I think it's because my dad never had a dad in his life.'" George Bush had become a sort of surrogate father to Bill Clinton. Barbara Bush thought that was part of the dynamic between the two men too.

"He's very hard not to warm up to," she said of Clinton. (The "brother of another mother" scenario would cast her as his stepmother, by the way.) "You can't dislike Bill Clinton."

Clinton gradually became closer with George W. Bush as well. The two had been born just forty-four days apart, in that first swell of the baby boom generation, and now they shared the rarefied status of former presidents. As he got to know the family better, Clinton recognized similarities between George W. and Barbara Bush when it came to developing a relationship. "She felt, I think, for a long time she had to be more guarded about me" than the elder George Bush did, Clinton told me. "So was W." Gaining the trust of mother and son took longer, but was worth it once you did: "I find in many ways he's like her. If you get by the barrier, you've got somebody who—she's real. And she's a sticker."

That is, a friend you can count on.

The warming feelings didn't include Hillary Clinton, who had an independent political career by then. She didn't accompany Bill when he visited Walker's Point each summer to play golf, have dinner, and gossip. She and Barbara Bush had first eyed each other under strained circumstances, when they were the loyal spouses of competing presidential candidates.

When that election was over, Barbara Bush moved quickly to invite Hillary Clinton to see the White House family quarters. She had never forgotten her annoyance when Nancy Reagan delayed her tour, waiting until January 11, 1989, just nine days before the inauguration. This time, the incoming First Lady was invited to visit two weeks after the election, on November 19, 1992.

"She was such a hostess, leading me through the White House, talking about living there, giving me advice," Hillary Clinton told me. "She said, 'It's actually a great way for your family to live, because your husband works so close to home,' which I thought was so charming, and it turned out to be absolutely accurate."

But Barbara Bush also lived up to her reputation for candor.

"She was also still pretty upset about the election results and didn't hide it. She basically said, 'I don't know how it happened, and I'm not over it yet,'" Hillary Clinton recalled. "She basically said to me, 'Well, did you think you were going to win? We were told we were going to win. I don't know what happened.' I said, 'Look, there was a real difficulty in figuring out that election, because of Ross Perot.' And she said, 'Yes, we thought he was going to drop out, and he never did.'"

She also vented her grievances with the press. "Stay away from them," she advised. "They're not your friends. They're not trying to help you."

In Hillary Clinton, Barbara Bush was reminded of the feminists who she felt had denigrated her role as a homemaker. During the 1992 campaign, Hillary had famously declared, "I suppose I could have stayed home and baked cookies and had teas, but what I decided to do was to fulfill my profession," saying she represented "a generational change." Barbara had never been one to bake cookies, but she saw the comment as a jab against women like her who chose to stay home with their children, and to focus on their husbands' careers rather than their own.

In Barbara Bush, Hillary Clinton saw a traditionalist who masked her influence in a way Hillary told a friend was fraudulent, calling it "backstage manipulation." The two women came to this debate—what's the proper role for a political wife to play?—reflecting the attitudes of their generations.

"I am not too sure that the American public likes the spouse to be too front and center," Barbara Bush wrote in her 1994 memoirs, published two years after Bill Clinton had won the White House. "Hillary Rodham Clinton is certainly very much a part of her husband's decision-making process. She seems much the stronger of the two. Does it make him seem weaker? I am afraid that when problems or controversy occur, and they will, the finger will be pointed at Hillary. I am not saying this is right or wrong. It just occurs to me that the American people also are going through an adjustment."

In the White House, Hillary Clinton was bridling at the criticism she was getting and the contrast that was being drawn between her and Barbara Bush. Hillary was a lightning rod, then and later. Her staff calculated that there were three and a half times more media references to her by September 1996 than there had been to Barbara Bush during her four years as First Lady.

Her predecessor had been powerful too, Hillary Clinton said, and so had Nancy Reagan and other previous First Ladies. The difference was that she was being honest about it.

She complained about that to her friend Diane Blair in a phone conversation on Thanksgiving Day, 1996. "She thinks press complete hypocrites," Blair wrote in contemporaneous notes. "Say they want the truth, want power to be transparent, but in fact they prefer the backstage manipulation of B. Bush, N. Reagan, B. Truman, R. Carter. It's the honesty of their partnership that's driving them nuts and making her a target. On her death bed, wants to be able to say she was true to herself and is not going to do phoney makeovers to please others."

Except for the skydiving, life got quieter.

When Bill Clinton called George Bush in January 2010 to ask him to launch another joint fund-raising campaign, this time for victims of a devastating earthquake in Haiti, Bush demurred. He no longer had the stamina, he said; call my son instead. George W. Bush had now joined the club of former presidents. (George W. Bush agreed, on the condition that the current president, Barack Obama, make the request, which he did.)

George Bush's late-in-life penchant for jumping out of planes to celebrate big birthdays was a small rebellion against the way he was slowing down. He had always been athletic. He loved movement and speed. Now a form of Parkinson's disease curtailed his mobility. He could no longer jog or play golf. But he could still get the adrenaline rush of skydiving.

The first parachute jump of his life hadn't been planned: The Japanese shot down his torpedo bomber over the Pacific during World War II. In 1997, at age seventy-two, he parachuted again, this time with the US Army Parachute Team, known as the Golden Knights, at the Army Proving Ground in Yuma, Arizona. On his eightieth birthday, he made two tandem jumps, again assisted by the Golden Knights. They landed on a grassy spot near his presidential library at Texas A&M. To mark his eighty-fifth birthday, he parachuted over Kennebunkport, landing near St. Ann's Episcopal Church. Then he made a final jump there at age ninety, in 2014.

Barbara Bush didn't protest, not that he had asked her permission. Her only sardonic comment was that it made sense to use the church grounds as his landing spot. Given the short distance to the sanctuary, she said, a funeral service could be held immediately afterward if things went wrong. "There was no choice," she told me. "I wasn't given a 'Do you mind if I jump?' No, just, 'I'm going to jump.' And that was fine." He loved the feeling once the parachute had deployed. "He says once the thing is up, it's the most peaceful thing you've ever known," she said. "He doesn't ask much in life."

What does he want to do now?

"Live," she responded. "That's all we're both trying to do."

They faced a distressing episode in 2017, when George Bush was brushed by the #MeToo movement, the exposure of powerful men in Hollywood, business, government, the news media, and other fields who stood accused of sexual harassment, especially in the workplace. Several women reported that Bush in recent years had groped them during picture-taking sessions.

"You wanna know my favorite book?" he asked novelist Christina Baker Kline at a fund-raiser in 2014 for the Barbara Bush Foundation for Family Literacy. "Yes, what is it?" she responded. She said Bush, sitting in his wheelchair, put his arm around her, low on her back. " 'David Cop-a-Feel,' " he said, "and squeezed my butt, hard, just as the photographer snapped the photo." Actresses Heather Lind and Jordana Grolnick described separate and similar incidents, in 2016 and 2013. Grolnick said Bush used a different version of the pun: "Do you know who my favorite magician is?" he asked, then said "David Cop-a-Feel" as he grabbed her rear. Another woman, Roslyn Corrigan, said she was sixteen years old when Bush groped her buttocks at a photo-taking session in 2003.

George Bush's spokesman issued a written statement acknowledging the incidents and apologizing for them. "To try to put people at ease, the president repeatedly tells the same joke—and on occasion, he has patted women's rears in what he intended to be a good-natured manner," Jim McGrath said. "Some have seen it as innocent; others clearly view it as inappropriate. To anyone he has offended, President Bush apologizes most sincerely."

Those close to him said Bush's judgment had been affected by his parkinsonism and the medications he was taking to treat it, a medical condition known as disinhibition. He didn't fully understand what the fuss was about, they said, but he was mortified by the idea that he had upset the women involved. Barbara Bush was dismayed, too, and outraged when news accounts included Bush in the same category as Hollywood producer Harvey Weinstein and other men accused of serious and persistent predatory behavior.

～ ～

On the first Monday of every month, whenever she was in Houston, Barbara Bush would join her oldest friends for lunch at the Bayou Club. They called themselves the 1925 Club; having that as the year of your birth was one requirement for membership. Some of them were women she had first met way back in Midland. "We're down to a very few," she told me. As their ranks thinned, they let their friend Ada Grundy join the group, even though she had been born in 1924 and so wasn't technically eligible.

They allowed me to attend the luncheon on the first Monday in February 2018, a month before Barbara Bush would fall, never to fully recover. Those around the table included Bessie Liedtke, a firecracker whose late husband, Bill, had been George Bush's business partner in Midland. And Barbara Riddell, whose late husband, John, was a fellow Yalie who had moved to Texas in 1948 to make his fortune in the oil business. Helen Vietor was there—she had founded the House at Pooh Corner, a beloved private preschool in Houston—and Ada Grundy. "Ada is as deaf as a doornail," Barbara Bush warned me beforehand. But she added, "I love them all."

They ate crab salad, though one of them grumbled that the kitchen was no longer serving it in an avocado half, and they gossiped. The old friends discussed an acquaintance whose obituary had run in that morning's *Houston Chronicle*; they speculated about who in their orbit had gotten a face-lift. Several of them, including Barbara Bush, bemoaned the fact that they had been forced to give up smoking decades earlier, most at the behest of their children. They reminisced about the days of sending telegrams and relying on the radio for family entertainment. They marveled over the new world of technology.

When her literacy foundation would host one of its signature "Celebration of Reading" events, she no longer joined in person, Barbara told them. "I Skype them. Isn't that a word?"

"I don't know what it means," one of her friends said.

"My aide does that," Barbara Bush explained. "You get it on your iPhone, iPad, and they see that fat little face [of mine] and I can see them and hear them, and I welcome them all to say I'm sorry I can't be there, and blah blah blah."

They nodded in amazement. By unspoken agreement, they skirted anything too political. Barbara Bush's caustic views of President Trump were well known by all of them, and not everyone agreed with her on that, so they talked about other things. ("I mean, look at the stock market," Bessie Liedtke mumbled to me in an aside, happy with its rise during Trump's first year in office.)

Then they passed around a plate of macaroons for dessert. The Bayou Club had the best macaroons, they assured me.

⌒　⌒

By now, the lives of George and Barbara Bush had a routine, a rhythm. They would head to Kennebunkport in May and return to Houston in October. They went to Astros games when they could; she would keep score, a skill she learned when watching him play first base for the Yale team. They frequented local restaurants—the Tex-Mex at Molina's and the liver-and-onions at Da Marco's were among their favorites—and welcomed visiting friends and former staffers and the occasional foreign official. They helped raise money for a few favorite causes, including literacy and cancer research, but neither was writing a book or delivering speeches anymore. They traveled less often, though almost on a lark they made their first transatlantic ship crossing in 2012, on the RMS *Queen Mary 2*.

By this point in their lives, Barbara Bush had become the effective head of Bush Inc. That is, she was the person who managed the household, decided what invitations to accept, designated the charitable donations, dealt with the demands and the crises. If George Bush had trouble hearing or speaking when they socialized, she would jump in and carry the conversation.

"I write the checks; I spend the money," she told me. "I'm the CEO of the family now." It was the sort of corporate job she might have excelled at if she had been born in another era. "I think I probably, with experience, would have been good," she agreed, ticking off her relevant attributes. "I'm bossy," she began. "Fairly" disciplined. And organized.

Did she like being in charge?

"Not particularly, but I don't mind it," she said. (The fact is, she had been in charge more often than not since elementary school, when she emerged as the unelected leader of her clique of a half dozen friends.) "Someone has to. I try to protect him." There were advantages to turning ninety, she noted. "Sometimes when someone asks me to do something I really don't want to do, I can say, 'I might not be alive.' It works."

When she turned ninety, Barbara Bush did move to resolve a secret predicament: She had been worshipping at St. Martin's Episcopal Church in Houston for more than a half century, and she had made arrangements to hold her funeral services there. But in a fit of pique decades earlier, she had backed out of being confirmed as an Episcopalian.

She had grown up attending First Presbyterian Church in Rye, and in Midland her family had attended a Presbyterian church. When they moved to Houston, they decided to join St. Martin's. George had grown up in the Anglican church, but she needed to take confirmation classes to become an Episcopalian. Attending with her was their good friend James Baker.

"Congratulations," the rector said at their last class. "You've all gone first-class."

His arrogant comment—the suggestion that Episcopalians enjoyed a more elite status than, say, Presbyterians—did not sit well with her. "That made me so mad," she told me. Fuming, she went home to talk to her husband. "I'm sorry, I can't join your church," she told him. Baker went through the confirmation ceremony before the congregation. She refused, though that didn't prevent her from being a member of the church. She didn't publicize what had happened; no one seemed to notice.

For decades, she worshipped at St. Martin's and taught Sunday school there. On Monday mornings, when she was in town, she attended the Saintly Stitchers, a group dedicated to needlepointing cushions with passages from the Scriptures for each of the three hundred kneelers in the church. Nearly everyone, including some in her family, simply assumed she was an Episcopalian.

Then, in 2015, the dean of Virginia Theological Seminary announced he was conferring upon Barbara Bush a high honor for Anglicans: the Dean's Cross for Servant Leadership in Church and Society Award. It was intended, of course, to go to an Episcopalian. She worried about accepting it under false premises. "Russ, we've got a bad problem here," she told the Reverend Dr. Russell J. Levenson Jr., who by then had become St. Martin's new rector. "I need to be an Episcopalian *today*." She asked if she needed to take a class. He told her she could teach the class, as far as he was concerned.

She and Levenson already had been discussing her desire to be confirmed, after all these years. As it happened, George Carey, a former Archbishop of Canterbury whom the Bushes knew, was scheduled to visit St. Martin's on May 15, 2015; that was the same day the Reverend J. Barney Hawkins IV of the Virginia Theological Seminary would be there to present the Dean's Cross.

At 10:15 a.m. that morning, in a small private room near the sanctuary, Barbara Bush knelt and Carey confirmed her as an Episcopalian, as George Bush and Neil Bush watched. Then, at the church service at 11:15 a.m., the congregation, unaware of that last-minute ceremony, watched as she sat in a front pew and accepted the award from Hawkins, her conscience clear.

She turned in her seat to thank the congregation for all the church had meant to her.

Barbara Bush adored Lady Bird Johnson, but she thought her funeral lasted too long.

"I came home and immediately Jean [Becker], Doro [Bush Koch], Kristan [King Nevins] and I agreed that we must meet to plan my funeral," she wrote in her diary after the service on July 14, 2007, referring to her daughter and two key staffers. "No TWO hours." She had put off planning the details before. Now she wanted to have some control over how long it would last, what hymns would be sung, and who would speak.

As always, she discounted her importance and underestimated her appeal. She wasn't convinced that a lot of people would want to attend. Maybe it should be held in the pretty side chapel at St. Martin's Episcopal Church, she suggested, rather than in the huge main sanctuary.

A few years earlier, she had written some preliminary notes, notable in part by how loose her instructions were. "When it comes to place the service is held please do what the survivors want," she wrote in instructions that were tucked in a box with her diaries from 2000 and 2001. "If I die in Houston that might be more convenient, but if I am smart enough to die in Maine, then I'd like the clergy of both the Congregational and St. Ann's By The Sea to officiate."

She recommended "Nearer My God to Thee" and "Amazing Grace" as hymns to be sung. "And please sing familiar songs…bright and cheery," she wrote. "Remember no living human ever had a better life. I adore my GOD, husband, children and friends."

It's not that she expected to die anytime soon, although she was seventy-five or so at that point and in chronic pain. She complained about her aches and pains to her diary; she tried to shield even her husband from knowing how awful she felt. "I am racked with ARTHRITIS," she wrote in March 2002. "My back is so bad, but every morning when I awaken I ache in hands and feet. My legs ache. I just refuse to accept this. I look at pictures and see a hump back. I am trying not to talk about my health and really don't think George has any inkling about how I feel."

Both of them went to the Mayo Clinic in Phoenix the next month for complete physicals. "Everything has gone left or right or worse DOWN," she wrote, bemoaning the effects of aging. "Bumps, brown spots, what look like red spider webs have appeared on my lovely body and a tummy that does not hold itself in."

Her mind was sharp to the end; it annoyed her that her body kept giving her trouble. She still sometimes had double vision, an effect of the Graves' disease that had been diagnosed when she was in the White House. She was getting shorter as her spine began to compress. She had been five feet eight inches tall when she was First Lady, but by 2016 she was down to five feet three inches tall, and still losing ground. Everything seemed to hurt. She used a walker, then a scooter; she resisted the suggestion that she use a wheelchair. Her congestive heart failure kept getting worse, leaving her gasping for breath. She had to use supplemental oxygen, at first removing the oxygen tubes from her nostrils when she was around other people. Then her deteriorating condition forced her to keep them in all the time.

The first time I interviewed Barbara Bush at her Houston home, in October 2017, she was sitting on the small front porch to welcome me; she didn't start using her oxygen until the interview began, and she removed the oxygen nose buds when we took a picture together. The second time, in November, she had just returned from a doctor's appointment that left her exhausted. "You're looking at what used to be Barbara Pierce Bush," she told me. "I spent all morning at the doctor being checked and pumped and poked and jabbed."

What had the doctor concluded?

"We know I'm alive," she responded. "But barely."

In December, she was optimistic that a new medical regimen was going to help. "I don't want to walk, necessarily, but what I want to do is feel energetic and push," she said. "I want to go back to the beach and push the cart." In January, she had just started taking a new drug. "I'm about to start upping my medication, and I'm going to be dancing soon," she told me, even more encouraged.

But a month later, on February 6, 2018, at what turned out to be our final interview, her spirits were flagging. At the start, she turned to tell assistant Neely Brunette that she wanted to cut back from two hair appointments a week to one, a message that pricked me for what it might signal. I asked how things were going. "Not so great," she replied, then changed the subject.

Two weeks later, her health took a final turn for the worse.

"During a nap after lunch, I evidently passed out and they could not awaken me," she wrote in her diary on February 20. The Secret Service agents and her husband's medical aide tried to revive her. "They were shaking me and had me on the floor and were working on getting me to respond. The local fire department came and were firm. They hustled me off to Methodist," the nearby hospital, where she spent the night. "Had every test known to man and was pricked and poked and every part ex-rayed."

Then, the night before we were scheduled to have our sixth interview on March 16, Barbara Bush lost her balance, fell backward, and hit her head and back on a side table in her bedroom. She fractured her vertebrae and was admitted again to the hospital. We rescheduled the interview for April, but she died on April 17, a week before we were to meet again.

She would not be dancing, nor taking another walk on the beach.

Barbara Bush wasn't afraid of dying, but she was afraid of leaving George Bush alone. She wanted to live one day, one hour longer than he did. Her husband felt the same way. Each wanted to stay alive at least in part for the sake of the other. The only time Pierce Bush saw his grandfather break down in sobs was when Barbara Bush had a health crisis and emergency surgery in 2008. She would be similarly distressed when he had health scares. "I feel like, weirdly, they're both still here because they want to be there for the other person," Pierce said.

Barbara Bush had tracked her husband's decline and tried to prepare their children for what was ahead. Nearly everyone had assumed that he would die first, though he would live seven months longer than she did, time enough to spend a final summer in Kennebunkport.

"I have warned all the children," she told me. "I just said, 'The quality of life is not good. We've got to think about this. First we've got to talk to him, though, about the quality of life.'" A form of Parkinson's had put George Bush in a wheelchair and made it difficult for him to speak more than a few words at a time. For the lifelong athlete, and someone who loved interacting with people, that was close to torture.

"George is sort of gently slipping away," Barbara Bush wrote a friend. She grieved for him. She was getting ready to let go, to pass away. But she realized that he wasn't ready.

Neil Bush, who lived across the street, would drop over every evening he was in town to check on his parents, to help his mother piece together one of her complicated jigsaw puzzles and to read aloud to them both. Neil had an easy manner and helpful instincts; his family nickname growing up, not entirely sarcastic, had been "Mr. Perfect." As a child, he had been less combative than George W., chattier than Jeb, less of a troublemaker than Marvin. She had always been comfortable with him.

"She's gone through three or four different kinds of interventions that haven't worked," Neil told me in an interview in December 2017, in the small office of his consulting firm in Houston. She had begun to talk to him about just not eating as a way to end her life. "I said, 'What about Dad?' She says, 'Well, I'm going to have him not eat too.'" Neil pointed out some potential problems with this plan. "When Dad says, 'Where's my dinner?' and she says, 'We're not eating tonight, George.' Dad says, 'Why?'—I can just imagine that conversation."

Neil took her comments seriously, and an indication of how much pain she was in every day. "She has very little quality of life as it relates to her physical condition right now," he told me four months before she died.

She talked about it with her other children too.

"She called me six months or nine months ahead and said, 'I'm ready to lie down,' is how she put it," George W. Bush told me in an interview in his Dallas office two months after she died. "I said, 'Well, let me tell you something. How are you going to lie down? What are you going to do, not eat?' She said, 'Well, that's an option.' I said, 'No, it's not. You've eaten all your life.'

"I was surprised she went before Dad, but she was ready to die. She had just worn out, you know? She was hurting," he said, then added the obvious. "Once she had made up her mind, Mother was pretty strong-willed," he said.

On a fine spring evening, Barbara and George Bush and old friends from his White House staff got together in the Bushes' apartment next to the Bush Library in College Station, on the campus of Texas A&M—John Sununu and Andy Card and Andy's wife, Kathleene. For two hours, they told stories and shared memories. George Bush declared that he wanted to live to be one hundred years old. "Not me," Barbara Bush responded. "I'm ready to go right now. If the Lord took me right now, I'm ready to go. I don't want to be some shriveled-up prune."

The others protested. She would hear none of it. "No, I'm confident," she said. A week later, she fell and broke her back, sending her to Houston Methodist Hospital, never to recover.

In the hospital, she began to draft a letter in her diary to give to her children, listing what she was grateful for—first of all, for them, "five men and one lady." She mentioned her husband's parents and her own, and especially her father. "My dad was the finest brightest man," she wrote.

"I am so grateful that our children and grand children all finished school and promptly went to work," she went on. "They did not feel entitled. They and their children support themselves and are now doing good works along with working in some cases." She was grateful for "so many friends," and for the Saintly Stitchers group at church. "They treat me as a normal person although they do spoil me," she said. She mentioned the 1925 Club—and noted the exception they had granted Ada Gandy, "although she was born in 1924." The letter was never finished, never sent.

She wrote the final, poignant entry in her diary on April 5, 2018, twelve days before she died.

"I've been in the hospital for forever and seem to not be getting any better, at least my breathing is not," she wrote. "Dr. Menderes [Amy Mynderse] came in and had a very sweet talk with me. As she rubbed my arm, she told me the most ghastly thing: She told me the next time I go home I will have hospice. I said, doesn't that mean I am dying? She said yes. It was like being hit in the solarplex. I asked her to keep it a secret."

Then, Barbara Bush did what she had done before. She pivoted from being hit in the solar plexus to embracing the joys and dealing with the minutiae of life. That's what she had done when Robin died; when she struggled with depression; when her husband lost the White House. "In any case, we had a great visit with Jeb, and then Neil read more of my book to us. And we are laughing about so much. When he had to leave, Jeb took over reading."

A few days later, while she was still in the hospital, George W. Bush visited. "I was needling her just to keep her spirits up," he told me. "The doctor walked in and out of the blue she said, 'You want to know why George W. turned out the way he did?' Sure, the doctor said. 'Because I drank and I smoked when I was pregnant with him.'" They all laughed.

"She could quip until death," her oldest son said. "No self-pity. She was herself."

She finally went home, receiving only palliative care. Her children and grandchildren called and visited to say their good-byes, though she tried to avoid the maudlin. Her brother Scott Pierce called from Florida for what would be their final conversation; both knew he was about to win the $5 bet they had made long ago on who would die first. He had told her that he loved her, he said, but he wasn't sure if he had told her that he had always been proud of her. She jokingly replied, "I don't know if I've told you that I've always thought of you as a pest."

Two days before she died, she and George Bush sat in the small den off the living room of their house, holding hands. They gave each other permission—for her to die, for him to live. "I'm not going to worry about you, Bar," George Bush told her. "I'm not going to worry about you, George," she told him.

Then she ordered a bourbon, her preferred drink. He had a vodka martini, his.

~ ~

Every seat was taken at St. Martin's Episcopal Church, and in the huge main sanctuary, not the side chapel, which she had once suggested would be enough. Her instructions were followed to the letter. Who would have dared to do otherwise? The memorial service started on time and ended on schedule, ninety minutes later. Sitting in the pews were four former presidents—the two Bushes, of course, and Bill Clinton and Barack Obama—as well as First Lady Melania Trump and three former First Ladies. Children of John F. Kennedy, Lyndon Johnson, Richard Nixon, and Gerald Ford attended. So did former British prime minister Sir John Major and former Canadian prime minister Brian Mulroney.

"The whole thing was like, 'This is my last statement and it's mine,'" Bill Clinton later said with admiration. "'This is who I am. This is what I believe. This is my life.'"

Her granddaughters read Bible verses. Her grandsons served as pall-bearers. Historian Jon Meacham, the first of three eulogists, called her "the First Lady of the Greatest Generation." Her close friend Susan Baker gave the second eulogy, saying Barbara Bush had been "the secret sauce" who held her sprawling family together.

Jeb Bush spoke last. He had known for years that this task would fall to him, but he had struggled to write a eulogy. "I'm like in total denial," he had told me two months earlier. "I've written more than one thing and I just don't like it." He predicted, "I'm afraid I'm going to end up doing the high school cramming the night before for the exam." He wanted to tell a story and use humor rather than get into the "deeply emotional part of it," for fear of breaking down. "I weep pretty easy," he said. That's a family trait, I observed. "I think it is," he agreed.

Four months after the memorial, in a subsequent interview, Jeb Bush told me he didn't write his eulogy the night before, as he had feared he might. He finished it about ten days in advance, in enough time that he could have read it to his mother. He decided against that idea, fearful that she might give him grief about what he planned to say. "I don't think she would've been comfortable with all the accolades," he said.

When the time came for him to deliver his eulogy, Jeb Bush did tell a story, and he used humor. "As I stand here today to share a few words about my mom, I feel her looming presence behind me and I know exactly what she's thinking right now: 'Jeb, keep it short; don't drag this out. People have already heard enough remarks already. And most of all, don't get weepy.'"

His voice caught once or twice, but he managed to avoid getting weepy.

"She called her style a benevolent dictatorship, but, honestly, it wasn't always benevolent," he said, a line that drew knowing laughter. "Barbara Bush filled our lives with laughter and joy, and in the case of her family, she was our teacher and role model on how to live a life of purpose" and on how to be "genuine and authentic."

After the service, the hearse carrying her casket looped through Memorial Park, where she had so often jogged and walked her dogs, for a final farewell. The procession drove past thousands of well-wishers who lined the one-hundred-mile route and gathered on highway overpasses. Finally, in a wooded grove near the George H. W. Bush Presidential Library in College Station, with only close family members and her minister present, she was laid to rest. Next to Robin.

When her body lay in repose at St. Martin's, the Secret Service agents who had been on the Bushes' detail had stood vigil beside her casket. After she was buried in College Station, they remained on duty at the gravesite through the night, though that was no longer required for any security reason. When everyone else had gone, the Secret Service team sent out a message, as they always did at the close of day. They used the code name Barbara Bush had been known by for decades, ever since that long-ago presidential campaign in 1980.

"Tranquility has reached her final destination."

Indispensable

Barbara Bush was on a publicity tour for her memoir in 1994 when she noticed something first thing in the morning as she was getting dressed. It stuck in her mind until that night, when she had a chance to sit down and write in her diary.

"I had one recurring thought all day which was that when I awakened this morning and turned on the TV and heard the news I KNEW EVERY SINGLE PERSON MENTIONED ON TV with the exception of Arafat," she wrote. Except for Palestinian leader Yasser Arafat, she had met every one of that day's global newsmakers at one time or another. She put the observation in all capital letters, a form of digital shouting that she reserved for the biggest outrages or greatest pleasures.

"That's the life George Bush has given me," she wrote. "Amazing life."

(By the way, three years later she met Arafat, too, when the Palestinian leader was in Houston and visited the former president.)

Was the reverse also true? Was this the life she had given George Bush?

George Herbert Walker Bush was a man of ambition and ability. Since he was a boy growing up in Greenwich, Connecticut, he had been seen by family and friends and teachers as a natural leader who was destined for big things. He would serve with distinction in World War II, build an oil business, win a seat in Congress, represent his country in the United Nations, head the CIA, become vice president, and, finally, be elected the forty-first president of the United States. He would see his son inaugurated as the forty-third president. George Bush wasn't perfect, as a person or as a president, but by any measure he had an amazing life indeed.

In doing dozens of interviews for this biography, I asked almost everyone I could this question: If George Bush hadn't married Barbara Pierce, would he have been able to achieve all that?

History isn't a computer game, of course. It can't be rerun with a different set of specs. If they hadn't met at that Christmas dance in 1941, he likely would have married someone else, someone with her own strengths and weaknesses, and her own story.

But he didn't. He married Barbara Pierce, and they would be partners for the seventy-three years that followed, through crisis and triumph and grief and joy.

George Bush and Barbara Bush both answered my question the same way.

And I believe both of them were wrong.

⌒ ⌒

When I asked Barbara Bush if her husband would have become president without her, she was immediate and emphatic.

"Yes, he would have," she declared. "He would. He was born to do his best in everything."

When I asked George Bush, he seemed to turn the question over in his mind. We were talking in his Houston office, in November 2017, almost exactly a year before his death at age ninety-four. It was the last interview he would do with a journalist. The effects of vascular parkinsonism had robbed him of mobility; he was using a wheelchair. He could understand questions and formulate responses, but to his frustration it was difficult for him to speak more than a few words at a time.

"Yeah, I think so," he said. "Good question, but I think so. You never know, but I think so."

His answer stopped me short. Just about any pol—maybe just about any husband—would know that the "right" answer to that question was no. I had expected him to say, "No, of course not. She was crucial. We were a team." But I was grateful that he hadn't simply delivered the politically correct answer. He had said what he thought.

On this, George Bush and Barbara Pierce Bush were true to their generation. They reflected the same attitude that had prompted her to be willing to follow him across the country and back, to uncomplainingly raise their family while he was so often on the road, to do everything she could to support his ambitions. *His* ambitions. In their era, women were more often seen as helpmates than partners, and rarely as equal partners.

Just asking the question prompted Bush's younger brother William, known to everyone as Bucky, to bristle a bit. I met with him on a bright New Year's Day in 2018, in West Palm Beach, Florida, where he spent winters. (At age seventy-nine, he was lively, lucid, and funny when I interviewed him, although he was annoyed that he recently had been forced to start using a walker for stability. The next month, he would die after a fall.) "I don't think she is the only reason he succeeded," he said, as though I was minimizing his brother's achievements. I assured him that wasn't my intent. "If you describe doing the job as a wife, she comes up pretty close to top of the charts," he said of his sister-in-law. But, no, he didn't see her role as crucial to his big brother's success in life.

In this decidedly unscientific survey, attitudes on this question were divided not by gender but by generation.

The younger the responder, the more certain the answer that Barbara Bush was a critical part of a team that propelled George Bush to the most powerful job in the world. Many of the millennials seemed a little perplexed about why the issue was worth a debate.

"She was pretty much like a part of the ticket," said grandson George P. Bush, the fourth generation of his family to win elective office. "She was not only the enforcer in the family but the enforcer politically. She would be the one that would remind, 'Hey, Gampy, this guy screwed you on this bill back when you were in Congress.'" If you're the one running for office, he noted, "sometimes you have to have amnesia."

Even among baby boomers, no longer a younger generation, only a few thought George Bush would have made it all the way to the White House without her. One of those was Andy Card, who served in the cabinet and on the White House staff of the elder Bush and as White House chief of staff for the younger Bush. He expressed enormous regard for Barbara Bush, but he said the instinct for public service had been inculcated in George Bush by his parents, his forceful mother and his father, a US senator. "I think it was in his blood," Card said.

Almost everyone else, including many of those who had worked most closely with George Bush during his political rise and his presidency, called Barbara Bush crucial for all that. Several of them independently settled on the same word: indispensable.

"She was indispensable, she was really indispensable," C. Boyden Gray, Bush's counsel as vice president and president, told me in an interview in his Washington law office, located a few blocks from the White House. "The anchor that she provided...allowed him the freedom and the assurance that there always was home, but he was free to pursue his dreams."

Then Gray revisited the original question. "Could he have become president without her?" he mused. "I don't know. I don't think so."

"He couldn't have done it without her," James A. Baker III, the Bushes' close friend and counselor, said in an interview in his Houston law office. "I really do believe that."

Barbara Bush was "somebody who would help toughen him at the right moments and somebody who would back him at the right moments, be in his corner," said Josh Bolten, who served on George H. W. Bush's White House staff and then as George W. Bush's chief of staff. "I bet he took some risks that he otherwise wouldn't have, had he not had the rock of Barbara Bush in his corner."

Former Canadian prime minister Brian Mulroney, an ally when the two men were in power and a good friend after they had left office, didn't hesitate.

"I can tell you, there's no doubt in my mind but that George Bush, for all his magnificent leadership qualities, became president of the United States because he married Barbara," he told me. "She was an indispensable part of his ascension to the highest office in the land. Without her, I tell you, I'm very doubtful we would have had a President George H. W. Bush."

He declared: "Nobody can be certain, but that's a no-brainer. Barbara made him as great as he became."

Those in the Bush family approached my query from a more personal perspective. Some found the question itself hard to fathom. "I can't imagine my grandfather without my grandmother," Barbara Pierce Bush, her namesake, replied. Perhaps that was an answer in itself.

"I think that was a marriage made in heaven," her nephew Jim Pierce said in an interview at his home in Houston, a short drive from where Aunt Bar and Uncle George lived. "That was the perfect union for him, 'cause she gave him the opportunity to pursue whatever he chose to pursue, and she supported him unequivocally. I don't think you can do what he did in his career without that kind of support valve."

That was a question he had thought through in his own life. In 1999, Jim Pierce had seriously considered running for Congress, for an open seat in the Houston district that George Bush had once represented. His wife, Dabney, told him she didn't want him to do that. "And that was the end of that, which is fine," he said without bitterness. It simply wasn't a move he wanted to make, or thought he could make, without his spouse's full support.

Jeb Bush wasn't entirely sure what the answer was, although he recognized the contribution his mother had made. "I think it's just an extraordinary team and the adversities they faced could have been a gigantic set of potholes, could have been a cliff," he told me. Given the complications of George Bush's life, the ambition and the successes and the setbacks, "to not have a partner, or to have a partner that was not as complete as my mom, that'd have been hard."

George W. Bush, like his father, considered the question about his parents before responding.

"It's unanswerable, but my guess is no," the forty-third president said finally. "I don't think he would have found somebody who, on the one hand, could help him raise a big family, which he wanted, and on the other hand, been [as willing to participate] in the many ventures he took on. This guy, he was willing to push the envelope of change. I doubt he could have ever found anybody who could have handled the change and the pressures of family the way Mom did."

He volunteered that he wouldn't have become president if he hadn't married Laura Welch. I asked another unanswerable question: Would he have become president if Barbara Bush hadn't been his mother?

Probably not, George W. Bush replied.

"She helped instill a lot of confidence in me. In order to run for president or governor in what seemed to be an impossible race, you [couldn't] be risk-averse. You've got to ask the question, why? How did I become such a confident person? Why wasn't I afraid to lose? Obviously, Dad had a huge influence in it because I watched him lose three times and know that life goes on, but Mother was a very encouraging person, you know?

"I remember her saying, 'Make sure you fight hard,'" he said. "'Don't give up.'"

—◠ ◡—

Bill Clinton knows something about the challenges of political life, and of achieving the presidency. He won two White House terms himself, then to almost everyone's surprise became a friend to two other presidents—the one he defeated, George Bush, and the one who succeeded him, George W. Bush.

What about the elder Bush? Would he have become president without Barbara?

"Not a shot," Clinton said flatly. Then the forty-second president delivered a discursive, Clintonesque explanation of why he thought that.

He began by imagining the proposition George Bush gave his bride just after World War II, a woman "who was born into remarkably comfortable circumstances." Here is what Clinton pictured Bush saying to her.

"I do not want a remarkably comfortable life. I want to get in this old car . . . and drive to West Texas—which you had never seen, which has no other institutions around which you have organized your life, with none of the women you have known. And I want you to go with me there and we have one child. I want to have a whole mess of 'em out there. And you will be there, and [in] what you may now think is a desolate place, raising all these kids while I first try to make it in the oil business and then try to make it in politics . . . The truth is our chances [of success] are rather remote. But it's what I want to do. I think it'll be a great adventure. Would you come?"

Clinton said Barbara Bush not only said yes but also "stuck when things went haywire and sideways," as they inevitably did at times.

While the answer to the question I had asked was unknowable, he said, he was sure he knew what the answer was. "It is no diminution of him whatever to say that it is unlikely he would have had the life without her," Clinton said, then added with a laugh, "In fact, it shows a certain strength that he wasn't afraid to marry her."

Throughout her life, Barbara Bush was consistently underestimated—by her mother, by her teachers, by her husband, by herself. The daughter who was easy to overlook ended up topping the list of women Americans most admire, though she would have responded to any suggestion that she was important or remarkable with a self-deprecating quip.

After the George Bush Presidential Library and Museum opened in 1997, some of those who admired Barbara Bush protested that she was given short shrift in it. The initial exhibit included photos of her with her dog Millie, and video of her reading to children. "What is lacking is an attempt to convey to the visitor how many issues Mrs. Bush devoted herself to and the impact that she had," one of her East Wing staffers wrote in a memo to museum curator Patricia Burchfield. "We have not conveyed this part of Mrs. Bush's work as First Lady in the exhibit and this is what needs to be improved."

Barbara Bush's contribution was again undervalued, though that was not a complaint she ever made. "She didn't in any way resent that she stood in his shadow," Laura Bush said of her mother-in-law. "I think that was typical of their generation, but also, Bar was happy to be that way," to have George Bush in the spotlight. "She adored him."

"Indispensable" is the right word. Barbara Pierce turned out to be George Bush's indispensable partner—not only as the wife and mother who provided a stable home but also as the gimlet-eyed adviser who weighed in on critical moments during his campaigns and his presidency. She was his conscience in addressing the AIDS crisis and his collaborator in creating personal relationships that facilitated negotiations to end the Cold War. She was a trusted adviser in private and a political asset in public. She stood by him through rocky times, after political defeat and family tragedy, as he stood by her.

He gave her an amazing life, and she returned the favor.

"Amazing life," she wrote in her diary that day in 1994. "Lucky lucky me."

Acknowledgments

The dedication at the beginning of this book was short. Fair warning:
The acknowledgments at the end of it are long.

The acknowledgments must begin with Barbara Pierce Bush, who
lived an interesting, complicated, and important life, and agreed to share
it with me. This book is an independent work, not an authorized biography, but when I contacted her in the summer of 2017 and asked for her
cooperation as I wrote this book, she agreed to meet with me. Eventually, we had five extended conversations in her Houston home during
the final six months of her life. She gave me permission to read the pro-
digious scrapbooks she kept through her life and to see her high school
transcripts—"although I fear she will be unimpressed," she wryly noted
in her letter to the archivist. Eventually, she granted me access to the
personal diaries and letters she began keeping in 1948. She wrote the
final, poignant diary entry seventy years later, just twelve days before her
death.

I am grateful to have had the opportunity to interview her husband of seventy-three years, George Bush, as well as her brother Scott
Pierce, and sons George W. Bush, Jeb Bush, and Neil Bush. My thanks
to Barbara P. Bush, George P. Bush, Marshall Bush, Pierce Bush, Jenna
Bush Hager, and Ellie LeBlond Sosa for sharing their perspectives on
their grandmother. Interviews with daughters-in-law Laura Bush and
Columba Bush and with brother-in-law William "Bucky" Bush helped
me to better understand Barbara Bush. So did my interviews with Bill
Clinton, Hillary Clinton, Dick Cheney, Karen Pence, James A. Baker

III, Brent Scowcroft, and Brian Mulroney. Marlin Fitzwater, Andy Card, Charlie Black, Peter Teeley, Ron Kaufman, John Sununu, Frank Fahrenkopf, Fred Malek, Sheila Tate, Karl Rove, Anita McBride, Tim McBride, Mary Kate Cary, Edward E. McNally, and Susan Porter Rose were crucial to my understanding more fully Barbara Bush's role in the White House and on the campaign trail. Benita Somerfield and Sharon Darling illuminated her work on literacy. Her assistants at the White House and during the years that followed—including Julie Cooke, Kristan King Nevins, Peggy Swift White, and Elizabeth Wise—gave me an invaluable look behind the scenes. Susan Baker, Betsy Heminway, and the Reverend Dr. Russell Levenson provided more personal insights. So did the women who make up the 1925 Club, a group of Texas girlfriends of a certain age who allowed me to join their monthly luncheon. My appreciation goes to Ada Grundy, Bessie Liedtke, Barbara Riddell, and Helen Vietor for their hospitality.

Jean Becker, chief of staff for President George H. W. Bush, was invaluable, a resource beyond any reasonable expectation. She helped on everything from tracking down the details to deliberating philosophical questions. So did President Bush's spokesman, Jim McGrath. I am indebted to them both. Among others in the Bush office, I appreciate the assistance of Neely Brunette and Evan Sisley. The staff at the George H. W. Bush Presidential Library and Museum in College Station, Texas, was cooperative and patient in dealing with a rookie researcher. My thanks to Director Warren Finch, Deborah Wheeler, R. Matthew Lee, Elizabeth Staats, and Cody McMillian. Audiovisual archivist Mary Finch was unfailingly helpful in managing access to Barbara Bush's diaries and the library's photo collection.

The intelligence and diligence of senior researcher Will Leubsdorf made this book more accurate and complete, not to mention delivered on time. My thanks also to researchers Sam Fontaine, working at the Ronald Reagan Presidential Library and Museum; Christine McCall, working at the William J. Clinton Presidential Library and Museum;

Andrew Brown and Laurence Nelson, working at the George H. W. Bush Presidential Library and Museum; Lori Berdak Miller of Redbird Research, working at the National Archives in St. Louis; and Kim White, working at the Ohio Historical Society.

Archives at libraries and special collections provided details and context for this biography. My appreciation goes to David Grinnell and the staff at University of Pittsburgh System Archives & Special Collections Department; Dale Rosengarten and the staff at Special Collections, Addlestone Library, College of Charleston; Jacky Johnson and the staff at Miami University of Ohio Special Collections and Archives; Allison Seyler and the B&O Railroad Museum Archives; Nanci Young and the staff at Smith College's Special Collections, Young Library; South Caroliniana Library, University of South Carolina; Leslie Nellis and the American University Archives and Special Collections; Virginia Historical Society; South Carolina Historical Society; Library of Congress, staff of Jefferson, Motion Picture & Television, and Newspaper & Current Periodicals reading rooms; the staff at the National Archives Microfilm Reading Room in Washington, DC; the Sharpsville Historical Society; and the White House Historical Association. Special thanks go to the George Washington University Gelman Library staff.

That said, any errors are mine alone.

This project began when one friend, Robin Sproul, suggested I consider writing a book and another friend, Karen Tumulty, set an inspirational example by signing a contract to write a biography of Nancy Reagan. Several friends who have written outstanding books, including Joan Biskupic and John A. Farrell, shared advice on how to proceed. Jon Meacham, author of the definitive biography of George H. W. Bush, *Destiny and Power: The American Odyssey of George Herbert Walker Bush*, was generous and encouraging. So was Myra G. Gutin, author of *Barbara Bush: Presidential Matriarch*. Robert Dallek and Matthew Dallek gave me a free tutorial on archival research and more. My thanks also go to Jeffrey A. Engel, Mark K. Updegrove, Michael Beschloss, and

Barbara A. Perry for giving me the benefit of their deep academic experience.

Cragg Hines provided the sharp eye and long memory of a journalist who covered the Bushes for decades for their hometown newspaper, the *Houston Chronicle*. Other colleagues in the press corps who covered the White House and presidential campaigns with me shared details and memories of key moments. My particular thanks to Kathy Lewis, Lou Cannon, Ira Allen, Terence Hunt, Thomas M. DeFrank, Howard Fineman, Walter Robinson, and Ann Compton.

Paul Morse, Evan Sisley, Pete Souza, David Shribman, Robert Deutsch, Tim Loehrke, and *USA TODAY* and the USA TODAY Network, including the *Indianapolis Star* and the *Clarion-Ledger* of Jackson, Mississippi, made it possible to reproduce the striking photographs and images illustrating Barbara Bush's remarkable life.

At *USA TODAY*, publisher Maribel Perez Wadsworth and editor in chief Joanne Lipman were generous in negotiating the flexibility of half-time leave for a year. That made it possible for me to remain engaged in coverage of Washington's dramatic current events while also undertaking this project to explore one of its former residents. Managing editor Lee Horwich provided encouragement, advice, and an editor's eye. I'm grateful to Nicole Carroll, Jeff Taylor, Wendy Benjaminson, and Kristen DelGuzzi for making this arrangement work when they became my new bosses in the interim.

My agents, Matt Latimer and Keith Urbahn, partners at Javelin DC, were crucial advisers and advocates, essential every step of the way. I'm grateful to Sean Desmond of Twelve for seeing the possibilities in a biography of Barbara Bush and then guiding it with great skill to completion. At Twelve, my thanks also extend to Paul Samuelson, Brian McLendon, Rachel Molland, and Rachel Kambury; and to Jarrod Taylor for designing a cover that captured the wisdom and the wariness of Barbara Bush.

Finally, and first, I am grateful beyond measure to my family for their support, patience, humor, and love. Ben Leubsdorf, Will Leubsdorf, and Carl Leubsdorf Jr. helped at key moments. Most of all, my husband,

Carl Leubsdorf, acted as memory bank, fact-checker, back-reader, and volunteer accountant. He was an encouraging voice when it mattered most. We've been married for thirty-seven years, which doesn't begin to compare to the seventy-three-year marriage of Barbara and George Bush. But it's a start.

Thank you.

Susan Page

Notes

Abbreviations used in endnotes

ATB: *All the Best, George Bush: My Life in Letters and Other Writings*, by George Bush

BB: *Barbara Bush: A Memoir*, by Barbara Bush

DP: *Destiny and Power: The American Odyssey of George Herbert Walker Bush*, by Jon Meacham

LF: *Looking Forward*, by George Bush with Victor Gold

MFMP: *My Father, My President: A Personal Account of the Life of George H. W. Bush*, by Doro Bush Koch

Introduction

"It was unbelievable"—Author interview with George W. Bush.

"The Secret Service is saying"—Author interview with David Rubenstein. Safari also discussed in *Reflections*, by Barbara Bush, pp. 321–22.

"Never ask anyone over seventy"—Barbara Bush interview on CNN's *Larry King Live*, November 22, 2010.

She was "a person with a strong sense of right and wrong"—Author interview with Bill Clinton.

"She's about the only voice"—Author interview with former White House press secretary Marlin Fitzwater.

"There is no George H. W. Bush"—Author interview with Pierce Bush.

"I talked to Susan Page"—Barbara Bush diary entry, December 19, 2017.

"I like her"—Barbara Bush diary entry, February 6, 2018.

Her distant cousin—Franklin Pierce was the fourth cousin, four times removed, of Barbara Pierce Bush.

"She is a strong woman"—*What I Saw at the Revolution*, by Peggy Noonan, p. 303.

"In a different time and a different era"—Author interview with Jeb Bush in 1990 for "Why America Loves Barbara Bush," by Susan Page, Newsday.

"She lived a full and exemplary life"—Author interview with Hillary Clinton.

Jeb Bush...described a common phenomenon—Author interview with Jeb Bush in 2018.

"At the end of your life"—Barbara Bush commencement address, Wellesley College, June 1, 1990.

"Mother was pretty good about dealing"—Author interview with George W. Bush.

"*The Fat Lady Sings Again*"—Author interview with Barbara Bush.

Chapter One: Six Brutal Months

"I don't know what to do"—*BB*, p. 39.

"You don't have a choice"—*DP*, p. 87.

When their teetotaling minister—*BB*, p. 40.

"I remember realizing"—Ibid., p. 45.

Patients were "diagnosed"—*Medical World News*, November 11, 1966, quoted in *The Emperor of All Maladies*, by Siddhartha Mukherjee, p. 12.

"Our big hope"—*DP*, p. 98.

highest white blood cell count—*LF*, p. 69.

"How we hated"—*BB*, p. 43.

"panicked, crying"—*DP*, p. 98.

"We used to laugh"—*BB*, p. 44.

"Someone had to look"—*ATB*, p. 102.

He often would arrive disheveled—*MFMP*, p. 53.

"What does your husband do"—*BB*, p. 42.

"Her eyes didn't sparkle"—*MFMP*, p. 52.

She found Ashley, huddled outside—*BB*, p. 42.

Sloan Kettering didn't charge—*Hope and Suffering*, by Gretchen Krueger, p. 102.

"Do you remember in the Bible where it says?"—The King James version of the Bible verse Matthew 19:14 reads, "But Jesus said, Suffer little children, and forbid them not, to come unto me: for of such is the kingdom of heaven."

"He raised our hopes"—*BB*, p. 42–43.

he was putty—Ibid., p. 43.

Many in Midland shied away—Ibid.

"I said, 'No, we've done enough to her'"—Interview with George Bush by Jon Meacham for *DP*, p. 99.

"One minute she was there"—*BB*, p. 44.

"Like an oak in the wind"—*What It Takes*, by Richard Ben Cramer, p. 244.

"I knew old so-and-so"—*BB*, p. 44.

It would be the first vivid memory of his life—Author interview with George W. Bush.

"We should have told him"—Author interview with Barbara Bush.

he had such terrifying nightmares—*First Son*, by Bill Minutaglio, pp. 46–47.

"I just needed somebody to blame"—*BB*, p. 46.

"I wouldn't let them cry in front of her"—Author interview with Barbara Bush.

"Time after time during the next six months"—*BB*, p. 45.

A study in the 1970s—*The Bereaved Parent*, by Harriet Sarnoff Schiff, p. 180.

another study concluded—"Research on the Effect of Parental Bereavement," by Lynn Videka-Sherman, Social Service Review, p. 102.

"I wanted to get back"—*BB*, p. 46.

"There is a sad part"—*MFMP*, p. 55.

"That, I think, was maybe one of the things"—Author interview with Susan Baker.

he wished he were Robin—*BB*, p. 46.

"He taught me something"—Author interview with Barbara Bush.

"I feel very close to George"—Author interview with Barbara Bush.

"We had a very, very close relationship"—Author interview with George W. Bush.

In the days before her own death—Author interview with Jean Becker.

"Mother's reaction"—"Don't Call Him Junior," by Patricia Kilday Hart, *Texas Monthly*, April 1989.

"That started my cure"—*BB*, p. 47.

"For a while after"—*Decision Points*, by George W. Bush, p. 7.

"I think kids who lose a sibling"—*First Son*, by Bill Minutaglio, p. 46.

"He felt he had to be the caretaker"—Author interview with Betsy Heminway.

"I always thought that was so sweet"—Author interview with granddaughter Barbara Pierce Bush.

"She was a constant memory"—Author interview with Neil Bush.

"It's a strange thing"—*MFMP*, p. 56.

She once told her mother—Author interview with Barbara Bush.

"There is about our house a need"—*ATB*, pp. 81–82.

"He just said, 'I've got to do something that's bigger'"—Author interview with Bessie Liedtke.

"Maybe all those things add up"—Author interview with Barbara Bush.

"It taught me that no matter"—*DP*, p. 101.

On December 20, 2017, she wrote—Barbara Bush diaries, December 2017.

Chapter Two: "The Fighting Pierces"

"Marked by seasickness"—*Coming Over*, by David Cressy, p. 159.

Notably for the time—One of the passengers on this voyage would have a bizarre intersection with another of Barbara Bush's ancestors. Nicholas Jennings, then twenty-two, arrived aboard the *Francis* with Coe in 1634. In 1661, in Lyme, Connecticut, Jennings and his wife, Margaret, were indicted for killing by witchcraft Marie Marvin, the wife of Reinhold Marvin, who was Barbara Bush's eighth-great-grandfather. Jennings and his wife were found not guilty, although most of the jury voted to convict them. *Witchcraft Trials of Connecticut*, by R. G. Tomlinson, pp. 24–25.

By the time Coe came ashore—*The Mayflower and Her Passengers*, by Caleb H. Johnson, p. 204.

As for Robert Coe—A fresco memorializing Hawkwood—holding a commander's baton and sitting astride a gray steed—is displayed in the Duomo in Florence, where he is buried. When John Coe returned to England, he established endowments at several churches in Essex for priests to celebrate Masses for Hawkwood's soul. *John Hawkwood*, by William Caferro, p. 40.

Puritans like Coe—Among them were Thomas and Elizabeth Pierce, who emigrated from England in 1633 or 1634. Their son, Thomas, would be the common ancestor of President Franklin Pierce and Barbara Bush. *Pierce Genealogy*, by Frederick C. Pierce, pp. 17–19.

After arriving in America—Another direct ancestor of Barbara Pierce Bush, Ezekiel Richardson, who emigrated from England in 1630, became a follower of two prominent dissenters in the Massachusetts Bay Colony, Anne Hutchinson and the Reverend John Wheelwright, in what was known as the Antinomian Controversy.

Five years later, in the wake of a disagreement—*History of the Colony of New Haven*, by Edward R. Lambert, p. 176.

Robert Coe was "a fine example"—*Robert Coe, Puritan*, by Joseph G. Bartlett, p. 76.

After yet another battle over church governance—Ibid., p. 74. The influential Puritan minister Cotton Mather described the diminutive Denton this way: "Though he were a little man, yet he had a great soul; his well-accomplished mind, in his lesser body, was as an Iliad in a nutshell." *Magnalia Christi Americana*, by Cotton Mather, p. 360.

There are indications—*The Skillmans of New York*, by Francis Skillman, p. 38.

His son Benjamin was among those who signed a letter—*Documents Relative to the Colonial History of the State of New York*, by Berthold Fernow, p. 492.

It was through this family line—Franklin Pierce was the fourth cousin, four times removed, of Barbara Bush.

The town was established in 1820 by James Sharp—*Golden Anniversary: 1874–1924; Borough of Sharpsville*. Sharp was rumored to be a bigamist; his older wife was said to have lived downstairs, the younger one upstairs. He reportedly fled with his younger wife.

"a wiry, well-spoken man"—"Great Mansion Is Fading Reminder of General Pierce," by Malry J. Wage, *Sharon Herald*, July 16, 1952

"indomitable energy"—"General James Pierce," *Record-Argus* (Greenville, PA), December 5, 1874.

By the time he died, he was worth $1.5 million—Ibid.

A local newspaper reported the jaw-dropping cost—Ibid.

The three-story mansion boasted thirty rooms—*History of Sharpsville, Pennsylvania*, pp. 7–8.

Soon after construction—*Record-Argus* (Greenville, PA), November 28, 1874; "Giant Mansion Is Fading Reminder of General Pierce," by Malry J. Wage, *Sharon Herald*, July 16, 1952.

All of them would be locally prominent—In 1884 Wallace Pierce presented a $5,000 promissory note to the McKeesport (PA) city council, saying he got it from a lawyer that the city owed money to. Neither the council nor the city had any record of the note ever existing, and it is strongly implied in the newspaper accounts of the time that Wallace forged the note (*Pittsburgh Daily Post*, December 15, 1884). In 1915, both Frank and James B. Pierce were accused of extorting $20,000 from a local businessman and his wife, though both Pierces were found not guilty by a jury (*Pittsburgh Press*, May 17, 1915; *Record-Argus* [Greenville, PA], December 4, 1915).

Weirdly, all except Frank—*History of Sharpsville*, Sharpsville Historical Society.

That would be the source of fascination—Author interviews with Barbara Bush and Scott Pierce.

He "withstood the war fever"—*A Twentieth Century History of Mercer County*, by John G. White, p. 930.

"the roughest and wickedest place"—*Bound to Be a Soldier*, by James Todd Miller, p. 7.

The hardtack biscuits—Ibid., p. 22.

After little more—Adjutant General's Office (1861–1862). Combined Military Service Report, 111th Pennsylvania Infantry, Jonas Pierce, RG 94, National Archives; Pennsylvania 111th Volunteer Infantry Regiment Orders Book (1861–1865), RG 94, National Archives.

Of the 1,549 men—*Regimental Losses in the American Civil War, 1861–1865*, by William F. Fox, p. 122.

Son Jonas Pierce had been a Democrat—*Pittsburgh Press*, October 16, 1884.

After he died, his widow and sons agreed—*Pierce v. Pierce*, 1885, 55 Mich. 629.

Efforts to dominate—"A Lively Contest in Western Pennsylvania," *New York Times*, January 12, 1883; *The Railroad That Never Was*, by Herbert H. Harwood Jr.

His four brothers and his mother—Sharpsville Railroad minute book, Box 406C-2, location 15.1.3, CSX Collection, Baltimore & Ohio Railroad Museum, Hays T. Watkins Research Library.

"Sharpsville will go down in history"—*Golden Anniversary: 1874–1924; Borough of Sharpsville*.

A lawsuit filed by Jonas Pierce—"Game Theory and Cumulative Voting for Corporate Directors," by Gerald J. Glasser, *Management Science*.

A second lawsuit, over 414 critical shares—*Jonas J. Pierce vs. First National Bank of West Greenville, the Sharpsville Railroad Company, and Walter Pierce*, Jonas J. Pierce Court Documents, Location 16.3.5., CSX Collection, Baltimore & Ohio Railroad Museum, Hays T. Watkins Research Library.

The *Pittsburgh Post-Gazette* headlined its story "The Fighting Pierces"—*Pittsburgh Post-Gazette*, May 15, 1884, p. 2.

Local law enforcement was less effective—Sharpsville Historical Society, III #3, September 9, 2014.

Jonas's brothers—*Pierce v. Pierce* 1885, 55 Mich. 629; *Pierce et al. v. Pierce*, 1892, *The Northwestern Reporter*, p. 851.

he left behind—"Trouble Following a Suicide," *Pittsburgh Dispatch*, February 29, 1892.

At a meeting—"Going out of Blast," *Pittsburgh Dispatch*, March 14, 1892.

Their unpaid debts were a factor—"The Iron Failures of the Week," *Iron Trade Review*, July 27, 1893, p. 7.

The city of Sharpsville filed—*Record-Argus* (Greenville, PA), October 3, 1905.

a bankrupt Jonas—Pension file, Jonas J. Pierce, pension application no. 1112261, Civil War Pension Index 1861–1934, Series T288; Roll 372. National Archives, Washington, DC. His pension would go up to $12 a month in April 1907, $15 a month in October 1909, and $19 a month in October 1912. The increase of pension from

$8 to $12 in 1907 was due to a change in law, which allowed soldiers to get pension based on old age, without having to demonstrate they were an invalid. Jonas's congressman, N. P. Wheeler, helped push the pension office to grant the increase to Jonas.

Chapter Three: The Football Star and the Campus Beauty

Gone was the comfortable life—*A Twentieth Century History of Mercer County*, by John G. White, pp. 931, 1909. Scott Pierce was the oldest of five children of Jonas Pierce and Kate Pritzl Pierce, an emigrant from Bavaria. Kate Pritzl's father was a civil engineer who had designed the pleasure ground of King Ludwig of Bavaria in Munich. Ludwig's son was the famous "Mad King." Scott may have been named after William Lawrence Scott, the railroad magnate who formed a partnership with his father in his legal battles against the rest of the family over control of the company.

He...worked for his father's company—*Index to "A Portrait and Biographical Record of Portage and Summit Counties,"* by James F. Caccamo, Jack Kauffmann Bowers, and Gwendolyn E. Mayer, p. 431.

the local newspapers published items—*Akron Beacon Journal*, October 26, 1895.

Another story chronicled a whist club—"A Whist Club," *Akron Beacon Journal*, October 21, 1897.

For a half dozen years—"Pierce Heard by the Salesmanship Class Last Night," *Hamilton Evening Journal*, March 19, 1915.

"Daddy's father, Scott Pierce, was not a success"—Letter written by Barbara Bush to her niece Gail Rafferty, but never sent; included in her diaries and dated January 30, 2017.

She remembered her grandfather—Author interview with Barbara Bush.

Handsome, graceful, and six feet tall—"Oxford Colonials to Meet Reserves," *Xenia Daily Gazette*, July 3, 1914.

None of the industrial titans in Dayton "loomed as large"—*You Have to Pay the Price*, by Earl H. Blaik, p. 13.

Athletic scholarships didn't exist—"A History of Recruiting: How Coaches Have Stayed a Step Ahead," by Andy Staples, *Sports Illustrated*, June 23, 2008.

A handwritten letter from George R. Eastman—Letter from George R. Eastman to A. E. Young, dated, March 27, 1912. Marvin Pierce File. Alumni/Alumni Affairs/Development, Individuals, Mo-Ste, Box 16. Miami University Libraries. Miami University Archives, Oxford, OH.

Marvin would support his parents financially—*BB*, p. 7.

On his father's sixtieth birthday—Letter from Raymond Hughes to Marvin Pierce, February 19, 1926. Raymond Mollyneaux Hughes Collection, Office Files, O-Z, 1925–26, Box 8. Miami University Archives, Oxford, OH.

His father warned—Letter from George R. Eastman to Prof. A. E. Young, dated March 27, 1912. Marvin Pierce File. Alumni/Alumni Affairs/Development, Individuals, Mo-Ste, Box 16. Miami University Libraries. Miami University Archives, Oxford, OH.

Professor A. E. Young forwarded the letter—Letter from A. E. Young to Raymond Hughes, dated March 29, 1912. Marvin Pierce File. Alumni/Alumni Affairs/Development, Individuals, Mo-Ste, Box 16. Miami University Libraries. Miami University Archives, Oxford, OH.

"I appreciate, however, the value"—Letter from Raymond Hughes to A.E. Young, dated March 30, 1912. Marvin Pierce File. Alumni/Alumni Affairs/Development, Individuals, Mo-Ste, Box 16. Miami University Libraries. Miami University Archives, Oxford, OH.

Blaik described him—*You Have to Pay the Price*, by Earl H. Blaik, p. 19.

a nine-letter man—*BB*, p. 8.

Marvin began playing—"Pierce Pitching Fine Ball," *Lima News*, July 6, 1914.

Then he was notified—"Pierce May Be Black Listed," *Xenia Daily Gazette*, June 26, 1915.

But Marvin was allowed to continue to play—*Hamilton Evening Journal*, June 25, 1915.

The other two players didn't return—College records show one of the students, junior Arthur Crist, did not return for his senior year, and later joined the Army in World War I. "Arthur J. Crist War Record" (Student 1912–14), Miami University Libraries. Miami University Archives, Oxford, OH. The other, junior Charles Landrey, also did not return to Miami the following year; no explanation was given. "Chances of State Championship Coming to Miami Are Great," *Miami Student* 40, no. 1 (September 23, 1915).

"a fine specimen"—"Marvin Pierce, the Star Player on Miami U Football Eleven Well Known to Many in Hamilton," *Hamilton Evening Journal*, October 30, 1913.

When Pierce was a senior—Graduation speech at Miami University of Ohio in 1951, by Marvin Pierce. Marvin Pierce File. Alumni/Alumni Affairs/Development, Individuals, Mo-Ste, Box 16. Miami University Libraries. Miami University Archives, Oxford, OH.

"March 8th—Pauline Robinson wears her hair back"—Miami University yearbook *Recensio*, 1915, p. 283.

Another entry seemed to make a juvenile joke—Miami University yearbook *Recensio*, 1916, p. 290.

As a freshman, Pauline accompanied Red Blaik—Scrapbook kept by Kenneth "Chief" Crawford, a football player and fraternity brother; he later played in the early National Football League. Miami University Libraries. Miami University Archives, Oxford, OH.

She played first violin—Miami University yearbook *Recensio*, 1916, pp. 110, 151.

When Marvin Pierce came courting—"Week-End Here," *Union County Journal*, June 12, 1917; "Week-End Guest," *Union County Journal*, July 3, 1917; "Guest in Marysville," *Marysville Journal-Tribune*, April 20, 1918.

A month after Congress—"United States, World War One Draft Registration Cards, 1917–1918." Marvin Pierce. Database with images. FamilySearch. http://Family Search.org: 11 July 2018. Citing NARA microfilm publication M1509. Washington, DC: National Archives and Records Administration, n.d.

Marvin and his unit boarded the transport ship—Company Number One History, Washington Barracks, S.A.R.D of Engineers, American Expeditionary Force, p. 3.

A few months after the Armistice—Daily Report of Casualties and Changes, April 6–12, 1919. Camp Hospital 40, American Expeditionary Force, World War I. National Archives at St. Louis, MO.

Robinson was born—"James E. Robinson," *Richwood Gazette*, June 22, 1899.

began running ads in local newspapers—"Professional Cards," *Richwood Gazette*, January 28, 1897.

"Always eloquent"—"Arguments Made in the Larkin Case," *Marysville Journal-Tribune*, January 23, 1914.

Her husband threatened—"About the Court House," *Weekly Marysville Tribune*, January 9, 1895.

Another said her husband—"J. J. Parish: A School Teacher, Wrote Spicy Love Letters," *Union County Journal*, March 27, 1902.

There was a woman—"Two Wives Ask the Court to Give Them Freedom from Erring Husbands," *Marysville Journal-Tribune*, October 22, 1901.

"Mr. Robinson's hustling qualities"—*Richwood Gazette*, June 22, 1899.

In one case—"Prosecutor Robinson Scared," *Richwood Gazette*, September 16, 1902.

Robinson took the case—"Wants to Be Separated from Joseph," *Richwood Gazette*, October 23, 1902.

A few months later—"Election Results in County," *Marysville Journal-Tribune*, November 5, 1902.

After the election, Robinson—"Nile Bland Purposely Casts an Illegal Vote in Milford Center," *Union County Journal*, November 13, 1902.

In that election, Robinson—"Election Results in County," *Marysville Journal-Tribune*, November 5, 1902.

His judicial philosophy—Rulings, Concurrences, and Dissents of Justice, James E. Robinson, Supreme Court of Ohio Law Library.

In at least two cases—"Judge Robinson," *Marysville Journal-Tribune*, January 27, 1932.

The whole notion—"Mexico Lures Four Widowed Grandmothers," United Press, November 30, 1939.

"She was very adventurous"—Author interview with Barbara Bush.

Chapter Four: Stuck in the Middle

"For a week, I wore"—Barbara Bush, American University Distinguished Lecture Series, May 1, 1985. "Sadat and Barbara Bush Lecture," Courtesy of University Archives and Special Collections, American University Library.

"He was the fairest man I knew"—*BB*, p. 29.

In a letter to a friend—Marvin Pierce letter to J. G. Kiefaber, March 22, 1948. George Bush Collection, World War II Correspondence, Box 2, George H. W. Bush Presidential Library.

a nice club, to be sure, but not the most elite—The Apawamis Club "was decidedly more upper-middle class than upper class." There was a $500 initiation fee and annual dues of $250 as of 1934. *In Pursuit of Privilege*, by Clifton Hood, pp. 312–14.

"Mrs. Pierce, she was tough"—Author interview with William "Bucky" Bush.

She told me she felt her father favored her—Author interview with Barbara Bush.

she was "probably the child least close to my mother"—*Simply Barbara Bush*, by Donnie Radcliffe, p. 84.

Even Miss Covington's Dancing School—*BB*, pp. 12–13.

"I remember my mother saying"—*BB*, pp. 6–7.

Her mother joked that Barbara had weighed a hundred pounds at birth—*First Ladies*, by Margaret Truman, p. 314.

"The best food in the world"—*BB*, p. 6.

In a youthful episode—*BB*, pp. 27–28.

June Biedler, a childhood pal—"Barbara's Backlash," by Marjorie Williams, *Vanity Fair*, August 1992.

"The meanest article I have ever read about me"—Barbara Bush diary entry, July 16, 1992.

In an interview a quarter century later—Author interview with Barbara Bush.

"She begged and borrowed"—Author interview with Barbara Bush.

"You have two choices in life"—*BB*, p. 31.

As a girl, Barbara was shocked—Author interview with Barbara Bush.

Marvin Pierce had been trained as an engineer—*Technology Review* 24, no. 1 (January 1922): 352.

He landed one at the McCall Corporation—*Betas of Achievement*, by William Raimond Baird; *Beta Lore: Sentiment, Song and Story in Beta Theta Pi*, by Francis W. Shepardson, p. 416; *Miami University Bulletin* 19, no. 6 (February 1921): p. 27; McCall 1922 Annual Report.

Pierce was hired—*Technology Review* 24, no. 1 (January 1922): 352.

Pierce didn't know much about recipes—*In Quiet Ways*, by Herrymon Maurer, p. 118.

He played a major role—*Inside the Founding of* Newsweek, by Thomas J. C. Martyn.

The week before Barbara Bush was married—Author interview with Barbara Bush.

"Part of my job after the operations"—Author interview with Scott Pierce.

Once, driving Scott to the hospital—Author interview and subsequent email exchange with Scott Pierce.

"In retrospect, I realize"—Author interview with Barbara Bush.

The treatment Scott received was considered appropriate—"Solitary Bone Cyst," by Bradley L. Coley and Norman L. Higinbotham, *Annals of Surgery*.

But under today's protocols—Dr. Michael S. Hughes, pediatric orthopedic surgeon.

"He was charming"—Author interview with Barbara Bush.

then was honorably discharged eighteen months later—James Robinson Pierce Army Air Corps Discharge Papers, July 14, 1943. War Department Adjutant General's Office, Form No. 55. National Archives at St. Louis, MO.

He worked for a time as a trainee—Russell, Burdsall and Ward, in Port Chester, N.Y. James Robinson Pierce Enlistment Papers, U.S. Navy, DSS Form No. 221, July 1944. National Archives at St. Louis, MO.

then enlisted in the Navy Reserves—James Robinson Pierce U.S. Navy Combined Service Record. National Archives at St. Louis, MO; Barbara Bush told me that Jimmy Pierce originally enlisted in the Canadian Air Force, a commitment her father helped extricate him from, but I was unable to find official records corroborating this.

A sanctioned history—*Ashley Hall*, by Ileana Strauch, p. 124.

Letters home written by Kathryn Noble—Kathryn Noble letter dated February 22, 1940. Taylor family. Taylor family papers, 1856–1981. (0574.00) South Carolina Historical Society.

Barbara started smoking—Author interview with Barbara Bush.

chronic lung disease—She was diagnosed with COPD, chronic inflammatory lung disease.

There were no African American students—*Charleston in Black and White*, by Steve Estes, p. 95.

Jewish girls were allowed to attend—Shera Lee Ellison Berlin, audio interview with Dale Rosengarten and Michael Samuel Grossman, 16 April 1997, Mss. 1035-144, Special Collections, College of Charleston, Charleston, SC.

Martha was a campus star—*Ashley Hall Cerberus*, June 1937. Ashley Hall Collection, College of Charleston Libraries, Charleston, SC.

Still, Martha was always "somewhat of a loner"—*BB*, p. 10.

In a short story—*Ashley Hall Cerberus*, December 1936, pp. 25–27. South Caroliniana Library, University of South Carolina.

As a senior—*Ashley Hall Cerberus*, June 1937, p. 149. Ashley Hall Collection, College of Charleston Libraries, Charleston, SC.

The group coordinated campaign volunteers—John Alsop was the younger brother of Washington political columnists Joseph and Stewart Alsop.

"Everybody liked her"—Author interview with Jane Lucas Thornhill.

But her grades were mediocre—Barbara Pierce Ashley Hall Cumulative Record. Ashley Hall Collection, College of Charleston Libraries, Charleston, SC.

"Although I fear she will be unimpressed"—Barbara Bush letter to College of Charleston, January 26, 2018.

"B. Pierce likes flowers"—*Ashley Hall Cerberus*, June 1942, p. 42. Ashley Hall Collection, College of Charleston Libraries, Charleston, SC.

When Barbara Bush was ninety-two years old—Author interview with Barbara Bush.

"Everytime I say beautiful"—Letter from George Bush to Barbara Pierce, December 12, 1943, *ATB*, p. 39.

Chapter Five: Love and War

George Bush was so young—"Consent-to-Wed Law for Males Is Upheld," by C. Gerald Fraser, *New York Times*, March 13, 1973.

"In wartime, the rules change"—*BB*, p. 22.

George Bush said they were living—*LF*, p. 31.

His reaction "was the same"—*Flight of the Avenger*, by Joe Hyams, p. 47.

"Although fighting had been going on"—*BB*, p. 15.

Decades later, George Bush could recall—*LF*, p. 31.

"She was so beautiful"—Author interview with George Bush.

By the time Barbara had gotten up—*BB*, p. 16.

"He was so afraid"—*BB*, p. 17.

"I think it was perfectly swell"—Barbara Bush scrapbooks, Book 12. George H. W. Bush Presidential Library.

After the prom—*BB*, p. 17.

During baseball practice—*MFMP*, p. 45.

"I couldn't breathe"—Author interview with Barbara Bush.

A year would pass before the Navy would confirm—The Navy confirmed it on May 1, 1943.

"She looked too cute for words"—*ATB*, p. 25.

"He looked like a baby"—Author interview with Barbara Bush.

"If she 'fluffed me off' "—Letter, George Bush to Nancy Bush, August 1942. George H. W. Bush personal papers, World War II Correspondence, Folder #2. George H. W. Bush Presidential Library; *ATB*, p. 33.

Bush biographies often say—"Chuck Downey, Youngest WWII Naval Pilot and Poplar Grove Resident, Dies," by Adam Poulisse, *Rockford Register Star*, February 21, 2016.

"I knew, of course, they would hate me"—*BB*, p. 19.

"He could kid her"—*DP*, p. 72.

His sister, Nancy, never got over thinking—*BB*, p. 91.

Because gasoline and tires were rationed—*BB*, p. 19.

Seventy-five years later, in 2018, George Bush—Conversation between George Bush and Jean Becker, July 27, 2018.

"We were secretly engaged"—*LF*, p. 31.

"When she came home"—Author interview with Barbara Bush.

"My dad knew he was going to be" president—Barbara Bush interview on NBC's *Tonight Show with Jay Leno*, November 18, 1994.

While traditional gender boundaries—"The Formation of Gay and Lesbian Identity," by Vincent F. Bonfitto, *Journal of Homosexuality*.

the announcement of their engagement—"Barbara Pierce Engaged to Wed," *New York Times*, December 12, 1943, p. 66.

"Bar, you have made my life"—*ATB*, p. 38.

"What do you both think"—*ATB*, letter dated January 11, 1944; p. 39.

"Incidentally if you see any shiny rocks"—*ATB*, p. 38.

In the shipyard, George gave Barbara—Author interview with Barbara Bush.

She would wear it until the day she died—Author interview with Jean Becker.

During the June 1944 campaign—*The Presidency of George H. W. Bush*, by John R. Greene, p. 13.

"We listened for every piece of news"—*BB*, p. 21.

"The minute we pushed over to dive"—"George Bush: A Sense of Duty," for Arts and Entertainment Network's *Biography* series, first broadcast November 1996. Quoted in *The Presidency of George H. W. Bush*, by John R. Greene, p. 13.

"The cockpit filled with smoke"—Letter from George Bush to his parents, dated September 3, 1944, quoted in *ATB*, p. 50.

"We were frantic"—*BB*, p. 22.

In the prisons there—*Sorties into Hell*, by Chester G. Hearn, pp. 112–22; *Hidden Horrors*, by Toshiyuki Tanaka, pp. 114–21.

Bush was allowed to return statewide—*DP*, pp. 66–67.

"This is the letter"—*ATB*, p. 57.

"Don't do what I did"—"Ex–First Lady Urges Women to Graduate," Associated Press, October 30, 1997.

She was one of six students—"Undergraduate Withdrawals During the Past Five Years," Office of the Registrar, Smith College, January 14, 1949, Office of the President Herbert John Davis Files, Box 7, Smith College Archives.

She hadn't declared a major yet—Email from Smith College Archives; Smith College Catalogue 1943, Smith College Archives.

As she ruefully told an interviewer decades later—"She Loves Being Mrs. George Bush," by Debra Scherban, *Daily Hampshire Gazette* (Northampton, MA), April 22, 1981.

The wedding date was set—*BB*, p. 22.

"There were tears"—*LF*, p. 41.

They had set a new wedding date—*George Bush*, by Herbert S. Parmet, p. 49.

The sensible Dorothy Walker Bush—Author interview with Barbara Bush.

Suddenly, a young man—*Simply Barbara Bush*, by Donnie Radcliffe, p. 99.

Barbara wore what the *New York Times* described—"Miss Pierce Is Wed to Lieut. G. H. Bush," *New York Times*, January 7, 1945, p. 36.

"When I fell in love with George Bush"—Author interview with Barbara Bush.

Chapter Six: "The Street Cop"

"Well, I never, never wondered"—Author interview with George H. W. Bush.

For the record, he never exactly asked—See chapter 5: "Love and War"; and chapter 9: "'What Are We Going to Do About Bar?'"

There, she sat in the special double-wide grandstand seat—"Big Man on Campus," by Mark A. Branch, *Yale Alumni Magazine*, March/April 2013.

"Doing well merely"—Letter from George H. W. Bush to FitzGerald Bemiss in June 1948, *ATB*, pp. 61–63.

"It was very important"—*BB*, p. 30.

Bush's father, Prescott, had been on the Dresser board—Prescott S. Bush Oral History, 1966, Columbia University Oral History Research Project, Eisenhower Administration Project.

"I've always wanted"—"How Bush Made It," by Richard Ben Cramer, *Esquire*, June 1991.

"Texas would be new"—Letter from George Bush to FitzGerald Bemiss in June 1948, *ATB*, pp. 61–63.

during what she called her "dormant" years—*Simply Barbara Bush*, by Donnie Radcliffe, p. 111.

"She jumped in"—Author interview with Susan Porter Rose.

"We were both"—"Barbara Bush," by Marty Primeau, *Dallas Morning News*, August 19, 1984.

One observer said—Author interview with Steve Clemons.

"When you are a couple"—*Simply Barbara Bush*, by Donnie Radcliffe, p. 105.

"I was glad to get away"—Author interview with Barbara Bush.

"We stepped off the plane"—*BB*, p. 54.

"We had the only bathroom"—Author interview with Barbara Bush.

"I thought we were being gassed"—Author interview with Barbara Bush.

"Still considered on the wrong side"—*BB*, p. 35.

"Dearest Mommy + Daddy"—Barbara Bush diaries, "Barbara Pierce Bush's letters to Family, 1948–1952."

"We lived in a duplex"—American University Distinguished Lecture Series, May 1, 1985. "Sadat and Barbara Bush Lecture," Courtesy of University Archives and Special Collections, American University Library.

Barbara's mother, Pauline Pierce, had been shipping—*BB*, p. 32.

"We lived in a motel"—*BB*, p. 35.

"Auto left road"—Pauline Robinson Pierce death certificate, Town of Harrison, New York, October 4, 1949.

The letter "is so loving"—Author interview with Barbara Bush.

"I think I have myself well enough in hand"—Letter from Marvin Pierce to Barbara Bush and his other children, October 1949. Letter provided to the author by Barbara Bush.

They had an almost visceral reaction—*BB*, p. 523.

"What a lonely, miserable time"—*BB*, p. 58.

But the other grandmother—BB, pp. 36–37.

"We had four kids"—Author interview with Bessie Liedtke.

"In our time it was different"—*What I Saw at the Revolution*, by Peggy Noonan, pp. 302–3.

"Bar is still not quite up to par"—George H. W. Bush letter to his mother, October 20, 1948, *ATB*, p. 65.

"Life seemed almost too good"—*BB*, p. 38.

"They kept having boys"—Author interview with Neil Bush.

"I would have liked one more"—Author interview with Barbara Bush.

She described it as a time—Barbara Bush, American University Distinguished Lecture Series, May 1, 1985. "Sadat and Barbara Bush Lecture," courtesy of University Archives and Special Collections, American University Library.

Sometimes she had the "feeling"—Ibid.

She once made an observation—"How Bush Made It," by Richard Ben Cramer, *Esquire*, June 1991.

"I remember Mother"—Author interview with George W. Bush.

"I can still picture us"—*Decision Points*, by George W. Bush, p. 7.

Neil Bush recalled the elaborate gift bags—Author interview with Neil Bush.

"George was away, so my friends held my hand"—"The Best Time of My Life Is Now,"
    by Jean L. Block, *Good Housekeeping*, November 1989, p. 255.
Jeb told me his mother—Author interview with Jeb Bush.
"Even when we were growing up"—"Barbara Bush: Supportive, Not a Maker of Politi-
    cal Waves," by Joyce Purnick, *New York Times*, July 18, 1980, p. 10.
"Somebody has to take care of the nest"—Ibid.
"Georgie has grown up to be"—Letter from George H. W. Bush to FitzGerald Bemiss,
    January 1, 1951. FitzGerald Bemiss Papers, 1943–1997. Mss1 B4252 c 1-50, Virginia
    Historical Society, Richmond, VA.
"She could get hot"—*Decision Points*, by George W. Bush, p. 7.
when he was a teenager—Author interview with Barbara Bush.
"I remember thinking"—*Decision Points*, by George W. Bush, p. 8.
"Don't worry, honey"—Ibid.
He told her they needed to talk—Author interview with Barbara Bush.
"Dad gets his energy"—Author interview with Neil Bush.
"Mom was the street cop"—Author interview with Jeb Bush.

Chapter Seven: How Hard Could It Be?

"In February 1962, just before Doro and I left"—*BB*, p. 57.
"I never even thought about it"—Author interview with Barbara Bush.
Her only complaint—*BB*, p. 56.
"I'd like to be President"—Barbara Bush diary and letters, January 7, 1966, quoted in
    DP, p. 129.
"exciting, overwhelming, intimidating"—*BB*, p. 65.
"I mean, that's me"—Author interview with Barbara Bush.
When Nixon aide Patrick Buchanan moved into the neighborhood—Author interview
    with Patrick Buchanan.
"He had some great friends in the House"—Author interview with Andy Card.
"Since George was unopposed"—*BB*, p. 73.
"Now the big question for us was"—*BB*, p. 80.
"I was born to the job"—*BB*, p. 87.
"When George was at the United Nations"—"Barbara Bush: The Plans in Her Life," by
    Barbara Gamarekian, *New York Times*, February 22, 1981.
She also began to volunteer—*BB*, p. 89.
In a letter to Nixon the next day—Letter from George H. W. Bush to President Nixon,
    November 11, 1972, quoted in *ATB*, pp. 162–64.
"but he was not lovable"—Author interview with Barbara Bush.
"I was very nervous!"—Author email exchange with Columba Bush.
"Their daughter, Robin"—"Return of the First Family," by Betty Cuniberti, *Los Ange-
    les Times*, November 20, 1988.
A *New York Times* story a few months later—"A Down-to-Earth Tenant for an Exclu-
    sive Address," by Bernard Weinraub, *New York Times*, January 15, 1989.
"That's baloney"—Author interview with Barbara Bush.

"Well, as the day got hotter"—*BB*, p.78.

"What you see is what you get"—"Barbara Bush Tends His Image Her Way," by Gerald M. Boyd, *New York Times*, May 5, 1988.

At the height of the scandal—President Nixon Phone Call with George H. W. Bush, April 30, 1973, White House Tapes, Richard Nixon Presidential Library.

Chapter Eight: Darkness

"I remember Camp David"—*LF*, p. 154.

"You have given him a post"—Memorandum of conversation, December 4, 1975, Gerald R. Ford Presidential Library, quoted in *DP*, p. 191.

"I felt terrible"—Author interview with Barbara Bush.

"I swore to myself"—*BB*, p. 135.

"I couldn't share"—Author interview with Barbara Bush.

"I thought that was a fourth ingredient"—Barbara Bush interview with Terry Gross on NPR's *Fresh Air*, September 13, 1994.

However, a woman who shared a friend's beach house—Author interview with a reliable firsthand source, speaking on condition of anonymity.

"I am looking forward"—*The China Diary of George H. W. Bush*, edited by Jeffrey A. Engel, p. 7.

But there were signs at the time—*BB*, p. 117.

"I asked if there was extra room"—Diary entry by George H. W. Bush on November 28, 1974, *The China Diary of George H. W. Bush*, edited by Jeffrey A. Engel, pp. 103–4. Note: *C'est la guerre* is a French phrase of resignation that translates as "It's war."

"I miss you more than tongue can tell"—Letter from George H. W. Bush to Barbara Bush, December 22, 1974; found in Barbara Bush diary.

"You didn't say anything"—Barbara Bush interview with Kenneth T. Walsh for *U.S. News & World Report*, May 28, 1990.

"Maybe I should have picked up"—*MFMP*, pp. 154–55.

"I remember Mom saying"—Author interview with Neil Bush.

"My 'code' told me"—*BB*, p. 135.

She began to volunteer again—"The Hidden Life of Barbara Bush," by Kenneth T. Walsh, *U.S. News & World Report*, May 28, 1990.

The only news coverage it attracted—"Stars Send the Blues Far Away," by Annie Gowen, *Washington Times*, March 1, 1991, p. E2. "Mrs. Bush recalled her own eight-month bout with depression in 1975. 'If I had known then what I know now…' she said."

"These are troubled times"—Text of Barbara Bush remarks to the National Foundation for Depressive Illness gala, February 27, 1991, at the National Building Museum in Washington, DC. OA/ID 08382. George H. W. Bush Presidential Library. The text says her depression occurred in 1975, but in her memoirs and interviews she identifies the year as 1976, when George Bush headed the CIA.

"I used to think that you could"—*BB*, p. 135.

"Would George Bush have run"—Author interview with Mary Kate Cary.

Chapter Nine: "What Are We Going to Do About Bar?"

"Strategy and timing were debated"—*BB*, p. 141.

By the time he formally announced—"The Long Journey of George Bush," by Paul Hendrickson, *Washington Post*, May 24, 1979.

She was outspoken and blunt—Author interview with Sheila Tate. "The problem is a strong wife makes her husband look weak," he told her. Tate replied, "There are those of us who think a strong wife is actually a sign of a strong husband."

"Mrs. Bush, people say"—*BB*, p. 148.

"They discussed how to make me snappier"—*BB*, p. 151.

"I tell you the truth"—"Barbara Bush Tends His Image Her Way," by Gerald M. Boyd, *New York Times*, May 5, 1988.

A profile in the *Cincinnati Enquirer*—"Barbara Bush: Traditionalist, Unspoiled," by Marian Christy, *Cincinnati Enquirer*, March 23, 1980.

tracking her itinerary—Appointment book found in a box of Barbara Bush's diaries, George H. W. Bush Presidential Library.

"I look at Bar's schedule"—*DP*, p. 239.

"She worked like hell"—Author interview with Pete Teeley.

When one of the CIA officers—*DP*, p. 205.

George Bush signed off—Ibid., p. 222.

He was suffering from "withdrawal symptoms"—*DP*, p. 226.

"I wonder if George"—Barbara Bush diary entry, October 22, 1976.

"The peripatetic Bushes"—Class Notes, February 1977, Class of 1947 Records, Box 2159, Smith College Archives.

"Look, George Bush never even exactly"—"Bushes Seem to Thrive in Hot Political Climate," by Loye Miller, *Press and Sun Bulletin* (Binghamton, NY), August 5, 1979, p. 39.

He resisted even when—Author interview with a senior campaign official, speaking on condition of anonymity.

"In all our years of campaigning"—*BB*, p. 152.

"Thoughts on abortion"—Four-page handwritten memo tucked into Barbara Bush's 1980 diaries.

"We heard footsteps"—Author interview with Walter Robinson. He later led the paper's Pulitzer Prize–winning investigation into sexual abuse by Catholic priests.

"I loved every minute"—*41: A Portrait of My Father*, by George W. Bush, p. 124.

An introvert by nature—Author interview with Jeb Bush.

"Our suite/room was a mad house"—Barbara Bush diary entry, January 22, 1980.

"George looked like the heavy"—Barbara Bush diary entry, February 26, 1980.

She told a friend—Letter from Barbara Bush to Elsie Hillman, February 25, 1980. Elsie H. Hillman Papers, 1920–2015, AIS.2013.02, Archives & Special Collections, University of Pittsburgh Library System.

"Take Sherman and cube it"—*The American Vice Presidency: From Irrelevance to Power*, by Jules Witcover, p. 449.

Jeb Bush, for one, argued—*LF*, p. 213.

"It was like a hundred degrees"—Author interview with Pete Teeley.

"It was brutal and you're melting"—Author interview with Karen Parfitt Hughes.

"The whole press corps is in the swimming pool"—Author interview with Pete Teeley.

"It was a tough decision"—Barbara Bush diary entry, summer 1980.

"I may have been mad"—Author interview with Barbara Bush.

"I feel we are very near"—Barbara Bush diary entry, March 10–11, 1980.

Chapter Ten: The Frost That Never Thawed

"She looked like a little girl"—"After Bush Had Gone to Bed, His Secret Dream Came True," by Bill Peterson, *Washington Post*, July 18, 1980.

"At the time, I didn't like George Bush"—*My Turn*, by Nancy Reagan, p. 212.

Barbara had arrived sporting—Author interview with Charlie Black.

"The bitter campaigns"—*My Turn*, by Nancy Reagan, p. 212.

"She really hated us"—Author interview with Barbara Bush.

"I found them both very attractive"—*BB*, p. 72.

He delivered his prepared remarks—Author interview with Jeb Bush.

"It was like a funeral"—*BB*, p. 154.

he and Barbara stepped into—"Bush Survived Frantic Night of Rumors," by Susan Page and Anthony Marro, *Newsday* (New York), July 18, 1980.

"Nancy Reagan was truly"—Foreword written by George Bush, dated April 20, 2017, published in *Lady in Red: An Intimate Portrait of Nancy Reagan*, by Sheila Tate.

the young couple bought the Washington house—*George Bush: An Intimate Portrait*, by Fitzhugh Green, p. 97.

His father welcomed his son and daughter-in-law—Barbara Bush diary entry, January 17 and 29, 1967.

Even after he had won the presidency—"For the Democrats, Pam's Is the Place for the Elite to Meet," by James M. Perry, *Wall Street Journal*, October 8, 1981.

"I think she was just insecure"—Author interview with Barbara Bush.

"George Bush is going to be a great, pleasant surprise"—"Mrs. Bush Happy to Settle for Second," by Bella Stumbo, *Los Angeles Times*, July 19, 1980.

"Nancy was so formal"—Author interview with Charlie Black.

"People say there is a big difference"—"Mrs. Bush Happy to Settle for Second," by Bella Stumbo, *Los Angeles Times*, July 16, 1980.

"Jack Steel got the Bayou Club to make lunch"—Author interview with Barbara Bush.

Nancy seemed more nonplussed—*First Father, First Daughter*, by Maureen Reagan, p. 260.

They "whisked through the Inner Harbor"—*Daily Times* (Salisbury, MD), September 16, 1980, p. 7.

"In May, we had bowed out"—*BB*, p. 158.

"George told me to go to New York"—Author interview with Barbara Bush.

"Thank heavens Nancy Reagan slipped the word to me"—*BB*, p. 160.

Not even Reagan's White House chief of staff Jim Baker—Author interview with James A. Baker III.

Barbara never saw the letter—Barbara Bush diary entry, April 11, 1994.

"That wasn't very nice"—Author interview with Barbara Bush.

"It burned me up"—Interview with George Bush by Jon Meacham, *DP*, p. 266.

On that day—*BB*, p. 165.

"Nancy does not like Barbara"—George Bush diary entry on June 12, 1988, after a conversation with Tom Arnold. He was a friend who had spoken with Lee and Walter Annenberg, who were close to both the Bushes and the Reagans. Quoted in *DP*, p. 324.

"I think it was a class thing"—Author interview with George Will.

In his 2003 satirical book—"Chapter 40: I Meet Former First Lady Barbara Bush and It Doesn't Go Well," in *Lies and the Lying Liars Who Tell Them*, by Al Franken, pp. 336–41. Franken was elected to the US Senate from Minnesota in 2008 and 2014, then resigned in 2018 after facing allegations of sexual misbehavior.

"She did some imitations"—Author interview with Lou Cannon.

When Kitty Kelley's tell-all biography—"Barbara Bush: The Steel Behind the Smile," by Ann McDaniel, *Newsweek*, June 21, 1992. Kitty Kelley's book was titled *Nancy Reagan: The Unauthorized Biography*.

When Kelley's tell-all book about the Bushes—*The Family*, by Kitty Kelley, pp. 375–76.

"A lot of Reagan people"—Author interview with Mark Weinberg, author of *Movie Nights with the Reagans*.

That was "one big difference"—Author interview with Sheila Tate.

"I think Mrs. Reagan felt"—Author interview with Mark Weinberg.

"Barbara Bush was just as devoted"—Author interview with George Will.

Nancy Reagan never disparaged—Author interview with Sheila Tate.

"Friend after friend"—Barbara Bush diary entry, April 11, 1994.

"I had gotten the word"—Barbara Bush diary entry, April 11, 1994.

The first draft of the invitation list—Guest List and Seating Chart, Prince and Princess of Wales Dinner, October/November 1985, Box OA 18719, White House Office of Social Affairs Records 1981–1989, Ronald Reagan Presidential Library.

When deputy White House chief of staff Michael Deaver—Interview with Deaver by Kati Marton, quoted in *Hidden Power*, by Kati Marton, p. 264.

The invitation list he presented—*Adventures of a Boy on the Bus* by Carl P. Leubsdorf, p. 199. (Note: Leubsdorf is author's spouse.)

his only concern that evening—Author phone conversation with Lee Verstandig.

"This was irritating"—Barbara Bush diary entry, April 11, 1994.

"We later learned"—Barbara Bush diary entry, April 11, 1994.

"We were campaigning"—Barbara Bush diary entry, April 11, 1994.

"I don't know"—Author interview with George H. W. Bush.

Chapter Eleven: Triumph

"Rich, when are you going"—Author conversations with Rich Bond in the 1990s.

"One very good thing"—*BB*, p. 147.

"She had the prematurely white hair"—Author interview with Fred Malek.

"This was my first suspicion"—Author interview with Marlin Fitzwater.

"I think I'm half Eleanor, half Bess"—"Barbara Bush: The President's Biggest Asset in a Time of Political Trouble," by Glenn F. Bunting, *Los Angeles Times*, May 31, 1992.

"Barbara is the memory bank"—Interview with Lud Ashley, *Hidden Power*, by Kati Marton, pp. 279–81.

"People were nervous"—Author interview with Marlin Fitzwater.

"There seemed to be a double standard"—*BB*, pp. 194–95.

The next morning, on their way—Author interviews with Ira Allen and Terence Hunt.

When the story about her comment moved on the wires—Author interview with Barbara Bush.

"What am I going to do?"—Author interview with Barbara Bush.

"For several years"—*BB*, p. 220.

"There were campaign flyers"—Author interview with James A. Baker III.

Within days, the nascent Bush campaign raised its head—"GOP Clock Ticks Toward '88 in Michigan," by Paul Taylor, *Washington Post*, September 23, 1985.

"George is obviously the most qualified"—Barbara Bush diaries, May 1986.

"I said to myself"—Author interview with Frank Fahrenkopf.

Now the rules about what news was fit to print—"Miami Woman Linked to Hart Candidate Denies Any Impropriety," by Jim McGee and Tom Fiedler, *Miami Herald*, May 3, 1987.

In 1981, when he was vice president, a bizarre allegation—*Washington Post*, March 22, 1981.

"The Power Behind Bush"—"The Power Behind Bush," by Ann Devroy, *Journal News* (White Plains, NY), January 24, 1982, p. AA4.

Time magazine published a similar—"Bush Does It His Way," by Douglas Brew, *Time*, February 22, 1982.

He gave a copy—*When Things Went Right*, by Chase Untermeyer, p. 157.

"My own opinion is that Jennifer"—Barbara Bush diary entry, January/February 1982.

In 1983, a trusted senior adviser—Author interview with a senior Bush adviser, speaking on condition of anonymity.

"They haven't got shit"—*DP*, p. 309; Jon Meacham interview with Roger Ailes.

But in his diary, Bush worried—George Bush diary, June 18, 1987; quoted in *DP*, p. 310.

Two *Newsweek* staffers—Author interview with Howard Fineman.

Newsweek ran a brief item—"Bush and the 'Big A Question,'" *Newsweek*, June 29, 1987.

the stories were "agony"—*DP*, pp. 310–11. From Bush's diary.

When a reporter for the *Houston Post*—*Houston Post* interview by Kathy Lewis published on October 11, 1987.

"There was nobody who worked"—Senior aide to President Bush, speaking on condition of anonymity.

The cover photo of Bush—"Bush Battles the 'Wimp Factor,'" by Margaret Warner, *Newsweek*, October 19, 1987.

"It was a cheap shot"—"Men Like Husband Needed, Barbara Bush Says," by Claudia Luther, *Los Angeles Times*, October 18, 1987.

"Bar looks beautiful"—George Bush diary entry, October 12, 1987, *ATB*, p. 368.

This campaign was different—*BB*, p. 221.

Gorbachev had a face "like Daddy's"—Barbara Bush diary entry, December 1987.

(Roger Ailes had suggested)—*DP*, p. 319; Jon Meacham interview with Roger Ailes.

"It was just plain ugly"—*BB*, p. 221.

"It's my hope"—George Bush diary, February 8, 1988, quoted in *ATB*, p. 377.

He received thirteen thousand fewer votes—Caucus History, *Des Moines Register*.

"What a difference eight years make"—*BB*, pp. 223–24.

Ailes screened it for the Bush team—Author interview with John Sununu.

"I don't think he wanted"—Author interview with John Sununu.

"She had rough edges"—Author interview with Andy Card.

"It was so unlike him"—Author interview with Barbara Bush.

Two weeks before Election Day—"On the Hustings with Barbara, Kitty," by Donnie Radcliffe, *Washington Post*, October 30, 1988.

Bush worried it would make them look desperate—*DP*, p. 332.

He dictated to his diary—George Bush diary entry, May 28, 1988, quoted in *George Bush*, by Herbert S. Parmet, p. 335.

"We were 17 points down"—Author interview with Charlie Black.

Bush was furious—Author interview with a source who witnessed the exchange and spoke on condition of anonymity.

"I finally just said"—Author interview with Charlie Black.

That month, Bush began using Willie Horton's name—"Bush Hammers Dukakis on Crime," by David Hoffman, *Washington Post*, June 23, 1988, in a speech to the National Sheriffs' Association in Louisville.

"Now you keep reading"—*DP*, p. 346, Bush diary.

"George used this heinous incident"—Barbara Bush diary entry, October 31, 1988.

"How do you defend against that"—Barbara Bush diary entry, October 19, 1988.

"I wasn't on the stock market"—"Dukakis Aide Quits; Remarks Are Disavowed," *Los Angeles Times*, October 21, 1988.

On *Live with Regis and Kathie Lee*—"Barbara Bush Blasts Rumors of Her Husband's Infidelity," by Ronnie Ramos, *Miami Herald*, October 22, 1988.

"Jim Baker was right"—Barbara Bush diary entry, October 20, 1988.

"We went to bed"—Barbara Bush diary entry, November 7, 1988.

Two days before the election—Author interview with Sheila Tate.

Chapter Twelve: First at Last

"A Down-to-Earth Tenant"—"A Down-to-Earth Tenant for an Exclusive Address," by Bernard Weinraub, *New York Times*, January 15, 1989, p. 1.

only Jacqueline Kennedy—YouGov.com poll, April 22–24, 2018.

"My mail tells me"—"Barbara Bush Being Herself," by Donnie Radcliffe, *Washington Post*, January 15, 1993.

in the first one hundred days—*BB*, p. 278.

"As a woman of a certain age"—"My Kind of First Lady," by Doris Willens, *New York Times*, December 11, 1988, p. 220.

"I will not treat her as Nancy Reagan has treated me"—Barbara Bush diary entry, December 6, 1988.

"It is something you are never prepared for"—"On Being First Lady," by Philip Shabecoff and Charles Mohr, *New York Times*, December 15, 1988, p. B20.

She acknowledged having "mixed feelings"—"For Reagans, a Season of Many Last Times," by Barbara Gamarekian, *New York Times*, December 13, 1988, p. B13.

A *Saturday Night Live* sketch—NBC's *Saturday Night Live*, January 21, 1989.

The Bushes held twenty-eight of the official black-tie dinners—White House Historical Association records.

"I am willing to turn it over"—"White House Gala a la Barbara Bush," by Marian Burros, *New York Times,* June 28, 1989.

"She said, 'You people know'"—"Bill Clinton and George W. Bush had the exact same reaction to one White House Chef's meal," by Linette Lopez, *Business Insider,* November 2, 2016.

"What does it matter?"—"White House Gala a la Barbara Bush," by Marian Burros, *New York Times*, June 28, 1989.

There was the time the kitchen was marinating duck—*BB*, p. 285.

She was seated to his left—Barbara Bush diary entry, quoted in *BB*, pp. 465–66.

A more serious faux pas loomed—*BB*, p. 287.

Lady Bird Johnson, a fellow Texan—Author interviews with Jean Becker and Julie Cooke.

One possibility was her volunteer work—The Washington Home for Incurables is now known as the Washington Home & Community Hospices.

"I've got to have a cause"—Author interview with Barbara Bush.

In what she called "one of my very few"—Author interview with Barbara Bush.

"It helped to have a First Lady whose passion"—Author interview with Lamar Alexander.

"It was a hidden secret"—Author interview with Sharon Darling.

"It wasn't cutesy little kids"—Author interview with Benita Somerfield.

Barbara Bush visited scores of literacy programs—*Barbara Bush: Presidential Matriarch*, by Myra G. Gutin, p. 75.

"There were a lot of other splashy things"—Author interview with Sharon Darling.

When the president signed the bill—Associated Press, July 25, 1991.

Sometimes she did more than praise—Author interview with Peggy Swift White.

Millie purportedly decided to do that—"Mrs Bush's Talking Points for *Millie's Book* Event, Houston, Texas," September 27, 1990, First Lady's Press Office, Barbara Bush Speeches, September–December 1990, IA/OA 07478, George H. W. Bush Presidential Library.

"They're naming a Literacy Plaza"—Author interview with Barbara Bush.

The last national literacy study—That reflected a shift in priority to STEM (science, technology, engineering, math) topics. In 2011–2012, another large-scale assessment of adult skills, the Program for the International Assessment of Adult Competencies, was done, which looked at adult skills in literacy, numeracy, and problem solving in technology-rich environments, rather than literacy in a standalone assessment.

A doctoral dissertation—"Literacy as Value: Cultural Capital in Barbara Bush's Foundation for Family Literacy," by Brandi Davis Westmoreland, PhD diss., Texas A&M University, p. 119.

"No matter how efficient you are"—Author interview with Jeb Bush.

"She never lost interest"—Author interview with Jean Becker.

Chapter Thirteen: Grandma's House

"I have always tried"—Gerald Ford at the Everett McKinley Dirksen Forum in Peoria, Illinois, March 5, 1976.

In her memoir—*The Times of My Life*, by Betty Ford, p. 223.

But he also refused—*Out for Good*, by Dudley Clendinen and Adam Nagourney, pp. 272, 276.

as president he said—Associated Press, June 20, 1977.

During his reelection campaign—*Gay and Lesbian Americans and Political Participation*, by Raymond A. Smith and Donald P. Haider-Markel, pp.149–50.

he won a straw poll—*Conduct Unbecoming*, by Randy Shilts, p. 368.

"My criticism is that"—Ibid.

His administration resisted calls—*And the Band Played On*, by Randy Shilts, p. 214.

At White House briefings—*When AIDS Was Funny*, a documentary by Scott Calonico, posted on VF.com in December 2015.

"Kiski? 1988?"—Letter from George Bush to Elsie Hillman, dated May 12, 1987. Elsie H. Hillman Papers, 1920–2015, AIS.2013.02, Archives & Special Collections, University of Pittsburgh Library System.

He supported Reagan's veto in 1987—"Big Defeat—Reagan's Veto of Rights Bill Is Overturned," *San Francisco Chronicle*, March 23, 1988. p. A1.

"I go home and tell George"—"Barbara Bush Chooses to Take a Back Seat," by Alan Sverdlik, *Atlanta Journal-Constitution*, October 16, 1987.

at her urging, George Bush—"Bush Endorses Premarital AIDS Testing," by Cragg Hines, *Houston Chronicle*, April 9, 1987, p. 2.

In June 1988—"Mrs. Bush Commits Early to Aids Benefit," by John Hawkins, *Dallas Morning News*, June 23, 1988.

His operatives reassured conservative columnists—"A Platform with Four Right Legs," by Rowland Evans and Robert Novak, *Washington Post*, August 12, 1988.

"She never championed"—Author interview with Kristan King Nevins.

"I work with a ton of AIDS activists"—Author interview with Barbara Pierce Bush, granddaughter.

"She didn't need to yell"—Author interview with Edward E. McNally. He would later serve in senior roles at the Department of Justice and as a US Attorney and, following the September 11 attacks in 2001, as general counsel for Homeland Security and Counter-Terrorism in the White House under President George W. Bush.

Indeed, she and George had hurriedly announced—See chapter 5: "Love and War."

When she was Second Lady—Author interview with Cragg Hines, then Washington Bureau chief of the *Houston Chronicle*, who attended a small luncheon where she made the remark.

As First Lady, when she walked offstage—Author interview with former White House aide to Barbara Bush, speaking on condition of anonymity.

"I would have been so sad"—Barbara Bush diaries, May 1990.

"When Robin got sick"—Author interview with Barbara Bush.

Then, during the first one hundred days of the new administration—Author interview with Julie Cooke.

During the transition from the Reagan administration—Email exchange with Jeffrey Vogt by author.

Debbie Tate, president of the group—Letter from Debbie Tate to David Demarest, director, Office of Public Affairs, Office of the President-Elect, dated February 1, 1989.

David Demarest, who had been director—Memo from David Demarest to Susan Porter Rose, dated February 12, 1989.

"She didn't come like she had a script"—interview on WUSA9 by correspondent Bruce Johnson, April 18, 2018.

Donovan would die not long afterward—"Barbara Bush Visited Our Facility for Children with HIV/AIDS. It Was Unforgettable," by Debbie Tate and Joan McCarley, *Washington Post*, April 21, 2018.

"Burt Lee told me"—Author interview with Barbara Bush.

Tate and McCarley—Interview on WUSA9 by correspondent Bruce Johnson, April 18, 2018.

"What joy it must have given"—"Thank You, Mrs. Bush," by Tom Rosshirt, June 20, 2012, Creators Syndicate; and a subsequent email exchange between the author and Rosshirt.

"Mrs. Bush, it is a fantastic thing"—Ibid.

"She had lost a little girl"—"The Unusual, Unforgettable Way Indy Buried Ryan White," by Will Higgins, *Indianapolis Star*, April 9, 2015.

The initiative, one of the most affirmative aspects of his legacy—That said, in his reelection campaign in 2004, George W. also stoked fears of same-sex marriage and endorsed a constitutional amendment to ban it.

"She was an activist"—Author interview with George W. Bush.

A few days later, he received—Author interview with Edward E. McNally. No other mentions of Robin were found in a search of the collected public papers of Bush's presidency.

A week later, Richard Land—"Bush and the Gay Lobby," by Rowland Evans and Robert Novak, *Washington Post*, May 25, 1990.

House Republican whip Newt Gingrich—Ibid.

"Quite frankly, the president's staff"—*First Son*, by Bill Minutaglio, p. 248.

"When I saw that"—Author interview with Paulette Goodman.

"I appreciate so much"—Letter from Barbara Bush to Paulette Goodman, dated May 10, 1990. Accessed University of North Texas Digital Library, special collections.

The lead to the AP story—Corvallis (Oregon) *Gazette-Times*, May 16, 1990, p. 6.

The letter was just two paragraphs long—"Barbara Bush Remembered as Gay Ally who Fought AIDS Stigma," by Chris Johnson, *Washington Blade*, April 18, 2018.

By the end of that summer, Wead was ordered—"Shadow and Substance," *Washington Times*, August 13, 1990.

"Doug was wearing his welcome out"—Author interview with Andy Card.

In his speech to the GOP convention—"Barbara Bush Remembered as Gay Ally Who Fought AIDS Stigma," by Chris Johnson, *Washington Blade*, April 18, 2018.

"How do we know?"—Author interview with Kristan King Nevins.

She told NPR's *Fresh Air*—*Fresh Air with Terry Gross*, September 13, 1994.

"I am not sure how Tim got here"—Barbara Bush diary entry, October 2, 2015.

Chapter Fourteen: The Reckoning

Southwest Community College—Now known as Southeast Kentucky Community & Technical College.

Her chief of staff—Barbara Bush diary entry, April 1990.

There had been a hint of controversy—"Visit Sparks Discussion over First Lady," by Brenda Elias, *Daily Hampshire Gazette* (Northampton, MA), September 7, 1989.

"I'm willing to say"—Author interview with Marlin Fitzwater.

"It was sort of humiliating"—Author interview with Julie Cooke.

"Each year the Senior Class"—Letter from Nannerl O. Keohane to Barbara Bush, December 22, 1989.

"We were all wondering"—Author interview with Susana Rosario Cardenas.

"We are outraged"—"Gentility, Gender, and Political Protest: The Barbara Bush Controversy at Wellesley College," by Rosanna Hertz and Susan M. Reverby, *Gender and Society* 9, no. 5 (1995): 594–611.

A stringer for the Associated Press—"Wellesley Students Oppose Barbara Bush Scheduled Commencement Speech," Associated Press, April 15, 1990.

"It seems to me that a truly educated person"—"A Defense of Mrs. Bush," by John Robinson, *Boston Globe*, April 17, 1990, p. 1.

More than seven thousand articles—"Gentility, Gender, and Political Protest at Wellesley College," by Rosanna Hertz and Susan M. Reverby, *Gender and Society* (1995): 594–611.

Senator Barbara Mikulski of Maryland—"Mrs. Bush's School Battle; The First-Lady Calm, in the Wellesley Storm," by Donnie Radcliffe, *Washington Post*, May 3, 1990.

"You tell those girls"—Barbara Bush interview on C-SPAN's *First Ladies: Influence and Image*, October 29, 2013.

"Some alumnae thought"—Author interview with Nannerl O. Keohane.

Bush was blunter in his diary—George Bush diary, April 16, 1990, quoted in *DP*, p. 405.

In public, Barbara Bush—"At Wellesley, a Furor over Barbara Bush," by Fox Butterfield, *New York Times*, May 4, 1990, p. 1.

"I have to remind myself"—Barbara Bush diaries, May 1990.

"I did not want to complain, explain, or apologize"—*BB*, p. 337.

She was irked—Author interview with Peggy Dooley, who was called on the carpet by Susan Porter Rose, Barbara Bush's chief of staff. Dooley, a researcher from the West Wing speechwriting shop who was a recent graduate of Wellesley and had been working on the speech, told her the story was mistaken; she hadn't asked the dean that question.

McNally raised his hand—Author interview with Edward E. McNally.

He noted the opening that day of their high-stakes summit—George Bush, toast at the State Dinner for Mikhail Gorbachev, May 31, 1990.

In a speech that lasted just eleven minutes—Text of remarks of Mrs. Bush at Wellesley College Commencement, June 1, 1990, *BB*, Appendix C, pp. 538–40.

An earlier draft had a different word—Author interview with Edward E. McNally.

The response was so great—*I Hope*, by Raisa Gorbachev, p. 60.

The East Wing staff, aware of how nervous—Author interview with Julie Cooke.

In a blistering *Boston Globe* column, Mike Barnicle—"Of Wellesley and Harvard," by Mike Barnicle, *Boston Globe*, April 26, 1990, p. 41.

"As we get older"—Author interview with Peggy Reid.

"All my married grandchildren"—Author interview with Barbara Bush.

Jenna Bush Hager told me—Author conversation with Jenna Bush Hager.

When TV host Charlie Rose noted—*Charlie Rose*, PBS, September 13, 1994.

She told me she had never read *The Feminine Mystique*—Author interview with Barbara Bush.

ABC White House correspondent Ann Compton once introduced her—Author interview with Ann Compton.

She complained that George Bush faced a double standard—Barbara Bush on PBS's *Talking with David Frost*, September 30, 1994.

"Do I believe"—Author interview with Barbara Bush.

"Oh, that's okay"—Author interview with Barbara Bush.

"All of this to tell you"—Barbara Bush diary entry, Memorial Day, 2006.

Chapter Fifteen: Détente

the mutual antagonism—*BB*, p. 210.

"I don't know how old"—Barbara Bush diary entry, recorded on December 11, 1987.

"We couldn't understand"—*BB*, pp. 213–14.

"They just never clicked"—*Lady in Red*, by Sheila Tate, p. 128.

"Who does that dame think she is?"—*For the Record*, by Donald Regan, p. 314.

Mikhail Gorbachev took umbrage—*Memoirs*, by Mikhail Gorbachev, p. 447.

"It was made clear"—*Simply Barbara Bush*, by Donnie Radcliffe, p. 16.

"I was supposed to take her"—Author interview with Barbara Bush.

"She understood where the president was"—Author interview with Marlin Fitzwater.

"She had been well briefed"—Barbara Bush diary entry, December 9, 1987.

Barbara Bush noted—Ibid.

George Bush's background in foreign affairs—*George Bush*, by Herbert S. Parmet, p. 148. Lud Ashley was "flabbergasted," asking his old friend, "George, what the fuck do you know about foreign affairs?" Bush replied, "You ask me that in ten days."

The national security archives—Gesprach des Bundeskandzlers Kohl mit Generalsekretar Gorbatschow, Bonn, 12 Juni 1989, in Hanns Jurgen Kusters and Daniel Hofmann, eds., *Deutsche Einheit: Sonderedition aus den Akten des Bundeskanzleramtes 1989/1990, Documente zur Deutschlandpolitik* (Munich: R. Oldenbourg Verlag, 1998), p. 281.

Later, in a separate phone conversation—Ibid.

"Helmut was the best retail politician"—Author interview with Brian Mulroney.

"If you understand there was no person"—Author interview with Brian Mulroney.

"If the First Ladies are on pretty good terms"—Author interview with James A. Baker III.

"Friends?"—Author interview with Barbara Bush.

"One thing I can promise you"—Barbara Bush letter to Scott Pierce, dated May 30, 1990, quoted in *BB*, pp. 338–39.

"I have the warmest feelings"—*I Hope*, by Raisa Gorbachev, p. 60.

When Barbara Bush died—Written statement released by Mikhail Gorbachev.

When they asked Raisa—*BB*, p. 341.

Barbara and Raisa changed into casual clothes—*BB*, p. 343.

During that day—Barbara Bush diary entry, June 3, 1990.

Raisa told Barbara—Barbara Bush diary entry, June 9, 1990.

"She once asked me why"—*BB*, p. 213.

"I had a couple different lipsticks"—Author interview with Peggy Swift White.

"I think she had been hurt"—*BB*, pp. 343–44.

When they met for dinner in Houston—Barbara Bush diary entry, May 15, 1992, quoted in *BB*, p. 460.

"I think they were empathetically close"—Author interview with Andy Card.

After Bush got the first CIA reports—Author interviews with Brian Mulroney.

"They wanted to stay on her good side"—Author interview with Brent Scowcroft.

"George wasn't very pleased"—Author interview with Brian Mulroney.

Two weeks after the invasion—*BB*, p. 355.

Those frantic days—*BB*, pp. 355–56.

"He said, 'No, never mind about that'"—Author interview with Derek Burney.

"It was as if the whole world"—*BB*, p. 384.

When he confided—Barbara Bush diary entry, January 16, 1991.

She reveled in the praise—Barbara Bush diary entry, March 2, 1991.

"I miss the tourists"—Barbara Bush diary entry, February 8, 1991.

Then, at a dinner at the Kremlin—*The Last Empire*, by Serhii Plokhy, p. 26.

In his memoirs, Mikhail Gorbachev said—*Memoirs*, by Mikhail Gorbachev, p. 624. He said Barbara Bush "was waiting for invitation from the Soviet President, the reception's host."

"During all this"—*The Last Empire*, by Serhii Plokhy, p. 26.

"Bigger than life"—Barbara Bush diary entry, July 1991.

During the uncertain days—Barbara Bush diary entry, August 19, 1991.

"Raisa never seemed exactly the same"—*Reflections*, by Barbara Bush, p. 63.

Chapter Sixteen: The Reluctant Campaign

"For the last few months"—Barbara Bush diary entry, May 1991.

"I did wonder sometimes"—*BB*, p. 454.

"I convinced myself"—*BB*, p. 283.

Mohr immediately suspected—Author interview with Lawrence Mohr.

Barbara Bush joked—*BB*, p. 283.

"She's just fine"—"First Lady Undergoes Radiation Treatment for Thyroid Illness," by Lawrence K. Altman, *New York Times*, April 13, 1989.

"She wasn't feeling great"—Author interview with Lawrence Mohr.

More than a year after—*BB*, p. 353.

"She was in such agony"—Author interview with Sharon Darling.

"Mine affected my eyes"—Author interview with Barbara Bush.

In her memoirs, Barbara Bush expressed—*BB*, p. 353.

"As I sat there"—*BB*, p. 410.

The fact that both were under stress—Book review by Dr. Ivor Jackson, *New England Journal of Medicine*, June 3, 1993, p. 1648. "Although conjugal thyrotoxicosis (perhaps now dignified with the eponym 'Bush disease') has no clear cause—though shared stress in genetically predisposed persons is as likely a candidate as any—and is quite uncommon."

Barbara Bush told me she was inclined—Author interview with Barbara Bush.

she reported that George W. Bush jokingly had called to say—*BB*, p. 412.

"They didn't want people"—Author interview with John Sununu.

"The campaign people"—Author interview with Marlin Fitzwater.

"If they hadn't had Graves' disease"—Author interview with Fred Malek.

He told Colin Powell—*My American Journey*, by Colin Powell and Joseph E. Persico, p. 560.

"He was sick"—Author interview with Marlin Fitzwater.

On the stump, she was—"In the News: Barbara Bush," by R. J. Reinhart, Gallup, April 18, 2018.

"Without counting the days"—*BB*, p. 366.

"I used to watch her at dinners"—Clayton Yeutter, oral history interview at the Miller Center of Public Affairs, University of Virginia.

In a story that may be apocryphal—Author conversation with Andy Card.

"I wish that John would realize"—Barbara Bush diary entry, October 26, 1991.

When Governor Gregg introduced Barbara Bush—C-SPAN, December 22, 1991.

"Barbara Bush Fighting Mad"—"Barbara Bush Fighting Mad in New Hampshire," Associated Press, December 19, 1991.

his approval rating soared—"Bush Job Approval Highest in Gallup History," by David W. Moore, September 24, 2001.

Barbara Bush would accuse Buchanan—*Charlie Rose*, PBS, September 13, 1994.

she would later admit—*BB*, p. 457.

a month after the election—"NBER Business Cycle Dating Committee Determines That Recession Ended in March 1991," National Bureau of Economic Research, December 22, 1992.

Elsie Hillman, chairwoman—Letter from Elsie Hillman to Rich Bond, February 19, 1992. Elsie H. Hillman Papers, 1920–2015, AIS.2013.02, Archives & Special Collections, University of Pittsburgh Library System.

"I've never been through a trial like this one"—Letter from George Bush to FitzGerald Bemiss, March 3, 1992. FitzGerald Bemiss Papers, 1943–1997. Mss1 B4252 c 1-50, Virginia Historical Society, Richmond, VA.

Jim Baker had a bold idea—Author interview with James A. Baker III. The idea of tapping Barbara Bush to deliver a message to Vice President Quayle was reported in *Quest for the Presidency 1992*, by Peter Goldman, Thomas M. DeFrank, Mark Miller, Andrew Murr, and Tom Mathews.

A just-published biography of a Washington lobbyist—*The Power House*, by Susan B. Trento.

"Why does the press shy away"—*Hillary's Choice*, by Gail Sheehy, pp. 204–5.

"There was no unfaithfulness"—Author interview with Scott Pierce.

One of Bush's old friends from Texas—Author interview with Dan Gillcrist.

A member of the Bushes' inner circle—Author interview with a member of the Bush inner circle, speaking on condition of anonymity.

"I used to think she was terrible"—Barbara Bush, quoted in *Inside Reagan's Navy*, by Chase Untermeyer, p. 138.

Only when Bush had won the White House—Author interview with a member of the Bush inner circle, speaking on condition of anonymity.

"I was very close to her for a while"—*DP*, p. 310. Note: Jennifer Fitzgerald didn't respond to requests for an interview by the author.

"I am flabbergasted"—Barbara Bush diary entry, September 28, 1992.

"Clinton's out there"—Author interview with Charlie Black.

"This morning I am absolutely convinced"—Barbara Bush diary entry, October 3, 1992.

"23 MORE DAYS TO GO!"—Barbara Bush diary entry, October 11, 1992.

"The spouses and families are brought in"—Author interview with Frank Fahrenkopf.

The Richmond debate "was the toughest"—*BB*, p. 491.

Campaign strategist Mary Matalin described him—"Convention Pulls Bush Clan into Limelight," by Ruth Rendon, *Houston Chronicle*, August 18, 1992.

"I tried to stay upbeat"—*41: A Portrait of My Father,* by George W. Bush, pp. 227–28.

"It really shook him"—Author interview with James A. Baker III.

"He was 90 percent popular a short time before"—Author interview with Barbara Bush.

"We all gathered in Dad and Mom's suite"—*MFMP*, p. 438.

Chapter Seventeen: Evicted

"Well, this is the day"—Barbara Bush diary entry, January 20, 1993.

The day before—Barbara Bush diary entry, January 20, 1993.

Then, she had tripped and cut her leg—*BB*, p. 185.

"The awful moment"—Barbara Bush diary entry, January 22, 1993.

"What did it feel like"—Interview of George W. Bush by Mark K. Updegrove, *The Last Republicans*, p. 247.

"He was right"—*BB*, p. 23.

"It's over"—Author interview with George W. Bush.

Since he was no longer commander in chief—For the flight to Houston, the Boeing 747 was now designed SAM 28000, for Special Air Mission.

"I honestly believe"—*BB*, p. 498.

"The press complained"—*BB*, p. 25.

"Everybody was so nice"—Author interview with Barbara Bush.

"I remember sensing a sadness"—Author interview with Pierce Bush.

Early in their marriage—*BB*, p. 539.

"It was the political equivalent"—Maureen Dowd and Frank Rich, *New York Times*, January 21, 1993, p. A11.

"It was ugly"—Barbara Bush diary entry, January 1993.

"I told her the press"—Barbara Bush diary entry, January 1993.

"And we did have your wonderful husband"—Author interview with Barbara Bush.

"I was dreading"—Barbara Bush diary entry, April 25, 1994.

"It just wasn't us"—Author interview with Barbara Bush.

In 2017, the house would be assessed—Harris County, Texas, tax assessor's office.

"Barbara is bustling"—Letter from George Bush to Patty Presock, January 22, 1993, quoted in *MFMP*, p. 461.

"Look out, world"—"No More Mr. President, Just a Texas Nice Guy," by Sam Howe Verhovek, *New York Times*, January 5, 1994, p. A10.

Only years later—Author interview with George W. Bush.

"It's hurt, hurt, hurt"—George Bush diary, November 4, 1992, quoted in *MFMP*, p. 572.

Bush got "fidgety"—Letter from Jack Fitch to Doro Bush Koch, quoted in *MFMP*, p. 460.

"Well, that's nice"—George Bush diary, January 20, 1993, quoted in *DP*, p. 533.

"Dear Vic"—Letter from George to Victor Gold, copied to Sheila Tate, May 18, 1998.

"I am truly back"—Barbara Bush diary entry, February 19, 1993.

George Bush made his first foray—*The Late Show with David Letterman*, September 13, 1994.

"They made a ton of money"—Author interview with Barbara Bush.

"We did not have a million dollars"—Author interview with Barbara Bush.

the value of his investments—Financial details based on "Running in the Green," by Jack Sirica, Gannett News Service, February 3, 1980. "Bush Bares Net Worth," UPI, August

18, 1984. "Bush Easily a Millionaire, but the Growth Was Slow," by David E. Rosen-
baum, *New York Times*, June 6, 1988. "Bucks for Bush," Associated Press, May 5, 1992.

"I felt like crying"—*Reflections*, by Barbara Bush, p. 8.

A White House usher overheard—*White House Usher*, by Christopher Emery.

Steven Clemons had no ties to Bush—Author interview with Steven Clemons. He later
became Washington editor-at-large for the *Atlantic* magazine. Note: The Nixon
Center is now called the Center for the National Interest.

In 1994, he gave a total of 111 speeches—*Reflections*, by Barbara Bush, p. 65.

Barbara Bush was amazed—Author interview with Barbara Bush.

She signed a contract—Source with firsthand knowledge who spoke on condition of
anonymity.

she had tea with best-selling mystery writer Mary Higgins Clark—*Reflections*, by Barbara Bush, p. 52.

Spoiler alert—Author interview with Jean Becker.

But Nancy sent word—Barbara Bush diary entry, April 11, 1994.

When Jean Becker relayed Nancy Reagan's query—Barbara Bush diary entry, April 11,
1994.

"First ladies have different styles"—*My Turn*, by Nancy Reagan, p. 31.

"On January 11 . . . she showed me everything"—*BB*, p. 258.

"Pat Nixon had made it"—*BB*, p. 277.

"Poor Nancy"—Author interview with Barbara Bush.

None of the Pierce children ever warmed to her—Author interview with Scott Pierce.

New York Times columnist Maureen Dowd—Author interview with Jill Abramson.

"Had Dad won in 1992"—*Decision Points*, by George W. Bush, p. 51.

"If it weren't a boost"—"Speak Softly, and Pack Quite a Punch," by Margo Hammond,
St. Petersburg Times, October 10, 1994.

In his suite at the Four Seasons Hotel in Austin—*Courage and Consequence*, by Karl
Rove, p. 97.

"The day after the election"—Barbara Bush interview with Jay Leno, NBC's *Tonight
Show with Jay Leno*, November 18, 1994.

Chapter Eighteen: First Son

"The most competitive living human"—*Simply Barbara Bush*, by Donnie Radcliffe,
p. 132.

"I used to say"—"Bush's 'Love Letter' to Dad and Message to Jeb: Run," by Susan Page,
USA TODAY, November 9, 2014.

"We have the same sense of humor"—*Decision Points*, by George W. Bush, p. 7.

"They're like the same person"—Author interview with Pierce Bush.

"Unfortunately, that's true"—Author interview with Barbara Bush.

During the 2000 campaign—"Spectators at a Son's Rise," by David Von Drehle, *Washington Post*, August 2, 2000.

"I was always impressed"—Author interview with Dick Cheney.

"Ugly words were being said"—Author interview with Andy Card.

"I happen to agree with what George says"—"The Gospel According to George W. Bush," *Weekly Standard*, March 22, 1999.

"For about six weeks"—*BB*, p. 92.

George Bush warned her—*BB*, p. 92.

"I thought, 'Nobody's ever going to come back here'"—Author interview with Marlin Fitzwater.

"That is a strange thing to say"—"Bush's Eldest Son Relishes Role as a Texas Delegate," *Houston Chronicle*, August 16, 1988.

"I'm rather hoping he won't"—"Mrs. Bush Advises Son Against Governor's Race," by Carl P. Leubsdorf, *Dallas Morning News*, April 28, 1989.

"For 42 years"—Ibid.

"That didn't discourage me"—Author interview with George W. Bush.

"George is confident"—Barbara Bush diary entry, October 27, 1994.

"You can say"—Barbara Bush, NBC's *Tonight Show with Jay Leno*, November 18, 1994.

"Mother, I'm really struggling"—Author interview with George W. Bush.

"I guess it is a normal instinct"—*Reflections*, by Barbara Bush, p. 308.

"I am sick of it"—Ibid., pp. 291–92.

"I advise them a lot"—ABC's *Good Morning America*, with Diane Sawyer, June 10, 1999.

When Jeb Bush was—Jeb Bush, "2003 Inaugural Address," January 7, 2003.

He wrote them a letter—George Bush letter footnote.

"He sort of intimated"—Barbara Bush diary entry, April 22, 2000.

Rove realized it was a difficult conversation—Author interview with Karl Rove.

The year before the 2000 election—*USA TODAY*, December 13, 1999.

After one primary debate in 1999—Barbara Bush diary entry, February 15, 1999.

He had questioned Bush's pitch—"'Compassionate Conservative' Says No Retreat on White House Bid," by Ron Fournier, Associated Press, June 12, 1999.

Baker and Barbara Bush knew each other—They served together on the Mayo Clinic board of directors from 1993 to 1997.

"She didn't like it one bit"—Author interview with Lamar Alexander.

"silver-haired, pearl-draped howitzer"—"Barbara Bush Joins G.O.P. Women on Stump to Try to Bridge Gender Gap," by Frank Bruni, *New York Times*, October 19, 2000.

A CBS News poll in 1999—"Popular and Full of Pride, Barbara Bush Campaigns," *New York Times*, January 21, 2000.

Her final swing—Letter to Elsie Hillman, November 4, 2000. Elsie H. Hillman Papers, 1920–2015, AIS.2013.02, Archives & Special Collections, University of Pittsburgh Library System.

"Miss Pessimistic (me)"—Barbara Bush diary entry, October 17, 2000.

The campaign and the recount had been "hard fought"—Author interview and subsequent email exchange with Bill Clinton.

On the night of September 10, 2001—*Reflections*, by Barbara Bush, pp. 386–89.

"I suddenly felt as though I had lost my son"—Letter from Barbara Bush to Elsie Hillman, September 27, 2001. Elsie H. Hillman Papers, 1920–2015, AIS.2013.02, Archives & Special Collections, University of Pittsburgh Library System.

"For the most part"—*Decision Points*, by George W. Bush, p. 243.

When George W. Bush called his parents—Author interview with Marlin Fitzwater.

"I almost hate to admit this"—Author interview with Andy Card.

Barbara Bush was incensed—Author interview with Steven Clemons.

"Barbara Bush is *allegedly* TICKED off"—*Washington Note*, by Steve Clemons, December 1, 2005.

"She'd say things like, 'Dick Cheney's changed'"—Author interview with George W. Bush. The exchange was first reported in *The Last Republicans*, by Mark Updegrove, pp. 343–44.

"He told me that"—Author interview with Barbara Bush.

He would appoint more women to the cabinet—"Diversity and Presidential Cabinet Appointments," by James D. King and James W. Riddlesperger Jr., *Social Science Quarterly*, 2014

"They were like mirror images"—Author interview with Karl Rove.

"I'm not getting involved"—Author interview with Sharon Darling.

When Barbara Bush would call—Author interview with Andy Card.

She could make a cutting remark—Author interview with senior White House aide to George W. Bush.

"He sits and listens"—ABC's *Good Morning America*, with Diane Sawyer, aired March 18, 2003.

"Almost everyone I've talked to"—NPR's *Marketplace*, September 5, 2005.

"I got taken out of context"—Barbara Bush diary entry, September 29, 2005.

Chapter Nineteen: A Second First Lady Named Bush

While she had chosen to become a teacher—"Laura Bush: A Twist on Traditional," by Lois Romano, *Washington Post*, May 14, 2000.

In the 1970s, she joined a women's consciousness-raising group—*Spoken from the Heart*, by Laura Bush, p. 92.

"There are a lot of myths"—"America's First Ladies: An Enduring Legacy," conference on November 15, 2011, at the George H. W. Bush Presidential Library Center at Texas A&M University.

"They are perfect for each other!!!"—Barbara Bush diary entry, October 8, 1977.

"Mother was thrilled"—Author interview with George W. Bush.

Laura Welch thought it helped—Author interview with Laura Bush.

"There was no time"—*Spoken from the Heart*, by Laura Bush, p. 95.

"When I married George"—Ibid, pp. 123–24.

"And what do you do?"—"The Good Wife," by Mimi Swartz, *Texas Monthly*, November 2004.

Laura's new brother-in-law Marvin joked—*MFMP*, p. 165.

"She is a darling even natured person"—Barbara Bush diary entry, September 11, 1983.

"Bar wanted me"—*Spoken from the Heart*, by Laura Bush, p. 124.

"It was really a bonding experience"—*MFMP*, p. 245.

Away from the chaos of Kennebunkport—*Spoken from the Heart*, by Laura Bush, p. 125.

"Bush didn't have to marry his mother"—"The Good Wife," by Mimi Swartz, *Texas Monthly*, November 2004.

"You have said"—ABC's *This Week*, December 19, 1999.

"You have Prescott, Forty-One, and Forty-Three"—Author interview with Karl Rove.

Barbara Bush sent word—Based on interviews with three contemporaneous sources, all speaking on condition of anonymity.

At the beginning of George W. Bush's first term—Author interview with an authoritative source, speaking on condition of anonymity.

"If you know her at all"—"Laura Bush: A Twist on Traditional," by Lois Romano, *Washington Post*, May 14, 2000.

"She saw it for years"—Author interview with Barbara Bush.

When asked during the 2000 campaign—"Laura Bush: A Twist on Traditional," by Lois Romano, *Washington Post*, May 14, 2000.

her poll ratings were never as high—"Laura Bush Approval Ratings Among Best for First Ladies," by Jeffrey M. Jones, Gallup News Service, February 9, 2006.

"She was very, very strong"—Author interview with Laura Bush.

She wrote that her mother-in-law—*Spoken from the Heart*, by Laura Bush, p. 124.

"Oh, only one friend"—Author interview with Barbara Bush.

"She ended with her own zinger"—*Sisters First*, by Jenna Bush Hager and Barbara Pierce Bush, p. 202.

"Were there some moments of tension?"—Author interview with George W. Bush.

"When I did something that she didn't approve of"—Author email exchange with Columba Bush.

"She felt it was her responsibility"—Author interview with Laura Bush.

"The thing that really bothered me"—Barbara Bush diary entry, June 16, 2001.

For the record, they may have been unhappy—*Sisters First*, by Jenna Bush Hager and Barbara Pierce Bush, p. 206.

When she was traveling to—*Abigail Adams*, by Woody Holton, p. 337.

Afterward, she wrote pointedly—*A Traveled First Lady*, by Louisa Catherine Adams, p. 112.

Her mother-in-law had warned her son—*Abigail Adams*, by Woody Holton, p. 337.

She was pretty—*Louisa*, by Louisa Thomas, p. 63.

"Had I steped"—*A Traveled First Lady*, by Louisa Catherine Adams, p. 93.

"Louisa quickly discovered"—Foreword by Laura Bush in ibid., p. xii.

"We did not understand one-another"—Ibid., p. 341.

"I admired that she was so natural"—Author interview with Laura Bush.

Chapter Twenty: Dynasty

"Don't ride on a name"—Author interview with George P. Bush.

"Hey, Pops, George P. is going to tell you"—Author interview with George P. Bush.

"One woman recently came up to me"—*Sisters First*, by Jenna Bush Hager and Barbara Pierce Bush, p. 202.

"She was the boss"—Author interview with Pierce Bush.

"It was on the back"—Author interview with Marshall Bush.

"When they were young"—Author interview by email with Columba Bush.

"My grandmother had just had double knee surgery"—Panel, George H. W. Bush Presidential Library, October 21, 2017.

"I was so damn mad"—Author interview with Barbara Bush.

"They were kind of dissipating"—Panel, George H. W. Bush Presidential Library, October 21, 2017.

she would tear up recalling the bigotry—"The Lonely Trials of Barbara Bush," by John Robinson, *Boston Globe*, September 17, 1994.

When he was nineteen or twenty years old—Author interview with Pierce Bush.

Doro went shopping for a new dress—Author interview with Jim Pierce.

"I mean, she's just always been"—Author interview with Marshall Bush.

"the rock of our family"—Author interview with Ellie LeBlond Sosa. She and Kelly Anne Chase coauthored *George and Barbara Bush: A Great American Love Story*, published in 2018.

In 2000, at age twenty-four—"America's Most Wanted," *People* magazine, July 10, 2000.

"What is the definition"—George P. Bush, George H. W. Bush Presidential Library panel, October 21, 2017.

"We heard footsteps"—Author interview with the younger Barbara Pierce Bush.

"From the very beginning"—Lizzie Andrews, George H. W. Bush Presidential Library panel, October 21, 2017.

"I have some relationship advice"—Sam LeBlond, George H. W. Bush Presidential Library panel, October 21, 2017.

"Such a big name for a little girl"—Author interview with the younger Barbara Pierce Bush.

"I mean seeing literally"—"Barbara Bush's Balancing Act," by Carl Swanson, *Elle*, September 24, 2013.

Her grandmother had provided a role model—Author interview with the younger Barbara Pierce Bush.

their joint memoir—*Sisters First: Stories from Our Wild and Wonderful Life,* by Jenna Bush Hager and Barbara Pierce Bush, published by Grand Central Publishing, October 2017.

That same month, the younger Barbara was set up on a blind date—"George W. Bush's Daughter Barbara Ties the Knot in Secret, Sentimental Wedding Ceremony," by Sandra Sobieraj Westfall, Diane Herbst, and Tierney McAfee, *People*, October 8, 2018.

When it comes to politics—*America's Political Dynasties*, by Stephen Hess.

On the list, in order—"America's Top Dynasty?" by Stephen Hess, *Washington Post*, September 13, 2009. The less familiar dynasties include the Frelinghuysens of New Jersey, who held elective office through six generations; the Breckinridges of Kentucky, whose members divided over the Civil War; and the Bayards of Delaware, who for decades had a family member in the US Senate.

(Stapleton's mother, Debbie Stapleton, is George Bush's first cousin.)—Walker Stapleton
     has political roots on his father's side of the family as well. His great-grandfather
     Benjamin F. Stapleton, a Democrat, was the five-term mayor of Denver.
When I asked Barbara Bush if she thought—Author interview with Barbara Bush.
"There are a lot of ways to serve"—Interview on C-SPAN's *First Ladies: Influence and
     Image*, October 29, 2013.
"I wouldn't call it a dynasty"—Author interview with George W. Bush.
"I think this generation is fabulous"—*Parade*, July 15, 2012. She presumably was refer-
     ring to "Race for the Cure," sponsored by the Susan G. Komen foundation, which
     funds breast cancer research.
Service was a lesson he learned—Panel, George Bush Library, October 21, 2017.
"I was born in 1986"—Author interview with Pierce Bush.
"The children, the grandchildren, the great-grandchildren"—Author interview with
     Barbara Bush.

Chapter Twenty-One: "We've Had Enough Bushes"

"Angst," she told me—Author interview with Barbara Bush.
"There's just a lot of angst"—Author interview with Jeb Bush.
"Jeb said, 'Mom, don't worry about things'"—Author interview with Barbara Bush.
"I pray for 44 a lot, too!!"—Letter from Elsie Hillman to Barbara Bush, October 7,
     2002; letter from Bush to Hillman, October 15, 2002. Elsie H. Hillman Papers,
     1920–2015, AIS 2013.02, Archives & Special Collections, University of Pittsburgh
     Library System.
"There are other people out there"—Barbara Bush interview on NBC's *Today* show,
     April 25, 2013.
"I never think ahead—Author interview with Barbara Bush.
"Thanks, Mom"—Author interview with Pierce Bush.
"It's a point of view"—Author interview with Jeb Bush.
"I think this is a great American country"—C-SPAN's *First Ladies: Influence and Image*,
     October 29, 2013.
"I said that *before* the *Today* show interview"—Author interview with Jeb Bush.
"This country, which is such a great country"—*Fox and Friends*, March 7, 2014.
"I just want to let you know"—Author interview with Jeb Bush.
"The real symbol of greed"—Barbara Bush diary entry, January 20, 1990.
"The Trumps are a new word"—Barbara Bush diary entry, February 25, 1990.
Trump had made a weird overture—George Bush diary entry, April 13–15, 1988,
     quoted in *DP*, p. 326.
"I don't understand"—Interview on CNN, February 5, 2016.
she expressed astonishment—Interview on CBS's *This Morning*, February 4, 2016.
     Trump and Kelly had tangled at the first Republican primary debate; he then criti-
     cized her, saying "there was blood coming out of her eyes, blood coming out of her
     wherever."
"I could not vote"—Barbara Bush diary entry, November 1, 2016.

"I thought that my values"—Author interview with George P. Bush.

"I think people didn't want anybody"—Author interview with Barbara Bush.

Trump "was very nice"—Barbara Bush diary entry, November 9, 2016

"I really wanted to write you earlier"—Author interview with Karen Pence. The full note: "Dear Karen, I really wanted to write you earlier to tell you how much fun I had as the wife of the VP. It is a lovely house. As the wife of the Vice President, nobody cared what I said or did. Every day, I tried to do something for somebody, like Grandma's House or the Salvation Army or different charities. It rarely got reported, but that's not why I did it. The day George got to be president, every word I said was news. Yikes. My mouth has gotten me in trouble ever since. God bless you and your husband. Have fun. Warmly, Barbara Bush."

"It said, 'Welcome to the First Ladies Club' "—Author interview with Barbara Bush.

Chapter Twenty-Two: "Hit in the Solarplex"

"I think George respects the presidency so"—ABC's *Good Morning America*, August 2, 2000.

"My-oh-my it was a tense evening"—Barbara Bush diary entry, November 12, 2000.

George Bush offered some advice—*The Presidents Club*, by Nancy Gibbs and Michael Duffy, p. 492.

"Aren't we a funny country?"—Barbara Bush diary entry, November 15, 2004.

"He leaves on Thursday"—Letters between Barbara Bush and Elsie Hillman, dated January 2005 and February 15, 2005. Elsie H. Hillman Papers, 1920–2015, AIS 2013.02, Archives & Special Collections, University of Pittsburgh Library System.

Clinton sat in the main cabin—Author interview with Jean Becker.

When talk show host Larry King asked her—Interview on CNN's *Larry King Live*, May 31, 2005.

"Bill Clinton came by in the afternoon"—Barbara Bush diary entry, September 2014.

George W. Bush and Neil Bush urged him—Author interview with Jean Becker.

"Dad has this amazing relationship"—Author interview with Neil Bush.

"He's very hard not to warm up to"—Author interview with Barbara Bush.

"She felt, I think, for a long time"—Author interview with Bill Clinton.

"She was such a hostess"—Author interview with Hillary Clinton.

"I am not too sure"—*BB*, pp. 213–14.

Her staff calculated—First Lady's Office, Press Office, and Lissa Muscatine, "FLOTUS Statements and Speeches 5/1/96–1/22/97 [Binder]: [Los Angeles Times Conference 9/26/1996]," Clinton Digital Library.

"She thinks press complete hypocrites"—Diane Blair recollection of phone call with Hillary Clinton, Thanksgiving Day, 1996. Diane Blair Papers, series 3, subseries, 3, box 1, folder 21. Special Collections, University of Arkansas Libraries, Fayetteville.

When Bill Clinton called George Bush—*The Presidents Club*, by Nancy Gibbs and Michael Duffy, p. 499.

"There was no choice"—Author interview with Barbara Bush.

"You wanna know my favorite book?"—"George H. W. Bush Groped Me, Too," by Christina Baker Kline, *Slate*, October 26, 2017.

Actresses Heather Lind and Jordana Grolnick—"Former President George H. W. Bush Accused by Heather Lind of Touching Her," Associated Press/NBC News; October 25, 2017.

Another woman, Roslyn Corrigan—"Woman Says George H. W. Bush Groped Her When She Was 16," by Aric Jenkins, *Time*, November 13, 2017.

"Ada is as deaf as a doornail"—Author interview with Barbara Bush.

There were advantages—"10 Questions with Barbara Bush," *Time*, June 4, 2015.

She and Levenson already had been discussing—Author interview with the Reverend Dr. Russell J. Levenson Jr.

George Carey, a former Archbishop of Canterbury—Two years later, in 2017, Carey resigned from his last formal role with the church after a finding that he had covered up sexual abuse allegations against Bishop Peter Ball.

"I came home"—Barbara Bush diary entry, July 14, 2007.

"I am racked with ARTHRITIS"—Barbara Bush diary entry, March 28, 2002.

"Everything has gone left or right"—Barbara Bush diary entry, March 28, 2002.

She had been five feet eight inches tall—Barbara Bush's elusive height was the subject of a funny essay, "I Have Reason to Believe Barbara Bush Is Four Feet Tall," by Laura Beck on the website *Jezebel*, November 1, 2016.

the night before we were scheduled—Interview by email with Evan Sisley, aide to George Bush.

The only time Pierce Bush—Author interview with Pierce Bush.

"I have warned all the children"—Author interview with Barbara Bush.

"George is sort of gently slipping away"—Letter from Barbara Bush to Elsie Hillman, May 19, 2012. Elsie H. Hillman Papers, 1920–2015, AIS.2013.02, Archives & Special Collections, University of Pittsburgh Library System.

"She's gone through three or four different kinds"—Author interview with Neil Bush.

"She called me six months or nine months ahead"—Author interview with George W. Bush.

George Bush declared that he wanted to live—Author interview with Andy Card.

"I've been in the hospital for forever"—Barbara Bush diary entry, April 5, 2018.

A few days later—Author interview with George W. Bush.

Her brother Scott Pierce called—Author email exchange with Scott Pierce.

Two days before she died—Author interviews with two sources who were present.

"The whole thing was like"—Author interview with Bill Clinton.

"I'm like in total denial"—Author interview with Jeb Bush.

In a subsequent interview, Jeb Bush told me—Author interview with Jeb Bush.

When everyone else had gone—Author interview with Jean Becker.

Epilogue: Indispensable

"I had one recurring thought all day"—Barbara Bush diary entry, September 11, 1994.

"Yes, he would have"—Author interview with Barbara Bush.

"Yeah, I think so"—Author interview with George Bush.

"I don't think she is the only reason he succeeded"—Author interview with William "Bucky" Bush.

"She was pretty much like a part of the ticket"—Author interview with George P. Bush.

He expressed enormous regard—Author interview with Andy Card.

"She was indispensable"—Author interview with C. Boyden Gray.

"He couldn't have done it without her"—Author interview with James A. Baker III.

"I bet he took some risks"—Author interview with Josh Bolten.

"Nobody can be certain"—Author interview with Brian Mulroney.

"I can't imagine"—Author interview with granddaughter Barbara Pierce Bush.

"I think that was a marriage made in heaven"—Author interview with Jim Pierce.

"I think it's just an extraordinary team"—Author interview with Jeb Bush.

"It's unanswerable, but my guess is no"—Author interview with George W. Bush.

"Not a shot"—Author interview with Bill Clinton.

"What is lacking"—Memo to Patricia Burchfield, George H. W. Bush Presidential Library and Museum, June 21, 2002.

"She didn't in any way resent"—Author interview with Laura Bush.

"Amazing life"—Barbara Bush diary entry, September 11, 1994.

Bibliography

Bush Family Interviews

Barbara Pierce Bush
George H. W. Bush
George W. Bush
Jeb Bush
Neil Bush
Columba Bush
Laura Bush

Barbara P. Bush
George P. Bush
Marshall Bush
Pierce Bush
Ellie LeBlond Sosa
William H. T. (Bucky) Bush

Scott Pierce
Janice Pierce
Jim Pierce
Hap Ellis
Robin Ellis
Dorothy (Debbie) Stapleton

Other Interviews

Jill Abramson
Lamar Alexander
Ira Allen
James A. Baker III
Stephen Bates
Susan Baker
Jean Becker
David Beckwith
Charlie Black
Josh Bolten
Patrick Buchanan
Neely Brunette
Derek Burney
Lou Cannon
Andy Card
Susana Rosario Cardenas
Mary Kate Cary
Dick Cheney
Steven Clemons
Bill Clinton
Hillary Clinton

Ann Compton
Julie Cooke
Sharon Darling
David Demarest
Thomas M. DeFrank
Lisa Drew
Peggy Dooley
Chris Emery
Jeffrey A. Engel
Frank Fahrenkopf
Howard Fineman
Marlin Fitzwater
Al Franken
Dan Gillcrist
Paulette Goodman
C. Boyden Gray
Judd Gregg
Kathy Gregg
Ada Grundy
Betsy Heminway
Cragg Hines

Karen Hughes
Michael S. Hughes
Terence Hunt
Ron Kaufman
Nannerl O. Keohane
Bill Kristol
Rev. Dr. Russell Levenson
Kathy Lewis
Bessie Liedtke
Melissa Luetke
Fred Malek
Chris Marden
Anita McBride
Tim McBride
Fred McClure
Jim McGrath
Edward E. McNally
Larry Mohr
Brian Mulroney
Kristan King Nevins
Bonnie Newman

Karen Pence

Roman Popadiuk

Todd Purdum

Tom Rath

Peggy Reid

Barbara Riddell

Peter Robinson

Walter Robinson

Susan Porter Rose

Tom Rosshirt

Karl Rove

Peter Roussel

David Rubenstein

Brent Scowcroft

Evan Sisley

Sam Skinner

Benita Somerfield

John Sununu

Sheila Tate

William Taubman

Pete Teeley

Charles A. Tesconi

Jane Thornhill

Mark K. Updegrove

Helen Vietor

Jeffrey Vogt

Mark Weinberg

Peggy Swift White

George Will

Elizabeth Wise

Manuscript Collections

Presidential Archives/Papers

George H. W. Bush Presidential Library and Museum, College Station, TX.

William J. Clinton Presidential Library, Little Rock, AR.

Ronald Reagan Presidential Library, Simi Valley, CA.

Richard M. Nixon Presidential Library, Yorba Linda, CA.

Public Papers of the Presidents of the United States: George Bush, 1989–1993. 8 vols. Washington, DC: United States Government Printing Office, 1990–93.

Public Papers of the Presidents of the United States: George W. Bush, 2001–2009. Washington, DC: United States Government Printing Office, 2007–09.

Public Papers of the Presidents of the United States: Gerald Ford, 1976–1977. Washington, DC: United States Government Printing Office, 1977.

Other Collections

University Archives and Special Collections, American University Library, Washington, DC.

Ashley Hall Collection, and Special Collections, College of Charleston, Charleston, SC.

FitzGerald Bemiss Papers, 1943–1997, Virginia Historical Society, Richmond, VA.

Diane Blair Papers, Special Collections, University of Arkansas Libraries, Fayetteville, AR.

CSX Collection, Baltimore & Ohio Railroad Museum, Hays T. Watkins Research Library, Baltimore, MD.

Walter Havighurst Special Collections & University Archives, Miami University Libraries, Oxford, OH.

Elsie H. Hillman Papers, 1920–2015, University of Pittsburgh Library System Archives & Special Collections, Pittsburgh, PA.

Jefferson Reading Room, Motion Picture & Television Room, and Newspaper & Current Periodicals Reading Room. Library of Congress, Washington, DC.

Civil War and Later Pension Files and Civil War Compiled Military Service Record, National Archives Building, Washington, DC.

World War I and World War II Military Records, National Archives at St. Louis, St. Louis, MO.

Smith College Archives Special Collections, Young Library, Northampton, MA.

South Caroliniana Library at the University of South Carolina, Columbia, SC.

George H. W. Bush Oral History Project, University of Virginia Miller Center.

Taylor Family Papers, 1856–1981, South Carolina Historical Society, Charleston, SC.

Books

Adams, Louisa Catherine. *A Traveled First Lady: Writings of Louisa Catherine Adams.* Edited by Margaret A. Hogan and C. James Taylor. Cambridge, MA: Harvard University Press, 2014.

Baker, James A., III. *The Politics of Diplomacy: Revolution, War, and Peace, 1989–1992.* With Thomas M. DeFrank. New York: G. P. Putnam's Sons, 1995.

———. *Work Hard, Study—and Keep Out of Politics! Adventures and Lessons from an Unexpected Public Life.* With Steve Fiffer. New York: G. P. Putnam's Sons, 2006.

Baird, William R. *Betas of Achievement: Being Brief Biographical Records of Members of the Beta Theta Pi Who Have Achieved Distinction in Various Fields of Endeavor.* New York: Beta Publishing, 1914.

Bartlett, Joseph G. *Robert Coe, Puritan: His Ancestors and Descendants, 1340–1910; with Notices of Other Coe Families.* Boston: Bartlett, 1911.

Blaik, Earl H. *You Have to Pay the Price.* New York: Holt, Rinehart and Winston, 1960.

Bradley, James. *Flyboys: A True Story of Courage.* Boston: Little, Brown, 2003.

Bush, Barbara. *Barbara Bush: A Memoir.* New York: Scribner, 1994.

———. *Reflections: Life After the White House.* New York: Scribner, 2003.

Bush, George H. W. *All the Best, George Bush: My Life in Letters and Other Writings.* New York: Scribner, 2013.

———. *Looking Forward.* With Victor Gold. Garden City, NY: Doubleday, 1987.

Bush, George H. W., and Brent Scowcroft. *A World Transformed.* New York: Knopf, 1998.

Bush, George W. *A Charge to Keep.* New York: William Morrow, 1999.

———. *Decision Points.* New York: Crown, 2010.

———. *41: A Portrait of My Father.* New York: Crown, 2014.

Caccamo, James F., Jack Kauffman Bowers, and Gwendolyn E. Mayer. *Index to "A Portrait and Biographical Record of Portage and Summit Counties, Ohio, 1898."* Hudson, OH: Hudson Genealogical Study Group, 2008.

Caferro, William. *John Hawkwood: An English Mercenary in Fourteenth-Century Italy.* Baltimore: Johns Hopkins University Press, 2015.

Clendinen, Dudley, and Adam Nagourney. *Out for Good: The Struggle to Build a Gay Rights Movement in America.* New York: Simon & Schuster, 1999.

Company Number One History, Washington Barracks, S.A.R.D. of Engineers, American Expeditionary Force. Liverpool: Daily Post Printers, 1919.

Cramer, Richard Ben. *What It Takes: The Way to the White House.* New York: Random House, 1992.

Cressy, David. *Coming Over: Migration and Communication Between England and New England in the Seventeenth Century*. Cambridge: Cambridge University Press, 1987.

Emery, Christopher B. *White House Usher: Stories from the Inside*. Washington, DC: Booklocker.com, 2018.

Engel, Jeffrey A., ed. *The China Diary of George H. W. Bush: The Making of a Global President*. Princeton, NJ: Princeton University Press, 2011.

Estes, Steve. *Charleston in Black and White: Race and Power in the South After the Civil Rights Movement*. Chapel Hill: University of North Carolina Press, 2015.

Fernow, Berthold. *Documents Relative to the Colonial History of the State of New York*. Vol. 14. Albany, NY: Weed, Parsons, 1883.

Ford, Betty. *The Times of My Life*. With Chris Chase. London: W. H. Allen, 1979.

Fox, William F. *Regimental Losses in the American Civil War, 1861–1865*. Albany, NY: Albany Printing, 1889.

Franken, Al. *Lies and the Lying Liars Who Tell Them: A Fair and Balanced Look at the Right*. New York: Dutton, 2003.

Gibbs, Nancy, and Michael Duffy. *The Presidents Club: Inside the World's Most Exclusive Fraternity*. New York: Simon & Schuster, 2012.

Golden Anniversary: 1874–1924; Borough of Sharpsville, Pennsylvania. Sharpsville, PA: Sharon Herald Printing, 1924.

Goldman, Peter Louis, Thomas M. DeFrank, Mark Miller, Andrew Murr, and Tom Mathews. *Quest for the Presidency, 1992*. College Station: Texas A&M University Press, 1994.

Gorbachev, Mikhail. *Memoirs*. New York: Doubleday, 1996.

Gorbachev, Raisa M. *I Hope: Reminiscences and Reflections*. Leicester: Charnwood, 1991.

Green, Fitzhugh. *George Bush: An Intimate Portrait*. New York: Hippocrene Books, 1989.

Greene, John R. *The Presidency of George H. W. Bush*. Lawrence: University Press of Kansas, 2015.

Gutin, Myra G. *Barbara Bush: Presidential Matriarch*. Lawrence: University Press of Kansas, 2008.

Hager, Jenna Bush, and Barbara Pierce Bush. *Sisters First: Stories from Our Wild and Wonderful Life*. New York: Grand Central, 2017.

Harwood, Herbert H., Jr. *The Railroad That Never Was: Vanderbilt, Morgan, and the South Pennsylvania Railroad*. Bloomington: Indiana University Press, 2010.

Hearn, Chester G. *Sorties into Hell: The Hidden War on Chichi Jima*. Westport, CT: Praeger, 2003.

Hess, Stephen. *America's Political Dynasties: From Adams to Clinton*. Washington, DC: Brookings Institution Press, 2016.

History of Sharpsville, Pennsylvania: Diamond Jubilee, 1949. Sharpsville, PA, 1949.

Holton, Woody. *Abigail Adams*. New York: Free Press, 2010.

Hood, Clifton. *In Pursuit of Privilege: A History of New York City's Upper Class and the Making of a Metropolis*. New York: Columbia University Press, 2017.

Hyams, Joe. *Flight of the Avenger: George Bush at War*. San Diego: Harcourt Brace Jovanovich, 1991.

Johnson, Caleb H. *The* Mayflower *and Her Passengers*. Philadelphia, PA: Xlibris, 2006.

Kelley, Kitty. *The Family: The Real Story of the Bush Dynasty*. London: Bantam, 2005.

———. *Nancy Reagan: The Unauthorized Biography*. New York: Pocket Star Books, 1992.

Kilian, Pamela. *Barbara Bush: A Biography*. Thorndike, ME: Thorndike Press, 1992.

Koch, Doro Bush. *My Father, My President: A Personal Account of the Life of George H. W. Bush*. New York: Warner, 2006.

Krueger, Gretchen. *Hope and Suffering: Children, Cancer, and the Paradox of Experimental Medicine*. Baltimore: Johns Hopkins University Press, 2008.

Küsters, Hanns J., and Daniel Hofmann, eds. *Deutsche Einheit: Dokumente zur Deutsch-landpolitik; Sonderedition aus den Akten des Bundeskanzleramtes 1989/90*. Berlin: Directmedia, 2004.

Lambert, Edward R. *History of the Colony of New Haven*. Whitefish, MT: Kessinger, 2008.

Leubsdorf, Carl P. *Adventures of a Boy on the Bus*. Washington, DC: Politics & Prose, 2018.

Marton, Kati. *Hidden Power: Presidential Marriages That Shaped Our Recent History*. New York: Anchor, 2002.

Martyn, Thomas J. C. *Inside the Founding of* Newsweek*: How a Hot-Tempered, One-Legged R.A.F. Pilot Launched an American Media Giant*. Edited by Anne M. Alexander. 2015. www.insidethefoundingofnewsweek.com.

Mather, Cotton. *Magnalia Christi Americana; or, The Ecclesiastical History of New-England*. Hartford, CT: Silas Andrus, 1820.

Maurer, Herrymon. *In Quiet Ways: George H. Mead, the Man and the Company*. Dayton, OH: Mead Corporation, 1970.

Meacham, Jon. *Destiny and Power: The American Odyssey of George Herbert Walker Bush*. New York: Random House, 2016.

Miller, James Todd. *Bound to Be a Soldier: The Letters of Private James T. Miller, 111th Pennsylvania Infantry, 1861–1864*. Edited by Jedediah Mannis and Galen R. Wilson. Knoxville: University of Tennessee Press, 2001.

Minutaglio, Bill. *First Son: George W. Bush and the Bush Family Dynasty*. New York: Random House, 1999.

Mukherjee, Siddhartha. *The Emperor of All Maladies: A Biography of Cancer*. London: HarperCollins, 2010.

Noonan, Peggy. *What I Saw at the Revolution: A Political Life in the Reagan Era*. New York: Random House, 1990.

Parmet, Herbert S. *George Bush: The Life of a Lone Star Yankee*. New York: Scribner, 1997.

Perry, Barbara A. *Rose Kennedy: The Life and Times of a Political Matriarch*. New York: Norton, 2013.

Pierce, Frederick C. *Pierce Genealogy, No. IV: Being the Record of the Posterity of Capt. Michael, John and Capt. William Pierce, Who Came to This Country from England*. Albany, NY: J. Munsell's Sons, 1889.

Plokhy, Serhii. *The Last Empire: The Final Days of the Soviet Union.* New York: Basic Books, 2014.

Powell, Colin L. *My American Journey.* With Joseph E. Persico. New York: Random House, 1995.

Radcliffe, Donnie. *Simply Barbara Bush: A Portrait of America's Candid First Lady.* New York: Warner, 1990.

Reagan, Maureen. *First Father, First Daughter: A Memoir.* Boston: Little, Brown, 2001.

Reagan, Nancy. *My Turn: The Memoirs of Nancy Reagan.* With William Novak. New York: Random House, 1989.

Regan, Donald T. *For the Record.* New York: Harcourt Brace Jovanovich, 1988.

Riker, James. *The Annals of Newtown, in Queens County, New-York.* Washington, DC: Library of Congress, 2015.

Rove, Karl. *Courage and Consequence: My Life as a Conservative in the Fight.* New York: Simon & Schuster, 2010.

Schiff, Harriet S. *The Bereaved Parent.* London: Souvenir Press, 1977.

Shepardson, Francis W. *Beta Lore: Sentiment, Song and Story in Beta Theta Pi.* Menasha, WI: George Banta, 1928.

Shilts, Randy. *And the Band Played On: Politics, People, and the AIDS Epidemic.* New York: Penguin, 2007.

———. *Conduct Unbecoming: Gays and Lesbians in the U.S. Military.* New York: St. Martin's Griffin, 2005.

Skillman, Francis. *The Skillmans of New York.* Salt Lake City: Genealogical Society of Utah, 1967.

Smith, Raymond A., and Donald P. Haider-Markel. *Gay and Lesbian Americans and Political Participation: A Reference Handbook.* Santa Barbara, CA: ABC-CLIO, 2002.

Sosa, Ellie LeBlond, and Kelly A. Chase. *George and Barbara Bush: A Great American Love Story.* Camden, ME: Down East Books, 2018.

Strauch, Ileana. *Ashley Hall.* Charleston, SC: Arcadia, 2003.

Tanaka, Toshiyuki. *Hidden Horrors: Japanese War Crimes in World War II.* New York: Rowman and Littlefield, 2018.

Tate, Sheila. *Lady in Red: An Intimate Portrait of Nancy Reagan.* New York: Crown Forum, 2018.

Thomas, Louisa. *Louisa: The Extraordinary Life of Mrs. Adams.* New York: Penguin, 2016.

Tomlinson, R. G. *Witchcraft Trials of Connecticut.* Hartford, CT: Bond Press, 1978.

Trento, Susan B. *The Power House: Robert Keith Gray and the Selling of Access and Influence in Washington.* New York: St. Martin's, 1992.

Truman, Margaret. *First Ladies: An Intimate Group Portrait of White House Wives.* New York: Ballantine, 1996.

Untermeyer, Chase. *Inside Reagan's Navy: The Pentagon Journals.* College Station: Texas A&M University Press, 2015.

———. *When Things Went Right: The Dawn of the Reagan-Bush Administration.* College Station: Texas A&M University Press, 2013.

Updegrove, Mark K. *The Last Republicans: Inside the Extraordinary Relationship Between George H. W. Bush and George W. Bush*. New York: HarperCollins, 2017.

Weinberg, Mark. *Movie Nights with the Reagans: A Memoir*. New York: Simon & Schuster, 2018.

White, John G., ed. *A Twentieth Century History of Mercer County, Pennsylvania: A Narrative Account of Its Historical Progress, Its People, and Its Principal Interests, Prepared Under the General Editorial Supervision of Mr. J. G. White*. Chicago: Lewis Publishing, 1909.

Witcover, Jules. *The American Vice Presidency: From Irrelevance to Power*. Washington, DC: Smithsonian Books, 2014.

Woodward, Bob. *The Commanders*. New York: Simon & Schuster, 1991.

Key Articles

Newspaper Articles

"Barbara Pierce Engaged to Wed." *New York Times*, December 12, 1943, p. 66.

Boyd, Gerald M. "Barbara Bush Tends His Image Her Way." *New York Times*, May 5, 1988.

Bradley, Carol. "Loyalty a Strong Suit for Barbara Bush." *White Plains Journal News*, October 17, 1988.

Bunting, Glenn F. "Barbara Bush: The President's Biggest Asset in a Time of Political Trouble." *Los Angeles Times*, May 31, 1992.

Butterfield, Fox. "At Wellesley, a Furor over Barbara Bush." *New York Times*, May 4, 1990, p. 1.

Christy, Marian. "Barbara Bush: Traditionalist, Unspoiled." *Cincinnati Enquirer*, March 23, 1980.

Devroy, Ann. "The Power Behind Bush." *White Plains Journal News*, January 24, 1982, p. AA4.

"Election Results in County." *Marysville Journal-Tribune*, November 5, 1902.

Elias, Brenda. "Visit Sparks Discussion over First Lady." *Daily Hampshire Gazette*, September 7, 1989.

"General James Pierce, the End of a Busy Life." *Record-Argus* (Greenville, PA), December 5, 1874.

Hines, Cragg. "Bush Endorses Premarital AIDS Testing." *Houston Chronicle*, April 9, 1987, p. 2.

Johnson, Chris. "Barbara Bush Remembered as Gay Ally Who Fought AIDS Stigma." *Washington Blade*, April 18, 2018.

Leubsdorf, Carl P. "Mrs. Bush Advises Son Against Governor's Race." *Dallas Morning News*, April 28, 1989.

"Miss Pierce Is Wed to Lieut. G. H. Bush." *New York Times*, January 7, 1945, p. 36.

Page, Susan. "Why America Loves Barbara Bush: She's Warm. She's Tough. She Looks Like Everybody's Grandmother—and She May Be Her Husband's Biggest Political Asset." *Newsday* (New York), November 11, 1990.

Page, Susan, and Anthony Marro. "Bush Survived Frantic Night of Rumors." *Newsday* (New York), July 18, 1980.

Peterson, Bill. "After Bush Had Gone to Bed, His Secret Dream Came True." *Washington Post*, July 18, 1980.

Primeau, Marty. "Barbara Bush." *Dallas Morning News*, August 19, 1984.

Radcliffe, Donnie. "Barbara Bush Being Herself." *Washington Post*, January 15, 1993.

———. "Mrs. Bush's School Battle; The First-Lady Calm, in the Wellesley Storm." *Washington Post*, May 3, 1990.

Romano, Lois. "Laura Bush: A Twist on Traditional." *Washington Post*, May 14, 2000.

Rosshirt, Tom. "Thank You, Mrs. Bush." Creators Syndicate, June 20, 2012.

Scherban, Debra. "She Loves Being Mrs. George Bush." *Daily Hampshire Gazette* (Northampton, MA), April 22, 1981.

Stumbo, Bella. "Mrs. Bush Happy to Settle for Second." *Los Angeles Times*, July 16, 1980.

Sverdlik, Alan. "Barbara Bush Chooses to Take a Back Seat." *Atlanta Journal-Constitution*, October 16, 1987.

Tate, Debbie, and Joan McCarley. "Barbara Bush Visited Our Facility for Children with HIV/AIDS. It Was Unforgettable." *Washington Post*, April 21, 2018.

Von Drehle, David. "Spectators at a Son's Rise." *Washington Post*, August 2, 2000.

Wage, Malry J. "Great Mansion Is Fading Reminder of General Pierce." *Sharon Herald*, July 16, 1952.

Weinraub, Bernard. "A Down-to-Earth Tenant for an Exclusive Address." *New York Times*, January 15, 1989.

"Wellesley Students Oppose Barbara Bush Scheduled Commencement Speech." Associated Press, April 15, 1990.

Magazine Articles

Block, Jean L. "The Best Time of My Life Is Now." *Good Housekeeping*, November 1989, p. 255.

Brew, Douglas. "Bush Does It His Way." *Time*, February 2, 1982.

Conason, Joe. "1,000 Reasons Not to Vote for George Bush." *Spy*, July/August 1992, pp. 29–38.

Cramer, Richard Ben. "How Bush Made It." *Esquire*, June 1991.

Fineman, Howard. "Bush and the 'Big A Question.'" *Newsweek*, June 29, 1987.

McDaniel, Ann. "Barbara Bush: The Steel Behind the Smile." *Newsweek*, June 22, 1992, p. 34.

Swanson, Carl. "Barbara Bush's Balancing Act." *Elle*, September 24, 2013.

Swartz, Mimi. "The Good Wife." *Texas Monthly*, November 2004.

Walsh, Kenneth T. "The Hidden Life of Barbara Bush." *U.S. News & World Report*, May 28, 1990.

Williams, Marjorie. "Barbara's Backlash." *Vanity Fair*, August 1992.

Academic Articles/Dissertations

Bonfitto, Vincent F. "The Formation of Gay and Lesbian Identity and Community in the Connecticut River Valley of Western Massachusetts, 1900–1970." *Journal of Homosexuality* 33, no. 1 (1997): 69–96.

Coley, Bradley L., and Norman L. Higinbotham. "Solitary Bone Cyst: The Localized Form of Osteitis Fibrosa Cystica." *Annals of Surgery* 99, no. 3 (1934): 432–48.

Glasser, Gerald J. "Game Theory and Cumulative Voting for Corporate Directors." *Management Science* 5 (1959): 151–56.

Jackson, Ivor. "Book Reviews—Thyroid Disease in Clinical Practice by I. Ross McDougall." *New England Journal of Medicine* 328, no. 22 (1993): 1648.

Hertz, Rosanna, and Susan M. Reverby. "Gentility, Gender, and Political Protest: The Barbara Bush Controversy at Wellesley College." *Gender and Society* 9, no. 5 (1995): 594–611.

King, James D., and James W. Riddlesperger Jr. "Diversity and Presidential Cabinet Appointments." *Social Science Quarterly* 96 (March 2015): 93–103.

Videka-Sherman, Lynn. "Research on the Effect of Parental Bereavement: Implications for Social Work Intervention," *Social Science Review* 61, no.1 (1987).

Westmoreland, Brandi Davis. "Literacy as Value: Cultural Capital in Barbara Bush's Foundation for Family Literacy." PhD diss., Texas A&M University, 2010.

Web Publications

Beck, Laura. "I Have Reason to Believe Barbara Bush Is Four Feet Tall." *Jezebel*, November 1, 2016.

Clemons, Steve. "Bush Gossip." *Washington Note*, December 1, 2005.

TV and Radio Interviews of Barbara Pierce Bush

ABC's *Good Morning America*, with Diane Sawyer, March 18, 2003.

ABC's *Good Morning America*, with Charlie Gibson, August 2, 2000.

ABC's *This Week* (joint interview with Laura Bush), December 19, 1999.

CBS's *The Late Show with David Letterman*, September 13, 1994.

CBS's *This Morning*, February 4, 2016.

CNN's *Anderson Cooper 360*, February 5, 2016.

CNN's *Larry King Live*, May 31, 2005.

CNN's *Larry King Live*, November 22, 2010.

C-SPAN's *First Ladies: Influence and Image*, October 29, 2013.

Fox News *Fox and Friends*, March 7, 2014.

NBC's *Today*, April 25, 2013.

NBC's *Tonight Show with Jay Leno*, November 18, 1994.

NPR's *Fresh Air*, with Terry Gross, September 13, 1994.

NPR's *Marketplace*, September 5, 2005.

PBS's *Talking with David Frost*, September 30, 1994.

PBS's *Charlie Rose*, September 13, 1994.

Speeches and Public Appearances

Barbara Bush commencement address, Wellesley College, June 1, 1990.

Barbara Bush speech, American University, May 1, 1985.

Barbara Bush filing, on behalf of her husband, for the New Hampshire Republican presidential primary. C-SPAN, December 22, 1991.

Panel with Laura and Barbara Bush at "America's First Ladies: An Enduring Legacy" conference on November 15, 2011, at the George H. W. Bush Presidential Library Center at Texas A&M University.

Grandchildren Panel including George P. Bush (son of Jeb); Pierce Bush and Ashley Bush (children of Neil); Lizzie Andrews (stepchild of Neil); Marshall Bush and Walker Bush (children of Marvin); and Sam LeBlond, Ellie LeBlond Sosa, Robert Koch, and Gigi Koch (children of Doro). George H. W. Bush Presidential Library, October 21, 2017.

Index

About the Author

Susan Page is an award-winning journalist and the Washington Bureau chief of *USA TODAY*, where she writes about politics and the White House. She has covered ten presidential elections and interviewed nine presidents (three after they had left office), from Richard Nixon through Donald Trump. During her career, she has reported from six continents and dozens of foreign countries. She drove to Three Mile Island hours after the nuclear mishap there was reported, traveled across Southeast Asia to chronicle the exodus of Vietnamese "boat people," and interviewed physicist Stephen Hawking through his computerized voice.

She has won every journalism award given specifically for coverage of the White House. She was twice awarded the Gerald R. Ford Prize for Distinguished Reporting on the Presidency, in 1990 for her coverage at *Newsday* of President George H. W. Bush and in 2001 for her coverage at *USA TODAY* of President George W. Bush. The White House Correspondents Association has honored her with the Merriman Smith Memorial Award for Deadline Reporting on the Presidency and with the Aldo Beckman Memorial Award, given for excellence in coverage of the White House. She was a member of a team that won the Sigma Delta Chi Award for Washington Correspondence. She has received the Excellence in Journalism Award from the American News Women's Club.

She has served as president of the White House Correspondents Association, chairman of the Robert F. Kennedy Journalism Awards, and president of the Gridiron Club, the oldest association of journalists in Washington. She twice has served as a juror for the Pulitzer Prizes.

A native of Wichita, Kansas, she received a bachelor's degree from Northwestern University, where she was editor-in-chief of the *Daily Northwestern*. She received a master's degree from Columbia University, where she was a Pulitzer Fellow. She is married to Carl Leubsdorf, a columnist with the *Dallas Morning News*. They have two sons, Ben and Will.